D0076287

www.wadsworth.com

www.wadsworth.com is the World Wide Web site for Wadsworth and is your direct source to dozens of online resources.

At www.wadsworth.com you can find out about supplements, demonstration software, and student resources. You can also send email to many of our authors and preview new publications and exciting new technologies.

www.wadsworth.com
Changing the way the world learns®

Voices of the
American Past

Documents in U.S. History

Volume II

Voices of the American Past

Documents in U.S. History

Volume II

Third Edition

Raymond M. Hyser

J. Chris Arndt

James Madison University

THOMSON
™
WADSWORTH

Australia • Canada • Mexico • Singapore • Spain • United Kingdom • United States

THOMSON
WADSWORTH

Publisher: Clark Baxter
Acquisitions Editor: Ashley Dodge
Senior Development Editor:
  Margaret McAndrew Beasley
Assistant Editor: Julie Yardley
Editorial Assistant: Anne Gittinger
Technology Project Manager: Melinda Newfarmer
Marketing Manager: Lori Grebe Cook
Marketing Assistant: Mary Ho
Advertising Project Manager: Stacey Purviance
Senior Project Manager, Editorial Production:
  Kimberly Adams

Print/Media Buyer: Rebecca Cross
Permissions Editor: Stephanie Lee
Production Service and Compositor:
  Lachina Publishing Services
Photo Researcher: Linda Sykes
Copy Editor: Lachina Publishing Services
Cover Designer: Lisa Henry
Cover Image: Smithsonian American Art Museum,
  Washington, DC/Art Resource, NY
Printer: Malloy Incorporated

COPYRIGHT © 2005 Wadsworth, a division of
Thomson Learning, Inc. Thomson Learning™ is a
trademark used herein under license.

ALL RIGHTS RESERVED. No part of this
work covered by the copyright hereon may be
reproduced or used in any form or by any
means—graphic, electronic, or mechanical, including but not limited to photocopying, recording,
taping, Web distribution, information networks, or
information storage and retrieval systems—without the written permission of the publisher.

Printed in the United States of America
1 2 3 4 5 6 7 08 07 06 05 04

For more information about
our products, contact us at:
**Thomson Learning Academic
Resource Center
1-800-423-0563**

For permission to use material from this text
or product, submit a request online at
http://www.thomsonrights.com.
Any additional questions about permissions
can be submitted by email to
thomsonrights@thomson.com.

**Library of Congress
Control Number:** 2004105197

ISBN: 0-534-64301-9

Thomson Wadsworth
10 Davis Drive
Belmont, CA 94002-3098
USA

Asia
Thomson Learning
5 Shenton Way #01-01
UIC Building
Singapore 068808

Australia/New Zealand
Thomson Learning
102 Dodds Street
Southbank, Victoria 3006
Australia

Canada
Nelson
1120 Birchmount Road
Toronto, Ontario M1K 5G4
Canada

Europe/Middle East/Africa
Thomson Learning
High Holborn House
50/51 Bedford Row
London WC1R 4LR
United Kingdom

To our children,

Kelsey, Marshall, and Christopher Hyser

and Olivia Arndt

Thanks for all of your love

and inspiration

✳

About the Authors

Raymond M. Hyser is a professor of history at James Madison University in Harrisonburg, Virginia, where he teaches courses in U.S. history, U.S. business history, Gilded Age America, and historical methods. He focuses his research interests on the study of race and ethnicity in the Gilded Age.

J. Chris Arndt is a professor of history at James Madison University in Harrisonburg, Virginia, where he teaches courses in U.S. history, the American Revolution, the early Republic, and historical methods. He focuses his research interests on the study of state's rights and economic change in antebellum America.

Contents

CHAPTER 22 Making the World Safe for Democracy 386

CHAPTER 23 The Return to "Normalcy" 404

CHAPTER 24 FDR and the New Deal 424

CHAPTER 25 Isolationism and World War II 443

CHAPTER 29 Society and Culture at Century's End 528

CHAPTER 30 Our Times 554

✳
Preface to the Third Edition

We are delighted with the opportunity to produce a revised third edition of *Voices of the American Past.* This allows us to better represent the ever-evolving approaches that historians employ to interpret the past, but it also enables us to provide more documents covering a greater variety of issues. Those who use this edition will find significant changes. Our selection of new documents was guided by a desire to provide greater diversity of voices while also offering readable selections that spoke to larger issues.

The revised reader offers well known primary sources such as *Federalist 10,* and President Eisenhower's farewell address, as well as Cotton Mather's admonitions on the evils of "self-pollution," a women's description of the southern homefront during the Civil War, John Muir's essay on American forests, and a critique of East Asians as the "model minority." The most significant change, however, is the addition of visual images. As historians have increasingly adopted more interdisciplinary approaches and expanded the types of sources they use both as scholars and in the classroom, we thought it essential to add a different type of primary source to the more traditional use of documents. The result is a collection of more than thirty images that provide a unique approach to interpreting and understanding the key issues of U.S. history.

We are again indebted to our colleagues in the James Madison University Department of History for their contributions and inspiration. Their high standards of teaching excellence coupled with their strong sense of collegiality provide the perfect atmosphere for quality instruction. Our students have contributed greatly by showing us where a document was contradictory or less readable, and perhaps more important, they helped to make us aware of the issues that are central to the current generation of young people. Many of our colleagues in the profession, particularly those who participate in the annual Advanced Placement U.S. History grading, have made more important contributions than they could ever realize. We appreciate the criticisms and suggestions of the following reviewers:

Sharon L. Arnoult, Midwestern State University
Robert A. Becker, Weber State University
Mario Bennekin, Georgia Perimeter College
Kirk Burnett, Mt. San Antonio College
Dominick Cavallo, Adelphi University

Stacy A. Cordery, Monmouth College

Brian Daugherity, University of Richmond

Gregory Michael Dorr, University of Alabama

Lisa Lindquist Dorr, University of Alabama

Harvey Green, Northeastern University

Robert R. Hollander, St. Louis Community College at Forest Park

Todd Kerstetter, Texas Christian University

Suzanne Marshall, Jacksonville State University

Timothy J. McMannon, North Seattle Community College

Stephen Middleton, North Carolina State University

William Howard Moore, University of Wyoming

Rick Moniz, Chabot College

John T. Payne, North Harris Montgomery Community College District/
Tomball College

Emily S. Rosenberg, Macalester College

Norman L. Rosenberg, Macalester College

Thomas Schoonover, University of Southwestern Louisiana

Sandra Strohhofer Pryor, University of Delaware

Paul Searls, University of Vermont

Vernon L. Volpe, University of Nebraska at Kearney

Their insight did much to improve this edition, enabling us to refocus our attention in some areas and leading us to some excellent documents in others. Special thanks go to our friends at Wadsworth Publishers. Margaret Beasley is a terrific editor with a wonderful sense of humor, a necessary ingredient for successfully bringing this project to fruition. Finally, we thank our wives, Pamela and Andi, for their love and support.

A Guide to Reading and Interpreting Documents and Images

This volume contains edited documents about American history. Historians refer to documents as written *primary sources*. These are the raw materials, the basic building blocks to reconstructing past events. In the same way that a detective searches a crime scene for clues, a historian draws on primary sources and uses the weight of the evidence to determine what happened, and to help support an interpretation of the event. While primary sources might be described as any evidence that is contemporary to the event described, historians rely heavily on first-hand, eyewitness accounts or recollections of events of the time, as well as speeches or official reports produced at that time. All primary sources, however, are not created equal. The closer the evidence is in time and space to the event described, the less bias that it contains, and the more reliable it tends to be. The interpretations that historians produce from these primary sources are called *secondary sources*. Secondary sources are books and articles written about past events, such as a textbook, the introductions to the documents in this volume, or a history of the American Civil War.

Reading and analyzing documents require particular skills. You should examine documents with a critical eye; that is, ask questions about the document. We recommend that you develop the ability to perform a twofold reading of a document. First, try to understand the document as the people in the time and place in which it was produced would have comprehended it. What did the document mean to them? Always remember that people live within a historical context—they inhabit a different time and place. They do not know what the future holds. Careful analysis of a document will enable you to examine the thoughts and actions of the people of a particular time. Second, read the document and consider the similarities and differences between that time period and your own. Students of history are often called upon to make judgments about the past. Documents should be analyzed to see how they fit into the broader sweep of history.

We have included the following pointers that will be useful in introducing you to this spirit of historical inquiry and enable you to better understand documents. It is our hope that equipped with these guidelines, you will be better able to read primary sources in a critical manner. And in so doing, you will gain more insight into past events, add some real-life views to historical facts, and better understand the complexities of the American past.

Interpreting Written Documents

1. **Context:** Each document has an introduction. You should read it, as well as review notes from your instructor's lecture. This will provide you with some background about events, people, and ideas of the time period in which the document was created.
   - What major political, social, and economic events may have affected the author of the document?
   - How does this document fit into the historical context?
   - How does this document better our understanding of the event?
   - Does the document help to explain the cause-and-effect relationship of this event?

2. **Thesis:** Most documents have a central point that is being conveyed. This is known as the thesis. It is critical for any reader to understand the core argument—the thesis—of a document. Identifying the thesis is the important first step in making sense of a document's overall impact.
   - Can you summarize the document in three or four sentences?
   - What is the thesis?
   - What does the author emphasize?
   - What are the key words that define the argument?

   Keep in mind that the meaning of words changes over time, so try to understand the use of language in the historical time period of the document. For example, students in the 21st century might refer to "icon" as a clickable symbol on their computer's desktop, while prior to the widespread use of computers, "icon" would refer to a sacred, religious image.

3. **Perspective:** The author's point of view, including his or her prejudices and beliefs, can dramatically affect the content of a document. It is essential to consider the author of a document when reading. Biographical information can be helpful in deciding the author's point of view. For example, a slave owner would have a different view of slavery than a slave. Factory workers would certainly have a different perception of life in America than the owner of the factory where they worked.
   - Who is the author of the document?
   - What is his or her background?
   - When was the document created?
   - Was it prepared during the event, immediately afterwards, within a short time period, or years later?

Such timing is important, as memories often fade or become distorted over time. An individual's life experience often shapes perspective or views about events in his or her time. Seek to determine the authors' gender, class, ethnicity (where appropriate), their regional background, and their political, economic, or social position.

- Do you detect any prejudices?
- What evidence indicates the bias of the author?
- Can you determine the author's motive in producing the document?
- What did he or she hope to accomplish?

4. **Audience:** Knowing the intended audience of an account can be useful in better understanding why the document was created.

- Was the document prepared for a specific audience—women, members of Congress, African Americans, wealthy businessmen, immigrants, a friend, for example?
- Was the document prepared for public distribution?
- Was it a speech, a newspaper or a magazine article or editorial, an official government report, a published memoir or autobiography, to name a few possibilities?
- Was it produced for personal and private reflection, such as a diary, journal entry, or an exchange of letters between friends?

Public consumption documents tend to be carefully worded, often guarded in presentation, while private ones tend to be less cautious and more honest. Classifying or identifying the document can be helpful in understanding its contents.

5. **Significance:** Finally, one should determine why a document is important.

- Why is the document important or significant?
- How has it shaped our understanding of the event?
- How has it shaped our understanding of historical change or continuity over time?
- What does it tell us about the historical time period?

Interpreting Visual Images

Many of the techniques used to interpret visual images are similar to those used to make sense of written documents. It is as important to ask questions about context, thesis, perspective, audience, and significance when analyzing an image as it is when reviewing a written text. The major difference with visual images is that there is more room for interpretation since the author/artist/photographer does not specifically describe what he or she is thinking. In analyzing visual images, one should consider the following:

- Carefully study the image. What is your overall impression? What thoughts or emotions does it conjure?
- What activities are depicted in the image? How and why are these activities significant?
- Does the artist make use of symbols? If so, what are they? What is the significance of these symbols?
- Who or what is portrayed positively? Negatively? What can you infer from this?

16

✴

Reconstruction

After the Civil War, the nation faced the enormous task of reconstructing the republic. In particular, policy makers had to determine the status of the former Confederate states and what to do with the recently freed slaves. Devastated by the war, the South also had to cope with the influx of northern troops, reformers, and profiteers, many of whom had their own ideas concerning the region's future. The diversity of opinions over Reconstruction deeply divided the North and occasionally brought a violent response from some southern whites. The ensuing selections reveal how Americans of different races and regions responded to Reconstruction.

120

A Northern Teacher's View of the Freedmen (1863–65)

Early in the Civil War, Union troops occupied the sea islands along South Carolina's coast near Beaufort. All property—plantations, cotton, and slaves—was confiscated and placed under the jurisdiction of Secretary of the Treasury Salmon P. Chase. Of particular concern was the welfare of the slaves, who at this early stage of the war were considered "contraband" if they were behind Union lines and were not returned to their owners. Sensing the opportunity to use these islands as an experiment for the future reconstruction of the South, Chase permitted benevolent organizations to send teachers, many of whom were women, to help educate the former slaves. In October 1863, the New England Freedmen's Aid Society sponsored Elizabeth Hyde Botume as a teacher in this experiment. Hyde became more than a teacher in the several years she spent among the ex-slaves, as her book, First Days Amongst the Contrabands, *revealed. Excerpted as follows is Hyde's description of the freedmen.*

Questions to Consider

1. In what ways did the slaves react to freedom?
2. What are the initial problems facing the freedmen?
3. What social, political, and economic issues confronting Reconstruction does Elizabeth Hyde Botume observe?

. . . Contrabands were coming into the Union lines, and thence to the town, not only daily, but hourly. They came alone and in families and in gangs,— slaves who had been hiding away, and were only now able to reach safety. Different members of scattered families following after freedom, as surely and safely guided as were the Wise Men by the Star of the East.

On New Year's Day I walked around amongst these people with Major Saxton. We went to their tents and other quarters. One hundred and fifty poor refugees from Georgia had been quartered all day on the wharf. A wretched and most pitiable gang, miserable beyond description. But when we spoke to them, they invariably gave a cheerful answer. Usually to our question, "How do you do?" the response would be, "Thank God, I live!"

Sometimes they would say, "Us ain't no wusser than we been."

These people had been a long time without food, excepting a little hominy and uncooked rice and a few ground-nuts. Many were entirely naked when they started, and all were most scantily clothed and we had already had some extremely cold days, which we, who were fresh from the North, found hard to bear.

It was the same old story. These poor creatures were covered only with blankets, or bits of old carpeting, or pieces of bagging, "crocus," fastened with thorns or sharp sticks. . . .

I went first to the negro quarters at the "Battery Plantation," a mile and a half away. A large number of Georgia refugees who had followed Sherman's army were quartered here. Around the old plantation house was a small army of black children, who swarmed like bees around a hive. There were six rooms in the house, occupied by thirty-one persons, big and little. In one room was a man whom I had seen before. He was very light, with straight red hair and a sandy complexion, and I mistook him for an Irishman. He had been to me at one time grieving deeply for the loss of his wife, but he had now consoled himself with a buxom girl as black as ink. His sister, a splendidly developed creature, was with them. He had also four sons. Two were as light as himself, and two were very black. These seven persons occupied this one room. A rough box bedstead, with a layer of moss and a few old rags in it, a hominy pot, two or three earthen plates, and a broken-backed chair, comprised all the furniture of the room. I had previously given one of the women a needle and some thread, and she now sat on the edge of the rough bedstead trying to sew the dress she ought, in decency, to have had on. . . .

The winter of 1864–1865 was a sad time, for so many poor creatures in our district were wretchedly ill, begging for help, and we had so little to give them. Many of the contrabands had pneumonia. Great exposure, with scanty clothing and lack of proper food, rendered them easy victims to the encroachments of any disease. I sent to Beaufort for help. The first doctor who came was exasperatingly indifferent. He might have been a brother of a "bureau officer," who was sent down especially to take care of the contrabands, and

Elizabeth Hyde Botume, *First Days Amongst the Contrabands* (Boston, 1893), 78–79, 82–83, 117–118, 168–169, 176–177.

who wished all the negroes could be put upon a ship, and floated out to sea and sunk. It would be better for them and for the world. When we expressed our surprise that he could speak so of human beings, he exclaimed, "Human beings! They are only animals, and not half as valuable as cattle."

When the doctor came, I went from room to room and talked with the poor sick people, whose entire dependence was upon us. Finally I could endure his apathy and indifference no longer.

"Leave me medicines, and I will take care of these people as well as I can," I said. . . .

I could not, however, excuse the doctor, a man in government employ, drawing a good salary with no heart in his work. Beaufort was reported to be a depot for officials whom government did not know what to do with. . . .

Early in February we went to Savannah with General and Mrs. Saxton, and members of the general's staff, and other officers. How it had become known that we were to make this trip I cannot tell, but we found a crowd of our own colored people on the boat when we went aboard. To our exclamations of surprise they said with glee,—

"Oh, we're goin' too, fur us has frien's there."

We found the city crowded with contrabands who were in a most pitiable condition. Nearly all the negroes who had lived there before the war had gone away. A large number went on with the army; those left were the stragglers who had come in from the "sand hills" and low lands. The people from the plantations too had rushed into the city as soon as they knew the Union troops were in possession.

A crowd of poor whites had also congregated there. All were idle and destitute. The whites regarded the negroes as still a servile race, who must always be inferior by virtue of their black skins. The negroes felt that emancipation had lifted them out of old conditions into new relations with their fellow beings. They were no longer chattels, but independent creatures with rights and privileges like their neighbors. . . .

Nothing in the history of the world has ever equalled the magnitude and thrilling importance of the events then transpiring. Here were more than four millions of human beings just born into freedom; one day held in the most abject slavery, the next, "de Lord's free men." Free to come and to go according to the best lights given them. Every movement of their white friends was to them full of significance, and often regarded with distrust. Well might they sometimes exclaim, when groping from darkness into light, "Save me from my friend, and I will look out for my enemy."

Whilst the Union people were asking, "Those negroes! what is to be done with them?" they, in their ignorance and helplessness, were crying out in agony, "What will become of us?" They were literally saying, "I believe, O Lord! help thou mine unbelief."

They were constantly coming to us to ask what peace meant for them? Would it be peace indeed? or oppression, hostility, and servile subjugation? This was what they feared, for they knew the temper of the baffled rebels as did no others.

121

Charleston, South Carolina at the Conclusion of the Civil War (1865)

The Civil War brought destruction to the South. With much of the fighting taking place in southern states, armies of both sides laid waste to the countryside and burned or destroyed communities as they struggled to win the war. While often not directly involved in the fighting, the civilian population felt the brunt of the war. The war also brought a dislocation of trade and business activities in the South, often resulting in shortages of food and clothing. Furthermore, the Civil War shattered the plantation economy of primarily cotton production based on the labor of African-American slaves. When the Confederacy surrendered in April 1865, the southern states faced significant social, political, and economic adjustments. At the war's conclusion, several northern journalists traveled throughout the South to report on conditions and people's reactions to the beginnings of Reconstruction. Sidney Andrews was one of these journalists; his observations appeared in the Chicago Tribune *and the* Boston Advertiser. *The reports from his three-month southern tour attracted such attention that they were compiled in book form,* The South Since the War, *which is excerpted as follows. Andrews' direct and well-written accounts were among the best commentaries on the immediate post-war South.*

Questions to Consider

1. What conditions did Andrews find in Charleston?

2. In what ways did residents of Charleston react to northerners? To Reconstruction policies? Would this be expected?

3. What issues and attitudes does Andrews reveal that become critical in Reconstruction?

A city of ruins, of desolation, of vacant houses, of widowed women, of rotting wharves, of deserted warehouses, of weed-wild gardens, of miles of grass-grown streets, of acres of pitiful and voiceful barrenness,—that is Charleston, wherein Rebellion loftily reared its head five years ago, on whose beautiful promenade the fairest of cultured women gathered with passionate hearts to applaud the assault of ten thousand upon the little garrison of Fort Sumter! . . .

We will never again have the Charleston of the decade previous to the war. The beauty and pride of the city are as dead as the glories of Athens. Five millions of dollars could not restore the ruin of these four past years; and that sum is so far beyond the command of the city as to seem the boundless measure of immeasurable wealth. Yet, after all, Charleston was

---

Sidney Andrews, *The South Since the War* (Boston, 1866), 1–9.

Charleston because of the hearts of its people. St. Michael's Church, they held, was the center of the universe; and the aristocracy of the city were the very elect of God's children of earth. One marks now how few young men there are, how generally the young women are dressed in black. The flower of their proud aristocracy is buried on scores of battlefields. If it were possible to restore the broad acres of crumbling ruins to their foretime style and uses, there would even then be but the dead body of Charleston. . . .

Of Massachusetts men, some are already in business here, and others came on to "see the lay of the land," as one of them said. "That's all right," observed an ex-rebel captain in one of our after-dinner chats,—"that's all right; let's have Massachusetts and South Carolina brought together, for they are the only two States that amount to anything."

"I hate all you Yankees most heartily in a general sort of way," remarked another of these Southerners; "but I find you clever enough personally, and I expect it'll be a good thing for us to have you come down here with your money, though it'll go against the grain of us pretty badly."

There are many Northern men here already, though one cannot say that there is much Northern society, for the men are either without families or have left them at home. Walking out yesterday with a former Charlestonian, . . . he pointed out to me the various "Northern houses"; and I shall not exaggerate if I say that this classification appeared to include at least half the stores on each of the principal streets. "The presence of these men," said he, "was at first very distasteful to our people, and they are not liked any too well now; but we know they are doing a good work for the city."

I fell into some talk with him concerning the political situation, and found him of bitter spirit toward what he was pleased to denominate "the infernal radicals." When I asked him what should be done, he answered: "You Northern people are making a great mistake in your treatment of the South. We are thoroughly whipped; we give up slavery forever; and now we want you to quit reproaching us. Let us back into the Union, and then come down here and help us build up the country." . . .

It would seem that it is not clearly understood how thoroughly Sherman's army destroyed everything in its line of march,—destroyed it without questioning who suffered by the action. That this wholesale destruction was often without orders, and often against most positive orders, does not change the fact of destruction. The Rebel leaders were, too, in their way, even more wanton, and just as thorough as our army in destroying property. They did not burn houses and barns and fences as we did; but, during the last three months of the war, they burned immense quantities of cotton and rosin. . . .

The city is under thorough military rule; but the iron hand rests very lightly. Soldiers do police duty, and there is some nine-o'clock regulation; but, so far as I can learn, anybody goes anywhere at all hours of the night without molestation. "There never was such good order here before," said an old colored man to me. The main street is swept twice a week, and all garbage is removed at sunrise. "If the Yankees was to stay here always and keep the city so clean, I don't reckon we'd have 'yellow jack' here any more," was a remark I overheard on the street. "Now is de fust time sense I can 'mem'er when brack men was safe in de street af'er nightfall," states the negro tailor in whose shop I sat an hour yesterday.

On the surface, Charleston is quiet and well-behaved; and I do not doubt that the more intelligent citizens are wholly sincere in their expressions of a desire for peace and reunion. The city has been humbled as no other city has been; and I can't see how any man, after spending a few days here, can desire that it shall be further humiliated enough for health is another thing. Said one of the Charlestonians on the boat, "You won't see the real sentiment of our people, for we are under military rule; we are whipped, and we are going to make the best of things; but we hate Massachusetts as much as we ever did." This idea of making the best of things is one I have heard from scores of persons. I find very few who hesitate to frankly own that the South has been beaten. "We made the best fight we could, but you were too strong for us, and now we are only anxious to get back into the old Union and live as happily as we can," said a large cotton factor. I find very few who make any special profession of Unionism; but they are almost unanimous in declaring that they have no desire but to live as good and quiet citizens under the laws.

122

African Americans Seek Protection (1865)

The emancipation of 4 million slaves in the South brought significant social, political, and economic adjustment for both African Americans and whites. Despite obtaining freedom from their masters and the rigors of plantation life, the former slaves lost their source of shelter, food, clothing, and occupation. In short, they had little but their freedom. Realizing that they remained at the mercy of their previous owners, many African Americans gathered in conventions in cities throughout the South to discuss the best methods of protecting their fragile freedom. Some of these conventions petitioned Congress for assistance, whereas others turned to local officials for help. Excerpted following is a petition from a convention of African Americans meeting in Alexandria, Virginia, in August 1865, which demonstrates the precarious position of the freedmen and how they proposed to protect themselves. This petition was the typical result of the conventions.

Questions to Consider

1. What types of protection does this convention seek?
2. For what reasons was the convention critical of "loyalty oaths" and the Freedmen's Bureau?
3. What does this document reveal about the situation for the freedmen at this time?

4. Compare and contrast the views of the post-war South expressed in this document with those in found in "A White Southern Perspective on Reconstruction" (Document 124).

We, the undersigned members of a convention of colored citizens of the State of Virginia, would respectfully represent that, although we have been held as slaves, and denied all recognition as a constituent of your nationality for almost the entire period of the duration of your government, and that by your permission we have been denied either home or country, and deprived of the dearest rights of human nature; yet when you and our immediate oppressors met in deadly conflict upon the field of battle—the one to destroy and the other to save your government and nationality, we, with scarce an exception, in our inmost souls espoused your cause, and watched, and prayed, and waited, and labored for your success. . . .

When the contest waxed long, and the result hung doubtfully, you appealed to us for help, and how well we answered is written in the rosters of the two hundred thousand colored troops now enrolled in your service; and as to our undying devotion to your cause, let the uniform acclamation of escaped prisoners, "Whenever we saw a black face we felt sure of a friend," answer.

Well, the war is over, the rebellion is "put down," and we are declared free! Four-fifths of our enemies are paroled or amnestied, and the other fifth are being pardoned, and the President has, in his efforts at the reconstruction of the civil government of the States, late in rebellion, left us entirely at the mercy of these subjugated but unconverted rebels, in everything save the privilege of bringing us, our wives and little ones, to the auction block. He has, so far as we can understand the tendency and bearing of his action in the case, remitted us for all our civil rights, to men, a majority of whom regard our devotions to your cause and flag as that which decided the contest against them! This we regard as destructive of all we hold dear, and in the name of God, of justice, of humanity, of good faith, of truth and righteousness, we do most solemnly and earnestly protest. Men and brethren, in the hour of your peril you called upon us, and despite all time-honored interpretation of constitutional obligations, we came at your call and you are saved; and now we beg, we pray, we entreat you not to desert us in this the hour of our peril!

We know these men—know them well—and we assure you that, with the majority of them, loyalty is only "lip deep," and that their professions of loyalty are used as a cover to the cherished design of getting restored to their former relation with the Federal Government, and then, by all sorts of "unfriendly legislation," to render the freedom you have given us more intolerable than the slavery they intended for us.

We warn you in time that our only safety is in keeping them under Governors of the military persuasion until you have so amended the Federal Constitution that it will prohibit the States from making any distinction

---

"The Late Convention of Colored Men," *New York Times,* August 13, 1865, p. 3.

between citizens on account of race or color. In one word, the only salvation for us besides the power of the Government, is in the possession of the ballot. Give us this, and we will protect ourselves. No class of men relatively as numerous as we were ever oppressed when armed with the ballot. But, 'tis said we are ignorant. Admit it. Yet who denies we know a traitor from a loyal man, a gentleman from a rowdy, a friend from an enemy? . . .

. . . All we ask is an equal chance with the white traitors varnished and japanned* with the oath of amnesty. Can you deny us this and still keep faith with us? "But," say some, "the blacks will be overreached by the superior knowledge and cunning of the whites." Trust us for that. We will never be deceived a second time. "But," they continue, "the planters and landowners will have them in their power, and dictate the way their votes shall be cast." We did not know before that we were to be left to the tender mercies of these landed rebels for employment. Verily, we thought the Freedmen's Bureau was organized and clothed with power to protect us from this very thing, by compelling those for whom we labored to pay us, whether they liked our political opinions or not! . . .

We are "sheep in the midst of wolves," and nothing but the military arm of the Government prevents us and all the truly loyal white men from being driven from the land of our birth. Do not then, we beseech you, give to one of these "wayward sisters" the rights they abandoned and forfeited when they rebelled until you have secured our rights by the aforementioned amendment to the Constitution.

Let your action in our behalf be thus clear and emphatic, and our respected President, who, we feel confident, desires only to know your will, to act in harmony therewith, will give you his most earnest and cordial cooperation; and the Southern States, through your enlightened and just legislation, will speedily award us our rights. Thus not only will the arms of the rebellion be surrendered, but the ideas also.

123

Thaddeus Stevens on Reconstruction and the South (1865)

The debate over Reconstruction began during the Civil War and became increasingly acute as the North moved toward victory. The lines were quickly drawn between the president and Congress, although various factions within the Republican party argued vociferously for certain positions. Some of the more important issues were: How should the secessionist states be reunited with the Union; what political and social status should be conveyed to the 4 million freedmen; how should whites who supported the Confederacy be treated; and who should control Reconstruction? Presidential Reconstruction, begun by Abraham Lincoln in December 1863 and slightly modified when

---

*A varnish that yields a hard brilliant finish.

Andrew Johnson assumed the presidency, was declared too lenient by Republicans. Within Congress, a powerful group called the Radical Republicans challenged presidential Reconstruction and began advocating their own agenda. Among the leaders of the Radical Republicans was Thaddeus Stevens, a representative from Lancaster, Pennsylvania, whose quick wit, honesty, political savvy, and belief that Reconstruction offered an opportunity to establish a better country made him a powerful supporter of Congressional Reconstruction. The following excerpt is Stevens' speech on the status of the South and what Congressional Reconstruction should encompass.

Questions to Consider

1. What political actions does Thaddeus Stevens propose for the South?
2. What does Stevens believe Congress should do for the freedmen?
3. In what ways do Stevens' proposals help shape Reconstruction policies?

. . . No one doubts that the late rebel states have lost their constitutional relations to the Union, and are incapable of representation in Congress, except by permission of the Government. It matters but little, with this admission whether you call them States out of the Union, and now conquered territories, or assert that because the Constitution forbids them to do what they did do, that they are therefore only dead as to all national and political action, and will remain so until the government shall breathe into them the breath of life anew and permit them to occupy their former position. In other words, that they are not out of the Union, but are only dead carcasses lying within the Union. In either case, it is very plain that it requires the action of Congress to enable them to form a State government and send representatives to Congress. Nobody, I believe, pretends that with their old constitutions and frames of government they can be permitted to claim their old rights under the Constitution. They have torn their constitutional States into atoms, and built on their foundations fabrics of a totally different character. Dead men cannot raise themselves. Dead States cannot restore their own existence "as it was." Whose especial duty is it to do it? In whom does the Constitution place the power? Not in the judicial branch of government, for it only adjudicates and does not prescribe laws. Not in the Executive, for he only executes and cannot make laws. Not in the Commander-in-Chief of the armies, for he can only hold them under military rule until the sovereign legislative power of the conqueror shall give them law. . . .

Congress alone can do it. But Congress does not mean the Senate, or the House of Representatives, and President, all acting severally. Their joint action constitutes Congress. . . . Congress must create States and declare when they are entitled to be represented. Then each House must judge whether the members presenting themselves from a recognized State possess the requisite qualifications of age, residence, and citizenship; and whether the election and returns are according to law. The Houses, separately, can judge of nothing

---

"Reconstruction," *Congressional Globe*, 39th Congress, 1st session, part 1 (December 18, 1865), 72–74.

else. It seems amazing that any man of legal education could give it any larger meaning.

It is obvious from all this that the first duty of Congress is to pass a law declaring the condition of these outside or defunct States, and providing proper civil governments to them. Since the conquest they have been governed by martial law. Military rule is necessarily despotic, and ought not to exist longer than is absolutely necessary. As there are no symptoms that the people of these provinces will be prepared to participate in constitutional government for some years, I know of no arrangement so proper for them as territorial governments. There they can learn the principles of freedom and eat the fruit of foul rebellion. Under such governments, while electing members to the Territorial Legislatures, they will necessarily mingle with those to whom Congress shall extend the right of suffrage. In Territories Congress fixes the qualifications of electors; and I know of no better place nor better occasion for the conquered rebels and the conqueror to practice justice to all men, and accustom themselves to make and obey equal laws. . . .

According to my judgment they ought never to be recognized as capable of acting in the Union, of being counted as valid States, until the Constitution shall have been so amended as to make it what its framers intended; and so as to secure perpetual ascendancy to the party of the Union; and so as to render our republican Government firm and stable forever. The first of those amendments is to change the basis of representation among the States from Federal numbers to actual voters. . . .

But this is not all that we ought to do before these inveterate rebels are invited to participate in our legislation. We have turned, or are about to turn, loose four million slaves without a hut to shelter them or a cent in their pockets. The infernal laws of slavery have prevented them from acquiring an education, understanding the commonest laws of contract, or of managing the ordinary business of life. This Congress is bound to provide for them until they can take care of themselves. If we do not furnish them with homesteads, and hedge them around with protective laws; if we leave them to the legislation of their late masters, we had better have left them in bondage. Their condition would be worse than that of our prisoners at Andersonville. If we fail in this great duty now, when we have the power, we shall deserve and receive the execration of history and of all future ages.

124

A White Southern Perspective on Reconstruction (1868)

Congressional or Radical Reconstruction imposed a new set of requirements on the South. It divided the region into five military districts and outlined how new governments were to be created—especially granting suffrage to African Americans. Complying with these guidelines, every southern state was readmitted into the Union by 1870. A Republican party coalition of African Americans, recently arrived northerners (carpetbaggers), and southern whites (scalawags) controlled nearly all of these state governments. Many former supporters of the Confederacy found these Republican governments to be offensive, corrupt, and expensive (they raised taxes to pay for new services like public education). One of the most outspoken and uncompromising opponents of Radical Reconstruction was Howell Cobb. Born into a wealthy Georgia cotton plantation family, Cobb devoted his life to public service. He served in the House of Representatives, was elected speaker in 1849, was governor of Georgia, served as secretary of the treasury under President James Buchanan, was a prominent secessionist, helped form the Confederate government, and was an officer in the war. After the war, Cobb maintained a self-imposed silence on political matters, which he broke with the following excerpted letter. Many white southerners would have agreed with Cobb's attack on Radical Reconstruction.

Questions to Consider

1. What are Howell Cobb's reasons to oppose Reconstruction policies?
2. Which policies does he particularly dispute? Why?
3. In what ways did white southerners react to Reconstruction?
4. In what ways might Howell Cobb have reacted to Sidney Andrews's commentary on conditions in Charleston, South Carolina ("Charleston, South Carolina at the Conclusion of the Civil War," Document 121)?

Macon [GA], 4 Jany., 1868

We of the ill-fated South realize only the mournful present whose lesson teaches us to prepare for a still gloomier future. To participate in a national festival would be a cruel mockery, for which I frankly say to you I have no heart, however much I may honor the occasion and esteem the association with which I would be thrown.

The people of the south, conquered, ruined, impoverished, and oppressed, bear up with patient fortitude under the heavy weight of their burdens. Disarmed and reduced to poverty, they are powerless to protect themselves against wrong and injustice; and can only await with broken spirits that destiny which the future has in store for them. At the bidding of their more powerful conquerors they laid down their arms, abandoned a hopeless struggle, and returned to their quiet homes under the plighted faith of a soldier's honor that they should be protected so long as they observed the obligations

Howell Cobb to J. D. Hoover, 4 January 1868, *Annual Report of the American Historical Association for the Year 1911*, vol. 2, *The Correspondence of Robert Toombs, Alexander H. Stephens, and Howell Cobb,* ed. U. B. Phillips (Washington D.C., 1913), 690–694.

imposed upon them of peaceful law-abiding citizens. Despite the bitter charges and accusations brought against our people, I hesitate not to say that since that hour their bearing and conduct have been marked by a dignified and honorable submission which should command the respect of their bitterest enemy and challenge the admiration of the civilized world. Deprived of our property and ruined in our estates by the results of the war, we have accepted the situation and given the pledge of a faith never yet broken to abide it. Our conquerors seem to think we should accompany our acquiescence with some exhibition of gratitude for the ruin which they have brought upon us. We cannot see it in that light. Since the close of the war they have taken our property of various kinds, sometimes by seizure, and sometime by purchase,—and when we have asked for remuneration have been informed that the claims of rebels are never recognized by the Government. To this decision necessity compels us to submit; but our conquerors express surprise that we do not see in such ruling the evidence of their kindness and forgiving spirit. They have imposed upon us in our hour of distress and ruin a heavy and burthensome tax, peculiar and limited to our impoverished section. Against such legislation we have ventured to utter an earnest appeal, which to many of their leading spirits indicates a spirit of insubordination which calls for additional burthens. They have deprived us of the protection afforded by our state constitutions and laws, and put life, liberty and property at the disposal of absolute military power. Against this violation of plighted faith and constitutional right we have earnestly and solemnly protested, and our protest has been denounced as insolent;—and our restlessness under the wrong and oppression which have followed these acts has been construed into a rebellious spirit, demanding further and more stringent restrictions of civil and constitutional rights. They have arrested the wheels of State government, paralized the arm of industry, engendered a spirit of bitter antagonism on the part of our negro population towards the white people with whom it is the interest of both races they should maintain kind and friendly relations, and are now struggling by all the means in their power both legal and illegal, constitutional and unconstitutional, to make our former slaves *our masters,* bringing these Southern states under the power of *negro supremacy.* To these efforts we have opposed appeals, protests, and every other means of resistance in our power, and shall continue to do so until the bitter end. If the South is to be made a pandemonium and a howling wilderness the responsibility shall not rest upon our heads. Our conquerors regard these efforts on our part to save ourselves and posterity from the terrible results of their policy and conduct as a new rebellion against the constitution of our country, and profess to be amazed that in all this we have failed to see the evidence of their great magnanimity and exceeding generosity. Standing today in the midst of the gloom and suffering which meets the eye in every direction, we can but feel that we are the victims of cruel legislation and the harsh enforcement of unjust laws. . . . We regarded the close of the war as ending the relationship of enemies and the beginning of a new national brotherhood, and in the light of that conviction felt and spoke of constitutional equality. . . . We claimed that the result of the war left us a state in the Union, and therefore under the protection of the constitution, rendering in return cheerful obedience to its requirements and bearing in common with the other states of the Union the burthens of government, submitting even as we were compelled to do to *taxation without representation;* but they tell us that a successful war to keep us in the Union left us out of the Union and that the pretension we put up for constitutional protection evidences bad temper on our part and a want of appreciation of the generous spirit which declares that the constitution is not over us for the purposes of protection. . . . In such reasoning is found a justification of the policy which seeks to put the South under negro supremacy. Better, they say, to hazard the consequences of negro supremacy in the south with its sure and inevitable results upon Northern prosperity than to put faith in the people of the south who though overwhelmed and conquered have ever showed themselves a brave and generous people, true to their plighted faith in peace and in war, in adversity as in prosperity. . . .

With an Executive who manifests a resolute purpose to defend with all his power the constitution of his country from further aggression, and a Judiciary whose unspotted record has never yet been tarnished with a base subserviency to the unholy demands of passion and hatred, let us indulge the hope that the hour of the country's redemption is at hand, and that even in the wronged and ruined South there is a fair prospect for better days and happier hours when our people can unite again in celebrating the national festivals as in the olden time.

125

The Ku Klux Klan during Reconstruction (1872)

The original Ku Klux Klan was formed in 1866 in Pulaski, Tennessee, as a social organization, but several former Confederates made the Klan a terrorist group. The Klan espoused white supremacy, the defeat of the Republican party in the South, and keeping African Americans "in their place." Incensed with the Republican party's control of state governments, especially African Americans voting and holding public office, and intrigued with the secrecy, unusual names, and disguises of the Klan, thousands joined the organization in the late 1860s. The Klan embarked on a terrorist campaign with intimidation, whippings, beatings, property destruction, shootings, or simply riding disguised in the countryside as its hallmarks. Blacks who affirmed their rights were the most common Klan targets, but white Republicans were also singled out. Much of the South was spared Klan activity, but locations where both races or political parties were almost equally balanced often witnessed Klan terrorism, especially near election time. In 1871, a congressional committee traveled in the South to investigate Klan activities and take statements from many of its victims. Excerpted as follows is Edward "Ned" Crosby's testimony on Klan intimidation in Mississippi.

Questions to Consider

1. What were the reasons for the Klan's intimidation of African Americans?

2. How were African Americans coerced into voting for the Democratic party?

3. What does this document reveal about race relations in the South during Reconstruction?

4. In what ways might Edward Crosby have reacted to Howell Cobb's commentary on conditions in the South ("A White Southern Perspective on Reconstruction," Document 124)?

Columbus, Mississippi, November 17, 1871

EDWARD CROSBY (colored) sworn and examined.

By the Chairman:

QUESTION. Where do you live?

ANSWER. Right near Aberdeen—ten miles east of Aberdeen.

QUESTION. State whether you were ever visited by the Ku-Klux; and, if so, under what circumstances.

ANSWER. I have been visited by them. They came to my house, and came into my house. . . . It looked like there were thirty-odd of them, and I didn't know but what they might interfere with me, and I just stepped aside, out in the yard to the smokehouse. They came up there and three of them got down and came in the house and called for me, and she told them I had gone over to Mr. Crosby's. . . . She didn't know but they might want something to do to me and interfere with me and they knocked around a while and off they went.

QUESTION. Was this in the night-time?

ANSWER. Yes, sir.

QUESTION. Were they disguised?

ANSWER. Yes, sir.

QUESTION. Had you been attempting to get up a free-school in your neighborhood?

ANSWER. Yes, sir.

QUESTION. Colored school?

ANSWER. Yes, sir.

U.S. Congress, *Testimony Taken by the Joint Select Committee to Inquire into the Condition of Affairs in the Late Insurrectionary States* (Washington, DC, 1872), 12: 1133–1134.

QUESTION. Do you know whether their visit to you had reference to this effort?

ANSWER. No, sir; I don't know only this: I had spoken for a school, and I had heard a little chat of that, and I didn't know but what they heard it, and that was the thing they were after.

QUESTION. Were their horses disguised?

ANSWER. Yes. Sir. . . .

QUESTION. Did you know any of the men?

ANSWER. No, sir; I didn't get close enough to know them. I could have known them, I expect, if I was close up, but I was afraid to venture.

QUESTION. Did they ever come back?

ANSWER. No, sir.

QUESTION. What do you know as to the whipping of Green T. Roberts?

ANSWER. Only from hearsay. He told me himself. They didn't whip him. They took him out and punched him and knocked him about right smart, but didn't whip him.

QUESTION. Was he a colored man?

ANSWER. He was a white man—a neighbor of mine.

QUESTION. Who took him out?

ANSWER. The Ku-Klux. . . .

QUESTION. What if anything do you know of any colored men being afraid to vote the republican ticket and voting the democratic ticket at the election this month, in order to save their property, and to save themselves from being outraged?

ANSWER. Well sir, the day of the election there was, I reckon, thirty or forty; I didn't count them, but between that amount; they spoke of voting the radical ticket. It was my intention to go for the purpose. I had went around and saw several colored friends on that business. . . . I knew some of the party would come in and maybe they would prevent us from voting as we wanted to. I called for the republican tickets and they said there was none on the ground. I knocked around amongst them, and I called a fellow named Mr. Dowdell and asked if there would be any there; he said he didn't know; he asked me how I was going to vote; I told him my opinion, but I was cramped for fear. They said if we didn't act as they wanted they would drop us at once. There is only a few of us, living amongst them like lost sheep where we can do the best; and they were voting and they stood back and got the colored population and pushed them in front and let them vote first, and told them there was no republican tickets on the ground. I didn't see but three after I voted. Shortly after I voted, Mr. James Wilson came with some, and a portion of the colored people had done voting. I met Mr. Henderson; I was going on to the other box at the Baptist church. He asked if there were any colored voters there; I told him there was thirty or forty, and there was no republican tickets there. Mr.

Wilson had some in his pocket, but I didn't see them. I saw that I was beat at my own game, and I had got on my horse and dropped out.

QUESTION. Who told you that unless the colored people voted the democratic ticket it would be worse for them?

ANSWER. Several in the neighborhood. Mr. Crosby said as long as I voted as he voted I could stay where I was, but he says, "Whenever Ned votes my rights away from me, I cast him down."

QUESTION. Was he a democrat?

ANSWER. A dead-out democrat.

QUESTION. Did you hear any other white men make the same declaration?

ANSWER. Not particular; I only heard them talking through each other about the colored population. I heard Mr. Jerome Lamb—he lived nigh Athens—tell a fellow named Aleck that lived on his place, he spoke to him and asked him if he was going to vote as he did; Aleck told him he was—he did this in fear, mind you—and Aleck went and voted, and after he voted he said, "Aleck, come to me;" says he, "Now, Aleck, you have voted?" Aleck says, "Yes sir;" he said, "Well, now, Aleck, you built some very nice houses. Now, I want you to wind your business up right carefully. I am done with you; off of my land."

QUESTION. Had Aleck voted the republican ticket?

ANSWER. Yes, sir.

QUESTION. Did all the colored men except these three vote the democratic ticket that day?

ANSWER. Up at Grub Springs all voted the democratic ticket. There was no republican ticket given to the colored people at all.

QUESTION. Did they vote the democratic ticket from fear that they would be thrown out of employment or injured?

ANSWER. That was their intention. You see pretty nigh every one of them was the same way I was, but there was none there; and them they were all living on white people's land, and were pretty fearful. The Ku-Klux had been ranging around through them, and they were all a little fearful.

QUESTION. Do you think they were all radical in sentiment, and would have been glad to have voted the radical ticket if uninfluenced?

ANSWER. They would. They had a little distinction up amongst themselves—the white and colored people. One of them said, "Ned, put in a republican ticket." Well, there was none on the ground, and I remarked, "If there is any radical tickets on the ground I will take one of them, and I will not take a democratic ticket, and I will fold them up and drop that in the box, and they will never tell the difference," and it got out that I had voted the radical ticket, and some were very harsh about it.

QUESTION. Would the colored people of your county vote the radical ticket if left alone?

ANSWER. Well, sir, I suppose they would have done it.

126

"The Problem at the South" (1871)

The end of the Civil War demanded federal efforts to remake the South, but efforts to bring the southern states back into the Union while helping the former slaves make the transition to freedom proved particularly problematic. By 1871, supporters of Reconstruction grew increasingly frustrated at their inability to achieve these two goals in the face of southern white opposition, weak Reconstruction governments, and Democratic challenges to their policies. As northerners debated Reconstruction policy, E. L. Godkin was a prominent commentator on the issue. A native of Great Britain, Godkin helped found The Nation *in July 1865 as a reform-minded political journal. The following excerpt from an 1871 selection offers his critique of Reconstruction as well as a suggestion concerning future policy toward the South.*

Questions to Consider

1. What does E. L. Godkin see as the major problems facing Reconstruction?
2. Are Godkin's suggested solutions prudent given the situation?
3. What does Godkin's commentary reveal about northern commitment to Reconstruction?

There is no doubt about the multiplicity and atrocity of the outrages committed by what are called the Ku-klux on the negroes and Unionists at the South. It appears to be equally certain that the persons who commit these outrages are not brought to Justice. The sheriffs do not arrest them, or, if they do, juries do not convict them—in other words, through a great part of the South there is no security for either life or property. That some such state of things would come to pass was foreseen after the war. It was said that if legislation and the election of officers were left solely to the Southern whites, the Southern blacks would be left without adequate protection. Consequently, the suffrage was given to the blacks. But this was not felt to be sufficient. A great proportion of the more experienced and intelligent people at the South were excluded by the State constitutions, and by an amendment to the United States Constitution, from all share in the government. In this way not only were the negroes and Unionists guaranteed a voice in the Government, but they were secured in the exclusive control of it. That is, to speak plainly, for the purpose of securing the poor and ignorant against oppression, not only were they admitted to an equality of rights with the rich and educated, but they were put in possession of the whole administrative machinery. Considering that a large body of the voters—in some States a majority—had recently emerged from slavery in its most brutal form, it must be admitted

E. L. Godkin, "The Problem at the South," *The Nation* (23 March 23, 1871): 192–193.

the experiment was a bold one; in fact, it was the boldest ever known. No similar rearrangement of the social organization has ever been attempted anywhere else. We do not blame those who attempted it. They were hot from a civil war which had ended in a social revolution, and they found themselves charged with the duty of securing a large and helpless population of freemen in possession of common civil rights, in the presence of their late masters, without having recourse to pure military coercion.

The experiment has, however, totally failed. The most influential portion of the Southern population, with whose support no government can in the long run dispense, as has been a thousand times proved, have not only given the new governments at the South no assistance, but have, naturally enough, been bitterly hostile to them. The new political system, indeed, was of a kind to rouse all their prejudices against it. The men who took part in and aided the rebellion, and who are therefore disfranchised, have within the last five years been reinforced by a powerful body of youths who were boys during the rebellion, and who have entered on manhood during a period of great disorder and uncertainty and poverty, in which few careers are open to them, and in which all the circumstances of their lives tend to exasperate and embitter them, and prepare them for turbulence and violence. They may therefore be said, without exaggeration, to have taken the field against the new regime. They have formed organizations somewhat similar to the Irish Whiteboys and Molly Maguires, the express object of which is to drive negroes and union men out of the South, and make all government through their instrumentality impossible. For this purpose they murder, rob, and maltreat, and they are too powerful, too skillful, and too firmly bound together, and enjoy too much of the sympathy of the local population, to make it possible for the State officers to bring them to justice. More than this, and, if possible, worse than this, they have at the North a powerful political party, which, if it cannot be said to be at their back, is certainly not disposed to blame them or call them to account, and whose chances of accession to power seem to improve as the passions excited by the war die out.

On the other hand, the new governments have done nothing to atone for the theoretical defects of their origin. We owe it to human nature to say that worse governments have seldom been seen in a civilized country. They have been largely composed of trashy whites and ignorant blacks. Of course, there have been in them men of integrity and ability of both races; but the great majority of the officers and legislators have been either wanting in knowledge or in principle, or both. That of South Carolina is one of the worst specimens, and, as such, we have often commented on it.

What is to be done? Congress having set those governments up, and having emancipated the negroes, and the negroes being, it is safe to say, the only men at the South who are really devoted to the Union, it seems as if it was the duty of Congress to see to their protection. Moreover, the experiment which is now on trial at the South being of Republican devising, it seems to be necessary to the credit of the party that it should be made to succeed, and at the same time, it seems as if the Ku-klux stories might be made to help the party by showing the necessity of such a prolongation of its power as would enable it to complete the work of Southern pacification. Accordingly, nearly every session of Congress there is a call either from philanthropists under the influence of feelings of humanity, or from mere politicians in search of "capital," for additional legislation "to protect life and property at the South." Of the sort of legislation demanded, the bill recently brought in by Butler is a fair specimen, and it consists simply in attempts to substitute for the state machinery, which is the only means of protecting life and property known to the Constitution of the United States, the machinery in use under the arbitrary and centralized governments of Europe—that is, the withdrawal of criminal cases from the jury, and their committal to single judges appointed by the central authority and armed with extraordinary powers, and the concession to mere official suspicion, and to legal presumptions, of a part in determining the question of guilt or innocence of a prominence hitherto unknown in Anglo-Saxon jurisprudence.

These are momentous changes to introduce into the administrative system of any free country; they are more momentous in this country than they would be in any other, because they not only increase the power of the central government, but they arm it with jurisdiction over a class of cases of which it has never hitherto had, and never pretended to have, any jurisdiction whatever. It would not simply furnish the Government at Washington with additional means of performing one of its well-known duties, such as the suspension of the *habeas corpus* in Ireland furnishes the British Government with, but it would impose upon it altogether new duties. But the separate States are, under the Constitution, as clearly charged with the duty of protecting life and property within their own borders, as the United States with the duty of making treaties with foreign powers. To impose the duty of protecting life and property on the Federal Government is, therefore, just as distinct and well-marked a novelty as, and a far more serious novelty than, the transfer of the power of negotiating treaties to the separate States would be. . . .

Is there, then, no remedy for local disorder at the South? If the state government does not protect a man, can he look nowhere else for redress? We answer, that if there be any value whatever in the theory on which American polity is based, the remedy of Southern disorders must come from the Southern people, through their experience of the folly and suffering of disorder. If this be not true, the whole American system is a mistake, and is destined ere long to perish. Our business is now to leave every Southern State to its own people, first, because this is the only practicable course, and secondly, because it is the only wise one. If they are so demoralized that they go on robbing, and murdering, and "Kukluxing" each other, we cannot interfere effectively, and had better not interfere at all. The American punishments for a State which permits these things are two—impoverishment and emigration. If a man cannot have freedom, security, and light taxation in New York, let him go to New Jersey; if he cannot have them in South Carolina, let him go to Virginia; if he cannot have them in either, let him go to Missouri. Those who stay behind, on seeing capital and population steadily leaving their State, and their property declining in value, will gradually mend their ways. This may be a slow remedy, but it is a sure one. It goes to the root of the disorder, while under coercion from the outside no state of things can grow up, or ever has grown up, in which coercion ceases to be necessary. Of course there is nothing in this theory to prevent the United States enforcing the Federal Constitution and laws. This ought to be done, *at whatever cost—* that is, by officers, and not by bill and resolution. If it be true that black men are kept from the polls by intimidation, we ought to see that going to the polls is made as safe as going to church; but to pass bills providing for this, without voting the men or the money to execute them, is a wretched mockery, of which the country and the blacks have had enough . . .

127

African-American Suffrage in the South (1867, 1876)

One of the critical and hotly debated issues of Reconstruction was the extension of civil rights to the freedmen. Mainly to protect the former slaves from possible retaliation at the hands of their former masters, the initial Reconstruction plans called for the protection of African-Americans' rights. Led by some Radical Republicans, Congress implemented its plan of Reconstruction, which required the new state governments in the South to guarantee the right to vote for male African Americans. In 1867, African Americans voted for the first time, often casting their ballots for Republican candidates and helping to establish the Republican party's control of state government. For white southerners, who mainly belonged to the Democratic party, this represented a revolutionary change and caused bitter resentment toward black voters and the Republican party. Some southern whites joined the Ku Klux Klan to intimidate Republicans, and other whites used their economic influence as landowners to intimidate African Americans. The two images that follow from Harper's Weekly, *a well-respected newspaper of the era, reflect the optimism of African Americans participating in the political process for the first time, as well as the reality of voter manipulation. The first image was the cover of the November 16, 1867 issue; the second image was a double-page illustration in the October 21, 1876 issue.*

Questions to Consider

1. How do the images differ in their depiction of African Americans' right to vote?

2. What appears to be the status of African Americans voting in the first image? How is the African American portrayed in the second image different? What might you deduce from these differences?

3. How does the second image portray southern whites? How do you account for this portrayal?

4. How do you think Howell Cobb, author of "A White Southern Perspective on Reconstruction" (Document 124), would respond to these images?

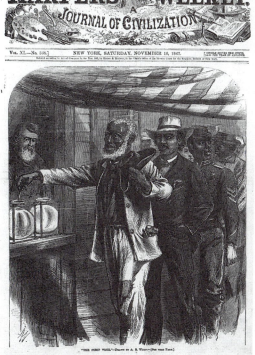

Harper's Weekly, November 16, 1867, p. 721. Reprinted by permission.

"The First Vote"

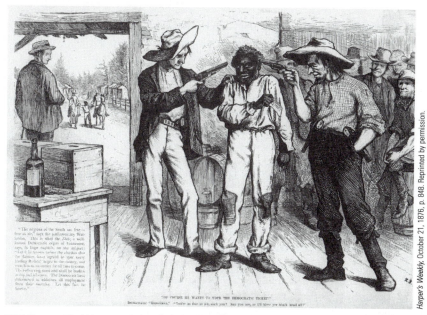

Harper's Weekly, October 21, 1876, p. 848. Reprinted by permission.

"Of Course He Wants to Vote the Democratic Ticket!"
Democratic "Reformer." "You're as free as air, ain't you? Say you are, or I'll blow yer black head off!"

17

✳

The West

Following the Civil War, many Americans expressed a renewed interest in the trans–Mississippi West. With the war concluded, construction proceeded on the trans–Mississippi railroad, and people began migrating to the Great Plains region. For many, especially those displaced by the war, the West offered a new beginning. The individuals who began to flood the West in the last third of the 19th century included Chinese and Irish laborers, African-American cowboys, white American farmers, and European immigrant miners, to name but a few. The land they entered was not an empty one, but one long inhabited by Native Americans and Mexicans. The meeting of these different groups triggered conflict over the region's future. The following documents describe the interactions of these groups in the western environment.

128

A Native American Remembers Life on the Great Plains (1870s)

After the Civil War, increased white migration through the Great Plains threatened the Native-American way of life. Available land and rumors of gold and silver deposits lured whites to the region, often in violation of earlier treaty agreements that protected Indian tribal hunting land. These white incursions threatened the nomadic lifestyle of many Native-American tribes on the Great Plains. Many Great Plains Indians traveled great distances in search of the American bison, or buffalo, their main source of food and shelter. In 1913, anthropologist Joseph Dixon recorded the accounts of Native Americans describing their lives, which he published as The Vanishing Race. *Excerpted as follows is a Native American describing a buffalo hunt conducted by his Blackfeet tribe.*

Questions to Consider

1. According to this account, how were the buffalo hunted?
2. What duties did the women and men perform? Why were there such distinctions?

3. In what ways did the buffalo influence this tribe?

4. How might William Ayer, the author of "A Western Newspaper Editorial on the Custer Massacre" (Document 130), respond to this selection?

. . . Then the chiefs sent for the leaders and warriors; we called them "crazy dogs." The leaders of the crazy dogs came into the tepee of Mountain Chief and Lame Bull, and my father, Mountain Chief, told these two crazy dogs to start before sunrise, and to take with them the other crazy dogs to find where there was a lot of good fresh water, and a lot of grass where they might camp, and also where they might find the nearest herd of buffalo. The crazy dogs found a good place where there was plenty of buffalo and water, and they marked the camp. . . . Four Bear went to the camp, told the people concerning their new camp, and the next morning the women took the medicine pipes and put them at the side of the tepee looking toward the direction where they were going to camp. Husbands told wives to go out and see on which side of the tepee the medicine pipes were placed, that they might know where they were going. Then the wives came in and told them that the medicine pipes pointed in a northerly direction. The husbands told the wives that the camp was going to move north. The camp broke up that very morning. . . . After everybody had left the camp, the chiefs followed the procession. When they thought it was noon they made a halt. They took their travois and saddles from the horses, and rested; then had their lunch. The chiefs then told Four Bear to get the camp in traveling shape again, and went on. Finally they came to the spot where the camping place was marked. . . . Four Bear was then told to get the people settled, to tie up the buffalo horses, and get ready for the hunt. Four Bear then told the people not to get a meal but to get a little lunch, and get ready for the hunt. Then the chiefs started out for the buffalo, the hunters following. They stopped halfway before they got to the herd, and told all the hunters not to start for the buffalo until they were ready and everybody had a fair chance. . . . If a hunter hit a buffalo with one arrow, he gave a scream, and that indicated that he had hit him just once. There were very few guns in those days and those were flint-locks. Sometimes when a hunter rode side by side with a buffalo, and shot the animal, the arrow would go clear through. The Indians were very proud and careful of their arrows. They did not wish to break them. That is the reason why they shot them on the side, so that when the buffalo fell the arrow would not be broken. Lots of the buffalo fell on their knees, and would begin to move from side to side. Then the Indian, for fear that the arrow would be broken, jumped off his horse and pulled it out. The hunter then tied his horse to the horns of the buffalo for fear that he might be attacked by enemies at any moment. After this they took out their knives and sharpened them on hard steel, like the flint with which they made fire. All the time they were sharpening their knives they were looking around for the

Joseph K. Dixon, ed., "Mountain Chief," *The Vanishing Race: The Last Great Indian Council* (Garden City, NY, 1913), 104–111.

approach of the enemy. The fire steel was scarce, we had to use rocks most of the time. The knives we procured from the Hudson Bay Company. When we killed a buffalo bull, we placed him on his knees, then we began to skin him down the back of the neck, down the backbone, splitting it on each side. The cows we laid on their backs, and cut down the middle. We used the buffalo cowhide for buffalo robes; the buffalo bull's hides were split down the back because from this hide we made war shields, parflesche bags, and saddle blankets. The husbands would tell the wives to take care of the heads. The wives took the brains out of the buffalo skull and mixed them with the largest part of the liver, and after mixing well, used the brains and liver in tanning hides. Then the wife was told to take out the tripe and skin it, for they used the skin as a bucket with which to carry water when they got home. They had strips of rawhide about three feet long and a quarter of an inch wide and tied the meat so that they could carry it home on the horses. They took the backbone after it had been cleaned of the flesh, and tied the meat to that and threw it over the back of the horse so that the load would not hurt the back of the horse. When we got home with the meat we unloaded. The men who had gone without their wives simply got off their horses and went into the tepee. The women rushed out to get the meat. Then the women took the horse with the meat on it to their father-in-law. Then the mother-in-law hurried to get the meal, taking the ribs of the buffalo, setting them up against the fire to roast. After the meal was cooked, it was cut in slices and placed in a wooden bowl, and the mother-in-law took the meat over to the lodge of her son-in-law. That was all we had for our meal. We had no coffee or anything else to eat, but we made a good meal from the meat of the buffalo. . . . About that time night came on, and the chiefs sent for Four Bear, and Four Bear would go around and tell the people that the grass in the camp was pretty well taken up. The next morning the women would take their medicine pipes and put them on the side, indicating where the next camp was going to be, and thus we went on from camp to camp.

129

A Century of Dishonor (1881)

In the years following the Civil War, problems with Native Americans in the West became increasingly difficult to resolve. The federal government policy of creating reservations by treaty with specific Indian tribes did not work. President Ulysses S. Grant endorsed the "peace policy," which called for "concentrating" most Plains Indians into two large reservations: one in the Indian Territory (Oklahoma) and the other in the Dakota Territory. Government management of these reservations was poor, and Native-American resentment increased. Other forces compounded the situation: New discoveries of gold and silver, westward railroad expansion, the destruction of the buffalo, and white demands for more land only heightened tensions. Struggling against these threats to

*their civilization, some Native Americans resisted. In a series of Indian wars, the U.S.
Army subdued hostile tribes and pushed Native Americans onto the reservations.
Alarmed at the plight of the Native American, Massachusetts-born Helen Hunt Jackson studied the history of Indian–white relations. Jackson's book,* A Century of Dishonor *(1881), chronicled the federal government's mistreatment of Native Americans.*

Questions to Consider

1. According to Jackson, what motivated whites to mistreat Native Americans?

2. What shaped whites' views about the Native Americans?

3. What does Jackson hope to accomplish with her book?

4. How would William Ayer, the author of "A Western Newspaper Editorial on the Custer Massacre" (Document 130), respond to Jackson's view of Indians? The federal government?

. . . It makes little difference, however, where one opens the record of the history of the Indians; every page and every year has its dark stain. The story of one tribe is the story of all, varied only by differences of time and place; but neither time nor place makes any difference in the main facts. Colorado is as greedy and unjust in 1880 as was Georgia in 1830, and Ohio in 1795; and the United States Government breaks promises now as deftly as then, and with an added ingenuity from long practice.

One of its strongest supports in so doing is the wide-spread sentiment among the people of dislike to the Indian, of impatience with his presence as a "barrier to civilization," and distrust of it as a possible danger. The old tales of the frontier life, with its horrors of Indian warfare, have gradually, by two or three generations' telling, produced in the average mind something like an hereditary instinct of unquestioning and unreasoning aversion which it is almost impossible to dislodge or soften.

There are hundreds of pages of unimpeachable testimony on the side of the Indian; but it goes for nothing, is set down as sentimentalism or partisanship, tossed aside and forgotten.

President after president has appointed commission after commission to inquire into and report upon Indian affairs, and to make suggestions as to the best methods of managing them. The reports are filled with eloquent statements of wrongs done to the Indians, of perfidies on the part of the Government; they counsel, as earnestly as words can, a trial of the simple and unperplexing expedients of telling truth, keeping promises, making fair bargains, dealing justly in all ways and all things. These reports are bound up with the Government's Annual Reports, and that is the end of them. It would probably be no exaggeration to say that not one American citizen out of ten thousand

---

Helen Hunt Jackson, *A Century of Dishonor* (New York, 1881), 337–340.

ever sees them or knows that they exist, and yet any one of them, circulated throughout the country, read by the right-thinking, right-feeling men and women of this land, would be of itself a "campaign document" that would initiate a revolution which would not subside until the Indians' wrongs were, so far as is now left possible, righted.

In 1869 President Grant appointed a commission of nine men, representing the influence and philanthropy of six leading States, to visit the different Indian reservations, and to "examine all matters pertaining to Indian affairs."

In the report of this commission are such paragraphs as the following: "To assert that 'the Indian will not work' is as true as it would be to say that the white man will not work.

"Why should the Indian be expected to plant corn, fence lands, build houses, or do anything but get food from day to day, when experience has taught him that the product of his labor will be seized by the white man tomorrow? The most industrious white man would become a drone under similar circumstances. Nevertheless, many of the Indians" (the commissioners might more forcibly have said 130,000 of the Indians) "are already at work, and furnish ample refutation of the assertion that 'the Indian will not work.' There is no escape from the inexorable logic of facts.

"The history of the Government connections with the Indians is a shameful record of broken treaties and unfulfilled promises. The history of the border white man's connection with the Indians is a sickening record of murder, outrage, robbery, and wrongs committed by the former, as the rule, and occasional savage outbreaks and unspeakably barbarous deeds of retaliation by the latter, as the exception.

"Taught by the Government that they had rights entitled to respect, when those rights have been assailed by the rapacity of the white man, the arm which should have been raised to protect them has ever been ready to sustain the aggressor.

"The testimony of some of the highest military officers of the United States is on record to the effect that, in our Indian wars, almost without exception, the first aggressions have been made by the white man; and the assertion is supported by every civilian of reputation who has studied the subject. In addition to the class of robbers and outlaws who find impunity in their nefarious pursuits on the frontiers, there is a large class of professedly reputable men who use every means in their power to bring on Indian wars for the sake of the profit to be realized from the presence of troops and the expenditure of Government funds in their midst. They proclaim death to the Indians at all times in words and publications, making no distinction between the innocent and the guilty. They irate the lowest class of men to the perpetration of the darkest deeds against their victims, and as judges and jurymen shield them from the justice due to their crimes. Every crime committed by a white man against an Indian is concealed or palliated. Every offence committed by an Indian against a white man is borne on the wings of the post or the telegraph to the remotest corner of the land, clothed with all the horrors which the reality or imagination can throw around it. Against such influences as these the people of the United States need to be warned." . . .

130

A Western Newspaper Editorial on the Custer Massacre (1876)

The country was still euphoric over the celebration of the Centennial when word of Colonel George A. Custer's massacre spread throughout the nation. Custer was part of a military operation to drive portions of the disgruntled Sioux (Lakota) tribe back to their reservation, when he ordered an attack on the Native-American encampment along the Little Big Horn River in present-day southeastern Montana. Custer and 264 of his men were killed in what became known as "Custer's Last Stand." William N. Byer, author of the editorial excerpted as follows, was considered a western "pioneer," having traveled and lived throughout the West. In 1859, he established the Rocky Mountain News, *the first newspaper in the Colorado territory, and he continued to edit and publish the paper for more than 19 years. In addition to his newspaper, Byer took an active role in pushing Colorado statehood and was closely identified with promoting the growth and development of Denver. His editorial reveals much about western attitudes of the time toward Native Americans and easterners.*

Questions to Consider

1. Whom does Byer blame for Custer's massacre?
2. Why does Byer fear the massacre will harm the "new west"?
3. In what ways does Byer's editorial reflect westerners' views about Native Americans and the development of the West?
4. On what issues would Byer and Helen Hunt Jackson ("*A Century of Dishonor,*" Document 129) disagree about the Native Americans?

The wish was father to the thought when yesterday we hazarded the assertion that the report of the annihilation of Custer's command bore the appearance of exaggeration, if not of entire fabrication. The details published in this morning's dispatches, although many of them emanate from not particularly trustworthy newspaper correspondents, forbid further incredulity, and we . . . accept the terrible truth in all its enormity, that some of the bravest officers in the service and a large fraction of one of the finest cavalry regiments, have fallen victim to the picayune policy that domineers in all matters appertaining to Indian affairs. The blood must boil in the veins of the most fishlike, at reading the horrible story of the massacre of three hundred United States soldiers at the hands of ten times that number of savages, when it is remembered that all this is the fruit of the do-nothing system of the Indian department. Custer and his men have been murdered, not by Indians,

"Extermination the Only Remedy," (Denver) *Rocky Mountain News,* July 8, 1876, p. 2.

who were only the instruments of their death, but by the sleek, smooth talking, Quaker advocates of the peace policy, who have always insisted that the
Indian was a man and a brother, and an elder brother, at that, with all the
rights of primogeniture. Had the Indian problem been treated properly, long
years since it would have been solved, and Custer would not now be a man-
gled corpse, from there being either no Indians alive to kill him, or the rem-
nants of the race so restrained within bounds that it would not be possible
for them to perpetrate the deed that they have. The Indian bureau has all
along realized Dicken's [sic] conception of the Circumlocution Office.*

How not to do it has ever been its aim, and the success with which it has
carried out its design is a blot on the entire fabric of government. What a
spectacle, indeed, is it for foreign nations to sneer at, when the great republic
of the west, for all its population of forty-four millions of people, allows its
soldiers to be overcome by odds of ten to one, although its antagonist numbers but a few paltry thousand of savages. The entire system pursued towards
the Indians, crowned as it is with this terrible disaster, is unworthy of the
government and a disgrace to the country.

While the entire nation has come to mourn the blot on its escutcheon
caused by the catastrophe to Custer, we of the new west have a right to feel
outraged, not for the sake of the honor that Falstaff dubbed but a word, but
for the wrong that is done as is preventing the increase of our population
and capital, by permitting the impression to gain ground abroad that our settlements are liable to hostile inroads. The states people have vague ideas of
distance, and the [location] in which Custer and those with him met their
death is liable to be located anywhere between Long and Pike's Peaks, while
very likely in the extreme east, the Platte is supposed to be the river from
which Gen. Reno at last got water, after suffering from a thirty-six hours'
thirst. The prosperity of the entire country from the Missouri river to the
Rocky Mountains is injured for years to come, more than it will easily be
believed, by the destruction of the Seventh cavalry. The shot that killed
Custer was heard around the world and everywhere that it aroused the
echoes, it frightened possible population and certain capital from the new
west. The injury done this entire region, indeed, will be almost irreparable,
unless the Sioux are at once exterminated. This is the only alternate. Do
what we will, it will be impossible to make it known in the states that Denver is as secure from Indian attack as New York, and that Custer fell half a
thousand miles form the northern boundary of Colorado. Distance leads
exaggeration to danger. No coward so great as capital, and even the con-
sumptive, flying from the deadly east winds of the coast will think twice
before he exposes himself to what he believes to be the scalping knives of
the Sioux.

In the name, then, of the people of the new west, we demand that instant
measures to taken to, at once and forever, prevent the possibility of the recent

---

*This is an allusion to Charles Dickens' *Bleak House*.

defeat of the troops being repeated. Let the story of Custer's death be lost in the terrible vengeance taken for it. Let real war be in order for once. Custer would never have met with his disaster had he been properly supported. In place of a few scattered companies of cavalry, at least three thousand frontiersmen, together with half that number of regular soldiers should scour the enemy's country, and no quarter should be given, as it certainly has not been taken. The extermination of the Sioux and the destruction of all that is theirs, is necessary for the future prosperity of the entire new west. For years we have had population and capital frightened away from us by fears of the Indians, and we call upon the government for redress at the eleventh hour. And by redress we mean the extermination of the hostile tribes.

131

Cultural Exchange on the Arizona Frontier (1874)

As Americans migrated to the West, they did not enter a vacant land, particularly in the Southwest, where various Native-American tribes had lived for several centuries. The Spanish explored the region as early as the 1540s and established trading posts and missions (Santa Fe was made the capital in 1619). As a far-flung northern province of Mexico, a distinct Spanish–Native-American culture evolved. Anglos (white traders and settlers) came to Arizona before the Civil War, but they remained a minority until the early 20th century. The influx of whites brought conflict with the Native Americans, and as outrages on both sides escalated, the U.S. Army was sent to maintain order. In 1874, Captain Jack Summerhayes' unit was dispatched to Arizona. Accompanying Summerhayes was his recent bride, Martha, a well-educated New England woman who kept an account of life in frontier Arizona, which she later published. The Summerhayeses spent four years on various outposts in Arizona, but one of their initial stops was Ehrenberg, a Colorado River town. In the selection that follows, Martha Summerhayes observes local (Mexican) customs.

Questions to Consider

1. Why was Summerhayes fascinated with Mexican customs, especially the activities of the women?

2. For what reasons does Summerhayes regret the American way of life in Arizona?

3. What does this document reveal about Anglo relations with local inhabitants in Arizona?

4. What does Summerhayes hope to accomplish with this account?

So work was begun immediately on the kitchen. My first stipulation was, that the new rooms were to have wooden *floors;* for, although the Cocopah Charley kept the adobe floors in perfect condition, by sprinkling them down and sweeping them out every morning, they were quite impossible, especially where it concerned white dresses and children, and the little sharp rocks in them seemed to be so tiring to the feet.

Life as we Americans live it was difficult in Ehrenberg. I often said: "Oh! if we could only live as the Mexicans live, how easy it would be!" For they had their fire built between some stones piled up in their yard, a piece of sheet iron laid over the top: this was the cooking-stove. A pot of coffee was made in the morning early, and the family sat on the low porch and drank it, and ate a biscuit. Then a kettle of *frijoles* was put over to boil. These were boiled slowly for some hours, then lard and salt were added, and they simmered down until they were deliciously fit to eat, and had a thick red gravy.

Then the young matron, or daughter of the house, would mix the peculiar paste of flour and salt and water, for *tortillas,* a species of unleavened bread. These *tortillas* were patted out until they were as large as a dinner plate, and very thin; then thrown onto the hot sheet-iron, where they baked. Each one of the family then got a *tortilla,* the spoonful of beans was laid upon it, and so they managed without the paraphernalia of silver and china and napery.

How I envied them the simplicity of their lives! Besides, the *tortillas* were delicious to eat, and as for the *frijoles,* they were beyond anything I had ever eaten in the shape of beans. I took lessons in the making of *tortillas.* A woman was paid to come and teach me; but I never mastered the art. It is in the blood of the Mexican, and a girl begins at a very early age to make the *tortilla.* It is the most graceful thing to see a pretty Mexican toss the wafer-like disc over her bare arm, and pat it out until transparent.

This was their supper; for, like nearly all people in the tropics, they ate only twice a day. Their fare was varied sometimes by a little *carni seca,* pounded up and stewed with *chile verde* or *chile colorado.*

Now if you could hear the soft, exquisite, affectionate drawl with which the Mexican woman says *chile verde* you could perhaps come to realize what an important part the delicious green pepper plays in the cookery of these countries. They do not use it in its raw state, but generally roast it whole, stripping off the thin skin and throwing away the seeds, leaving only the pulp, which acquires a fine flavor by having been roasted or toasted over the hot coals.

The women were scrupulously clean and modest, and always wore, when in their *casa,* a low-necked and short-sleeved white linen *camisa,* fitting neatly, with bands around neck and arms. Over this they wore a calico skirt; always white stockings and black slippers. When they ventured out, the younger women put on muslin gowns, and carried parasols. The older women wore a linen towel thrown over their heads, or, in cool weather, the black *riboso.* I often cried: "Oh! if I could only dress as the Mexicans do! Their necks and arms do look so cool and clean."

Martha Summerhayes, *Vanished Arizona: Recollections of the Army Life of a New England Woman,* 2nd ed. (Salem, MA, 1911), 144–148.

I have always been sorry I did not adopt their fashion of house apparel. Instead of that, I yielded to the prejudices of my conservative partner, and sweltered during the day in high-necked and long-sleeved white dresses, kept up the table in American fashion, ate American food in so far as we could get it, and all at the expense of strength. . . .

There was no market, but occasionally a Mexican killed a steer, and we bought enough for one meal; but having no ice, and no place away from the terrific heat, the meat was hung out under the *ramada* with a piece of netting over it, until the first heat had passed out of it, and then it was cooked.

The Mexican, after selling what meat he could, cut the rest into thin strips and hung it up on ropes to dry in the sun. It dried hard and brittle, in its natural state, so pure is the air on that wonderful river bank. They called this *carni seca,* and the Americans called it "jerked beef."

Patrocina often prepared me a dish of this, when I was unable to taste the fresh meat. She would pound it fine with a heavy pestle, and then put it to simmer, seasoning it with the green or red pepper. It was most savory. There was no butter at all during the hot months, but our hens laid a few eggs, and the Quartermaster was allowed to keep a small lot of commissary stores, from which we drew our supplies of flour, ham, and canned things. We were often without milk for weeks at a time, for the cows crossed the river to graze, and sometimes could not get back until the river fell again, and they could pick their way back across the shifting sand bars.

The Indian brought the water every morning in buckets from the river. It looked like melted chocolate. He filled the barrels, and when it had settled clear, the *ollas* were filled, and thus the drinking water was a trifle cooler than the air. One day it seemed unusually cool, so I said: "Let us see by the thermometer how cool the water really is." We found the temperature of the water to be 86 degrees; but that, with the air at 122 in the shade, seemed quite refreshing to drink.

132

A Native American Remembers the Ghost Dance (1890)

By 1890, the Great Plains Indian tribes had experienced severe hardships. Whites had invaded their traditional lands, the American bison (buffalo) was nearly exterminated, new diseases ravaged some tribes, often with fatal results, and the Native Americans were placed on reservations with unfilled promises of government assistance. Disenchanted and witnessing the collapse of their culture, many Plains Indians embraced the preachings of a Paiute messiah named Wovoka (also known as Jack Wilson), who led a revival of the Ghost Dance on a Nevada reservation. A religious movement soon spread throughout the West. Wovoka taught the Ghost Dance ceremony and instructed the Native Americans to live peacefully with one another and with the whites. Many tribes sent delegations to meet with Wovoka to learn the Ghost Dance, so that the promised return of the old ways could be achieved. Among those who consulted Wovoka was Rising Wolf, who retold his Ghost Dance participation to novelist Hamlin Garland. Rising Wolf was interviewed while Garland toured the West to gather materials for future writing projects. Rising Wolf's account, excerpted as follows, was published in the popular McClure's *Magazine. Garland later won the Pulitzer Prize (1921) and was known for his realistic depiction of western life.*

Questions to Consider

1. For what reasons were the Plains Indians attracted to the Ghost Dance?
2. What were the reactions of whites to the Ghost Dance?
3. What does this account reveal about the significance of the Ghost Dance?
4. How might John D. Rockefeller ("The Success of Standard Oil," Document 139) have responded to this document?

One night there came into our midst a Snake messenger with a big tale. "Away in the west," he said to us in sign talk, "a wonderful man has come. He speaks all languages and he is the friend of all red men. He is white, but not like other white men. He has been nailed to a tree by the whites. I saw the holes in his hands. He teaches a new dance, and that is to gather all the Indians together in council. He wants a few head men of all tribes to meet him where the big mountains are, in the place where the lake is surrounded by pictured rocks. There he will teach us how to make mighty magic and drive away the white man and bring back the buffalo."

All that he told us we pondered long, and I said: "It is well, I will go to see this man. I will learn his dance." . . .

A day passed, and he did not come; but one night when we sat in council over his teachings, he suddenly stepped inside the circle. He was a dark man, but not so dark as we were. He had long hair on his chin, and long, brown head-hair, parted in the middle. I looked for the wounds on his wrists; I could not see any. He moved like a big chief, tall and swift. He could speak all tongues. He spoke Dakota, and many understood. I could understand the language of the Cut-throat people, and this is what he said: My people, before the white man came you were happy. You had many buffalo to eat and tall grass for your ponies. You could come and go like the wind. When it was cold, you could go into the valleys to the south, where the healing springs are; and when it grew warm, you could return to the mountains in the north. The white man came. He dug the bones of our mother, the earth. He tore her bosom with steel. He built big trails and put iron horses on them. He fought you and beat you, and put you in barren places where a horned toad would die. He said you must stay there; you must not hunt in the mountains.

Then he breathed his poison upon the buffalo, and they disappeared. They vanished into the earth. One day they covered the hills, the next nothing but their bones remained. Would you remove the white man? Would you have the buffalo come back? Listen, and I will tell you how to make great magic. I will teach you a mystic dance, and then let everybody go home and dance. When the grass is green, the change will come. Let everybody dance four days in succession, and on the fourth day the white man will disappear and the buffalo come back; our dead will return with the buffalo. . . .

You have forgotten the ways of the fathers; therefore great distress is upon you. You must throw away all that the white man has brought you. Return to the dress of the fathers. You must use the sacred colors, red and white, and the sacred grass, and in the spring, when the willows are green, the change will come. . . .

Then he taught us the song and the dance which white people call the ghost dance, and we danced all together, and while we danced near him he sat with bowed head. No one dared to speak to him. The firelight shone on him. Suddenly he disappeared. No one saw him go. Then we were sorrowful, for we wished him to remain with us. . . .

At last we reached home, and I called a big dance, and at the dance I told the people what I had seen, and they were very glad. "Teach us the dance," they cried to me. . . .

Then they did as I bid, and when the moon was round as a shield, we beat the drum and called the people to dance. . . .

The agent came to see us dance, but we did not care. He was a good man, and we felt sorry for him, for he must also vanish with the other white people. He listened to our crying, and looked long, and his interpreter told him we prayed to the great Spirits to destroy the white man and bring back the buffalo. Then he called me with his hand, and because he was a good man I went to him. He asked me what the dance meant, and I told him, and he said, "It must stop." "I cannot stop it," I said. "The Great Spirits have said it. It must go on." . . .

On the fourth night, while we danced, soldiers came riding down the hills, and their chiefs, in shining white hats, came to watch us. All night we prayed and danced. We prayed in our songs.

But the agent smiled, and the soldiers of the white chiefs sat not far off, their guns in their hands, and the moon passed by, and the east grew light, and we were very weary, and my heart was heavy. I looked to see the red come in the east. "When the sun looks over the hills, then it will be," I said to my friends. "The white man will become as smoke. The wind will sweep him away."

As the sun came near we all danced hard. My voice was almost gone. My feet were numb, my legs were weak, but my heart was big. . . .

But the sun came up, the soldiers fired a big gun, and the soldier chiefs laughed. Then the agent called to me, "Your Great Spirit can do nothing. Your Messiah lied." . . .

All day I lay there with my head covered. I did not want to see the light of the sun. I heard the drum stop and the singing die away. Night came, and then on the hills I heard the wailing of my people. Their hearts were gone. Their bones were weary.

When I rose, it was morning. I flung off my blankets, and looked down on the valley where the tepees of the white soldiers stood. I heard their drums and their music. I had made up my mind. The white man's trail was wide and dusty by reason of many feet passing thereon, but it was long. The trail of my people was ended.

133

Life on the Prairie Farms (1893)

The Homestead Act of 1862 and its promise of 160 acres of free land if it were improved for five consecutive years enticed people to settle the Great Plains. This vast grassland, once considered "desert" and uninhabitable, was passed over by earlier westward migrants. But new agricultural techniques, such as dry farming, the chilled iron plow, drought- and disease-resistant wheat helped transform the region into America's breadbasket. Despite these changes, many settlers found that economic survival was difficult: Their homestead did not contain enough land to grow wheat or corn profitably, as overproduction drove prices down. Responses to the plight of the farmer were frequently politically or economically motivated, but journalist E. V. Smalley, author of the following excerpt, focused on the social aspect of agriculture. His depiction of life on prairie farms gave readers of the respected Atlantic Monthly *a sense of the solitude facing families on the Great Plains.*

Questions to Consider

1. According to E. V. Smalley, what factors led to the farm family isolation on the Great Plains?
2. Explain the living and working conditions for the small farmer on the Great Plains.
3. For what reasons does Smalley believe that farm life on the Great Plains will improve?
4. Why would easterners or immigrants be attracted to the conditions described by Smalley?

. . . Every homesteader must live upon his claim for five years to perfect his title and get his patent; so that if there were not the universal American custom of isolated farm life to stand in the way, no farm villages would be possible in the first occupancy of a new region in the West without a change in our land laws. If the country were so thickly settled that every quarter section of land (160 acres) had a family upon it, each family would be half a mile from any neighbor, supposing the houses to stand in the center of the farms; and in any case the average distance between them could not be less. But many settlers own 320 acres, and a few have a square mile of land, 640 acres. Then there are school sections, belonging to the state, and not occupied at all; and everywhere you find vacant tracts owned by Eastern speculators or by mortgage companies, to which former settlers have abandoned their claims, going to newer regions and leaving their debts and their land behind. Thus the average space separating the farmsteads is, in fact, always more than a half a mile, and many settlers must go a mile or two to reach a neighbor's house. This condition obtains not on the frontiers alone but in fairly well-peopled agricultural districts.

If there be any region in the world where the natural gregarious instinct of mankind should assert itself, that region is our Northwestern prairies, where a short, hot summer is followed by a long, cold winter and where there is little in the aspect of nature to furnish food for thought. On every hand the treeless plain stretches away to the horizon line. In summer, it is checkered with grain fields or carpeted with grass and flowers, and it is inspiring in its color and vastness; but one mile of it is almost exactly like another, save where some watercourse nurtures a fringe of willows and cottonwoods. When the snow covers the ground, the prospect is bleak and dispiriting. No brooks babble under icy armor. There is no bird life after the wild geese and ducks have passed on their way south. The silence of death rests on the vast landscape, save when it is swept by cruel winds that search out every chink and cranny of the buildings and drive through each unguarded aperture the dry powdery snow.

In such a region, you would expect the dwellings to be of substantial construction, but they are not. The new settler is too poor to build of brick or stone. He hauls a few loads of lumber from the nearest railway station and puts up a frail little house of two, three, or four rooms that looks as though the prairie winds would blow it away. Were it not for the invention of tarred building paper, the flimsy walls would not keep out the wind and snow. With this paper the walls are sheathed under the weatherboards. The barn is often a nondescript affair of sod walls and straw roof. Lumber is much too dear to be used for dooryard fences, and there is no enclosure about the house. . . .

In this cramped abode, from the windows of which there is nothing more cheerful in sight than the distant houses of other settlers, just as ugly and lonely, and stacks of straw and unthreshed grain, the farmer's family must live. In the summer there is a school for the children, one, two, or three miles away; but in winter the distances across the snow-covered plains are too great for them to travel in severe weather; the schoolhouse is closed, and there is nothing for them to do but to house themselves and long for spring. Each family must live mainly to itself, and life, shut up in the little wooden farmhouses, cannot well be very cheerful.

A drive to the nearest town is almost the only diversion. There the farmers and their wives gather in the stores and manage to enjoy a little sociability.

E. V. Smalley, "The Isolation of Life on Prairie Farms," *Atlantic Monthly* 72 (September 1893): 378–382.

The big coal stove gives out a grateful warmth, and there is a pleasant odor of dried codfish, groceries, and ready-made clothing. The women look at the display of thick cloths and garments and wish the crop had been better so that they could buy some of the things of which they are badly in need. The men smoke corncob pipes and talk politics. It is a cold drive home across the windswept prairies, but at least they have had a glimpse of a little broader and more comfortable life than that of the isolated farm.

There are few social events in the life of these prairie farmers to enliven the monotony of the long winter evenings; no singing schools, spelling schools, debating clubs, or church gatherings. Neighborly calls are infrequent because of the long distances which separate the farmhouses and because, too of the lack of homogeneity of the people. They have no common past to talk about. They were strangers to one another when they arrived in this new land, and their work and ways have not thrown them much together.

Often the strangeness is intensified by differences of national origin. There are Swedes, Norwegians, Germans, French Canadians, and perhaps even such peculiar people as Finns and Icelanders, among the settlers, and the Americans come from many different states. It is hard to establish any social bond in such a mixed population, yet one and all need social intercourse, as the thing most essential to pleasant living, after food, shelter, and clothing. . . .

The plains of the West extend from the Gulf of Mexico to the valley of the Saskatchewan in the British territory. A belt about 300 miles wide on the eastern side of this vast region receives sufficient rainfall for farming. This belt is the granary of the continent, and even with its present sparse settlement it produces an enormous yearly surplus of wheat and corn. Its cultivators have thus far been engaged in a hard struggle to establish themselves on the soil, procure the necessaries of existence, and pay off their mortgages. They are getting ahead year by year; and in the older settled districts good houses are taking the places of the pioneer shanties, and the towns show thrift and progress. Before long these prairie people will begin to grapple with the problems of a higher civilization. . . .

134

"The Significance of the Frontier in American History" (1893)

Since the first permanent English settlement was established in Jamestown, Virginia, in 1607, white settlers had moved steadily westward for nearly 300 years, encroaching on Native-Americans' land and pushing the tribes farther west. Many Americans believed that an ever-advancing frontier line enabled a superior white culture to exploit the resources of the West. In 1890, the director of the U.S. Census Bureau announced that the country's "unsettled area has been so broken into by isolated bodies of settlement that there can hardly be said to be a frontier line." This announcement that the frontier period of American history had ended prompted the young historian, Frederick Jackson Turner, to present a paper entitled "The Significance of the Frontier in American History" at the annual meeting of the American Historical Association in Chicago in July 1893. Excerpted as follows is the essay that became known as the Turner frontier thesis.

Questions to Consider

1. How does Frederick Jackson Turner describe the frontier?
2. Do Turner's views seem closer to those of Helen Hunt Jackson ("A Century of Dishonor," Document 129) or William Byer ("A Western Newspaper Editorial on the Custer Massacre," Document 130)?
3. How would Turner respond to the question "What is an American?"
4. What does this document reveal about late-19th-century white Americans' views of their culture?

In this advance, the frontier is the outer edge of the wave—the meeting point between savagery and civilization. Much has been written about the frontier from the point of view of border warfare and the chase, but as a field for the serious study of the economist and the historian it has been neglected.

The American frontier is sharply distinguished from the European Frontier—a fortified boundary line running through dense populations. The most significant thing about the American frontier is, that it lies at the hither edge of free land. . . .

. . . The wilderness masters the colonist. It finds him a European in dress, industries, tools, modes of travel, and thought. It takes him from the railroad car and puts him in the birch canoe. It strips off the garments of civilization and arrays him in the hunting shirt and the moccasin. It puts him in the log cabin of the Cherokee and Iroquois and runs an Indian palisade around him. Before long he has gone to planting Indian corn and plowing with a sharp stick; he shouts the war cry and takes the scalp in orthodox Indian fashion. In short, at the frontier the environment is at first too strong for the man. He must accept the conditions which it furnishes, or perish, and so he fits himself into the Indian clearings and follows the Indian trails. Little by little he transforms the wilderness, but the outcome is not the old Europe, not simply the development of Germanic germs, any more than the first phenomenon was a case of reversion to the Germanic mark. The fact is, that here is a new product that is American. At first, the frontier was the Atlantic coast. It was the frontier of Europe in a very real sense. Moving westward, the frontier became more and more American. . . .

Frederick Jackson Turner, "The Significance of the Frontier in American History," *Annual Report of the American Historical Association for 1893* (Washington, DC, 1894), 199-227.

First, we note that the frontier promoted the formation of a composite nationality for the American people. The coast was predominately English, but the later tides of continental immigration flowed across to the free lands. . . .

But the most important effect of the frontier has been in the promotion of democracy here and in Europe. As has been indicated, the frontier is productive of individualism. Complex society is precipitated by the wilderness into a kind of primitive organization based on the family. The tendency is anti-social. It produces antipathy to control, and particularly to any direct control. The tax-gatherer is viewed as a representative of oppression. Prof. Osgood, in an able article, has pointed out that the frontier conditions prevalent in the colonies are important factors in the explanation of the American Revolution, where individual liberty was sometimes confused with absence of all effective government. The same conditions aid in explaining the difficulty of instituting a strong government in the period of the confederacy. The frontier individualism has from the beginning promoted democracy.

The frontier States that came into the Union in the first quarter of a century of its existence came in with democratic suffrage provisions, and had reactive effects of the highest importance upon the older States whose peoples were being attracted there. An extension of the franchise became essential. It was *western* New York that forced an extension of suffrage in the constitutional convention of that State in 1821; and it was *western* Virginia that compelled the tide-water region to put a more liberal suffrage provision in the constitution framed in 1830, and to give to the frontier region a more nearly proportionate representation with the tide-water aristocracy. The rise of democracy as an effective force in the nation came in with western preponderance under Jackson and William Henry Harrison, and it meant the triumph of the frontier—with all of its good and with all of its evil elements. . . .

So long as free land exists, the opportunity for a competency exists, and economic power secures political power. But the democracy born of free land, strong in selfishness and individualism, intolerant of administrative experience and education, and pressing individual liberty beyond its proper bounds, has its dangers as well as its benefits. Individualism in America has allowed a laxity in regard to governmental affairs which has rendered possible the spoils system and all the manifest evils that follow from the lack of a highly developed civic spirit. In this connection may be noted also the influence of paper currency and wild-cat banking. The colonial and revolutionary frontier was the region whence emanated many of the worst forms of an evil currency. The West in the War of 1812 repeated the phenomenon on the frontier of that day, while the speculation and wild-cat banking of the period of the crisis of 1837 occurred on the new frontier belt of the next tier of States. Thus each one of the periods of lax financial integrity coincides with periods when a new set of frontier communities had arisen, and coincides in area with these successive frontiers, for the most part. The recent Populist agitation is a case in point. Many a State that now declines any connection with the tenets of the Populists, itself adhered to such ideas in an earlier stage of the development of the State. . . .

From the conditions of frontier life came intellectual traits of profound importance. The works of travelers along each frontier from colonial days onward describe certain common traits, and these traits have, while softening down, still persisted as survivals in the place of their origin, even when a higher social organization succeeded. The result is that to the frontier the American intellect owes its striking characteristics. That coarseness and strength combined with acuteness and inquisitiveness; that practical, inventive turn of mind, quick to find expedients; that masterful grasp of material things, lacking in the artistic but powerful to effect great ends; that restless, nervous energy; that dominant individualism, working for good and for evil, and withal that buoyancy and exuberance which comes with freedom—there are traits of the frontier, or traits called out elsewhere because of the existence of the frontier. . . . But never again will such gifts of free land offer themselves. For a moment, at the frontier, the bonds of custom are broken and unrestraint is triumphant. There is not *tabula rasa*. The stubborn American environment is there with its imperious summons to accept its conditions; the inherited ways of doing things are also there; and yet, in spite of environment, and in spite of custom, each frontier did indeed furnish a new field of opportunity, a gate of escape from the bondage of the past; and freshness, and confidence, and scorn of older society, impatience of its restraints and its ideas, and indifference to its lessons, have accompanied the frontier. What the Mediterranean Sea was to the Greeks, breaking the bond of custom, offering new experiences, calling out new institutions and activities, that, and more, the ever retreating frontier has been to the United States directly, and to the nations of Europe even more remotely. And now, four centuries from the discovery of America, at the end of a hundred years of life under the Constitution, the frontier has gone, and with its going has closed the first period of American history.

18

✳

The Expansion of Big Business

The Market Revolution that transformed America before the Civil War brought about even greater changes after the war. This postwar Industrial Revolution included the spread of many prewar economic developments as well as the emergence of new technologies, which expanded economic production. In particular, the railroads would help create a national market for American goods with inexpensive transportation costs. Mass production of items through increased mechanization and commercial applications of inventions such as electricity, the telephone, and steel production helped fuel the economic growth. The economic transformation of the late 19th century occurred in an environment where government policy was "laissez-faire" and business followed the creed of "survival of the fittest." The following selections describe some of the new technologies and chronicle the attitudes of those who benefited from the new economic realities.

135

The Cattle Industry (1884)

The post–Civil War period witnessed the acceleration of economic developments that had begun before the conflict. The relationship between agricultural and manufacturing enterprises grew closer and encouraged mass-production techniques in both economic sectors. For example, farmers increased wheat production with the adaptation of the wheat reaper, and flour mills grew larger and more mechanized. Assisting economic growth and helping to forge a link between agriculture and manufacturing after the Civil War was the expansion of the railroads, primarily into the West. The railroads could move agricultural products profitably to markets in the East. Fitting into this situation was the new growth industries of cattle ranching in the West and eastern meat processors, primarily those located in Chicago. In 1884, G. Pomeroy Keese wrote an article, excerpted following, for the popular Harper's New Monthly Magazine *describing how cattle raised on western ranges becomes beef for the family meal. His account was based on riding the range with cowboys in the West and observing work in the "shambles," or slaughterhouses, in Chicago.*

Questions to Consider

1. In what ways does Keese regard economic development in the West?
2. How do the meat processing plants in Chicago address the need to mass produce beef profitably?
3. What economic impact does the railroad have on the beef business?
4. In what ways does Keese's account of conditions in the cattle industry compare with that described in "The Impact of Mechanization" (Document 136) or "*The Jungle*" (Document 162)?

An establishment in Chicago which combines the operations of "shipping" and of "canning" beef has a slaughtering capacity of 400,000 head annually. When we add to this the requirements of other similar although smaller concerns, and the large number shipped eastward on the hoof, we have a grand total of not far from 2,500,000 head marketed in the city of Chicago alone. . . . Whence does it come? Let the five great trunk lines which have their termini on the borders of Lake Michigan answer. Like the outstretched fingers of a hand, they meet in the central palm, Chicago. All from the West, but from the extreme northern and southern portions, Texas representing the latter, and the utmost limits of Montana the former. Ten thousand miles of rail at least are occupied in the transit. . . .

There are several ways of becoming interested in the cattle business on a northern range. One may commence by buying out a small herd, with the ranch and primitive equipments which accompany it, and with this nucleus build up by natural increase and additional purchases from time to time. . . . Or, again, one may contract in Texas during the winter for a given number of one or two year old steers, to be delivered on a certain range in Wyoming or Montana the coming summer. Having previously made an arrangement for their herding for two or more years, for which he pays annually one dollar per head, including all expenses, all he has to do is to await their arrival about midsummer, see them counted and branded, and then turn them loose upon the range. Or, thirdly, he may become a stockholder in one of the organized gigantic companies already existing. . . .

If the second method is adopted, . . . we will suppose a purchase made in Texas, say the 1st of February, of two thousand steers, . . . to be delivered on a range in Wyoming the following summer. These would be well bought at fifteen and eighteen dollars a head respectively, and then only as part of a larger drive of perhaps ten or twelve thousand going through to the same locality. . . .

The word "drive" is a misnomer as applied to the trail. It is exactly this which should not be done. Cattle once gathered, and headed in the direction of their long journey, should be allowed to "drift" rather than be urged.

G. Pomeroy Keese, "Beef, from the Range to the Shambles," *Harper's New Monthly Magazine* 69 (July 1884): 202–301.

Walking as they feed, they will accomplish their twelve or fifteen miles a day with but little exertion to themselves, and with very much less care and anxiety on the part of the herder. . . .

There are several distinct trails across the plains, and the pathways are as distinctly marked as a road could be, pressed by the hoofs of thousands for years past.

. . . As previously stated, the expense of herding a "bunch" of cattle is one dollar per head annually, which includes all charges after they are turned loose upon the range until they are delivered as "beeves" at the nearest railroad shipping point. . . .

Cattle trains arrive in Chicago early in the morning. They are unloaded, the cattle are classified and entered upon the stock-yard books in the name of the consignee, and after they are fed and watered in their respective pens, are ready for inspection of the buyer. . . .

As we come within the gate, we reach first the outer inclosure or pen, where may be gathered one hundred head of choice "shippers." They come in quietly and without excitement, and in a few minutes perhaps one-third of them are driven into a narrow alleyway adjoining the single pens. . . . A few seconds later a mild-looking man with a short carbine in his hand drops the muzzle to a point in the center of the forehead, just below the horns, and pulls the trigger. The steer falls without a struggle or groan . . . a hooking chain passed around the neck, and the animal is drawn out upon a broad platform about fourteen feet wide, at the bottom of which runs a shallow trough to catch the blood. Suspended by the hind feet, the sticking knife completes the bleeding process, and then two men step forward and disconnect the head. Four follow, stripping down the hide, two others, in the mean while, taking off the feet. Sawing the breast and haunch bones is the next operation, and then the carcass is hoisted preparatory to taking out the innards. This accomplished, a number are detailed to do the trimming, cleaning and turning to account every scrap and particle connected with the animal, so that nothing is wasted, down to the horns and hoofs. While these several operations are in progress, the carcass has been moving along a distance of some two hundred feet, being attached to a track overhead. The men at work maintain their relative positions as one after another of the carcasses come before them, and in the brief space of fourteen minutes from the time of the fatal shot to the animal is hung up, "drawn and quartered," and then left to cool in the chill room for forty-eight hours preparatory to shipping. . . .

Perhaps the most satisfactory part of the operations we have witnessed is the scrupulous cleanliness observed throughout. The pure creamy fat and dark rich red meat attest the perfection and purity attained, which the most expert stall-man in Fulton Market can not excel. . . .

The canning and packing department is another branch of the business entirely distinct from that of shipping. Up to a certain point the process is substantially the same, until it comes to cutting up the quarters into suitable pieces for these uses. Here division of labor takes complete possession of the work and it is carried to the perfection of economy. A man will stand by the hour giving but a single turn to his knife, which separates a joint. . . . A hundred others are on the same floor with him, each doing what may seem a trifling portion of the work, but before the carcass, which came in on one side in quarters, leaves the room, it is entirely bereft of bones, and then wheeled away in small pieces ready for the curing and the canning. . . . In this case the division is made into the various pieces familiar to household providers, viz., loins, ribs . . . "Extra mess" is composed of chucks, plates, rumps and flanks, and the time of curing is twenty-four days. All hams are cut into three pieces, or "one-set"; time of curing, sixty days. Plates are cut into five pieces. Loins, ribs, and shoulders are also sold to the city butchers. "Prime" tallow is made from the kidney and caid fat only, while "regular" tallow is made from the other fat, bones and trimmings. Glue factories and fertilizing establishments use up the bones and refuse, and the hides find their way to the tanneries. Not a scrap of the animal is wasted, or fails to yield some revenue to the buyer.

136

The Impact of Mechanization (1889)

The rapid adaptation of machinery for mass production created significant transformations in the American economy in the post–Civil War period. The author of the following excerpt, David A. Wells, realized the consequences of the machine age for both the business community and society. His background as an inventor, publisher of scientific information, political activist, and a foremost economist who advised Presidents Lincoln, Garfield, and Grant on business and currency matters gave Wells a unique perspective to observe the technological changes taking place and to analyze their implications. In his book Recent Economic Changes, *Wells offered a commentary on the growing size of businesses and how that affected the nature of enterprise. Wells was also among the first economists to recognize that machines displaced workers—creating "technological unemployment"—and that business was changing American society. His observations indicate that both business and society were adjusting to the technological progress of the time.*

Questions to Consider

1. According to David A. Wells, what were the most dramatic changes taking place?
2. For what reasons does Wells call these changes a "total revolution"?
3. To what extent can the common person participate in the economic advances described here?
4. In what ways would the American people respond to the new methods of doing business?

Machinery is now recognized as essential to cheap production. Nobody can produce effectively and economically without it, and what was formerly known as domestic manufacture is now almost obsolete. But machinery is one of the most expensive of all products, and its extensive purchase and use require an amount of capital far beyond the capacity of the ordinary individual to furnish. There are very few men in the world possessed of an amount of wealth sufficient to individually construct and own an extensive line of railway or telegraph, a first-class steamship, or a great factory. It is also to be remembered that, for carrying on production by the most modern and effective methods, large capital is needed, not only for machinery but also for the purchasing and carrying of extensive stocks of crude material and finished products.

. . . Hence, from such conditions have grown up great corporations or stock companies, which are only forms of associated capital organized for effective use and protection. They are regarded to some extent as evils; but they are necessary, as there is apparently no other way in which the work of production and distribution, in accordance with the requirements of the age, can be prosecuted. The rapidity, however, with which such combinations of capital are organizing for the purpose of promoting industrial and commercial undertakings on a scale heretofore wholly unprecedented, and the tendency they have to crystalize into something far more complex than what has been familiar to the public as corporations, with the impressive names of syndicates, trusts, etc., also constitute one of the remarkable features of modern business methods. It must also be admitted that the whole tendency of recent economic development is in the direction of limiting the area within which the influence of competition is effective.

And when once a great association of capital has been effected, it becomes necessary to have a mastermind to manage it—a man who is competent to use and direct other men, who is fertile in expedient and quick to note and profit by any improvements in methods of production and variations in prices. Such a man is a general of industry, and corresponds in position and functions to the general of an army.

What, as a consequence, has happened to the employees? Coincident with and as a result of this change in the methods of production, the modern manufacturing system has been brought into a condition analogous to that of a military organization, in which the individual no longer works as independently as formerly, but as a private in the ranks, obeying orders, keeping step, as it were, to the tap of the drum, and having nothing to say as to the plan of his work, of its final completion, or of its ultimate use and distribution. In short, the people who work in the modern factory are, as a rule, taught to do one thing—to perform one, and generally a simple, operation;

David A. Wells, *Recent Economic Changes* (New York, 1889), 91–94, 98, 109, 111.

and when there is no more of that kind of work to do, they are in a measure helpless. The result has been that the individualism or independence of the producer in manufacturing has been in a great degree destroyed, and with it has also in a great degree been destroyed the pride which the workman formerly took in his work—that fertility of resource which formerly was a special characteristic of American workmen, and that element of skill that comes from long and varied practice and reflection and responsibility. Not many years ago every shoemaker was or could be his own employer. The boots and shoes passed directly from an individual producer to the consumer. Now this condition of things has passed away. Boots and shoes are made in large factories; and machinery has been so utilized, and the division of labor in connection with it has been carried to such an extent, that the process of making a shoe is said to be divided into sixty-four parts, or the shoemaker of to-day is only the sixty-fourth part of what a shoemaker once was. . . .

Another exceedingly interesting and developing feature of the new situation is that, as machinery has destroyed the handicrafts and associated capital has placed individual capital at a disadvantage, so machinery and associated capital in turn, guided by the same common influences, now war upon machinery and other associated capital. Thus the now well-ascertained and accepted fact, based on long experience, that power is most economically applied when applied on the largest possible scale, is rapidly and inevitably leading to the concentration of manufacturing in the largest establishments and the gradual extinction of those which are small. . . .

The same influences have also to a great degree revolutionized the nature of retail trade. . . . Experience has shown that, under a good organization of clerks, shopmen, porters, and distributors, it costs much less proportionally to sell a large amount of goods than a small amount; and that the buyer of large quantities can, without sacrifice of satisfactory profit, afford to offer to his retail customers such advantages in respect to prices and range of selection as almost to preclude competition on the part of dealers operating on a smaller scale, no matter how otherwise capable, honest, and diligent they may be. The various retail trades in the cities and larger towns of all civilized countries are accordingly being rapidly superseded by vast and skillfully organized establishments . . . which can sell at little over wholesale prices a great variety of merchandise, dry goods, manufactures of leather, books, stationery, furs, ready-made clothing, hats and caps, and sometimes groceries and hardware, and at the same time give their customers far greater conveniences than can be offered by the ordinary shopkeeper or tradesman. . . .

From these specimen experiences it is clear that an almost total revolution has taken place, and is yet in progress, in every branch and in every relation of the world's industrial and commercial system. Some of these changes have been eminently destructive, and all of them have inevitably occasioned, and for a long time yet will continue to occasion, great disturbances in old methods and entail losses of capital and changes of occupation on the part of individuals. . . .

137

Progress and Poverty (1882)

In the post–Civil War era, the United States experienced remarkable economic growth. This new Industrial Revolution included the expansion of many prewar economic developments, the emergence of new technologies, the mass production of goods through mechanization, and the growth of an integrated railroad network that helped create a national market for American products. Such dramatic growth did lead to a "boom and bust" economic cycle: A period of rapid expansion was often followed by economic contraction or depression (a "panic," as they were called at the time) as the economy adjusted. The dazzling economic achievements did much to increase the wealth and improve the lives of many Americans, but progress was not universal. Among the earliest critics of this new industrial order was California newspaperman Henry George. In 1879, he published the angry critique, Progress and Poverty, *which offered a "single tax" on land as the solution to social ills. In this selection taken from* Progress and Poverty, *George explains that not everyone participated in the "progress."*

Questions to Consider

1. Why does George consider the ownership of land to be critical?
2. What are some of the contradictions of the new economy of this era?
3. According to George, why does labor not benefit from the progress?
4. How would William Graham Sumner, author of "The Forgotten Man" (Document 138), respond to George's views?

The present century has been marked by a prodigious increase in wealth-producing power. The utilization of steam and electricity, the introduction of improved processes and labor-saving machinery, the greater subdivision and grander scale of production, the wonderful facilitation of exchanges, have multiplied enormously the effectiveness of labor. . . .

Now, however, we are coming into collision with facts which there can be no mistaking. From all parts of the civilized world come complaints of industrial depression; of labor condemned to involuntary idleness; of capital massed and wasting; of pecuniary distress among business men; of want and suffering and anxiety among the working classes. . . .

This association of poverty with progress is the great enigma of our times. It is the central fact from which spring industrial, social, and political difficulties that perplex the world, and with which statesmanship and philanthropy and education grapple in vain. From it come the clouds that overhang the future of the most progressive and self-reliant nations. It is the riddle

Henry George, *Progress and Poverty* (Cambridge, MA, 1882), 3–10, 282–283, 287–288, 295–296.

which the Sphinx of Fate puts to our civilization, and which not to answer is to be destroyed. So long as all the increased wealth which modern progress brings goes but to build up great fortunes, to increase luxury and make sharper the contrast between the House of Have and the House of Want, progress is not real and cannot be permanent. The reaction must come. . . .

In every direction, the direct tendency of advancing civilization is to increase the power of human labor to satisfy human desires—to extirpate poverty, and to banish want and the fear of want. All the things in which progress consists, all the conditions which progressive communities are striving for, have for their direct and natural result the improvement of the material (and consequently the intellectual and moral) condition of all within their influence. . . .

But labor cannot reap the benefits which advancing civilization thus brings, because they are intercepted. Land being necessary to labor, and being reduced to private ownership, every increase in the productive power of labor but increases rent—the price that labor must pay for the opportunity to utilize its powers; and thus all the advantages gained by the march of progress go to the owners of land, and wages do not increase. Wages cannot increase; for the greater the earnings of labor the greater the price that labor must pay out of its earnings for the opportunity to make any earnings at all. The mere laborer has thus no more interest in the general advance of productive power than the Cuban slave has in advance in the price of sugar. . . .

The simple theory which I have outlined (If indeed it can be called a theory which is but the recognition of the most obvious relations) explains this conjunction of poverty with wealth, of low wages with high productive power, of degradation amid enlightenment, of virtual slavery in political liberty. It harmonizes, as results flowing from a general and inexorable law, facts otherwise most perplexing, and exhibits the sequence and relation between phenomena that without reference to it are diverse and contradictory. It explains why interest and wages are higher in new than in older communities, though the average, as well as the aggregate, production of wealth is less. It explains why improvements which increase the productive power of labor and capital increase the reward of neither. It explains what is commonly called the conflict between labor and capital, while proving the real harmony of interest between them. It cuts the last inch of ground from under the fallacies of protection, while showing why free trade fails to benefit permanently the working classes. It explains why want increases with abundance, and wealth tends to greater and greater aggregations. It explains the periodically recurring depressions of industry without recourse either to the absurdity of "over-production" or the absurdity of "over-consumption." It explains the enforced idleness of large numbers of would-be producers, which wastes the productive force of advanced communities, without the absurd assumption that there is too little work to do or that there are too many to do it. It explains the ill effects upon the laboring classes which often follow the introduction of machinery, without denying the natural advantages which the use of machinery gives. It explains the vice and misery which show themselves amid dense population, without attributing to the laws of the All-Wise and All-Beneficent defects which belong only to the short-sighted and selfish enactments of men. . . .

. . . It is not in the relations of capital and labor; it is not in the pressure of population against subsistence, that an explanation of the unequal development of our civilization is to be found. The great cause of inequality in the distribution of wealth is inequality in the ownership of land. The ownership of land is the great fundamental fact which ultimately determines the social, the political, and consequently the intellectual and moral condition of a people. And it must be so. For land is the habitation of man, the storehouse upon which he must draw for all his needs, the material to which his labor must be applied for the supply of all his desires; for even the products of the sea cannot be taken, the light of the sun enjoyed, or any of the forces of nature utilized, without the use of land or its products. On the land we are born, from it we live, to it we return again—children of the soil as truly as is the blade of grass or the flowers of the field. Take away from man all that belongs to land, and he is but a disembodied spirit. Material progress cannot rid us of our dependence upon land, it can but add to the power of producing wealth from land; and hence, when land is monopolized, it might go on to infinity without increasing wages or improving the condition of those who have but their labor. It can but add to the value of land and the power which its possession gives. Everywhere, in all times, among all peoples, the possession of land is the base of aristocracy; the foundation of great fortunes, the source of power.

138

"The Forgotten Man" (1883)

In the Gilded Age, Social Darwinism became the prevailing force in American thought: It was the application of Charles Darwin's theory of evolution to society. The leading advocate of this new intellectual tenet was Englishman Herbert Spencer, who argued that society operated in competitive ways so that only the strongest and "fittest" individuals would survive. Even though this competition could be harsh, the long-term evolution for humans would be a better society. Social Darwinists argued that this competition must occur naturally; there should be no interference in this process. The most prominent American Social Darwinist was Yale sociologist William Graham Sumner. He argued that competition was natural and that it sentenced the unfit to poverty and blessed the fit with wealth and power. Sumner's arguments of noninterference in the "natural selection" process held a powerful place in America. Excerpted as follows is a speech Sumner gave to a Brooklyn, New York, audience in 1883. Entitled "The Forgotten Man," it addresses some of the issues of Social Darwinism.

Questions to Consider

1. For what reasons does Sumner defend the "Forgotten Man" and oppose efforts to help the "good-for-nothing"?
2. Why does Sumner oppose reformers and their legislation?
3. How might Henry George, author of "Progress and Poverty" (Document 137), respond to Sumner's views?
4. Why was Social Darwinism so appealing in the Gilded Age?

Now who is the Forgotten Man? He is the simple, honest laborer, ready to earn his living by productive work. We pass him by because he is independent, self-supporting, and asks no favors. He does not appeal to the emotions or excite the sentiments. He only wants to make a contract and fulfill it, with respect on both sides and favor on neither side. He must get his living out of the capital of the country. The larger the capital is, the better living he can get. Every particle of capital which is wasted on the vicious, the idle, and the shiftless is so much taken from the capital available to reward the independent and productive laborer. But we stand with our backs to the independent and productive laborer all the time. We do not remember him because he makes no clamor; but I appeal to you whether he is not the man who ought to be remembered first of all, and whether, on any sound social theory, we ought not to protect him against the burdens of the good-for-nothing. . . . Every man is bound to take care of himself and his family and to do his share in the work of society. It is totally false that one who has done so is bound to bear the care and charge of those who are wretched because they have not done so. The silly popular notion is that the beggars live at the expense of the rich, but the truth is that those who eat and produce not, live at the expense of those who labor and produce. The next time that you are tempted to subscribe a dollar to a charity, I do not tell you not to do it, because after you have fairly considered the matter, you may think it right to do it, but I do ask you to stop and remember the Forgotten Man and understand that if you put your dollar in the savings bank it will go to swell the capital of the country which is available for division amongst those who, while they earn it, will reproduce it with increase. . . .

Let us take another class of cases. So far we have said nothing about the abuse of legislation. We all seem to be under the delusion that the rich pay the taxes. . . . Now the state and municipality go to great expense to support policemen and sheriffs and judicial officers, to protect people against themselves, that is, against the results of their own folly, vice, and recklessness. Who pays for it? Undoubtedly the people who have not been guilty of folly, vice, or recklessness. Out of nothing comes nothing. We cannot collect taxes from

William Graham Sumner, *The Forgotten Man and Other Essays*, Albert G. Keller, ed. (Freeport, NY, 1969), 476–481, 492–493.

people who produce nothing and save nothing. The people who have something to tax must be those who have produced and saved.

When you see a drunkard in the gutter, you are disgusted, but you pity him. When a policeman comes and picks him up you are satisfied. You say that "society" has interfered to save the drunkard from perishing. Society is a fine work, and it saves us the trouble of thinking to say that society acts. The truth is that the policeman is paid by somebody, and when we talk about society we forget who it is that pays. It is the Forgotten Man again. It is the industrious workman going home from a hard day's work, whom you pass without noticing, who is mulcted [penalized by fining or demanding forfeiture] of a percentage of his day's earnings to hire a policeman to save the drunkard from himself. All the public expenditure to prevent vice has the same effect. Vice is its own curse. If we let nature alone, she cures vice by the most frightful penalties. It may shock you to hear me say it, but when you get over the shock, it will do you good to think of it: a drunkard in the gutter is just where he ought to be. Nature is working away at him to get him out of the way, just as she sets up her processes of dissolution to remove whatever is a failure in its line. . . .

Another class of cases is closely connected with this last. There is an apparently invincible prejudice in people's minds in favor of state regulation. All experience is against state regulation and in favor of liberty. The freer the civil institutions are, the more weak and mischievous state regulation is. . . .

Now we have a great many well-intentioned people among us who believe that they are serving their country when they discuss plans for regulating the relations of employer and employee, or the sanitary regulations of dwellings, or the construction of factories, or the way to behave on Sunday, or what people ought not to eat or drink or smoke. All this is harmless enough and well enough as a basis of mutual encouragement and missionary enterprise, but it is almost always made a basis of legislation. The reformers want to get a majority, that is, to get the power of the state and so to make other people do what the reformers think it right and wise to do. . . .

It is plain enough that the Forgotten Man and the Forgotten Woman are the very life and substance of society. They are the ones who ought to be first and always remembered. They are always forgotten by sentimentalists, philanthropists, reformers, enthusiasts, and every description of speculator in sociology, political economy, or political science. If a student of any of these sciences ever comes to understand the position of the Forgotten Man and to appreciate his true value, you will find such student an uncompromising advocate of the strictest scientific thinking on all social topics, and a cold and hard-hearted skeptic towards all artificial schemes of social amelioration. If it is desired to bring about social improvements, bring us a scheme for relieving the Forgotten Man of some of his burdens. He is our productive force which we are wasting. Let us stop wasting his force. Then we shall have a clean and simple gain for the whole society. The Forgotten Man is weighted down with the cost and burden of schemes for making everybody happy, with the cost of public beneficence, with the support of all the loafers, with the loss of all the economic quackery, with the cost of all the jobs. Let us remember him a little while. Let us take some of the burdens off him. Let us turn our pity on him instead of on the good-for-nothing. It will be only justice to him, and society will greatly gain by it. . . .

139

The Success of Standard Oil (1899)

The early petroleum industry was filled with chaotic inefficiency and fierce competition among numerous refiners. John D. Rockefeller and his associates transformed this business into a stable and orderly enterprise, with their company, Standard Oil, dominating the industry. Forming the Standard Oil Trust (the first of its kind) in 1882 to permit legal ownership of companies in several states and to allow continued consolidation of his enterprise, Rockefeller came to control about 90 percent of the petroleum industry. In 1900, Standard Oil's net profit was $55.5 million. Naturally, the success of the Standard Oil Trust led other businessmen to use the trust to create monopolies within certain industries (sugar, tobacco, for example), and the term trust *became synonymous with monopoly. Alarmed at the growth and economic influence of trusts, Congress formed the Industrial Commission in 1898 to investigate. Although many businessmen testified before this body, Rockefeller's business tactics and Standard Oil were particularly scrutinized. Excerpted following is part of Rockefeller's response to questions about Standard Oil's success.*

Questions to Consider

1. According to John D. Rockefeller, what made Standard Oil a successful business enterprise?

2. Why does Rockefeller believe "combinations" are a necessity for American business prosperity?

3. What does Rockefeller's testimony reveal about business activity during the Gilded Age?

4. Would William Graham Sumner ("The Forgotten Man," Document 138) approve of Rockefeller's views? Would Bill Gates ("Bill Gates and Microsoft," Document 230) approve of Rockefeller's views?

3. Q. Did the Standard Oil Company or other affiliated interests at any time before 1887 receive from the railroads rebates on freight shipped, or other special advantages?

A. The Standard Oil Company of Ohio, of which I was president, did receive rebates from the railroads prior to 1880, but received no special advantages for which it did not give full compensation. The reason for rebates was that such was the railroad's method of business. A public rate was made and collected by the railway companies, but so far as my knowledge extends, was never really retained in full, a portion of it was repaid to the shippers as a rebate. By this method the real rate of freight which any shipper paid was not known by his competitors nor by the other railway companies, the amount being in all cases a matter of bargain with the carrying company. Each shipper made the best bargain he could, but whether he was doing better than his competitor was only a matter of conjecture. Much depended upon whether the shipper had the advantage of competition of carriers. The Standard Oil Company of Ohio, being situated at Cleveland, had the advantage of different carrying lines, as well as water transportation in the summer, and taking advantage of those facilities made the best bargains possible for its freights. All other companies did the same, their success depending largely upon whether they had the choice of more than one route. The Standard sought also to offer advantages to the railways of the purpose of lessening rates of freight. It offered freights in large quantity carloads and trainloads. It furnished loading facilities and discharging facilities. It exempted railways from liability for fire. For these services it obtained contracts for special allowances on freights. These never exceeded, to the best of my present recollections, 10 per cent. But in almost every instance it was discovered subsequently that our competitors had been obtaining as good, and, in some instances, better rates of freight than ourselves. . . .

9. Q. To what advantages, or favors, or methods of management do you ascribe chiefly the success of the Standard Oil Company?

A. I ascribe the success of the Standard to its consistent policy to make the volume of its business large through the merits and cheapness of its products. It has spared no expense in finding, securing, and utilizing the best and cheapest methods of manufacture. It has sought for the best superintendents and workmen and paid the best wages. It has not hesitated to sacrifice old machinery and old plants for new and better ones. It has placed its manufactories at the points where they could supply markets at the least expense. It has not only sought markets for its principal products, but for all possible by-products, sparing no expense in introducing them to the public. It has not hesitated to invest millions of dollars in methods for cheapening the gathering and distribution of oils by pipe lines, special cars, tank steamers, and tank wagons. It has erected tank stations at every important railroad station to cheapen the storage and delivery of its products. It has spared no expense in forcing its products into the markets of the world among people civilized and uncivilized. It has had faith in

U.S. Congress, Industrial Commission, "John D. Rockefeller, Answers to Interrogatories," *Reports of the Industrial Commission*, vol. 2, *Hearings before the Industrial Commission* (Washington, DC, 1900), 794–797.

American oil, and has brought together millions of money for the purpose of making it what it is, and holding its market against the competition of Russia and all the many countries which are producers of oil and
competitors against American oil. . . .

It is too late to argue about advantages of industrial combinations.
They are a necessity. And if Americans are to have the privilege of extending their business in all the States of the Union, and into foreign countries
as well, they are a necessity on a large scale, and require the agency of
more than one corporation. . . .

I speak from my experience in the business with which I have
been intimately connected for about 40 years. Our first combination was
a partnership and afterwards a corporation in Ohio. That was sufficient
for a local refining business. But dependent solely upon local business we
should have failed long ago. We were forced to extend our markets and
to seek for export trade. This latter made the seaboard cities a necessary
place of business, and we soon discovered that manufacturing for export
could be more economically carried on at the seaboard, hence refineries
at Brooklyn, at Bayonne, at Philadelphia, and necessary corporations in
New York, New Jersey, and Pennsylvania.

We soon discovered as the business grew that the primary method
of transporting oil in barrels could not last. The package often cost more
than the contents, and the forests of the country were not sufficient to
supply the necessary material for an extended length of time, hence we
devoted attention to other methods of transportation, adopted the pipe-
line system, and found capital for pipe-line construction equal to the
necessities of the business.

To operate pipe-lines required franchises from the States in which
they were located and consequently corporations in those States, just as
railroads running through different States are forced to operate under
separate State charters. To perfect the pipe-line system of transportation
required in the neighborhood of fifty millions of capital. This could not
be obtained or maintained without industrial combination. The entire
oil business is dependent upon this pipe-line system. Without it every well
would shut down and every foreign market would be closed to us. . . .

I have given a picture rather than a detail of the growth of one
industrial combination. It is a pioneer, and its work has been of incalcu-
lable value. There are other American products besides oil for which the
markets of the world can be opened, and legislators will be blind to our
best industrial interests if they unduly hinder by legislation the combination
of persons and capital requisite for the attainment of so desirable an end.

11. Q. What are the chief disadvantages or dangers to the public arising from
them?

A. The dangers are that the power conferred by combination may be abused;
that combinations may be formed for speculation in stocks rather than for
conducting business, and that for this purpose prices may be temporarily

raised instead of being lowered. These abuses are possible to a greater or less extent in all combinations, large or small, but this fact is no more of an argument against combinations than the fact that steam may explode is an argument against steam. Steam is necessary and can be used comparatively safe. Combination is necessary and its abuses can be minimized; otherwise our legislators must acknowledge their incapacity to deal with the most important instrument of industry. Hitherto most legislative attempts have been an effort not to control but to destroy; hence their futility.

140

The Gospel of Wealth (1889)

A new intellectual tenet—Social Darwinism—helped justify the position of wealthy businessmen while simultaneously explaining poverty, misery, and unemployment. Social Darwinists, led by Englishman Herbert Spencer, who coined the phrase "survival of the fittest," broadened the theory of evolution to include all phenomena, especially society. Spencer argued that industrial leaders were products of natural selection: the best prospered while the unfit fell by the wayside. Any attempt to criticize or limit these survivors was contrary to natural law, and those less fortunate were the price modern society had to pay for progress. Andrew Carnegie, who amassed a fortune from the steel industry and was one of the few immigrant "rags to riches" examples of the era, understood that Social Darwinism could weaken democratic ideals. He published "Wealth," excerpted as follows, in the prominent journal, North American Review, *in an effort to encourage businessmen to administer their wealth properly. Carnegie set the example and followed his "Gospel of Wealth" until the day he died.*

Questions to Consider

1. How does Andrew Carnegie justify the contrast between the wealthy and the working poor?

2. According to Carnegie, what is the "proper administration of wealth"?

3. On what issues would Carnegie agree with William Graham Sumner's speech on "The Forgotten Man" (Document 138)?

4. Why would some people criticize Carnegie's proposal?

Andrew Carnegie, "Wealth," *North American Review* 148 (1889): 653–664.

The problem of our age is the proper administration of wealth, so that the ties of brotherhood may still bind together the rich and poor in harmonious relationship. The conditions of human life have not only been changed, but revolutionized, within the past few hundred years. . . . The contrast between the palace of the millionaire and the cottage of the laborer with us to-day measures the change which has come with civilization. . . .

This change, however, is not to be deplored, but welcomed as highly beneficial. It is well, nay, essential for the progress of the race, that the houses of some should be homes for all that is highest and best in literature and the arts, and for all the refinements of civilization, rather than that none should be so. Much better this great irregularity than universal squalor. . . .

The price which society pays for the law of competition, like the price it pays for cheap comforts and luxuries, is also great; but the advantages of this law are also greater still, for it is to this law that we owe our wonderful material development, which brings improved conditions in its train. But . . . the law may be sometimes hard for the individual, it is best for the race, because it insures the survival of the fittest in every department. We accept and welcome, therefore, as conditions to which we must accommodate ourselves, great inequality of environment, the concentration of business, industrial and commercial, in the hands of a few, and the law of competition between these, as being not only beneficial, but essential for the future progress of the race. . . .

We start, then, with a condition of affairs under which the best interest of the race are promoted, but which inevitably gives wealth to the few. Thus far, accepting conditions as they exist, the situations can be surveyed and pronounced good. The question then arises, . . . What is the proper mode of administering wealth after the laws upon which civilization is founded have thrown it into the hands of the few? . . .

There are but three modes in which surplus wealth can be disposed of. It can be left to the families of the decedents; or it can be bequeathed for public purposes: or, finally, it can be administered during their lives by its possessors. Under the first and second modes most of the wealth of the world that has reached the few has hitherto been applied. Let us in turn consider each of these modes. The first is the most injudicious. In monarchical countries, the estates and the greatest portion of the wealth are left to the first son, that the vanity of the parent may be gratified by the thought that his name and title are to descend to succeeding generations unimpaired. The condition of this class in Europe to-day teaches the futility of such hopes or ambitions. The successors have become impoverished through their follies or from the fall in the value of land. . . .

As to the second mode, that of leaving wealth at death for public uses, it may be said that this is only a means for the disposal of wealth, provided a man is content to wait until he is dead before it becomes of much good in the world. Knowledge of the results of legacies bequeathed is not calculated to inspire the brightest hopes of much posthumous good being accomplished. The cases are not few in which the real object sought by the testator is attained, nor are they few in which his real wishes are thwarted. In many cases the bequests are so used as to become only monuments of his folly. . . .

There remains, then, only one mode of using great fortunes; but in this we have the true antidote for the temporary unequal distribution of wealth, the reconciliation of the rich and the poor—a reign of harmony—another ideal, differing, indeed, from that of the communist in requiring only the further evolution of existing conditions, not the total overthrow of our civilization. It is founded upon the present most intense individualism, and the race is prepared to put it in practice by degrees whenever it pleases. Under its sway we shall have an ideal state, in which the surplus wealth of the few will become, in the best sense, the property of the many, because administered for the common good, and this wealth, passing through the hands of a few, can be made a much more potent force for the elevation of our race than if it had been distributed in small sums to the people themselves. . . .

This, then, is held to be the duty of the man of Wealth: First, to set an example of modest, unostentatious living, shunning display or extravagance; to provide moderately for the legitimate wants of those dependent upon him; and after doing so to consider all surplus revenues which come to him simply as trust funds, which he is called upon to administer, and strictly bound as a matter of duty to administer in the manner which, in his judgment, is best calculated to produce the most beneficial results for the community—the man of wealth thus becoming the mere agent and trustee for his poorer brethren, bringing to their service his superior wisdom, experience, and ability to administer, doing for them better than they would or could do for themselves. . . .

In bestowing charity, the main consideration should be to help those who will help themselves; to provide part of the means by which those who desire to improve may do so; to give those who desire to rise the aids by which they may rise; to assist, but rarely or never to do all. Neither the individual nor the race is improved by alms-giving. . . . He is the only true reformer who is as careful and as anxious not to aid the unworthy as he is to aid the worthy, and, perhaps, even more so, for in alms-giving more injury is probably done by rewarding vice than by relieving virtue. . . .

Thus is the problem of Rich and Poor to be solved. The laws of accumulation will be left free; the laws of distribution free. Individualism will continue, but the millionaire will be but a trustee for the poor; intrusted for a season with a great part of the increased wealth of the community, but administering it for the community far better than it could or would have done for itself. The best minds will thus have reached a stage in the development of the race in which it is clearly seen that there is no mode of disposing of surplus wealth creditable to thoughtful and earnest men into whose hands it flows save by using it year by year for the general good. This day already dawns . . . yet the man who dies leaving behind him millions of available wealth, which was his to administer during life, will pass away "unwept, unhonored, and unsung," no matter to what uses he leaves the dross which he cannot take with him. Of such as these the public verdict will then be: "The man who dies thus rich dies disgraced."

Such, in my opinion, is the true gospel concerning Wealth, obedience to which is destined some day to solve the problem of the Rich and the Poor, and to bring "Peace on earth, among men Good-Will."

141

Views on the Trusts (1889, 1899)

The rapid growth of corporations and their profound influence on everyday life concerned many Americans in the Gilded Age. Through a variety of means, some corporations began to acquire former competitors, or they began to acquire other companies in a process of consolidation. Following the example of the Standard Oil Trust, many of these large companies reorganized as trusts, wherein a few individuals could control many businesses, or, in some cases, dominate an entire industry. Trusts came to be seen as monopolies, corporate entities that stifled competition and wielded power beyond the business world. Some Americans believed that the trusts threatened freedom, democracy, and even the government. The two cartoons reveal a public perspective on the trusts. The first cartoon appeared in the January 23, 1889 issue of Puck, *and was drawn by Joseph Keppler, who was known for his powerful imagery. The second cartoon appeared in the May 22, 1899 issue of* The Verdict.

Questions to Consider

1. Why are the capitalists depicted as such large figures in the first image? Why do the legislators seem so small by comparison?

2. Why are the capitalists portrayed in the second image depicted as they are?

3. Why are these two cartoons so negative in their portrayal of the trusts?

4. Based on a careful consideration of these images, what appear to be some of the problems with the United States?

"The Bosses of the Senate"

"One Sees His Finish Unless Good Government Retakes the Ship"

19

✳

How the Other Half Lives

The extraordinary growth of the American economy after the Civil War had another side. The new, more capital-intensive industries prevented many people from taking advantage of the emerging opportunities. With businesses determined to secure a profit and a government that refused to intervene, many Americans had increasingly less control over their lives, working longer hours in more dangerous jobs for comparatively less pay. Despite this situation, millions of immigrants flooded into the country. The influx of these newcomers compounded problems of race and ethnicity that had plagued the nation throughout its history, and recent immigrants joined African Americans in experiencing new, more virulent forms of discrimination and exploitation. The following documents provide a glimpse into some of the conditions these workers, recent immigrants, and African Americans faced, as well as chronicle their responses.

142

Preamble to the Constitution of the Knights of Labor (1878)

Faced with the growing size and complexity of business, small groups of skilled workers began to form labor organizations or societies to protect their jobs and gain a share of the wealth that business generated. Many of the early societies were secretive in order to protect against employer retaliation. These organizations were often small, confined to certain industries, and usually failed to achieve their goals. Among the earliest labor organizations that created a national following was the Knights of Labor. Begun as a secret trade union of tailors in Philadelphia in 1869, the Knights grew slowly until Terrence V. Powderly assumed the leadership in 1879. Powderly advocated including all workers—regardless of trade—and women and African Americans (although in separate locals) into the Knights. He also believed in arbitration of disputes and the use of boycotts, but opposed the use or threat of a strike when confronting business. Powderly, who served three terms as mayor of Scranton, Pennsylvania, while leading the Knights, assisted in writing the preamble to the constitution of the Knights of Labor, which is excerpted as follows.

Questions to Consider

1. What key issues did the Knights of Labor want addressed?

2. In what ways do the Knights of Labor propose to achieve their demands?

3. What does this document reveal about the conditions for many workers in America at this time?

4. How do you suppose John D. Rockefeller, author of "The Success of Standard Oil" (Document 139), would respond to sentiments expressed in this selection?

The recent alarming development and aggression of aggregated wealth, which, unless checked, will invariably lead to the pauperization and hopeless degradation of the toiling masses, render it imperative, if we desire to enjoy the blessings of life, that a check should be placed upon its power and upon unjust accumulation, and a system adopted which will secure to the laborer the fruits of his toil; and as this much-desired object can only be accomplished by the thorough unification of labor, and the united efforts of those who obey the divine injunction that "In the sweat of thy brow shalt thou eat bread," we have formed the * * * * * with a view of securing the organization and direction, by co-operative effort, of the power of the industrial classes; and we submit to the world the object sought to be accomplished by our organization, calling upon all who believe in securing "the greatest good to the greatest number" to aid and assist us:

  I. To bring within the folds of organization every department of productive industry, making knowledge a standpoint for action, and industrial and moral worth, not wealth, the true standard of individual and national greatness.

 II. To secure to the toilers a proper share of the wealth that they create; more of the leisure that rightfully belongs to them; more societary advantages; more of the benefits, privileges, and emoluments of the world; in a word, all those rights and privileges necessary to make them capable of enjoying, appreciating, defending, and perpetuating the blessings of good government.

III. To arrive at the true condition of the producing masses in their educational, moral, and financial condition, by demanding from the various governments the establishment of bureaus of Labor Statistics.

 IV. The establishment of co-operative institutions, productive and distributive.

  V. The reserving of the public lands—the heritage of the people—for the actual settler;—not another acre for railroads or speculators.

Terrence V. Powderly, *Thirty Years of Labor* (Columbus, OH, 1889), 243–245.

VI. The abrogation of all laws that do not bear equally upon capital and labor, the removal of unjust technicalities, delays, and discriminations in the administration of justice, and the adopting of measures providing for the health and safety of those engaged in mining, manufacturing, or building pursuits.

VII. The enactment of laws to compel chartered corporations to pay their employes weekly, in full, for labor performed during the preceding week, in the lawful money of the country.

VIII. The enactment of laws giving mechanics and laborers a first lien on their work for their full wages.

IX. The abolishment of the contract system of national, State, and municipal work.

X. The substitution of arbitration for strikes, whenever and wherever employers and employes are willing to meet on equitable grounds.

XI. The prohibition of the employment of children in workshops, mines, and factories before attaining their fourteenth year.

XII. To abolish the system of letting out by contract the labor of convicts in our prisons and reformatory institutions.

XIII. To secure for both sexes equal pay for equal work.

XIV. The reduction of the hours of labor to eight per day, so that the laborers may have more time for social enjoyment and intellectual improvement, and be enabled to reap the advantages conferred by the labor saving machinery which their brains have created.

XV. To prevail upon governments to establish a purely national circulating medium based upon the faith and resources of the nation, and issued directly to the people, without the intervention of any system of banking corporations, which money shall be a legal tender in payment of all debts, public or private.

143

The "Long Turn" in Steel (1910)

The steel industry was an integral part of the Industrial Revolution in the United States, because it supplied essential materials to the railroads and later the automobile industry. The techniques of steel production, however, had changed little since the introduction of the Bessemer process and the open-hearth method in the 1860s. Steel mills relied almost exclusively on an unskilled male workforce because the hours were long and the work was physically demanding under the most severe conditions. Steelworkers were often recent immigrants to America and received relatively little pay. There was frequent turnover in the workforce. Starting in 1907, several individuals conducted the "Pittsburgh Survey," an investigation that focused on the life and labor of steelworkers in and around Pittsburgh, Pennsylvania, the premier steel city in America. John A. Fitch was a part of this survey and wrote The Steel Workers *based on his research of work in the mills. The following selection is his interview with a long-time steelworker and a description of the "long turn," a labor practice common throughout the industry.*

Questions to Consider

1. According to John Fitch, what changes were taking place in the steel mill workforce? Why?
2. What were the purposes of the Sunday "long turn"?
3. What can you deduce about labor conditions from this document?
4. How do you suppose Andrew Carnegie, author of the "Gospel of Wealth" (Document 140), would respond to this essay?

John Griswold is a Scotch-Irish furnace boss who came to America and got a laborer's position at a Pittsburgh blast furnace when the common labor force was largely Irish. Those were the days before the advent of the "furriners." I sat in Griswold's sitting room in his four-room cottage one evening and he told me about the men who work at the furnaces, and about the "long turn."

"Mighty few men have stood what I have, I can tell you. I've been twenty years at the furnaces and been workin' a twelve-hour day all that time, seven days a week. We go to work at seven in the mornin' and we get through at night at six. We work that way for two weeks and then we get the long turn and change to the night shift of thirteen hours. The long turn is when we go on at seven Sunday mornin' and work up through the whole twenty-four hours up to Monday mornin'. That puts us onto the night turn for the next two weeks, and the other crew onto the day. The next time they get the long turn and we get twenty-four hours off, but it don't do us much good. I get home at about half past seven Sunday mornin' and go to bed as soon as I've had breakfast. I get up at noon so as to get a bit o' Sunday to enjoy, but I'm tired and sleeps all the afternoon. Now, if we had eight hours it would be different. I'd start work, say, at six and I'd be done at two and I'd come home, and after dinner me and the missus could go to the park if we wanted to, or I could take the childer to the country where there ain't any saloons. That's the danger,—the childer runnin' on the streets and me with no time to take them any place else. That's what's driven the Irish out of the industry. It ain't the Hunkies,—they couldn't do it,—but the Irish don't have to work this way. There was fifty of them here with me sixteen years ago and now where are they? I meet 'em sometimes around the city, ridin' in carriages and all of them wearin' white shirts, and here I am with these Hunkies. They don't seem like men to me hardly. They can't talk United States. You tell them something and they just look at you and say 'Me no fustay, me no fustay,' that's all you can get out of 'em. And I'm here with them all the time, twelve hours a day

John A. Fitch, *The Steel Workers* (New York, 1910), 11–12, 174–176.

and every day and I'm all alone,—not a mother's son of 'em that I can talk to. Everybody says I'm a fool to stay here,—I dunno, mebbe I am. It don't make so much difference though. I'm gettin' along, but I don't want the kids ever to work this way. I'm goin' to educate them so they won't have to work twelve hours." . . .

For other departments it was harder to make estimates, but the situation as regards Sunday work is by no means set forth when we have discussed blast furnaces and open-hearth plants. The heating furnaces are never allowed to grow cold. Whether the suspension be the ordinary one, from Saturday night to Sunday night, or whether it be a shut-down for many weeks, the fires are not allowed to go out, and men are on duty tending gas, changing the flame from one side of the furnace to the other. In the open-hearth department the second helpers take turns tending gas on Saturday nights. In the soaking-pits and the re-heating furnaces, either the heater or some of his assistants remain with the furnaces all through the period of suspension. Sometimes this involves a twenty-four-hour shift, and sometimes that is avoided, but Sunday work is inevitable. In 1907–8 Sunday was the repair day. Repairs were made through the week, but everything that could possibly wait was left until Sunday, so that no time might be lost in the mills, and so that the repair men might work without being endangered or impeded by moving machinery. The practice was not defended by some of the men in authority, but the efforts made to stop it were without practical result. In a normal year the steel mills are crowded with work. Sunday was, the year of my inquiry, a day for clearing up, for tardy departments to get even with swifter ones. Often the mills rolled out the finished product faster than the shears or the transportation department could take care of it. Then there was great activity of traveling cranes and narrow-gauge or dinkey engines, and when the rolling mills began again on Sunday evening everything was cleared away, and all departments were ready for another week. Whenever there was construction work of any sort it was customary for it to go on without interruption until it was finished. Loading cars and unloading them frequently continued on Sunday, and for all this work many laborers, crane men, engineers, firemen, millwrights and machinists, besides the regular mill watchmen, were on duty seven nights in the week. . . .

Added to and intensifying the evils of Sunday work is the "long turn" of twenty-four hours that comes every second week to 60 per cent of the blast furnace workers and to many others. This is involved in the variations referred to on a previous page. The men average seven working days a week by working six days one week and the next week eight. Every Sunday the shifts change about. The men on the night shift give place on Sunday morning to the men on the day shift, and these work through until Monday morning, a full twenty-four hours, so as to change to the night shift for the week succeeding, while the old night shift changes to the day. The men who get through Sunday morning have a twenty-four hour interval. Theoretically they have a day of rest, but they must choose between trying to take advantage of it without resting from a twelve hour night of work, or going to bed and waking, later, to find most of the precious day of freedom gone. . . .

144

Views of Urban Life (1890s)

In the post–Civil War period, cities swelled in population as a twin migration of immigrants and rural Americans flocked to the glittering urban environment. For many, especially those lacking urban work skills, the city offered a difficult life amid squalid living conditions. Although poor districts have always existed in urban areas, never had poverty affected so many people in America. Danish-born newspaper reporter Jacob Riis made millions aware of the urban slums. As a New York City police reporter, Riis frequently entered the tenement districts to gather evidence for his stories, but the wretched life of the people shocked him into writing about life in the tenement slums. His photographs were particularly powerful in revealing urban conditions. The first image captures immigrant workers in a sweatshop in the Ludlow Street tenement. The photograph was included in Riis's first book, How The Other Half Lives, *which gave many Americans their first description of life in the tenement slums of New York City. The second photograph was taken on a street in New York City between 1900 and 1906.*

Questions to Consider

1. What can you deduce from the photographs about urban life?

2. How would William Graham Sumner, author of "The Forgotten Man" (Document 138), respond to these photographs?

3. How might these photographs challenge middle-class Americans' views of immigrants? How might the pictures confirm middle-class stereotypes of foreign-born Americans?

4. Why do you think these pictures were taken?

Library of Congress, Prints and Photographs Division, LC-USZ62-23305

From Jacob Riis,
*How the Other
Half Lives,*
chapter 11.

Library of Congress, Prints and Photographs Division, LC-D401-13645

"The close of a career in New York"

145

Lynching in the South (1895)

Starting in the late 1880s, race relations in the South changed quickly. Southern states disenfranchised African-American voters and passed Jim Crow laws, which legally segregated the races. This "color line" was often enforced through intimidation and violence. African Americans who transgressed the community standards for race relations, perhaps breaking some race etiquette or Jim Crow law, were sometimes lynched as a powerful message to the black community. Many lynchings were public rituals where the victim was hanged or burned alive by mobs. In the 1890s, when one black person was lynched nearly every two days, some African Americans began to campaign against these heinous murders. One of the leaders of the antilynching campaign was Ida B. Wells-Barnett of Memphis, Tennessee. Born into a slave family, she came to own and edit a weekly newspaper, the Memphis Free Speech and Headlight. *She condemned lynchings in her paper until threats of violence forced her to flee to the North. She continued the antilynching crusade, publishing editorials and conducting a lengthy speaking tour in Europe. The following selection is from Wells-Barnett's powerful pamphlet,* A Red Record.

Questions to Consider

1. According to Wells–Barnett, what were the reasons for lynching in the South?

2. Why had the reasons changed over time?

3. In what ways does Wells-Barnett propose to end lynching?

4. What does this document reveal about the status of African Americans and white attitudes in this time period?

Not all nor nearly all of the murders done by white men, during the past thirty years in the South, have come to light, but the statistics as gathered and pre-served by white men, and which have not been questioned, show that during these years more than ten thousand Negroes have been killed in cold blood, without the formality of judicial trial and legal execution. . . .

The first excuse given to the civilized world for the murder of unoffending Negroes was the necessity of the white man to repress and stamp out alleged "race riots." For years immediately succeeding the war there was an appalling slaughter of colored people, and the wires usually conveyed to northern peo-ple and the world the intelligence, first, that an insurrection was being planned by Negroes, which, a few hours later, would prove to have been vigorously resisted by white men, and controlled with a resulting loss of several killed and wounded. It was always a remarkable feature in these insurrections and riots that only Negroes were killed during the rioting, and that all the white men escaped unharmed. . . .

Then came the second excuse, which had its birth during the turbulent times of reconstruction. By an amendment to the Constitution the Negro was given the right of franchise, and, theoretically at least, his ballot became his invaluable emblem of citizenship. In a government "of the people, for the people, and by the people," the Negro's vote became an important factor in all matters of state and national politics. But this did not last long. The south-ern white man would not consider that the Negro had any right which a white man was bound to respect, and the idea of a republican form of gov-ernment in the southern states grew into general contempt. It was maintained that "This is a white man's government," and regardless of numbers the white man should rule. "No Negro domination" became the new legend on the sanguinary banner of the sunny South, and under it rode the Ku Klux Klan, the Regulators, and the lawless mobs, which for any cause chose to murder one man or a dozen as suited their purpose best. . . .

The white man's victory soon became complete by fraud, violence, intim-idation and murder. The franchise vouchsafed to the Negro grew to be a "barren ideality," and regardless of numbers, the colored people found them-selves voiceless in the councils of those whose duty it was to rule. With no longer the fear of "Negro Domination" before their eyes, the white man's second excuse became valueless. With the Southern governments all sub-verted and the Negro actually eliminated from all participation in state and national elections, there could be no longer an excuse for killing Negroes to prevent "Negro Domination."

Brutality still continued; Negroes were whipped, scourged, exiled, shot and hung whenever and wherever it pleased the white man so to treat them, and as the civilized world with increasing persistency held the white people

Ida B. Wells-Barnett, *A Red Record* (Chicago, 1895), 8–15.

of the South to account for its outlawry, the murderers invented the third excuse—that Negroes had to be killed to avenge their assaults upon women. There could be framed no possible excuse more harmful to the Negro and more unanswerable if true in its sufficiency for the white man. . . .

A word as to the charge itself. In considering the third reason assigned by the Southern white people for the butchery of blacks, the question must be asked, what the white man means when he charges the black man with rape. Does he mean the crime which the statutes of the civilized states describe as such? Not by any means. With the Southern white man, any mesalliance existing between a white woman and a colored man is a sufficient foundation for the charge of rape. The Southern white man says that it is impossible for a voluntary alliance to exist between a white woman and a colored man, and therefore, the fact of an alliance is a proof of force. In numerous instances where colored men have been lynched on the charge of rape, it was positively known at the time of lynching, and indisputably proven after the victim's death, that the relationship sustained between the man and woman was voluntary and clandestine, and that in no court of law could even the charge of assault have been successfully maintained. . . .

During all the years of slavery, no such charge was ever made, not even during the dark days of the rebellion, when the white man, following the fortunes of war went to do battle for the maintenance of slavery. While the master was away fighting to forge the fetters upon the slave, he left his wife and children with no protectors save the Negroes themselves. And yet during those years of trust and peril, no Negro proved recreant to his trust and no white man returned to a home that had been dispoiled.

Likewise during the period of alleged "insurrection," and alarming "race riots," it never occurred to the white man, that his wife and children were in danger of assault. Nor in the Reconstruction era, when the hue and cry was against "Negro Domination," was there ever a thought that the domination would ever contaminate a fireside or strike to death the virtue of womanhood. It must appear strange indeed, to every thoughtful and candid man, that more than a quarter of a century elapsed before the Negro began to show signs of such infamous degeneration. . . .

It is his regret, that, in his own defense, he must disclose to the world that degree of dehumanizing brutality which fixes upon America the blot of a national crime. Whatever faults and failings other nations may have in their dealings with their own subjects or with other people, no other civilized nation stands condemned before the world with a series of crimes so peculiarly national. It becomes a painful duty of the Negro to reproduce a record which shows that a large portion of the American people avow anarchy, condone murder and defy the contempt of civilization.

These pages are written in no spirit of vindictiveness, for all who give the subject consideration must concede that far too serious is the condition of that civilized government in which the spirit of unrestrained outlawry constantly increases in violence, and casts its blight over a continually growing area of territory. We plead not for the colored people alone, but for all victims of the terrible injustice which puts men and women to death without form of law.

During the year 1894, there were 132 persons executed in the United States by due form of law, while in the same year, 197 persons were put to death by mobs who gave the victims no opportunity to make a lawful defense. No comment need be made upon a condition of public sentiment responsible for such alarming results. . . .

146

"The Negro Question in the South" (1892)

The People's party (Populist) faced the problem of all new political organizations: convincing voters to abandon the traditional political parties and join their cause. In the South, this task was especially difficult because race relations had to be considered. The Democratic party had established white solidarity in the state governments as the Radical Reconstruction governments collapsed, while the Republican party, comprising mostly African Americans and some disaffected whites, was disintegrating. Some Populists sought the African-American vote to remove the Democrats from office and establish a new political power in the South. Among the more fervent supporters of this approach was Tom Watson of Georgia. Known for his combative nature and charismatic speeches, Watson served one term in Congress before joining the Populist party. In 1892, he explained the reasons for creating a fusion party of black and white voters in the South to readers of the national magazine, Arena. *Watson's article is excerpted following.*

Questions to Consider

1. According to Tom Watson, what will be the foundation of the proposed fusion party?
2. In what ways will the People's Party address the race issue?
3. What does this document portray about economic conditions and race relations in the South?
4. For what reasons would some whites and blacks oppose this proposal?

The Negro Question in the South has been for nearly thirty years a source of danger, discord, and bloodshed. It is an ever-present irritant and menace. . . . Now consider: here were two distinct races dwelling together, with political equality established between them by law. They lived in the same section; won their livelihood by the same pursuits; cultivated adjoining fields on the same terms; enjoyed together the bounties of a generous climate; suffered together the rigors of cruelly unjust laws; spoke the same language; bought and sold in the same markets; classified themselves into churches under the same denominational teachings; neither race antagonizing the other in any

---

Thomas E. Watson, "The Negro Question in the South," *Arena* 6 (October 1892): 540–550.

branch of industry; each absolutely dependent on the other in all the avenues of labor and employment; and yet, instead of being allies, as every dictate of reason and prudence and self-interest and justice said they should be, they were kept apart, in dangerous hostility, that the sordid aims of partisan politics might be served!

So completely has this scheme succeeded that the Southern black man almost instinctively supports any measure the Southern white man condemns, while the latter almost universally antagonizes any proposition suggested by a Northern Republican. We have, then, a solid South as opposed to a solid North; and in the South itself, a solid black vote against the solid white.

That such a condition is most ominous to both sections and both races is apparent to all. . . .

Having given this subject much anxious thought, my opinion is that the future happiness of the two races will never be assured until the political motives which drive them asunder, into two distinct and hostile factions, can be removed. There must be a new policy inaugurated, whose purpose is to allay the passions and prejudices of race conflict, and which makes its appeal to the sober sense and honest judgment of the citizen regardless of his color.

To the success of this policy two things are indispensable—a common necessity acting upon both races, and a common benefit assured to both—without injury or humiliation to either.

. . . The two races can never act together permanently, harmoniously, beneficially, till each race demonstrates to the other a readiness to leave old party affiliations and to form new ones, based upon the profound conviction that, in acting together, both races are seeking new laws which will benefit both. On no other basis under heaven can the "Negro Question" be solved.

Now, suppose that the colored man were educated upon these questions just as the whites have been; suppose he were shown that his poverty and distress came from the same sources as ours; suppose we should convince him that our platform principles assure him an escape from the ills he now suffers, and guarantee him the fair measure of prosperity his labor entitles him to receive,—would he not act just as the white Democrat who joined us did? . . .

The People's Party will settle the race question. First, by enacting the Australian ballot system. Second, by offering to white and black a rallying point which is free from the odium of former discords and strifes. Third, by presenting a platform immensely beneficial to both races and injurious to neither. Fourth, by making it to the interest of both races to act together for the success of the platform. Fifth, by making it to the interest of the colored man to have the same patriotic zeal for the welfare of the South that the whites possess.

The white tenant lives adjoining the colored tenant. Their houses are almost equally destitute of comforts. Their living is confined to bare necessities. They are equally burdened with heavy taxes. They pay the same high rent for gullied and impoverished land. . . .

Now the People's Party says to these two men, "You are kept apart that you may be separately fleeced of your earnings. You are made to hate each other because upon that hatred is rested the keystone of the arch of financial despotism which enslaves you both. You are deceived and blinded that you may not see how this race antagonism perpetuates a monetary system which beggars both."

This is so obviously true it is no wonder both these unhappy laborers stop to listen. No wonder they begin to realize that no change of law can benefit the white tenant which does not benefit the black one likewise; that no system which now does injustice to one of them can fail to injure both. Their every material interest is identical. The moment this becomes a conviction, mere selfishness, the mere desire to better their conditions, escape onerous taxes, avoid usurious charges, lighten their rents, or change their precarious tenements into smiling happy homes, will drive these two men together, just as their mutually inflamed prejudices now drive them apart.

Concede that in the final event, a colored man will vote where his material interests dictate that he should vote; concede that in the South the accident of color can make no possible difference in the interests of farmers, croppers, and laborers; concede that under full and fair discussion the people can be depended upon to ascertain where their interests lie—and we reach the conclusion that the Southern race question can be solved by the People's Party on the simple proposition that each race will be led by self-interest to support which benefits it, when so presented that neither is hindered by the bitter party antagonisms of the past. . . .

The question of social equality does not enter into the calculation at all. That is a thing each citizen decides for himself. No statute ever yet drew the latch of the humblest home—or ever will. Each citizen regulates his own visiting list—and always will.

The conclusion, then, seems to me to be this: The crushing burdens which now oppress both races in the South will cause each to make an effort to cast them off. They will see a similarity of cause and similarity of remedy. They will recognize that each should help the other in the work of repealing bad laws and enacting good ones. They will become political allies, and neither can injure the other without weakening both. It will be to the interest of both that each should have justice. And on these broad lines of mutual interest, mutual forbearance, and mutual support the present will be made the stepping-stone to future peace and prosperity.

<hr>

147

W.E.B. Du Bois on Race Relations (1903)

Among a group of African-American intellectuals who opposed the accommodationist views of Booker T. Washington was W.E.B. Du Bois. Born and raised in Massachusetts, Du Bois studied with many of the leading thinkers of the day and later earned a Ph.D. in history at Harvard University. He taught at several universities, committed his life to ending segregation and discrimination, and helped shape the modern African-

American identity. Du Bois believed that only by confronting and educating whites about the inequity of discrimination and segregation could the overall condition for African Americans improve. He also believed that the black elite had a responsibility to help fellow African Americans. In 1903, while an Atlanta University professor, Du Bois published The Souls of Black Folk, which included a chapter that criticized Booker T. Washington's approach to race relations. In 1909–10, Du Bois would join white and black intellectuals to found the National Association for the Advancement of Colored People (NAACP). He became the NAACP director of publicity and editor of its journal, The Crisis.

Questions to Consider

1. What are the reasons for Du Bois' criticism of Booker T. Washington and his approach to race relations?
2. What does Du Bois propose to African Americans?
3. What does this document reveal about race relations at the turn of the 20th century?
4. How do you think a California legislator who supported restricting the immigration of Chinese ("The Unwanted Immigrants: The Chinese," Document 148) would respond to DuBois' views?

Mr. Washington represents in Negro thought the old attitude of adjustment and submission; but adjustment at such a peculiar time as to make his programme unique. This is an age of unusual economic development, and Mr. Washington's programme naturally takes an economic cast, becoming a gospel of Work and Money to such an extent as apparently almost completely to overshadow the higher aims of life. Moreover, this is an age when the more advanced races are coming in closer contact with the less developed races, and the race-feeling is therefore intensified; and Mr. Washington's programme practically accepts the alleged inferiority of the Negro races. Again, in our own land, the reaction from the sentiment of war time has given impetus to race-prejudice against Negroes, and Mr. Washington withdraws many of the high demands of Negroes as men and American citizens. In other periods of intensified prejudice all the Negro's tendency to self-assertion has been called forth; at this period a policy of submission is advocated. In the history of nearly all other races and peoples the doctrine preached as such crises has been that manly self-respect is worth more than lands and houses, and that a people who voluntarily surrender such respect, or cease striving for it, are not worth civilizing.

In answer to this, it has been claimed that the Negro can survive only through submission. Mr. Washington distinctly asks that black people give up, at least for the present, three things,—

W.E.B. Du Bois, *The Souls of Black Folk* (Chicago, 1903), 50–52, 57–59.

First, political power,

Second, insistence on civil rights,

Third, higher education of Negro youth,—

and concentrate all their energies on industrial education, the accumulation of wealth, and the conciliation of the South. This policy has been courageously and insistently advocated for over fifteen years, and has been triumphant for perhaps ten years. As a result of this tender of the palm-branch, what has been the return? In these years there have occurred:

1. The disfranchisement of the Negro.

2. The legal creation of a distinct status of civil inferiority for the Negro.

3. The steady withdrawal of aid from institutions for the higher training of the Negro.

These movements are not, to be sure, direct results of Mr. Washington's teachings; but his propaganda has, without a shadow of doubt, helped their speedier accomplishment. The question then comes: Is it possible, and probable, that nine millions of men can make effective progress in economic lines if they are deprived of political rights, made a servile caste, and allowed only the most meagre chance for developing their exceptional men? If history and reason give any distinct answer to these questions, it is an emphatic *No.* And Mr. Washington thus faces the triple paradox of his career:

1. He is striving nobly to make Negro artisans business men and property-owners; but it is utterly impossible, under modern competitive methods, for workingmen and property-owners to defend their rights and exist without the right of suffrage.

2. He insists on thrift and self-respect, but at the same time counsels a silent submission to civic inferiority such as is bound to sap the manhood of any race in the long run.

3. He advocates common-school and industrial training, and depreciates institutions of higher learning; but neither the Negro common-schools, nor Tuskegee itself, could remain open a day were it not for teachers trained in Negro colleges, or trained by their graduates. . . .

It would be unjust to Mr. Washington not to acknowledge that in several instances he has opposed movements in the South which were unjust to the Negro; he sent memorials to the Louisiana and Alabama constitutional conventions, he has spoken against lynching, and in other ways has openly or silently set his influence against sinister schemes and unfortunate happenings. Notwithstanding this, it is equally true to assert that on the whole he distinct impression left by Mr. Washington's propaganda is, first, that the South is justified in its present attitude toward the Negro because of the Negro's degradation; secondly, that the prime cause of the Negro's failure to rise more quickly is his wrong education in the past; and, thirdly, that his future rise depends primarily on his own efforts. Each of these propositions is a dangerous half-truth. The supplementary truths must never be lost sight of: first, slavery and race-prejudice are potent if not sufficient causes of the Negro's position; second, industrial and common-school training were necessarily slow in planting because they had to await the black teachers trained by higher institutions,—it being extremely doubtful if any essentially different development was possible, and certainly a Tuskegee was unthinkable before 1880; and third, while it is a great truth to say that the Negro must strive and strive mightily to help himself, it is equally true that unless his striving be not simply seconded, but rather aroused and encouraged, by the initiative of the richer and wiser environing group, he cannot hope for great success.

In his failure to realize and impress this last point, Mr. Washington is especially to be criticised. His doctrine has tended to make the whites, North and South, shift the burden of the Negro problem to the Negro's shoulders and stand aside as critical and rather pessimistic spectators; when in fact the burden belongs to the nation, and the hands of none of us are clean if we bend not our energies to righting these great wrongs.

The South ought to be led, by candid and honest criticism, to assert her better self and do her full duty to the race she has cruelly wronged and is still wronging. The North—her co-partner in guilt—cannot salve her conscience by plastering it with gold. We cannot settle this problem by diplomacy and suaveness, by "policy" alone. If worse come to worst, can the moral fibre of this country survive the slow throttling and murder of nine millions of men?

The black men of America have a duty to perform, a duty stern and delicate,—a forward movement to oppose a part of the work of their greatest leader. So far as Mr. Washington preaches Thrift, Patience, and Industrial Training for the masses, we must hold up his hands and strive with him, rejoicing in his honors and glorying in the strength of this Joshua called of God and of man to lead the headless host. But so far as Mr. Washington apologizes for injustice, North or South, does not rightly value the privilege and duty of voting, belittles the emasculating effects of caste distinctions, and opposes the higher training and ambition of our brighter minds,—so far as he, the South, or the Nation, does this,—we must unceasingly and firmly oppose them. By every civilized and peaceful method we must strive for the rights which the world accords to men, clinging unwaveringly to those great words which the sons of the Fathers would fain forget: "We hold these truths to be self-evident: That all men are created equal; that they are endowed by their Creator with certain unalienable rights; that among these are life, liberty, and the pursuit of happiness."

148

The Unwanted Immigrants: The Chinese (1878)

Fleeing political and economic hardships, Chinese immigrants came to the West Coast and settled first in California. Initially, the California gold rush attracted Chinese immigrants, but the western railroad companies actively recruited many Chinese immigrants to construct their tracks. Known for their willingness to work long hours for little pay, these "coolies," as whites called them, filled many manual labor jobs when railroad construction declined. White workers came to resent the industrious Chinese and their different customs and lifestyle, and the white workers began pressuring state governments for action. Even though the Chinese composed 1 percent of California's population in 1878 (and only .002 percent of the nation's), the California legislature investigated the nature and impact of Chinese immigration. The committee's report, excerpted as follows, warned the nation about the "evils" of the Chinese and reflected the racism that had developed; four years later, Congress passed the Chinese Exclusion Act (1882), which suspended Chinese immigration for 10 years.

Questions to Consider

1. According to this California state government report, in what ways do Californians oppose the Chinese immigrants?
2. For what reasons were the Chinese, and not other immigrant groups, singled out?
3. Why would Congress pass the Chinese Exclusion Act, if the Chinese are identified as a problem in California?
4. How might Ida Wells-Barnett ("Lynching in the South," Document 145) respond to the sentiments contained in this document?

The Chinese have now lived among us, in considerable numbers, for a quarter of a century, and yet they remain separate, distinct from, and antagonistic to our people in thinking, mode of life, in tastes and principles, and are as far from assimilation as when they first arrived.

They fail to comprehend our system of government; they perform no duties of citizenship; they are not available as jurymen; cannot be called upon as a *posse comitatus* to preserve order, nor be relied upon as soldiers.

They do not comprehend or appreciate our social ideas, and they contribute but little to the support of any of our institutions, public or private. They bring no children with them, and there is, therefore, no possibility of influencing them by our ordinary educational appliances.

There is, indeed, no point of contact between the Chinese and our people through which we can Americanize them. The rigidity which characterizes these people forbids the hope of any essential change in their relations to our own people or our government.

We respectfully submit the admitted proposition that no nation, much less a republic, can safely permit the presence of a large and increasing element among its people which cannot be assimilated or made to comprehend the responsibilities of citizenship.

California, Senate, Special Committee on Chinese Immigration, "An Address to the American People of the United States upon the Evils of Chinese Immigration," *Report of the Special Committee on Chinese Immigration to the California State Senate, 1878*, 8–9, 25, 35, 46–47.

The great mass of the Chinese residents of California are not amenable to our laws. It is almost impossible to procure the conviction of Chinese criminals, and we are never sure that a conviction, even when obtained, is in accordance with justice.

This difficulty arises out of our ignorance of the Chinese language and the fact that their moral ideas are wholly distinct from our own. They do not recognize the sanctity of an oath, and utterly fail to comprehend the crime of perjury. Bribery, intimidation, and other methods of baffling judicial action, are considered by them as perfectly legitimate. It is an established fact that the administration of justice among the Chinese is almost impossible, and we are, therefore, unable to protect them against the persecutions of their own countrymen, or punish them for offenses against our own people. This anomalous condition, in which the authority of law is so generally vacated, imperils the existence of our republican institutions to a degree hitherto unknown among us. . . .

We now come to an aspect of the question more revolting still. We would shrink from the disgusting details did not a sense of duty demand that they be presented. Their lewd women induce, by the cheapness of their offers, thousands of boys and young men to enter their dens, very many of whom are inoculated with venereal diseases of the worst type. Boys of eight and ten years of age have been found with this disease, and some of our physicians treat a half dozen cases daily. The fact that these diseases have their origin chiefly among the Chinese is well established. . . .

But we desire to call your attention to the sanitary aspect of the subject. The Chinese herd together in one spot, whether in city or village, until they transform the vicinage into a perfect hive—there they live packed together, a hundred living in a space that would be insufficient for an average American family.

Their place of domicile is filthy in the extreme, and to a degree that cleansing is impossible except by the absolute destruction of the dwellings they occupy. But for the healthfulness of our climate, our city populations would have long since been decimated by pestilence from these causes. And we do not know how long this natural protection will suffice us.

In almost every house is found a room devoted to opium smoking, and these places are visited by white boys and women, so that the deadly opium habit is being introduced among our people. . . .

We now call attention to an aspect of the subject of such huge proportions, and such practical and pressing importance, that we almost dread to enter upon its consideration, namely, the effect of Chinese labor upon our industrial classes. We admit that the Chinese were, in the earlier history of the State, when white labor was not attainable, very useful in the development of our peculiar industries; that they were of great service in railroad building, in mining, gardening, general agriculture, and as domestic servants.

We admit that the Chinese are exceedingly expert in all kinds of labor and manufacturing; that they are easily and inexpensively handled in large numbers.

We recognize the right of all men to better their condition when they can, and deeply sympathize with the overcrowded population of China. . . .

Our laborers cannot be induced to live like vermin, as the Chinese and these habits of individual and family life have ever been encouraged by our statesmen as essential to good morals.

Our laborers require meat and bread, which have been considered by us as necessary to that mental and bodily strength which is thought to be important in the citizens of a Republic which depends upon the strength of its people, while the Chinese require only rice, dried fish, tea, and a few simple vegetables. The cost of sustenance to the whites is four-fold greater than that of the Chinese, and the wages of the whites must of necessity be greater than the wages required by the Chinese. The Chinese are, therefore, able to underbid the whites in every kind of labor. They can be hired in masses; they can be managed and controlled like unthinking slaves. But our laborer has an individual life, cannot be controlled as a slave by brutal masters, and this individuality has been required of him by the genius of our institutions, and upon these elements of character the State depends for defense and growth. . . .

As a natural consequence the white laborer is out of employment, and misery and want are fast taking the places of comfort and plenty.

Now, to consider and weigh the benefits returned to us by the Chinese for these privileges and for these wrongs to our laboring classes. They buy little or nothing from our own people, but import both their food and clothing from China; they send their wages home; they have not introduced a single industry peculiar to their own country; they contribute nothing to the support of our institutions; can never be relied upon as defenders of the State; they have no intention of becoming citizens; they acquire no homes, and are a constant tax upon the public treasury. . . .

149

An Italian Immigrant's Experience in America (1902)

In the Gilded Age, the nature of European immigration to America changed. The number of immigrants increased dramatically, and the ethnic composition changed. Unlike earlier immigrants who came from northern and western Europe, these "New Immigrants" came from southern and eastern Europe. These Italians, Russian Jews, Poles, and Slovaks, to name a few, brought languages, religions, and customs that sharply contrasted with native-born American lifestyles. The new immigrants clustered into the growing cities, often forming easily identified ethnic neighborhoods (Little Italy, for example) as a refuge from the realities of life in America. Often uneducated and lacking job skills, many immigrants found work in low-paying, menial occupations. One example of an immigrant's experience was Rocco Corresca's. Raised as an orphan in Italy, Corresca was forced to beg and steal in the streets for a living. Corresca and his friend Francisco fled to America, where they fell victim to the exploitive padrone system. In 1902, the news magazine The Independent *published Rocco Corresca's account of life in America, which is excerpted as follows.*

Questions to Consider

1. What services did the *padrone* (Bartolo) provide to Rocco and Francisco?
2. In what ways did Rocco and Francisco adapt to life in America? How did they not adapt?
3. What does this account reveal about the Italian immigrant experience?
4. To what extent do the photographs of urban life ("Views of Urban Life," Document 144) corroborate the information contained in this document? Are there discrepancies between the written and photographic account?

. . . Now and then I had heard things about America—that it was a far off country where everybody was rich and that Italians went there and made plenty of money, so that they could return to Italy and live in pleasure ever after. One day I met a young man who pulled out a handful of gold and told me he had made that in America in a few days.

I said I should like to go there, and he told me that if I went he would take care of me and see that I was safe. I told Francisco and he wanted to go too. . . .

. . . We were all landed on an island and the bosses there said that Francisco and I must go back because we had not enough money, but a man named Bartolo came up and told them that we were brothers and he was our uncle and would take care of us. He brought two other men who swore that they knew us in Italy and that Bartolo was our uncle. I had never seen any of them before, but even then Bartolo might be my uncle, so I did not say anything. The bosses of the island let us go out with Bartolo after he had made the oath. . . .

Most of the men in our room worked at digging the sewer. Bartolo got them the work and they paid him about one quarter of their wages. Then he charged them for board and he bought the clothes for them, too. So they got little money after all.

Bartolo was always saying that the rent of the room was so high that he could not make anything, but he was really making plenty. He was what they call a padrone and is now a very rich man. The men that were living with him had just come to the country and could not speak English. They had all been sent by the young man we met in Italy. Bartolo told us all that we must work for him and that if we did not the police would come and put us in prison. . . .

We were with Bartolo nearly a year, but some of our countrymen who had been in the place a long time said that Bartolo had no right to us and we could get work for a dollar and a half a day, which, when you make it *lire* (reckoned in the Italian currency) is very much. So we went away one day to Newark and got work on the street. Bartolo came after us and made a great

Rocco Corresca, "The Biography of a Bootblack," *The Independent* 54 (December 4, 1902): 2863–2867.

noise, but the boss said that if he did not go away soon the police would have him. Then he went, saying that there was no justice in this country.

We paid a man five dollars each for getting us the work and we were with that boss for six months. He was Irish, but a good man and he gave us our money every Saturday night. We lived much better than with Bartolo, and when the work was done we each had nearly $200 saved. Plenty of the men spoke English and they taught us, and we taught them to read and write. That was at night, for we had a lamp in our room, and there were only five other men who lived in that room with us. . . .

When the Newark boss told us that there was no more work Francisco and I talked about what we would do and we went back to Brooklyn to a saloon near Hamilton Ferry, where we got a job cleaning it out and slept in a little room upstairs. There was a bootblack named Michael on the corner and when I had time I helped him and learned the business. Francisco cooked the lunch in the saloon and he, too, worked for the bootblack and we were soon able to make the best polish.

Then we thought we would go into business and we got a basement on Hamilton avenue, near the Ferry, and put four chairs in it. We paid $75 for the chairs and all the other things. We had tables and looking glasses there and curtains. We took the papers that have the pictures in and made the place high toned. Outside we had a big sign that said:

THE BEST SHINE FOR TEN CENTS.

Men that did not want to pay ten cents could get a good shine for five cents, but it was not an oil shine. We had two boys helping us and paid each of them fifty cents a day. The rent of the place was $20 a month, so the expenses were very great but we made money from the beginning. We slept in the basement, but got our meals in the saloon till we could put a stove in our place, and then Francisco cooked for us all. That would not do, tho, because some of our customers said that they did not like to smell garlic and onions and red herrings. I thought that was strange, but we had to do what the customers said. So we got the woman who lived upstairs to give us our meals and paid her $1.50 a week each. She gave the boys soup in the middle of the day—five cents for two plates. . . .

We had said that when we saved $1,000 each we would go back to Italy and buy a farm, but now that the time is coming we are so busy and making so much money that we think we will stay. We have opened another parlor near South Ferry, in New York. We have to pay $30.00 a month rent, but the business is very good. The boys in this place charge sixty cents a day because there is so much work.

At first we did not know much of this country, but by and by we learned. There are here plenty of Protestants who are heretics, but they have a religion, too. Many of the finest churches are Protestant, but they have no saints and no altars, which seems strange. . . .

I and Francisco are to be Americans in three years. The court gave us papers and said we must wait and we must be able to read some things and tell who the ruler of the country is.

There are plenty of rich Italians here, men who a few years ago had nothing and now have so much money that they could not count all their dollars in a week. The richest ones go away from the other Italians and live with the Americans. . . .

I am nineteen years of age now and have $700. saved. Francisco is twenty-one and has about $900. We shall open some more parlors soon. I know an Italian who was a bootblack ten years ago and now bosses bootblacks all over the city, who has so much money that if it was turned into gold it would weigh more than himself. . . .

I often think of Ciguciano and Teresa [in Italy]. He is a good man, one in a thousand, and she was very beautiful. Maybe I shall write to them about coming to this country.

150

"The Story of a Sweatshop Girl" (1902)

The adaptation of machines to methods of production brought changes to the workforce as well as to how goods were made. The garment industry was among those businesses affected by the change. The development of standard clothing sizes, the use of the electrically powered sewing machine, and the availability of low-wage workers allowed for the mass production of inexpensive clothes for both men and women. In most instances, garment businesses were located in cities. Often taking over a floor or floors of a former warehouse, numerous workers and machines were crammed into these floors, creating crowded and dangerous work conditions that became known as the "sweatshop." The workforce was usually young females, often recent immigrants, because the garment trades offered women one of the few sources of income that were available outside the home. These women assembled parts of clothing, performing the same sewing task repetitiously for hours on end. In 1902, Sadie Frowne, a Polish immigrant, told her story as a sweatshop girl to a reporter from the news magazine The Independent. *Excerpts of her account follow.*

Questions to Consider

1. How does Sadie Frowne describe her work and the conditions in the "sweatshop"?

2. In what ways does Sadie Frowne seek to improve her life?

3. What does this document reveal about life and work for recent immigrant women?

4. How is Sadie Frowne's experience similar to that expressed in "An Italian Immigrant's Experience in America" (Document 149)? How is it different?

"The Story of a Sweatshop Girl," *The Independent* 54 (September 25, 1902): 2279–2282. 19-38

. . . Aunt Fanny had always been anxious for me to get an education, as I did not know how to read or write, and she thought that was wrong. Schools are different in Poland from what they are in this country, and I was always too busy to learn to read and write. So when mother died I thought I would try to learn a trade and then I could go to school at night and learn to speak the English language well.

So I went to work in Allen street (Manhattan) in what they call a sweat-shop, making skirts by machine. I was new at the work and the foreman scolded me a great deal.

"Now, then," he would say, "this place is not for you to be looking around in. Attend to your work. That is what you have to do."

I did not know at first that you must not look around and talk, and I made many mistakes with the sewing, so that I was often called a "stupid animal." But I made $4 a week by working six days in the week. For there are two Sabbaths here—our own Sabbath, that comes on a Saturday, and the Christian Sabbath that comes on Sunday. It is against our law to work on our own Sabbath, so we work on their Sabbath. . . .

Two years ago I came to this place, Brownsville, where so many of my people are, and where I have friends. I got work in a factory making under-skirts—all sorts of cheap underskirts, like cotton and calico for the summer and woolen for the winter, but never the silk, satin or velvet underskirts. I earned $4.50 a week and lived on $2 a week, the same as before. . . .

It isn't piecework in our factory, but one is paid by the amount of work done just the same. So it is like piecework. All the hands get different amounts, some as low as $3.50 and some of the men as high as $16 a week. The factory is in the third story of a brick building. It is in a room twenty feet long and fourteen broad. There are fourteen machines in it. I and the daughter of the people with whom I live work two of these machines. The other operators are all men, some young and some old. . . .

I get up at half-past five o'clock every morning and make myself a cup of coffee on the oil stove. I eat a bit of bread and perhaps some fruit and then go to work. Often I get there soon after six o'clock so as to be in good time, tho the factory does not open till seven. I have heard that there is a sort of clock that calls you at the very time you want to get up, but I can't believe that because I don't see how the clock would know.

At seven o'clock we all sit down to our machines and the boss brings to each one the pile of work that he or she is to finish during the day, what they call in English their "stint." This pile is put down beside the machine and as soon as a skirt is done it is laid on the other side of the machine. Sometimes the work is not all finished by six o'clock and then the one who is behind must work overtime. Sometimes one is finished ahead of time and gets away at four or five o'clock, but generally we are not done till six o'clock. The machines go like mad all day, because the faster you work the more money you get. Sometimes in my haste I get my finger caught and the needle goes right through it. It goes so quick, tho, that it does not hurt much. I bind the finger up with a piece of cotton and go on working. We all have accidents like that. Where the needle goes through the nail it makes a sore finger, or where it splinters a bone it does much harm. Sometimes a finger has to come off. Generally, tho, one can be cured by a salve.

All the time we are working the boss walks about examining the finished garments and making us do them over again if they are not just right. So we have to be careful as well as swift. But I am getting so good at the work that within a year I will be making $7 a week, and then I can save at least $3.50 a week. I have over $200 saved now.

The machines are all run by foot power, and at the end of the day one feels so weak that there is a great temptation to lie right down and sleep. But you must go out and get air, and have some pleasure. So instead of lying down I go out, generally with Henry. Sometimes we go to Coney Island, where there are good dancing places, and sometimes we go to Ulmer Park to picnics. . . .

I am going back to night school again this winter. Plenty of my friends go there. Some of the women in my class are more than forty years of age. Like me, they did not have a chance to learn anything in the old country. It is good to have an education; it makes you feel higher. Ignorant people are all low. People say now that I am clever and fine in conversation.

We have just finished a strike in our business. It spread all over and the United Brotherhood of Garment Workers was in it. That takes in the cloak-makers, coatmakers, and all the others. We struck for shorter hours, and after being out four weeks won the fight. We only have to work nine and a half hours a day and we get the same pay as before. So the union does good after all in spite of what some people say against it—that it just takes our money and does nothing.

I pay 25 cents a month to the union, but I do not begrudge that because it is for our benefit. The next strike is going to be for a raise of wages, which we all ought to have. But tho I belong to the Union I am not a Socialist or an Anarchist. I don't know exactly what those things mean. There is a little expense for charity, too. If any worker is injured or sick we all give money to help. . . .

20

✳

Imperialism

The Social Darwinist attitudes that supported economic exploitation and white Anglo-Saxon superiority in the United States combined to buttress a new imperialism abroad. Although traditionally expansionistic, the United States had previously confined its ambitions to the North American continent. During the 1890s, however, the "closing" of the frontier, a search for new economic opportunities, national pride, and competition with European rivals caused many Americans to champion a more aggressive policy overseas. America's new role in world affairs became a matter of serious debate by the turn of the 20th century. The next several documents show the varying sentiments, both foreign and domestic, concerning the new imperialism.

151

Our Country (1891)

In the late 19th century, America's westward expansion had occupied much of the available lands within the continental United States. In fact, the U.S. Census Bureau announced the official "closing" of the frontier in 1890. Some individuals, noting the shrinking potential for territorial expansion and the need for new outlets for both manufacturing and agricultural products, came to believe that seeking new overseas markets and possibly acquiring foreign possessions would benefit the country. Certainly, the European countries' scramble to acquire colonial empires helped convince some Americans that the United States should participate or be left out. Such developments helped generate increasing interest in foreign policy. Adding another dimension to the argument for overseas expansion were Protestant missionaries who hoped to spread Christianity. Protestant minister Josiah Strong touched on missionary work in his book, Our Country, *which captured the concerns and hopes of many American Protestants who had witnessed dramatic social, economic, and intellectual change while offering the moral reassurance that America could still become a model Christian nation. In this excerpt from* Our Country, *Strong depicts the role of America in the world.*

Questions to Consider

1. For what reasons does Josiah Strong predict a bright future for America?
2. In what ways does Strong believe the Anglo-Saxon race is prepared to "influence the world's future"?
3. In what ways would this document shape ideas about overseas expansion?
4. How do you think the author of this document would respond to the views found in "The Unwanted Immigrants: The Chinese" (Document 148)?

. . . It is not necessary to argue to those for whom I write that the two great needs of mankind, that all men may be lifted up into the light of the highest Christian civilization, are, first, a pure, spiritual Christianity, and second, civil liberty. Without controversy, these are the forces which, in the past, have contributed most to the elevation of the human race, and they must continue to be, in the future, the most efficient ministers to its progress. It follows, then, that the Anglo-Saxon, as the great representative of these two ideas, the depository of these two greatest blessings, sustains peculiar relations to the world's future, is divinely commissioned to be, in a peculiar sense, his brother's keeper. Add to this the fact of his rapidly increasing strength in modern times, and we have well-nigh a demonstration of his destiny. . . .

There can be no reasonable doubt that North America is to be the great home of the Anglo-Saxon, the principal seat of his power, the center of his life and influence. . . . Our continent has room and resources and climate, it lies in the pathway of the nations, it belongs to the zone of power, and already, among Anglo-Saxons, do we lead in population and wealth. . . .

Again, another marked characteristic of the Anglo-Saxon is what may be called an instinct or genius for colonizing. His unequaled energy, his indomitable perseverance, and his personal independence, made him a pioneer. He excels all others in pushing his way into new countries. It was those in whom this tendency was strongest that came to America, and this inherited tendency has been further developed by the westward sweep of successive generations across the continent. So noticeable has this characteristic become that English visitors remark it. Charles Dickens once said that the typical American would hesitate to enter heaven unless assured that he could go farther west.

Again, nothing more manifestly distinguishes the Anglo-Saxon than his intense and persistent energy, and he is developing in the United States an energy which, in eager activity and effectiveness, is peculiarly American.

This is due partly to the fact that Americans are much better fed than Europeans, and partly to the undeveloped resources of a new country, but more largely to our climate, which acts as a constant stimulus. . . . Moreover, our social institutions are stimulating. In Europe the various ranks of society

Josiah Strong, *Our Country* (New York, 1891), 200–218.

are, like the strata of the earth, fixed and fossilized. There can be no great change without a terrible upheaval, a social earthquake. Here society is like the waters of the sea, mobile; as General Garfield said, and so signally illustrated in his own experience, that which is at the bottom to-day may one day flash on the crest of the highest wave. Every one is free to become whatever he can make of himself; free to transform himself from a rail-splitter or a tanner or a canal-boy, into the nation's President. Our aristocracy, unlike that of Europe, is open to all comers. Wealth, position, influence, are prizes offered for energy; and every farmer's boy, every apprentice and clerk, every friendless and penniless immigrant, is free to enter the list. Thus many causes co-operate to produce here the most forceful and tremendous energy in the world.

What is the significance of such facts? These tendencies unfold the future; they are the mighty alphabet with which God writes his prophecies. May we not, by a careful laying together of the letters, spell out something of his meaning? It seems to me that God, with infinite wisdom and skill, is training the Anglo-Saxon race for an hour sure to come in the world's future. Heretofore there has always been in the history of the world a comparatively unoccupied land westward, into which the crowded countries of the East have poured their surplus populations. But the widening waves of migration, which millenniums ago rolled east and west from the valley of the Euphrates, meet to-day on our Pacific coast. There are no more new worlds. The unoccupied arable lands of the earth are limited, and will soon be taken. The time is coming when the pressure of population on the means of subsistence will be felt here as it is now felt in Europe and Asia. Then will the world enter upon a new stage of its history—*the final competition of races, for which the Anglo-Saxon is being schooled.* Long before the thousand millions are here, the mighty *centrifugal* tendency, inherent in this stock and strengthened in the United States, will assert itself. Then this race of unequaled energy, with all the majesty of numbers and the might of wealth behind it—the representative, let us hope, of the largest liberty, the purest Christianity, the highest civilization—having developed peculiarly aggressive traits calculated to impress its institutions upon mankind, will spread itself over the earth. If I read not amiss, this powerful race will move down upon Mexico, down upon Central and South America, out upon the islands of the sea, over upon Africa and beyond. And can any one doubt that the result of this competition of races will be the "survival of the fittest"? . . .

In my own mind, there is no doubt that the Anglo-Saxon is to exercise the commanding influence in the world's future; but the exact nature of that influence is, as yet, undetermined. How far his civilization will be materialistic and atheistic, and how long it will take thoroughly to Christianize and sweeten it, how rapidly he will hasten the coming of the kingdom wherein dwelleth righteousness, or how many ages he may retard it, is still uncertain; but *is now being swiftly determined.* Let us weld together in a chain the various links of our logic which we have endeavored to forge. Is it manifest that the Anglo-Saxon holds in his hands the destinies of mankind for ages to come? Is it evident that the United States is to be the home of this race, the principal seat of his power, the great center of his influence? Is it true that the great West is to dominate the nation's future? Has it been shown that this generation is to determine the character, and hence the destiny of the West? Then may God open the eyes of this generation! . . . Notwithstanding the great perils which threaten it, I cannot think our civilization will perish; but I believe it is fully in the hands of the Christians of the United States, during the next ten or fifteen years, to hasten or retard the coming of Christ's kingdom in the world by hundreds, and perhaps thousands, of years. We of this generation and nation occupy the Gibraltar of the ages which commands the world's future.

152

The Sinking of the *Maine* (1898)

In 1895, the Cuban revolution against Spain flared up again. Spain sent troops under General Valeriano Weyler to quell the revolt, and he began a policy of reconcentrado, assembling peasants into camps before laying waste to the countryside. The revolt was bloody and savage on both sides. Sensational American newspapers, especially William Randolph Hearst's New York Journal *and Joseph Pulitzer's* New York World, *began publishing lurid—and often exaggerated—accounts and drawings of Spanish atrocities in an effort to increase circulation. This "yellow journalism" only created more American interest and sympathy in the Cuban revolt. When riots broke out in Havana, Cuba, in 1898, and American citizens might be endangered, the U.S. battleship* Maine *arrived in the harbor, supposedly on a courtesy call. On February 15, 1898, the* Maine *exploded and sank, with the loss of 260 sailors. Rumors circulated that Spain sunk the battleship, and the tabloid newspapers blared headlines accusing Spain while clamoring for war. The following selection is the* New York Journal's *editorial on the sinking of the* Maine.

Questions to Consider

1. According to the *New York Journal,* in what ways was the *Maine* an "object lesson" to the United States?

2. What reasons does the *New York Journal* give for U.S. intervention in Cuba?

3. In what ways did the sinking of the *Maine* move the United States closer to war with Spain?

4. How do you think William Graham Sumner, author of "The Forgotten Man" (Document 138), would have responded to the views contained in this essay?

The prudent, proper and patriotic policy for the United States Government to adopt in dealing with the Cuban question is not changed by the disaster to the Maine. What the Journal said months ago is perfectly applicable to the situation today. It is the duty of the United States to intervene in Cuba, not because an American war ship has been destroyed in Havana harbor by a suspicious "accident," but because every dictate of national self-protection, every impulse of humanity compels such intervention.

The disaster to the Maine is an object lesson to the Administration rather than a present cause for war. If the inquiry which begins this week shall show it to have been the result of the faulty construction of the vessel, or of carelessness, it of course offers no reason for attack upon Spain. If it be shown to be the work of irresponsible individuals, malignant fanatics or murderous Weylerites the United States will demand full reparation and a money indemnity from Spain, the refusal of which would necessarily lead to war. If, what is almost incredible, the explosion should be shown to have been caused with connivance or by the act of responsible Spanish officers, a declaration of war would be instant and the war would be one of chastisement and revenge.

There are countless reasons to believe that the second hypothesis will be supported by the finding of the court of inquiry; but, even so, reliance upon it would defer tediously the time of American intervention in Cuba. After the time spent in investigation would come the delay attendant upon diplomatic correspondence with a nation which never does to-day what it can put off until to-morrow. That is why the disaster to the Maine is not to be regarded as an immediate cause for war.

But it is an object lesson which the Administration may well heed. For two years the Spaniards have carried on in Cuba a warfare which has outraged humanity and violated the laws of civilized nations. They have destroyed American property and imprisoned and murdered American citizens. The navy of the United States has been forced to do police duty on the seas that the Spaniards might prosecute their outrages the more securely. The commerce of the United States with Cuba has been destroyed. American vessels have been illegally fired upon and the United States flag insulted. To-day the revolution is no nearer suppression than it ever was. Spanish power in Cuba is a myth—it extends just far enough to give Spanish officials an opportunity to enrich themselves by plundering their own troops.

These reasons why the United States should intervene have existed ever since the McKinley Administration came into power. Had the right course been promptly taken the Spaniards would have been driven out of Cuba at probably a [lower] cost to the United States in lives than the "accident" to the Maine entailed. Are we to wait now until the ship sent to take the place of the Maine also meets with an "accident"? Shall we give Spain time to complete her projected alliance with the Spanish-American republics against the United States?

"Enforce Peace in Cuba," *New York Journal*, February 21, 1898, p. 10.

The result of the inquiry at Havana may make instant war with Spain inevitable. But the reasons why the United States should insure peace in their hemisphere by enforcing peace in Cuba would be as forceful to-day if the gallant Maine and her noble crew were still floating in Havana harbor.

153

Aguinaldo's Call for Philippine Independence (1899)

The Spanish-American War began with a stunning naval victory in the Philippines. The plan was to inflict severe damage on the Spanish colony of the Philippines in order to coerce Spain to liberate Cuba. Commodore George Dewey and the Asiatic squadron destroyed the Spanish fleet in Manila Bay, but lacking sufficient numbers of troops, they could not occupy territory until an expeditionary force arrived from America. Helping liberate the countryside was Filipino nationalist Emilio Aguinaldo. He had been leading a rebellion against the Spanish colonial government before the war broke out in 1898. Understanding that the American motive in the war was to liberate Cuba from Spanish colonial rule, Aguinaldo assumed that helping American forces remove Spanish troops might mean independence for the Philippines. Aguinaldo and his supporters even established a temporary government. When they realized that America would not leave the Philippines, Aguinaldo issued a call for independence and rebelled against the United States, touching off a war that lasted nearly three years. His declaration of independence, as presented in The Outlook, *a popular news magazine, is as follows.*

Questions to Consider

1. What are Aguinaldo's reasons for waging war against the United States?

2. In what ways does Aguinaldo use references about America to support his case for Filipino independence?

3. For what reasons does Aguinaldo dismiss "this autonomy America offers"?

4. On what issues would Aguinaldo agree with Senator George F. Hoar ("An Anti-Imperialist Perspective," Document 154)? On what issues would they disagree?

Filipinos: Beloved daughter of the ardent sun of the tropics, commended by Providence to the care of noble Spain, be not ungrateful to her salute who warmed you with the breath of her own culture and civilization. It is true she sought to crush thy aspiration for independence, as a loving mother opposes separation forever from the daughter of her bosom. This but proves the excess of affection and love Spain feels for thee, Filipinos! Delicate flower of the East, scarcely eight months weaned from the breast of thy mother,

"Pleas for Independence," *The Outlook* 62 (July 22, 1899): 677.

thou hast dared to brave a great and powerful nation such as is the United States, after barely organizing and disciplining thy little army. Yet we reply, we will be slaves to none, nor allow ourselves to be deceived by soft words. Let us continue to defend our fatherland till independence is assured, for this is justice. We shall see at last that the great American Nation will acknowledge the right which is on our side. That doctrine of the great Monroe, that America is for Americans, is not forgotten: just as we affirm that the Philippines are for the Filipinos. Some States of the American Union have arisen in our favor. Especially is the Democratic party convinced that both victors and vanquished will lose precious lives. Thus many of the people and many statesmen censure President McKinley as inhuman for having ordered his military representatives at Manila to seek means to bring about hostilities with the Filipinos. These facts prove that they wish to try us, to see if we are able to live up to the second color of our banner, red, which signifies courage, heroism, and martyrdom. Therefore we should not resent this struggle with the Americans. In spite of their expressed desire to dominate all the Philippines, well convinced are they that we fight with justice and right on our side, and that autonomy is all a show of deceit, only serving to save certain accumulated wealth. We have never concealed our aspirations, that we aspire but to independence, that we will struggle on to obtain it, perhaps from those who are now our enemies and to-morrow will be our allies, as they were for the overthrowal of the power of Spain. We might well accept this autonomy America offers, but what can we do with it if our ambition is independence, and if we are to accept it only to later overthrow by force of arms the sovereignty of America? As I believe it is the intention of the autonomists to make use of treachery and deceit, we cannot accept such a procedure. We do not wish to be traitors afterward. We wish to show our character of frankness and sincerity, and nothing more. Let us avoid the example of those natives who, having at one time been colonists, accepted autonomy to enable them to make their work surer once everything was prepared. History has given us an example of this in recent events. Let us persist in our idea, which is only the legitimate and noble aspiration of a people which is desirous at all cost to preserve its national honor spotless and as pure as crystal. Thus, then, there will not be a single Filipino autonomist. Those who are so are in the eyes of the people but time-servers, fearful of losing their riches threatened by risks of war. Filipinos! Let us be constant! Let us strengthen the bonds of our union! . . .

154

An Anti-Imperialist Perspective (1899)

Congress declared war against Spain in April 1898, to establish Cuban independence, but the opening battle of the war was fought halfway around the world when Commodore George Dewey attacked the Spanish fleet in Manila, Philippines. The Spanish surrendered Manila to the Americans, while Filipino insurgent leader Emilio Aguinaldo, working with the Americans, liberated the countryside and established a temporary government. The war's end left the Philippines under joint American-Filipino control, but the future of the country was in the hands of Congress. The Philippine annexation issue—perhaps the most important foreign policy decision of the time—became hotly debated, as the sides were sharply drawn between imperialists and anti-imperialists. Among the first to denounce annexation was George F. Hoar, an aged, four-term Republican senator from Massachusetts. Hoar's political career spanned nearly 50 years: He helped form the Republican party, he oversaw the Republican party's shift to support business, and he denounced the popular election of senators. His speech, excerpted following, was given as the Senate considered ratifying the Treaty of Paris, which officially ended the war and made the Philippines an American possession.

Questions to Consider

1. For what reasons does George F. Hoar oppose the annexation of the Philippines?

2. Why does Hoar believe the imperialists are hypocrites?

3. On what issues would Hoar disagree with Senator Albert K. Beveridge's views in "The New Manifest Destiny" (Document 155)?

4. Compare and contrast Hoar's views with those expressed by W.E.B. DuBois ("On Race Relations," Document 147).

Mr. President, the persons who favor the ratification of this treaty without conditions and without amendment differ among themselves certainly in their views, purposes, and opinions. . . . In general, the state of mind and the utterance of the lips are in accord. If you ask them what they want, you are answered with a shout: "Three cheers for the flag! Who will dare haul it down? Hold on to everything you can get. The United States is strong enough to do what it likes. The Declaration of Independence and the counsel of Washington and the Constitution of the United States have grown rusty and musty. They are for little countries and not for great ones. There is no moral law for strong nations. America has outgrown Americanism." . . .

If you can not take down a national flag where it has once floated in time of war, we were disgraced when we took our flag down in Mexico, and in Vera Cruz, or after the invasion of Canada; England was dishonored when she took her flag down after she captured this capital; and every nation is henceforth pledged to the doctrine that where ever it puts its military foot or its naval power with the flag over it, that must be a war to the death and to extermination or the honor of the state is disgraced by the flag of that nation being withdrawn. . . .

"Acquisition of Territory," *Congressional Record*, 55th Congress, 3rd session (January 9, 1899), 493–503.

Now Mr. President, there are Senators here yet hesitating as to what their action may be in the future, who will tell you that they loathe and hate this doctrine that we may buy nations at wholesale; that we may acquire imperial powers or imperial regions by conquest; that we may make vassal states and subject peoples without constitutional restraint, and against their will, and without any restraint but our own discretion. . . .

The Monroe Doctrine is gone. Every European nation, every European alliance, has the right to acquire dominion in this hemisphere when we acquire it in the other. The Senator's doctrine put anywhere in practice will make our beloved country a cheap-jack country, raking after the cart for the leaving of European tyranny. . . .

Our fathers dreaded a standing army; but the Senator's doctrine put in practice anywhere, now or hereafter, renders necessary a standing army, to be reenforced by a powerful navy. Our fathers denounced the subjection of any people whose judges were appointed or whose salaries were paid by a foreign power; but the Senator's doctrine, whenever it shall be put in practice, will entail upon us a national debt larger than any now existing on the face of the earth, larger than any ever known in history.

Our fathers dreaded the national taxgatherers; but the doctrine of the Senator from Connecticut, if it be adopted, is sure to make our national taxgatherers the most familiar visitant to every American home. . . .

. . . My proposition, summed up in a nut shell is this: I admit you have the right to acquire territory for constitutional purposes, and you may hold land and govern men on it for the constitutional purpose of a seat of government or for the constitutional purpose of admitting it as a State. I deny the right to hold land or acquire any property for any purpose not contemplated by the Constitution. The government of foreign people against their will is not a constitutional purpose, but a purpose expressly forbidden by the Constitution. Therefore I deny the right to acquire this territory and to hold it by the Government for that purpose. . . .

Now, I claim that under the Declaration of Independence you can not govern a foreign territory, a foreign people, another people than your own, that you can not subjugate them and govern them against their will, because you think it is for their good, when they do not: because you think you are going to give them the blessings of liberty. You have no right at the cannon's mouth to impose on an unwilling people your Declaration of Independence and your Constitution and your notions of freedom and notions of what is good. . . .

But read the account of what is going on in Iloilo. The people there have got a government, with courts and judges, better than those of the people of Cuba, who, it was said, had a right to self-government, collecting their customs; and it is proposed to turn your guns on them, and say 'We think that our notion of government is better than the notion you have got yourselves.' I say that when you put that onto them against their will and say that freedom as we conceive it, not freedom as they conceive it, public interest as we conceive it, not as they conceive it, shall prevail and that if it does not we are to force it on them at the cannon's mouth—I say that the nation which undertakes that plea and says it is subduing these men for their good, will encounter the awful and terrible rebuke, 'Beware of the leaven of the Pharisees, which is hypocrisy.'

155

The New Manifest Destiny (1900)

In the Philippine annexation debates, one of the most forceful advocates of imperialism was Albert J. Beveridge, a first-term Republican senator from Indiana. Known for powerful political oratory and Anglo-Saxon supremacy before arriving in the Senate, Beveridge broke with tradition and gave a major speech as a freshman senator. In order to obtain information about the Philippine issue, Beveridge traveled to the islands and conducted a personal investigation. This inquiry added credibility to his annexationist position. Excerpted following is Beveridge's eloquent Senate speech on the question of Philippine annexation. Beveridge served two terms in the Senate and was often considered one of the original Progressive Republicans. He lost a re-election bid in 1911, and became a distinguished historian. His best work was The Life of John Marshall *(four volumes), for which he received the Pulitzer Prize for historical biography.*

Questions to Consider

1. According to Albert J. Beveridge, for what reasons should the United States annex the Philippines?

2. In what ways does Beveridge address the anti-imperialist issues of constitutional authority and intent of the Founders?

3. Compare Beveridge's argument for annexing the Philippines to the position of George F. Hoar ("An Anti-Imperialist Perspective," Document 154).

4. Why is Beveridge's speech significant to the annexation movement?

Mr. President, the times call for candor. The Philippines are ours forever, "territory belonging to the United States," as the Constitution calls them. And just beyond the Philippines are China's illimitable markets. We will not retreat from either. We will not repudiate our duty in the archipelago. We will not abandon our opportunity in the Orient. We will not renounce our part in the mission of our race, trustee, under God, of the civilization of the world. And we will move forward to our work, not howling out regrets like slaves

---

"Policy Regarding the Philippines," *Congressional Record,* 56th Congress, 1st session (January 9, 1900), 704–712.

whipped to their burdens, but with gratitude for a task worthy of our strength, and thanksgiving to Almighty God that He has marked us as His chosen people, hence forth to lead in the regeneration of the world.

This island empire is the last land left in all the oceans. If it should prove a mistake to abandon it, the blunder once made would be irretrievable. If it proves a mistake to hold it, the error can be corrected when we will. Every other progressive nation stands ready to relieve us.

But to hold it will be no mistake. Our largest trade henceforth must be with Asia. The Pacific is our ocean. More and more Europe will manufacture the most it needs, secure from its colonies the most it consumes. Where shall we turn for consumers of our surplus? Geography answers the question. China is our natural customer. She is nearer to us than to England, Germany, or Russia, the commercial powers of the present and the future. They have moved nearer to China by securing permanent bases on her borders. The Philippines give us a base at the door of all the East.

Lines of navigation from our ports to the Orient and Australia; from the Isthmian Canal to Asia; from all Oriental ports to Australia, converge at and separate from the Philippines. They are a self-supporting, dividend-paying fleet, permanently anchored at a spot selected by the strategy of Providence, commanding the Pacific. And the Pacific is the ocean of the commerce of the future. Most future wars will be conflicts for commerce. The power that rules the Pacific, therefore, is the power that rules the world. And, with the Philippines, that power is and will forever be the American Republic. . . .

Here, then, Senators, is the situation. Two years ago there was no land in all this world which we could occupy for any purpose. Our commerce was daily turning toward the Orient, and geography and trade developments made necessary our commercial empire over the Pacific. And in that ocean we had no commercial, naval, or military base. To-day we have one of the three great ocean possessions on the globe, located at the most commanding commercial, naval, and military points in the eastern seas, within hail of India, shoulder to shoulder with China, richer in its own resources than any equal body of land on the entire globe, and peopled by a race which civilization demands shall be improved. Shall we abandon it? That man little knows the common people of the Republic, little understands the instincts of our race, who thinks we will not hold it fast and hold it forever, administering just government by simplest methods. . . .

But Senators, it would be better to abandon this combined garden and Gibraltar of the Pacific, and count our blood and treasure already spent a profitable loss, than to apply any academic arrangement of self-government to these children. They are not capable of self-government. How could they be? They are not of a self-governing race. They are Orientals, Malays, instructed by Spaniards in the latter's worst estate.

They know nothing of practical self-government except as they have witnessed the weak, corrupt, cruel, and capricious rule of Spain. What magic will anyone employ to dissolve in their minds and characters those impression of governors and governed which three centuries of misrule has created? What alchemy will change the oriental quality of their blood and set the self-government currents of the American pouring through their Malay veins? How shall they, in the twinkling of an eye, be exalted to the heights of self-governing peoples which required a thousand years, Anglo-Saxon though we are? . . .

No one need fear their competition with our labor. No reward could beguile, no force compel, these children of indolence to leave their trifling lives for the fierce and fervid industry of high wrought America. The very reverse is the fact. One great problem is the necessary labor to develop these islands—to build the roads, open the mines, clear the wilderness, drain the swamps, dredge the harbors. The natives will not supply it. . . .

Senators in opposition are estopped from denying our constitutional power to govern the Philippines as circumstances may demand, for such power is admitted in the case of Florida, Louisiana, Alaska. How, then, is it denied in the Philippines? Is there a geographical interpretation to the Constitution? Do degrees of longitude fix constitutional limitations? Does a thousand miles of ocean diminish constitutional power more than a thousand miles of land? . . .

Mr. President, this question is deeper than any question of party politics; deeper than any question of the isolated policy of our country even; deeper even than any question of constitutional power. It is elemental. It is racial. God has not been preparing the English-speaking and Teutonic peoples for a thousand years for nothing but vain and idle self-contemplation and self-admiration. No! He has made us the master organizers of the world to establish a system where chaos reigns. He has given us the spirit of progress to overwhelm the forces of reaction throughout the earth. He has made us adept in government that we may administer government among savage and senile peoples. Were it not for such a force as this the world would relapse into barbarism and night. And of all our race He has marked the American people as His chosen nation to finally lead in the regeneration of the world. This is the divine mission of America, and it holds for us all the profit, all the glory, all the happiness possible to man. We are the trustees of the world's programs, guardians of its righteous peace. The judgment of the Master is upon us: "Ye have been faithful over a few things; I will make you ruler over many things."

What shall history say of us? Shall it say that we renounced that holy trust, left the savage to his base condition, the wilderness to the reign of waste, deserted duty, abandoned glory, forget our sordid profits even, because we feared our strength and read the charter of our powers with the doubter's eye and the quibbler's mind? Shall it say that, called by events to captain and command the proudest, ablest, purest race of history in history's noblest work, we declined that great commission? Our fathers would not have had it so. No! They founded no paralytic government, no sluggard people, passive while the world's work calls them. They established no reactionary nation. They unfurled no retreating flag. . . .

Mr. President and Senators, adopt the resolution offered, that peace may quickly come and that we may begin our saving, regenerating, and uplifting work. . . . Reject it, and the world, history, and the American people will know where to forever fix the awful responsibility for the consequences that will surely follow such failure to do our manifest duty. How dare we delay when our soldier's blood is flowing?

156

"A Colombian View of the Panama Canal Question" (1903)

*Since the 1840s, Americans had considered constructing a central American canal to facilitate inter-ocean transportation, but little was done until the 20th century. A French company—*Compagnie Universelle du Canal de Panama—*obtained the rights to build a canal in the Colombian province of Panama in 1881, but the effort ended in bankruptcy. When an American commission recommended construction of a canal in Nicaragua, representatives of the defunct French company, who held the rights to a Panama canal, lobbied Congress to adopt their route. When the group, led by Philippe Bunau-Varilla, lowered their asking price for the rights to build in Panama from $109 million to $40 million, Congress authorized construction of a Panama canal. In early 1903, Congress ratified the Hay-Herran Treaty and presented it to the Colombian government. The treaty authorized an American canal zone 10 miles wide for $10 million and an annual payment of $250,000. As the Colombian government considered the treaty, Raul Perez, Colombia's ambassador to the United States, published the following excerpted article in* The North American Review. *Although not representing Colombia's official position, the article indicates apprehension over America's intervention as well as Colombia's potential loss from the canal.*

Questions to Consider

1. For what reasons does Raul Perez oppose the Hay-Herran Treaty?
2. In what ways does Perez propose a better treaty for Colombia?
3. What happens to Colombia's interest in the canal a few months after this article appeared?
4. How would Albert J. Beveridge, author of "The New Manifest Destiny" (Document 155), respond to Perez's views?

Raul Perez, "A Colombian View of the Panama Canal Question," *The North American Review* 177 (July 1903): 63–68.

The most important matter to be settled with regard to opening the canal is that of exactly defining the status of the party that will carry on the enterprise. It is evident at a glance that there is a wide difference between a private corporation, such as the *Compagnie Universelle du Canal de Panama,* and the powerful government to the United States of America. The Company has been doing and was to do business under the protection of the Colombian laws, subject to those laws in every detail; being considered simply as any other "juridical person"—that is, any Colombian citizen. . . .

If the substitution of the United States government for the *Compagnie Universelle* were once affected, and the consequent transference of rights carried out, would the United States submit to be considered merely a "juridical person," with no more rights than any other Colombian citizen carrying on business in Colombian territory, under protection of the Colombian Laws and subject to those laws in every respect? Such is not the spirit of the Herran-Hay treaty; and, even if it were, Colombians would have plausible reasons for misgivings or apprehensions on that point. No one willing to consider the situation with absolute impartiality can criticise those who desire that the status of Panama Canal builders should be most clearly defined, particularly in a case where a World Power is to be the builder. . . .

Let it be well understood that the Colombians . . . are decidedly favorable to the opening of the canal by the United States, should the negotiations be concluded in a manner that would result in real and lasting good to their country. . . .

The ten millions of dollars that Colombia would receive as the only compensation is considered inadequate, and the same would be the case if the sum were increased to fifty millions. This may sound preposterous on first consideration, but not to those who know that the money would be distributed among the dictator's clique and the religious orders. . . .

There is also a very erroneous impression to the effect that the canal when completed will have a great beneficial influence on our country. The conditions as they exist to-day place Colombia in the position of the owner of a bridge, over which an immense traffic is constantly passing. There are many steamship lines converging on the ports of Panama and Colon that load and unload there enormous quantities of merchandise in transit, while large numbers of passengers are compelled to stop at both ends of the trans-Isthmian railroad. . . . Such will not be the case when the canal is opened. Steamers will go through as rapidly as possible, the passengers dreading the unhealthy climate. There will be no loading of cargoes. . . .

The facts stated are perfectly well known to Colombians, who from the time of Bolivar have imagined that within the narrow strip linking the two American continents, Colombia held her great trump card. It would be an unspeakable disappointment to them to see that advantage fall into other hands, with no return but a few millions of dollars to be employed not for but against their welfare and prosperity. Indeed, so strong is this sentiment that it seems more patriotic to feel that no compensation at all would be preferable. There are many who maintain that a seizure of the Isthmus by a world Power would be more satisfactory, inasmuch as Colombians would be in a position to repeat in all coming years the phrase: "*Tout est perdu, fors L'honneur*" [all is lost except honor]. The rights of Colombia in that case would hold good forever, and the day might come when they would be revindicated; but no such hope could be entertained if the dishonest band of clericals, who act as the government of Colombia, give a seemingly legal consent to the transaction.

The members of that band are in favor of the canal . . . simply because they see the possibility of securing ten millions of dollars to be applied to their own purposes. They argue more or less thus: "The Isthmus is a segregated limb of the country where we have not full sway. We may just as well abandon it in exchange for ten millions of dollars with which to establish our uncontested dominion in the rest of the territory."

The other enthusiastic supporters of the canal treaty as it stands are the shortsighted inhabitants of the Isthmus, who long to kill the goose that lays the golden eggs. They see in the near future a boom for their region—excavation contracts, which they imagine will be as profitable as were those of the good old times of the *Compagnie Universelle;* an increase in the value of property; thousands of people coming to make their fortunes, and all the business opportunities attending an undertaking of this kind. . . .

What the Colombians would like to do about the canal would be to have their country hold a permanent interest in the enterprise as a partner of the United States, deriving an income that would benefit not a few officials and one political party but all the people for generations to come. There is no reason why a partnership of that nature could not be successfully carried out, in the same way as a partnership between individuals. All details could be deliberately and safely settled between the two countries to the entire satisfaction of both, bearing in mind that a century in the life of a nation counts no more than one year in the life of a man, and that the canal must be of vast consequence for ages. The desire to cut the canal open as rapidly as possible is praiseworthy, but it is more important to lay first the solid foundations of the transaction and establish the exact limitations of the rights of those concerned, so as to avoid all possible friction in the future.

157

Roosevelt Corollary to the Monroe Doctrine (1904)

Victory in the Spanish-American War thrust the United States into the new position of world power, but problems in the Western Hemisphere attracted American interests.

Many Caribbean countries were plagued with political instability, and violent revolutions often broke out. Compounding the problem was the poor financial state of these countries. Concerned with stability in the region, and wary that hostile foreign powers might use military force to collect debts from these countries and establish a presence in the hemisphere, President Theodore Roosevelt intervened in the domestic affairs of neighboring countries to provide stability and order. This intervention also created investment opportunities for American bankers and businessmen. Such shortsighted activities became a pattern and helped create a legacy of distrust between Latin American nations and the United States. In his 1904 annual message to Congress, excerpted as follows, Roosevelt offered an explanation for intervention in his famous "corollary" to the Monroe Doctrine.

Questions to Consider

1. According to Roosevelt, for what reasons would the United States intervene in a Caribbean basin country's affairs?

2. What are the potential problems of becoming an "international police power"?

3. In what instances would the Roosevelt Corollary to the Monroe Doctrine be used?

4. Compare and contrast the views expressed in this selection with those found in "Our Country" (Document 151). How are they similar? Different?

It is not true that the United States feels any land hunger or entertains any projects as regards the other nations of the Western Hemisphere save such as are for their welfare. All that this country desires is to see the neighboring countries stable, orderly, and prosperous. Any country whose people conduct themselves well can count upon our hearty friendship. If a nation shows that it knows how to act with reasonable efficiency and decency in social and political matters, if it keeps order and pays its obligations, it need fear no interference from the United States. Chronic wrongdoing, or an impotence which results in a general loosening of the ties of civilized society, may in America, as elsewhere, ultimately require intervention by some civilized nation, and in the Western Hemisphere the adherence of the United States to the Monroe Doctrine may force the United States, however reluctantly, in flagrant cases of such wrongdoing or impotence, to the exercise of an international police power. If every country washed by the Caribbean Sea would

"Theodore Roosevelt, Fourth Annual Message," *The State of the Union Messages of the Presidents, 1790–1966,* ed. Fred L. Israel, vol. 2, *1861–1904* (New York, 1967), 2134–2135.

show the progress in stable and just civilization which with the aid of the Platt amendment Cuba has shown since our troops left the island, and which so many of the republics in both Americas are constantly and brilliantly showing, all question of interference by this Nation with their affairs would be at an end. Our interests and those of our southern neighbors are in reality identical. They have great natural riches, and if within their borders the reign of law and justice obtains, prosperity is sure to come to them. While they thus obey the primary laws of civilized society they may rest assured that they will be treated by us in a spirit of cordial and helpful sympathy. We would interfere with them only in the last resort, and then only if it became evident that their inability or unwillingness to do justice at home and abroad had violated the rights of the United States or had invited foreign aggression to the detriment of the entire body of American nations. It is a mere truism to say that every nation, whether in America or anywhere else, which desires to maintain its freedom, its independence, must ultimately realize that the right of such independence can not be separated from the responsibility of making good use of it.

In asserting the Monroe Doctrine, in taking such steps as we have taken in regard to Cuba, Venezuela, and Panama, and in endeavoring to circumscribe the theater of war in the Far East, and to secure the open door in China, we have acted in our own interest as well as in the interest of humanity at large. There are, however, cases in which, while our own interests are not greatly involved, strong appeal is made to our sympathies. Ordinarily it is very much wiser and more useful for us to concern ourselves with striving for our own moral and material betterment here at home than to concern ourselves with trying to better the condition of things in other nations. We have plenty of sins of our own to war against, and under ordinary circumstances we can do more for the general uplifting of humanity by striving with heart and soul to put a stop to civic corruption, to brutal lawlessness and violent race prejudices here at home than by passing resolutions about wrongdoing elsewhere. Nevertheless there are occasional crimes committed on so vast a scale and of such peculiar horror as to make us doubt whether it is not our manifest duty to endeavor at least to show our disapproval of the deed and our sympathy with those who have suffered it. The cases must be extreme in which such a course is justifiable. There must be no effort made to remove the mote from our brother's eye if we refuse to remove the beam from our own. But in extreme cases action may be justifiable and proper. What form the action shall take must depend upon the circumstances of the case; that is, upon the degree of the atrocity and upon our power to remedy it. The cases in which we could interfere by force of arms as we interfered to put a stop to intolerable conditions in Cuba are necessarily very few.

158

Perspectives on Imperialism

The quick victory in the war against Spain in 1898 revealed that the United States was an emerging global power. The war sparked considerable debate over the acquisition of foreign territory, specifically the Philippines, which America wrested from Spanish control. Some Americans wanted to keep the Philippines as an American possession to expand trade in Asia and to bring American democracy to the islands rather than turn over the country to the Filipino people. Others opposed this imperialistic annexation as immoral and unconstitutional. The war also highlighted growing American interests in Latin America, specifically concerns about Caribbean-basin nations. While American businesses expanded trade with Latin American countries, considerable economic dislocation and political turmoil characterized the region. European nations were also active in Latin America; they extended considerable loans to some nations and hoped to increase trade. Observing this European activity and fearful that it could lead to further involvement, the United States made strong references to the Monroe Doctrine. The first cartoon appeared in Joseph Pulitzer's New York World *in November 1898, as Congress debated the annexation of the Philippines. The second cartoon appeared in* Puck *in October 1901.*

Questions to Consider

1. What can you deduce from the first image about the artist's attitudes toward American imperialism?

2. What can you deduce from the first image about the artist's attitudes toward race?

3. What can you deduce from the second image about American nationalism?

4. What can you conclude from these images about the morality of American expansion?

New York World, November 13, 1898, p. 5.

"Civilization Begins at Home"

Puck, October 9, 1901 20-29

"His Foresight"
Europe: "You're not the only rooster in South America."
Uncle Sam: "I was aware of that when I cooped you up."

21

✳

The Progressive Movement

The polarization of society into rich and poor, assimilable and unassimilable in the late 19th century prompted many middle-class Americans into action. The reformers who emerged to cure these ills came to be known as the progressives. Eschewing the laissez-faire approach of the past, the movement believed that through the expansion of democracy, active government, and the regulation of business to create opportunity, a new class of well-trained professionals could solve society's problems. Although some contemporaries criticized the progressives' efforts as radical, the leaders of the movement actually sought a more centrist approach in solving these problems. The next group of documents illustrates the problems facing and solutions advocated by the progressives.

159

An Insider's View of Hull House

One of the initial efforts to bring about progressive reform came with individuals such as Jane Addams, who helped establish the settlement house movement in America. Part of a first generation of college-educated women, Addams declined marriage and motherhood and devoted her life to the poor and to social reform. In 1889, she and a college friend, Ellen Starr, bought the Hull House mansion in a Chicago immigrant neighborhood and created a model settlement house that offered services to the poor in the neighborhood. But Addams realized that such neighborhood activities were futile unless laws were reformed to address larger problems, so she campaigned to pass state and local laws that would improve conditions in urban neighborhoods. Addams publicized Hull House and social reform with lecture tours and writing. Hilda S. Polacheck, the author of the excerpted selection, was a recent Polish immigrant who discovered Hull House and its offerings. Her account presents a unique insider's view of Hull House and the services it provided for immigrants in the neighborhood. Polacheck credits Hull House, and especially Jane Addams, with making her life in America better.

Questions to Consider

1. In what ways did Hull House help immigrants and urban dwellers?

2. For what reasons did Hilda Polacheck visit and then work at Hull House?

3. What did Jane Addams hope to accomplish at Hull House?

4. What do you think Jane Addams and Hilda Polacheck shared in common? How were they different? What can you deduce about the differences between native and foreign-born Americans from this document?

She took me up a flight of stairs and then down a flight and we came to the Labor Museum. The museum had been opened a short time before and it was a very special addition to the work at Hull-House and very dear to her heart. As I look back, and this may be wishful thinking, I feel that she sensed what I needed most at that time. . . .

There were many classes connected with the Labor Museum. Here we could learn how to cook and sew and also learn about millinery and embroidery. . . .

There was still another function that the Labor Museum filled. Miss Addams found that there was a definite feeling of superiority on the part of children of immigrants toward their parents. As soon as the children learned to speak English, they were prone to look down on those who could not speak the language. I am grateful that I never had that feeling toward my parents, but I often talked to playmates who would disdainfully say: "Aw, she can't talk English."

I recall having an argument with a girl whose mother could speak German, French, Russian, and Polish but had not yet learned to speak English. That girl did not realize that her mother was a linguist. To her, the mother was just a greenhorn.

For such children the Labor Museum was an eye-opener. When they saw crowds of well-dressed Americans standing around admiring what Italian, Irish, German, and Scandinavian mothers could do, their disdain for their mothers often vanished.

The Labor Museum did not solve all the problems of immigrant parents and their children. There were many problems that were not easy to solve. Children, by going to school and to work, did come in contact with forces in American life and had a better chance of becoming Americanized. But I am sure the Labor Museum reduced the strained feelings on the part of immigrants and their children. . . .

I soon branched out into other activities. I joined a reading class that was conducted by Miss Clara Landsberg. . . .

. . . She opened new vistas in reading for me. In her class we would be assigned a book, which we were to read during the week and then discuss

Hilda Satt Polacheck, *I Came a Stranger: The Story of a Hull-House Girl*, ed. Dena J. Polacheck Epstein (Urbana, IL, 1989), 63–67, 70–73, 91–92, 102. Copyright 1989 by the Board of Trustees of the University of Illinois. Used with permission of the University of Illinois Press.

the following session of the class. The class met once a week. I not only read the assigned books but every book I could borrow. Dickens, Scott, Thackeray, Louisa May Alcott, Victor Hugo, Alexander Dumas, and many others now became my friends. The daily monotony of making cuffs was eased by thinking of these books and looking forward to evenings at Hull-House.

For ten years I spent most of my evenings at Hull-House. The first three years of that time I saw Jane Addams almost every night. As more and more people found their way to this haven of love and understanding, she began to relegate the work to other people and to seek rest at the home of friends. But her presence was always felt, whether she was there in person or in spirit. . . .

Bad housing of the thousands of immigrants who lived near Hull-House was the concern of Jane Addams. Where there were alleys in back of the houses, these alleys were filled with large wooden boxes where garbage and horse manure were dumped. In most cases these boxes did not have covers and were breeding places for flies and rats. The city gave contracts to private scavengers to collect the garbage. Its responsibility seemed to end there. There was no alley inspection and no one checked on these collectors.

When Jane Addams called the attention of the health department to the unsanitary conditions, she was told that the city had contracted to have the garbage collected and it could do nothing else. When the time came to renew contracts for garbage collection, Miss Addams, with the backing of some businessmen, put in a bid to collect garbage. Her bid was never considered, but she was appointed garbage inspector for the ward. I have a vision of Jane Addams, honored by the great of the world, acclaimed as the first citizen of Chicago, following a filthy garbage truck down an alley in her long skirt and immaculate white blouse. . . .

Being allowed to teach English to immigrants at Hull-House did more for me than anything that I imparted to my students. It gave me a feeling of security that I so sorely needed. What added to my confidence in the future was that my class was always crowded and the people seemed to make good progress. From time to time Jane Addams would visit the class to see what I was doing, and she always left with that rare smile on her face; she seemed to be pleased. . . .

But to come back to the subject of textbooks, since there were none, I decided to use the Declaration of Independence as a text. It was a distinct success. The students did not find the words difficult; so in addition to learning English, we all learned the principles of Americanism.

I next introduced the manual on naturalization and the class learned English while studying how to become a citizen. It was all very exciting and stimulating.

My students were now beginning to confide in me. Classes at Hull-House were never just classes where people came to learn a specific subject. There was a human element of friendliness among us. Life was not soft or easy for any of them. They worked hard all day in shops and factories and made this valiant effort to learn the language of their adopted country. At times they needed real help, and they knew that somewhere in this wonderful house on Halsted Street they would get it. . . .

As time went on, I discovered that Hull-House was the experimental laboratory for Jane Addams's interests and services. To create opportunities for young people of the neighborhood, to bring a little sunshine into otherwise bleak lives of older immigrants, to point out the evils of miserable housing; in short, to tell Chicago what its responsibility to the poor was, was just first aid to the problem. She traveled through America spreading the gospel of a better life than she had found on South Halsted Street. As a result, social settlements sprang up all over the country. Chicago became dotted with playgrounds. Social centers were added to these playgrounds and became the responsibility of the city government.

160

Boss Government at Work (1903)

In the early 20th century, a group of investigative journalists began writing exposés about the social, political, and economic problems of the nation. They considered their work scientific and objective. President Theodore Roosevelt contemptuously nicknamed them "muckrakers" from a character in John Bunyan's Pilgrim's Progress *who "could look no way but downward with a muckrake in his hands" as he dug up filth rather than see more important issues by looking up. The beginning of muckraking journalism is often associated with* McClure's Magazine, *when it published a series of Lincoln Steffens' articles on municipal corruption in various American cities. The articles, which were later collected in a book,* The Shame of the Cities, *focused national attention on the problem and helped bring about reform. Steffens spent his career as a reporter and editor with New York newspapers and magazines and prided himself on objective reporting that was not self-righteous. The final article in the* McClure's *series, which is excerpted as follows, focused on the Democratic party machine—Tammany Hall—in New York City and how this boss government operated.*

Questions to Consider

1. According to Steffens, in what ways does Tammany Hall obtain and preserve political power?

2. For what reasons is Steffens suspicious of "municipal reform"?

3. What circumstances in urban America allowed boss governments like Tammany Hall to be blatantly dishonest and politically powerful?

4. How might Hilda Polacheck, author of "An Insider's View of Hull House" (Document 159), have described Tammany Hall? How do you account for these differences?

Tammany is bad government; not inefficient, but dishonest; not a party, not a delusion and a snare, hardly known by its party name—Democracy; having little standing in the national councils of the party and caring little for influence outside of the city. Tammany is Tammany, the embodiment of corruption. All the world knows and all the world may know what it is and what it is after. For hypocrisy is not a Tammany vice. Tammany is for Tammany, and the Tammany men say so. Other rings proclaim lies and make pretensions; other rogues talk about the tariff and imperialism. Tammany is honestly dishonest. Time and time again, in private and in public, the leaders, big and little, have said they are out for themselves and their own; not for the public, but for "me and my friends"; not for New York, but for Tammany. Richard Croker said under oath once that he worked for his own pockets all the time, and Tom Grady, the Tammany orator, has brought his crowds to their feet cheering sentiments as primitive, stated with candor as brutal. The man from Mars would say that such an organization, so self-confessed, could not be very dangerous to an intelligent people. Foreigners marvel at it and at us, and even Americans—Pennsylvanians, for example—cannot understand why we New Yorkers regard Tammany as so formidable. I think I can explain it. Tammany is corruption with consent; it is bad government founded on the suffrages of people. . . . Tammany rules, when it rules, by right of the votes of the people of New York. . . .

Tammany's democratic corruption rests upon the corruption of the people, the plain people, and there lies its great significance; its grafting system is one in which more individuals share than any I have studied. The people themselves get very little; they come cheap, but they are interested. Divided into districts, the organization subdivides them into precincts or neighborhoods, and their sovereign power, in the form of votes, is brought up by kindness and petty privileges. They are forced to a surrender, when necessary, by intimidation, but the leader and his captains have their hold because they take care of their own. They speak pleasant words, smile friendly smiles, notice the baby, give picnics up the River or the Sound, or a slap on the back; find jobs, most of them at the city's expense, but they have also newsstands, peddling privileges, railroad and other business places to dispense, they permit violations of the law, and, if a man has broken the law without permission, see him through the court. Though a blow in the face is as readily given as a shake of the hand, Tammany kindness is real kindness, and will go far, remember long, and take infinite trouble for a friend.

The power that is gathered up thus cheaply, like garbage, in the districts is concentrated in the district leader, who in turn passes it on through a general committee to the boss. This is a form of living government, extra-legal, but very actual, and, though the beginnings of it are purely democratic, it develops at each stage into an autocracy. . . .

Lincoln Steffens, *Shame of the Cities* (New York, 1904), 279–294, 302–303. Originally published as "New York: Good Government to the Test," *McClure's Magazine* 22 (November 1903): 84–92.

Tammany leaders are usually the natural leaders of the people in these districts, and they are originally good-natured, kindly men. No one has a more sincere liking than I for some of those common but generous fellows; their charity is real, at first. But they sell out their own people. They do give them coal and help them in their private troubles, but, as they grow rich and powerful, the kindness goes out of the charity and they not only collect at their saloons or in rents—cash for their "goodness"; they not only ruin fathers and sons and cause the troubles they relieve; they sacrifice the children in the schools; let the Health Department neglect the tenements, and, worst of all, plant vice in the neighborhood and in the homes of the poor.

This is not only bad; it is bad politics; it has defeated Tammany. Woe to New York when Tammany learns better. Honest fools talk of the reform of Tammany Hall. It is an old hope, this, and twice it has been disappointed, but it is not vain. That is the real danger ahead. The reform of a corrupt ring means, as I have said before, the reform of its system of grafting and a wise consideration of certain features of good government. . . .

161

"The American Forests" (1901)

For some progressive reformers, a key issue was conservation. The approach of greedy Americans who had long believed that the nation's natural resources were unlimited and could be selfishly plundered helped prompt the conservation movement. By the late 19th century, it became clear that the natural landscape was altered in potentially harmful ways and that limited resources were being depleted at an alarming rate. How to best approach, or even define, conservation divided progressives. Gifford Pinchot led one camp of conservationists. A specialist in forestry management, Pinchot headed the newly created U.S. Forest Service and would advocate a program that natural resources be used efficiently. He regulated the use of government land through user fees, created a competitive bidding process for lumbering on government lands, and insisted on an efficient harvest of the forest crop that should be replenished for future generations. Taking the approach of preservation was John Muir. Born in Scotland and raised in Wisconsin, Muir was a naturalist and advocate of protecting land from human interference. In 1897, Muir published the article excerpted as follows in the respected Atlantic Monthly, *and would later include the article in* Our National Parks *(1901), in which he outlined the preservationist approaches to conservation. He was one of the principle founders of the Sierra Club and served as its first president.*

Questions to Consider

1. In what ways does Muir characterize the activities of man in the forest?
2. According to Muir, what do forests provide humankind?

3. For what reasons does Muir argue for federal government involvement in forest lands?

4. In what ways are the two positions on conservation (Muir's and Pinchot's) relevant today?

. . . American forests! the glory of the world! Surveyed thus from the east to the west, from the north to the south, they are rich beyond thought, immortal, immeasurable, enough and to spare for every feeding, sheltering beast and bird, insect and son of Adam; and nobody need have cared had there been no pines in Norway, no cedars and deodars on Lebanon and the Himalayas, no vine-clad selves in the basin of the Amazon. With such variety, harmony, and triumphant exuberance, even nature, it would seem, might have rested content with the forests of North America, and planted no more.

So they appeared a few centuries ago when they were rejoicing in wildness. The Indians with stone axes could do them no more harm than could gnawing beavers and browsing moose. Even the fires of the Indians and the fierce shattering lightning seemed to work together only for good in clearing spots here and there for smooth garden prairies, and openings for sunflowers seeking the light. But when the steel axe of the white man rang out on the startled air their doom was sealed. Every tree heard the bodeful sound, and pillars of smoke gave the sign in the sky.

I suppose we need not go mourning the buffaloes. In the nature of things they had to give place to better cattle, though the change might have been made without barbarous wickedness. Likewise many of nature's five hundred kinds of wild trees had to make way for orchards and cornfields. In the settlement and civilization of the country, bread more than timber or beauty was wanted; and in the blindness of hunger, the early settlers, claiming Heaven as their guide, regarded God's trees as only a larger kind of pernicious weeds, extremely hard to get rid of. Accordingly, with no eye to the future, these pious destroyers waged interminable forest wars; chips flew thick and fast; trees in their beauty fell crashing by millions, smashed to confusion, and the smoke of their burning has been rising to heaven more than two hundred years. . . .

The legitimate demands on the forests that have passed into private ownership, as well as those in the hands of the government, are increasing every year with the rapid settlement and up-building of the country, but the methods of lumbering are as yet grossly wasteful. In most mills only the best portions of the best trees are used, while the ruins are left on the ground to feed great fires, which kill much of what is left of the less desirable timber, together with the seedlings, on which the permanence of the forest depends. Thus every mill is a centre of destruction far more severe from waste and fire than from use. The same thing is true of the mines, which consume and destroy indirectly immense quantities of timber with their innumerable fires, accidental

John Muir, *Our National Parks* (Boston, 1901), chapter 10, "The American Forests." Originally published as John Muir, "The American Forests," *The Atlantic Monthly* 80 (August 1897): 145–157.

or set to make open ways, and often without regard to how far they run. The prospector deliberately sets fires to clear off the woods just where they are densest, to lay the rocks bare and make the discovery of mines easier. Sheep-owners and their shepherds also set fires everywhere through the woods in the fall to facilitate the march of their countless flocks the next summer, and perhaps in some places to improve the pasturage. The axe is not yet at the root of every tree, but the sheep is, or was before the national parks were established and guarded by the military, the only effective and reliable arm of the government free from the blight of politics. . . .

Notwithstanding all the waste and use which have been going on unchecked like a storm for more than two centuries, it is not yet too late—though it is high time—for the government to begin a rational administration of its forests. About seventy million acres it still owns,—enough for all the country, if wisely used. These residual forests are generally on mountain slopes, just where they are doing the most good, and where their removal would be followed by the greatest number of evils; the lands they cover are too rocky and high for agriculture, and can never be made as valuable for any other crop as for present crop of trees. . . .

In their natural condition, or under wise management, keeping out destructive sheep, preventing fires, selecting the trees that should be cut for lumber, and preserving the young ones and the shrubs and sod of herbaceous vegetation, these forests would be a never failing fountain of wealth and beauty. . . .

. . . The wonderful advance made in the last few years, in creating four national parks in the West, and thirty forest reservations, embracing nearly forty million acres; and in the planting of the borders of streets and highways and spacious parks in all the great cities, to satisfy the natural taste and hunger for landscape beauty and righteousness that God has put, in some measure, into every human being and animal, shows the trend of awakening public opinion. . . .

All sorts of local laws and regulations have been tried and found wanting, and the costly lessons of our own experience, as well as that of every civilized nation, show conclusively that the fate of the remnant of our forests is in the hands of the federal government, and that if the remnant is to be saved at all, it must be saved quickly.

Any fool can destroy trees. They cannot run away; and if they could, they would still be destroyed,—chased and hunted down as long as fun or a dollar could be got out of their bark hides, branching horns, or magnificent bole backbones. Few that fell trees plant them; nor would planting avail much towards getting back anything like the noble primeval forests. During a man's life only saplings can be grown, in the place of the old trees—tens of centuries old—that have been destroyed. It took more than three thousand years to make some of the trees in these Western woods,—trees that are still standing in perfect strength and beauty, waving and singing in the mighty forests of the Sierra. Through all the wonderful, eventful centuries since Christ's time—and long before that—God has cared for these trees, saved them from drought, disease, avalanches, and a thousand straining, leveling tempests and floods; but he cannot save them from fools,—only Uncle Sam can do that.

162

The Jungle (1906)

*Early in the 20th century, some individuals questioned the quality of food and medi-
cine production in America. The "embalmed beef" scandal of the Spanish-American War,
involving tainted provisions for troops, and muckraking exposés of patent medicines
and the "beef trust" had alerted the American people that some problems existed. But
when Upton Sinclair's novel,* The Jungle, *was published in January 1906, it created an
immediate furor. The novel was intended to advocate socialism as it depicted the difficult life of Lithuanian immigrant Jurgis Rudkus and his friends in the fictitious Packingtown. Sinclair also included some descriptions of conditions in the meatpacking
houses where Jurgis worked. These shocking descriptions, some of which are excerpted
following, appalled the American people. President Theodore Roosevelt read the book
and then sent two agents to investigate Chicago's meatpacking houses to learn if Sinclair's depiction was accurate—and it was. Within six months, the Pure Food and
Drug Act was passed. Sinclair later wrote about his novel: "I aimed at the public's
heart and by accident hit it in the stomach."*

Questions to Consider

1. What is more shocking, the work conditions or the preparation of meat
   for the American consumers? Why?

2. In what ways could government regulation address the situations in the
   meatpacking industry?

3. Compare Sinclair's description with that found in "The Cattle Industry" (Document 135). In what ways had conditions changed?

4. How would labor and immigrant rights' advocates have responded to
   this selection?

. . . so Jurgis learned a few things about the great and only Durham canned
goods, which had become a national institution. They were regular alchemists
at Durham's; they advertised a mushroom catsup, and the men who made it
did not know what a mushroom looked like. They advertised "potted
chicken,"—and it was like the boarding-house soup of the comic papers,
through which a chicken had walked with rubbers on. Perhaps they had a
secret process for making chickens chemically—who knows? Said Jurgis's
friends; the things that went into the mixture were tripe, and the fat of pork,
and beef suet, and hearts of beef, and finally the waste ends of veal, when
they had any. They put these up in several grades, and sold them at several
prices; but the contents of the cans all came out of the same hopper. And

Upton Sinclair, *The Jungle* (New York, 1906), 115–120. Copyright held by the estate of Upton Sinclair.

then there was "potted game" and "potted grouse," "potted ham" and "dev-illed ham"—de-vyled, as the men called it. "De-vyled" ham was made out of the waste ends of smoked beef that were too small to be sliced by the machines; and also tripe, dyed with chemicals so that it would not show white; and trimmings of hams and corned beef; and potatoes, skins and all; and finally the hard cartilaginous ingenious mixture was ground up and flavoured with spices to make it taste like something. Anybody who could invent a new imitation had been sure of a fortune from old Durham. . . .

There was another interesting set of statistics that a person might have gathered in Packingtown—those of the various afflictions of the workers. When Jurgis had first inspected the packing plants with Szedvilas, he had marvelled while he listened to the tale of all the things that were made out of the carcasses of animals, and of all the lesser industries that were maintained there; now he found that each one of these lesser industries was a separate little inferno, in its way as horrible as the killing beds, the source and fountain of them all. The workers in each of them had their own peculiar diseases. And the wandering visitor might be sceptical about all the swindles, but he could not be sceptical about these, for the worker bore the evidence of them about on his own person—generally he had only to hold out his hand.

There were the men in the pickle rooms, for instance, where old Antanas had gotten his death; scarce a one of these that had not some spot of horror on his person. Let a man so much as scrape his finger pushing a truck in the pickle rooms, and he might have a sore that would put him out of the world; all the joints in his fingers might be eaten by the acid, one by one. Of the butchers and floorsmen, the beef-boners and trimmers, and all those who used knives, you could scarcely find a person who had the use of his thumb; time and time again the base of it had been slashed, till it was a mere lump of flesh against which the man pressed the knife to hold it. The hands of these men would be criss-crossed with cuts, until you could no longer pretend to count them or to trace them. They would have no nails—they had worn them off pulling hides; their knuckles were swollen so that their fingers spread out like a fan. There were men who worked in the cooking rooms, in the midst of steam and sickening odours, by artificial light; in these rooms the germs of tuberculosis might live for two years, but the supply was renewed every hour. There were the beef-luggers, who carried two-hundred-pound quarters into the refrigerator cars—a fearful kind of work, that began at four o'clock in the morning, and that wore out the most powerful men in a few years. There were those who worked in the chilling rooms, and whose special disease was rheumatism; the time limit that a man could work in the chilling rooms was said to be five years. There were the wool-pluckers, whose hands went to pieces even sooner than the hands of the pickle men; for the pelts of the sheep had to be painted with acid to loosen the wool, and then the pluckers had to pull out this wool with their bare hands, till the acid had eaten their fingers off. There were those who made the tins for the canned meat; and their hands, too, were a maze of cuts, and each cut represented a chance for blood poisoning. Some worked at the stamping machines, and it was seldom that one could work long there at the pace that was set, and not give out and forget himself, and have a part of his hand chopped off. There were the "hoisters," as they were called, whose task it was to press the lever which lifted the dead cattle off the floor. They ran along upon a rafter, peering down through the damp and the steam; and as old Durham's architects had not built the killing room for the convenience of the hoisters, at every few feet they would have to stoop under a beam, say four feet above the one they ran on; which got them into the habit of stooping, so that in a few years they would be walking like chimpanzees. Worst of any, however, were the fertilizer-men, and those who served in the cooking rooms. These people could not be shown to the visitor, for the odour of a fertilizer-man would scare any ordinary visitor at a hundred yards; and as for the other men, who worked in tank rooms full of steams, and in some of which there were open vats near the level of the floor, their peculiar trouble was that they fell into the vats; and when they were fished out, there was never enough of them left to be worth exhibiting—sometimes they would be overlooked for days, till all but the bones of them had gone out to the world as Durham's Pure Leaf Lard!

163

The New Nationalism of Theodore Roosevelt (1912)

Disappointed with William Howard Taft's conservative nature and his unwillingness to pursue progressive policies, former President Theodore Roosevelt began challenging Taft's position while offering a new brand of Progressivism. Roosevelt gave a series of speeches throughout the country in which he gradually formulated his program—the "New Nationalism." Roosevelt called for expanding the federal government's powers to control and regulate big business, new measures of direct democracy, and a program of labor and social legislation. In February 1912, Roosevelt addressed the Ohio Constitutional Convention and offered one of the clearest explanations of the "New Nationalism." The speech is excerpted as follows. Several days after the address, Roosevelt announced that he would seek the Republican party's presidential nomination in 1912. When the Republicans chose Taft, Roosevelt bolted the party and established the Progressive or Bull Moose party, which used the New Nationalism as its platform.

Questions to Consider

1. What problems does Theodore Roosevelt identify in the American political process?

2. For what purposes does Roosevelt propose to expand democracy in the United States?

3. In what ways will the functions of government change as a result of the reforms Roosevelt offered in this speech?

4. In what ways does Roosevelt's speech reflect progressive ideals?

This is the reason why I have for so many years insisted, as regards our national government, that it is both futile and mischievous to endeavor to correct the evils of big business by an attempt to restore business conditions as they were in the middle of the last century, before railways and telegraphs rendered larger business organizations both inevitable and desirable. . . .

All business into which the element of monopoly in any way or degree enters, and where it proves in practice impossible totally to eliminate this element of monopoly, should be carefully supervised, regulated and controlled by governmental authority; and such control should be exercised by administrative, rather than judicial officers. No effort should be made to destroy a big corporation merely because it is big, merely because it has shown itself a particularly efficient business instrument.

But we should not fear, if necessary, to bring the regulation of big corporations to the point of controlling conditions so that the wage-worker shall have a wage more than sufficient to cover the basic cost of living, and hours of labor not so excessive as to wreck his strength by the strain of unending toil and leave him unfit to do his duty as a good citizen in the community. Where regulation by competition (which is, of course, preferable), proves insufficient, we should not shrink from bringing governmental regulation to the point of control of monopoly prices if it should ever become necessary to do so, just as in exceptional cases railway rates are now regulated. . . .

The people have nothing whatever to fear from giving any public servant power so long as they retain their own power to hold him accountable for his use of the power they have delegated to him. You will get the best service where you elect only a few men, and where each man has his duties and responsibilities, and is obliged to work in the open, so that the people who know who he is and what he is doing, and have the information that will enable them to hold him to account for his stewardship.

I believe in providing for direct nominations by the people, including therein direct presidential primaries for the election of delegates to the national nominating conventions. Not as a matter of theory, but as a matter of plain and proved experience, we find that the convention system, while it often records the popular will, is also often used by adroit politicians as a method of thwarting the popular will. In other words, the existing machinery for nominations is cumbrous, and is not designed to secure the real expression of a majority of the people, but we do not like to acquiesce in a nomination secured by adroit political management in defeating the wish of the majority of people.

"Roosevelt Would Give People Right to Recall Judges' Decisions: Favors Initiative and Referendum, Carefully Safeguarded," *The Ohio State Journal* (Columbus), February 22, 1912, p. 4.

I believe in the election of United States senators by direct vote. Just as actual experience convinced our people that presidents should be elected (as they are now in practice, although not in theory) by direct vote of the people instead of by indirect vote through an untrammeled electoral college, so actual experience has convinced us that senators should be elected by direct vote of the people instead of indirectly through the various legislatures.

I believe in the initiative and the referendum, which should be used not to destroy representative government, but to correct it whenever it become misrepresentative. Here again I am concerned not with theories but with actual facts. If in any state the people are themselves satisfied with their present representative system, then it is, of course, their right to keep that system unchanged; and it is nobody's business but theirs.

But in actual practice it has been found in very many states that legislative bodies have not been responsive to the popular will. Therefore I believe that the state should provide for the possibility of direct popular action in order to make good such legislative failure.

The power to invoke such direct action, both by initiative and referendum, should be provided in such fashion as to prevent its being wantonly or too frequently used. I do not believe that it should be made the easy or ordinary way of taking action. In the great majority of cases it is far better that action on legislative matters should be taken by those specifically delegated to perform the task. . . . But where the men thus delegated fail to perform their duty, then it should be in the power of the people themselves to perform the duty. . . .

I do not believe in adopting the recall save as a last resort, when it has become clearly evident that no other course will achieve the desired result. But either the recall will have to be adopted or else it will have to be made much easier than it now is to get rid, not merely of a bad judge, but of a judge who, however virtuous, has grown so out of touch with social needs and facts that he is unfit longer to render good service on the bench. . . .

When the supreme court of the state declares a given statute unconstitutional, because in conflict with the state or the national constitution, its opinion should be subject to revision by the people themselves. Such an opinion ought always to be created with great respect by the people, and unquestionably in the majority of cases would be accepted and followed by them. But actual experience has shown the vital need of the people reserving to themselves the right to pass upon such opinion. . . .

I do not say that the people are infallible. But I do say that the American people are more often sound in their decisions than is the case with any of the governmental bodies to whom, for their convenience, they have delegated portions of their power. If this is not so, then there is no justification for the existence of our government; and if it is so, then there is no justification for refusing to give the people the real, and not merely the nominal, ultimate decision on questions of constitutional law. . . . [S]o I hold that now the American people as a whole have shown themselves wiser than the courts in the way they have approached and dealt with such vital questions of our day as those concerning the proper control of the big corporations and of securing their rights to industrial workers.

164

"A Progressive Illusion" (1912)

By the presidential election of 1912, Americans were well aware of progressive reform efforts to cure some social, political, and economic ills that resulted from the rapid industrialization and urbanization of the late 19th century. Essentially an optimistic middle-class movement, progressive reformers argued that through active government, the expansion of democracy, and the regulation of business to create opportunity, a new class of well-trained professionals could solve many of society's problems. Consequently, progressives enacted legislation on the state, local, and national government levels to impose order and combat problems. Issues such as boss control of urban government, regulation of railroads and the meatpacking industry, child labor, women's suffrage, and work conditions, hours, and wages were part of the progressive reforms. Some contemporaries criticized the reformers as too radical or too moralistic. In the last month of the hotly contested 1912 presidential election, which made progressivism a central issue, The Nation, *a popular news magazine, published the following editorial on progressive reform.*

Questions to Consider

1. In what ways does *The Nation* react to the reforms of the Progressive movement?
2. According to this editorial, what is the role of government?
3. How do you suppose *The Nation* responded to Theodore Roosevelt's "New Nationalism" (Document 163)?
4. What does this editorial reveal about popular support for proposed reforms?

It seems worth while to enter a mild protest against the rapidly growing tendency to imagine that until there grew up a movement that called itself progressive—with a big P—no progress was being made in the matters to which the Progressive label is now attached. Men and women who have labored for workmen's compensation, acts for limitation of women's working hours, for child-labor laws, for tenement and factory laws, and have achieved great results in a comparatively short time, have not been shouting from the housetops that they are Progressives, and have accomplished much progress in many States without attacking in any way the foundations of our system of government.

A curious minor instance of the tendency to which we refer is the widely prevailing belief—for which Judge Linsey, we hasten to say, is not in the least responsible—that the idea of the juvenile court originated at Denver, whereas this institution had been in operation on a large scale in Chicago before it was introduced in the Colorado city. The commission form of government is a bold experiment, which was put into motion at Galveston under the stress of a practical exigency, and which rapidly spread to scores of other cities, without any stimulus from rhapsodical Progressivism. Public service commissions have been instituted in State after State, either under the pressure of general public sentiment or through the energetic labors of able and high-minded leaders like Gov. Hughes, who have not at all worn the label of the professional Progressive. That the Progressive movement, dating back to such agitations as that of La Follette in Wisconsin, has been an important factor in some or all of these things, we would not deny; but there is all the difference in the world between recognizing this influence and imagining that without it we should all have stood still or gone backward. And there is a practical difference between seeing the thing as it is and viewing it through a magnifying and distorting haze. In the one case we shall walk carefully and firmly, whereas in the other we are in danger of rushing into all sorts of follies under the impression that only so can we make any advance.

That our governmental machinery in State and nation has fallen far short of the ideal requirements of representative government is, unfortunately, only too true. Nevertheless, the degree of its shortcoming in relation to the great questions of public welfare with which the Progressive programme is concerned may easily be exaggerated; and, furthermore, there exists a widespread confusion of thought concerning the nature and the origin of its defects. A parliamentary system may fail to be representative either because it is hopelessly dominated by a ruling class, or because it is permeated by corruption. In our own country, in so far as representative institutions have failed, this has been chiefly because of the corrupting influence of machine politics and the boss system, and it would be a strange confession of ineradicable national weakness to suppose that this state of things is incapable of remedy. It is true that powerful interests have here and there controlled machines and bosses in order to block legislation demanded by the welfare of the masses; but it is far from true that the wealthy or prosperous classes as a whole, or in any great part, have taken their stand with these forces. The most that can be alleged as against these classes is indifference or inertia; which may, indeed, be reprehensible, but is so far from being invincible that it yields readily to any genuine and earnest effort for humane and beneficent legislation or administrative improvement.

It would be easy to cite innumerable examples of this, some of them very striking. One of the most recent is the enactment by the Maryland Legislature of a law limiting the hours of labor of women, which was carried to success in a short, and spirited campaign, conducted chiefly by a few women, and in large measure by the enthusiastic efforts of a young girl hardly out of college. In Louisiana a few years ago one woman got the credit of having procured the enactment of a child-labor law by a Legislature which, at the beginning of its session, was regarded as immovably opposed to it. These, to be sure, are piecemeal achievements; but it has been the way of reforms in this country, to the need of which the public mind has been thoroughly awakened, to make rapid though piecemeal progress until they have, in a short time, covered the whole extent of the Union. This was the case, for example, with the Australian ballot, which has effected a fundamental and essential, though simple, reform in our whole political machinery; and workmen's compensation, the regulation of public service corporations, direct primaries, control of campaign expenditures, are now going through the same history.

Imperfect as may be the representative character of our legislative systems, they do respond infallibly, though doubtless with some unnecessary delay, to the clearly and deliberately adopted desires of the community. And if legislation by direct vote of the people would expedite the process, it would, on the other hand, make possible conditions which cannot be viewed by sober-minded people without serious solicitude. There are proposals of a wholly different nature from any of those which we have mentioned—grave proposals which should not be adopted until it is known that they have the unmistakable approval of a deliberate, well-considered, and permanent public sentiment. When this is the case, they are sure, with more or less delay—delay essential to the establishment of this certainty—to be adopted under our present machinery. Our Government may respond slowly, but it responds surely, to any demand truly bottomed on a sincere and solid public sentiment, truly representative of the settled desire of the community. But it does not permit the sweeping away of old institutions, or the establishment of fundamental and irreversible innovations, by a mere count of noses at a single popular election. It compels these new things to show their credentials. If they have the staying power necessary to overcome the natural resistance with which they are met at first, a second, and perhaps a third and fourth time, they will be adopted; if they have not, they fail because they have failed to prove their title in a manner befitting the gravity of the issues involved.

165

"Why Women Should Vote" (1910)

In the several decades after the Seneca Falls Convention (1848), women argued that suffrage was a natural right, a position that threatened male political dominance and was therefore denied. At the dawn of the 20th century, the women's suffrage campaign languished, but a less threatening expediency argument emerged to help revive the movement. Frustrated with combating state and local politicians to bring about social improvement, the settlement house women realized they needed the vote in order to challenge the politicians and to make America better. The best-known settlement house woman was Jane Addams, who published the article excerpted as follows in the Ladies' Home Journal *in 1910. Addams placated the middle-class female audience of this magazine by arguing that the woman's domain remained the home and cultural affairs, but that women voting could help with the larger problems of social housekeeping. With this argument (and others like it), coupled with new publicity generated by the actions of radical suffragettes, a revitalized moderate suffragist organization, and women's good deeds in wartime, public support for women's suffrage grew rapidly. In 1920, the 19th Amendment, granting women the right to vote, was ratified.*

Questions to Consider

1. In what ways does Jane Addams argue for giving women the right to vote?

2. For what reasons does Addams soften the perceived threat to male political power?

3. How radical a change in women's roles does Addams advocate?

4. How would women and men react to this article?

This paper is an attempt to show that many women today are failing to discharge their duties to their own households properly simply because they do not perceive that as society grows more complicated it is necessary that woman shall extend her sense of responsibility to many things outside of her own home if she would continue to preserve the home in its entirety. One could illustrate in many ways. A woman's simplest duty, one would say, is to keep her house clean and wholesome and to feed her children properly. Yet if she lives in a tenement house, as so many of my neighbors do, she cannot fulfill these simple obligations by her own efforts because she is utterly dependent upon the city administration for the conditions which render decent living possible. . . . In a crowded city quarter, however, if the street is not cleaned by the city authorities no amount of private sweeping will keep the tenement free from grime; if the garbage is not properly collected and destroyed a tenement-house mother may see her children sicken and die of diseases from which she alone is powerless to shield them, although her tenderness and devotion are unbounded. . . . In short, if woman would keep on with her old business of caring for her house and rearing her children she will have to have some conscience in regard to public affairs lying quite outside of her immediate household. The individual conscience and devotion are no longer effective. . . .

If women follow only the lines of their traditional activities there are certain primary duties which belong to even the most conservative women, and which no one woman or group of women can adequately discharge unless they join the more general movements looking toward social amelioration through legal enactment.

The first of these . . . is woman's responsibility for the members of her own household that they may be properly fed and clothed and surrounded by hygienic conditions. The second is a responsibility for the education of

Jane Addams, "Why Women Should Vote," *Ladies' Home Journal* 27 (January 1910): 21–22. 21–30 children: (a) that they may be provided with good schools; (b) that they may be kept free from vicious influences on the street; (c) that when working they may be protected by adequate child-labor legislation.

(a) The duty of a woman toward the schools which her children attend is so obvious that it is not necessary to dwell upon it. But even this simple obligation cannot be effectively carried out without some form of social organization as the mothers' school clubs and mothers' congresses testify, and to which the most conservative women belong because they feel the need of wider reading and discussion concerning the many problems of childhood. It is, therefore, perhaps natural that the public should have been more willing to accord a vote to women in school matters than in any other, and yet women have never been members of a Board of Education in sufficient numbers to influence largely actual school curriculi. . . .

(b) But women are also beginning to realize that children need attention outside of school hours; that much of the petty vices in cities is merely the love of pleasure gone wrong, the overrestrained boy or girl seeking improper recreation and excitement. It is obvious that a little study of the needs of children, a sympathetic understanding of the conditions under which they go astray, might save hundreds of them. Women traditionally have had an opportunity to observe the plays of children and the needs of youth, and yet in Chicago, at least, they had done singularly little in this vexed problem of juvenile delinquency until they helped to inaugurate the Juvenile Court movement a dozen years ago. . . .

(c) As the education of her children has been more and more transferred to the school, so that even children four years old go to the kindergarten, the woman has been left in a household of constantly-narrowing interests, not only because the children are away, but also because one industry after another is slipping from the household into the factory. . . . Because many thousands of those working in factories and shops are girls between the ages of fourteen and twenty-two there is a necessity that older women should be interested in the conditions of industry. The very fact that these girls are not going to remain in industry permanently makes it more important that some one should see to it that they shall not be incapacitated for their future family life because they work for exhausting hours and under insanitary conditions.

. . . If conscientious women were convinced that it was a civic duty to be informed in regard to these grave industrial affairs, and then to express the conclusions which they had reached by depositing a piece of paper in a ballot-box, one cannot imagine that they would shirk simply because the action ran counter to old traditions. . . .

This is, perhaps, the attitude of many busy women who would be glad to use the ballot to further public measures in which they are interested and for which they have been working for years. It offends the taste of such a woman to be obliged to use indirect "influence" when she is accustomed to well-bred, open action in other affairs, and she very much resents the time spent in persuading a voter to take her point of view, and possibly to give up his own, quite as honest and valuable as hers, although different because resulting from a totally different experience. Public-spirited women who wish to use the ballot, as I know them, do not wish to do the work of men nor to take over men's affairs. They simply want an opportunity to do their own work and to take care of those affairs which naturally and historically belong to women, but which are constantly being overlooked and slighted in our political institutions. . . .

In closing, may I recapitulate that if woman would fulfill her traditional responsibility to her own children; if she would educate and protect from danger factory children who must find their recreation on the street; if she would bring the cultural forces to bear upon our materialistic civilization; and if she would do it all with the dignity and directness fitting one who carries on her immemorial duties, then she must bring herself to the use of the ballot—that latest implement for self-government. May we not fairly say that American women need this implement in order to preserve the home?

22

✴

Making the World Safe for Democracy

The values of the progressive movement were expressed on a wider scale when the United States entered the First World War. Government-employed professionals using a centrist approach to solve problems now directed their methods against the United States' foreign enemies. The ensuing crusade to save democracy set off a similar movement at home, in which those who lacked this progressive sense of patriotism, particularly leftists, were subject to persecution by both the government and private citizens. The dislocation that followed the war only heightened the sense of urgency perceived by many Americans, many of whom yearned for a return to a simpler time. The following set of documents captures the various moods and issues of the era.

166

Woodrow Wilson's Declaration of War Message (1917)

When the First World War broke out in August 1914, President Woodrow Wilson gave the routine declaration of neutrality and urged Americans to be "impartial in thought as well as action." This stance would prove difficult to maintain. As the largest neutral nation with huge economic resources available, the United States was vulnerable to efforts to control trade from both sides in the conflict. The British, whose surface fleet controlled the Atlantic, were very successful at maintaining trade with the United States. To counter British naval supremacy and throttle trade with Great Britain, the Germans began submarine warfare. The U-boat violated traditional naval warfare practices by sinking merchant ships without warning. When American lives were lost, especially when the passenger liner Lusitania *was sunk in 1915, the Wilson administration protested and the Germans agreed to limit their submarine attacks. In late January 1917, in an attempt to win the war, the Germans announced unrestricted submarine warfare against any ship bound for Great Britain. Several American ships were sunk in February and March. Even though he was reelected in 1916 on the slogan "He kept us out of war," Wilson asked Congress for a declaration of war on April 2, 1917. Excerpted as follows is Wilson's war message.*

Questions to Consider

1. Why is Woodrow Wilson asking for a declaration of war?
2. Who is the audience of this speech?
3. Why is it significant that Wilson wants war declared against the German government, but not the German people?
4. What is the purpose of America's war effort?

The present German submarine warfare against commerce is a warfare against mankind.

It is a war of all nations. American ships have been sunk, American lives taken, in ways which it has stirred us very deeply to learn of, but the ships and people of other neutral and friendly nations have been sunk and overwhelmed in the waters in the same way. There has been no discrimination. The challenge is to all mankind. Each nation must decide for itself how it will meet it. The choice we make for ourselves must be made with a moderation of counsel and a temperance of judgment befitting our character and our motives as a nation. We must put excited feeling away. Our motive will not be revenge or the victorious assertion of the physical might of the nation, but only the vindication of right, of human right, of which we are only a single champion. . . .

With a profound sense of the solemn and even tragical character of the step I am taking and of the grave responsibilities which it involves, but in unhesitating obedience to what I deem my constitutional duty, I advise that the Congress declare the recent course of the Imperial German Government to be in fact nothing less than war against the government and people of the United States; that it formally accept the status of belligerent which has thus been thrust upon it; and that it take immediate steps, not only to put the country in a more thorough state of defense but also to exert all its power and employ all its resources to bring the Government of the German Empire to terms and end the war. . . .

Our object now, as then, is to vindicate the principles of peace and justice in the life of the world as against selfish and autocratic power and to set up among the really free and self-governed peoples of the world such a concert of purpose and of action as will henceforth ensure the observance of those principles. Neutrality is no longer feasible or desirable where the peace of the world is involved and the freedom of its peoples, and the menace to that peace and freedom lies in the existence of an autocratic government backed by an organized force which is controlled wholly by their will, not the will of their people. We have seen the last of neutrality in such circumstances. We are at the beginning of an age in which it will be insisted that the same standards of conduct and of responsibility for wrong done shall be observed among

---

"Address by the President of the United States," *Congressional Record*, 65th Congress, 1st session (April 2, 1917), 102–104.

nations and their governments that are observed among the individual citizens of civilized states.

We have no quarrel with the German people. We have no feeling toward them but one of sympathy and friendship. It was not upon their impulse that their government acted in entering this war. It was not with their previous knowledge or approval. It was a war determined as wars used to be determined in the old, unhappy days when peoples nowhere consulted by their rulers and wars were provoked and waged in the interest of dynasties or of little groups of ambitious men who were accustomed to use their fellowmen as pawns and tools. . . .

The world must be made safe for democracy. Its peace must be planted upon the tested foundations of political liberty. We have no selfish ends to serve. We desire no conquest, no domination. We seek no indemnities for ourselves, no material compensation for the sacrifices we shall freely make. We are but one of the champions of the rights of mankind. We shall be satisfied when those rights have been made as secure as the faith and the freedom of nations can make them. . . .

It will be all the easier for us to conduct ourselves as belligerents in a high spirit of right and fairness because we act without animus, not in enmity toward a people or with the desire to bring any injury or disadvantage upon them, but only in armed opposition to an irresponsible government which has thrown aside all considerations of humanity and of right and is running amuck. We are, let me say again, the sincere friends of the German people, and shall desire nothing so much as the early reestablishment of intimate relations of mutual advantage between us—however hard it may be between them, for the time being, to believe that this is spoken from our hearts. We have borne with their present government through all these bitter months because of that friendship,—exercising a patience and forebearance which would otherwise have been impossible. We shall, happily, still have an opportunity to prove that friendship in our daily attitude and actions toward the millions of men and women of German birth and native sympathy who live among us and share our life, and we shall be proud to prove it toward all who are in fact loyal to their neighbors and to the Government in the hour of test. They are, most of them, as true and loyal Americans as if they had never known any other fealty or allegiance. . . .

It is a distressing and oppressive duty, gentlemen of Congress, which I have performed in thus addressing you. There are, it may be, many months of fiery trial and sacrifice ahead of us. It is a fearful thing to lead this great peaceful nation into war, into the most terrible and disastrous of all wars, civilization itself seeming to be in the balance. But the right is more precious than peace, and we shall fight for the things which we have always carried nearest our hearts,—for democracy, for the right of those who submit to authority to have a voice in their own governments, for the rights and liberties of small nations, for a universal dominion of right by such a concert of free peoples as shall bring peace and safety to all nations and make the world itself at last free. To such a task we can dedicate our lives and our fortunes, everything that we are and everything that we have, with the pride of those who know that the day has come when America is privileged to spend her blood and her might for the principles that gave her birth and happiness and the peace which she has treasured. God helping her, she can do no other.

167

The Question of First Amendment Rights (1919)

America's entry into the First World War produced widespread nationalism among the American people. The Woodrow Wilson administration helped mold this reaction when it launched an extraordinarily successful propaganda campaign to rally support for the war crusade. Capitalizing on this popular mood and eager to protect war mobilization, Congress passed the Espionage Act (1917), which imposed severe penalties on persons who were found guilty of obstructing the war effort. Despite the patriotic fervor, some individuals and groups opposed the war, with certain members of the Socialist party being the most conspicuous. In 1917, Socialist Charles Schenck was arrested and found guilty of violating the Espionage Act. He appealed the decision to the Supreme Court, where Justice Oliver Wendell Holmes, Jr. delivered the court's opinion in Schenck v. U.S. *Holmes devoted his entire life to studying the law, becoming one of the great legal minds of the 20th century, who was best known for his liberal dissenting opinions on the Supreme Court. Holmes argued that interpretations of the law should be based not simply on legal precedents but on the conditions of the time. In this selection taken from* Schenck v. U.S., *Holmes introduces the "clear and present danger" test for limitations on free speech.*

Questions to Consider

1. According to Oliver Wendell Holmes, Jr., how had Charles Schenck violated the Espionage Act?
2. Were the Socialist leaflets really that menacing?
3. How does Holmes interpret the First Amendment in this case?
4. What are the consequences of such a decision?

This is an indictment in three counts. The first charges a conspiracy to violate the Espionage Act of June 15, 1917, by causing and attempting to cause insubordination, etc., in the military and naval forces of the United States, and to obstruct the recruiting and enlistment service of the United States, when the United States was at war with the German Empire; to wit, that the defendant wilfully conspired to have printed and circulated to men who had been called and accepted for military service under the Act of May 18, 1917, a document set forth and alleged to be calculated to cause such insubordination

---

Schenck v. United States, 249 *US Reports* 47–53 (1919).

and obstruction. The count alleges overt acts in pursuance of the conspiracy, ending in the distribution of the document set forth. The second count alleges a conspiracy to commit an offense against the United States; to wit, to use the mails for the transmission of matter declared to be nonmailable by title 12, of the Act of June 15, 1917. . . . The third count charges an unlawful use of the mails for the transmission of the same matter and otherwise as above. The defendants were found guilty on all the counts. They set up the 1st Amendment to the Constitution, forbidding Congress to make any law abridging the freedom of speech or of the press, and, bringing the case here on that ground, have argued some other points also of which we must dispose.

It is argued that the evidence, if admissible, was not sufficient to prove that the defendant Schenck was concerned in sending the document. According to the testimony Schenck said he was general secretary of the Socialist party and had charge of the Socialist headquarters from which the documents were sent. He identified a book found there as the minutes of the executive committee of the party. The book showed a resolution of August 13, 1917, that 15,000 leaflets should be printed on the other side of one of them in use, to be mailed to men who had passed examination boards, and for distribution. Schenck personally attended to the printing. . . . and there was a resolve that Comrade Schenck be allowed $125 for sending the leaflets through the mail. He said that he had about fifteen or sixteen thousand printed. . . . Without going into confirmatory details that were proved, no reasonable man could doubt that the defendant Schenck was largely instrumental in sending the circulars about. . . .

The document in question, upon its first printed side, recited the 1st section of the 13th Amendment, said that the idea embodied in it was violated by the Conscription Act, and that a conscript is little better than a convict. In impassioned language it intimated that conscription was despotism in its worst form and a monstrous wrong against humanity, in the interest of Wall street's chosen few. It said: "Do not submit to intimidation;" but in form at least confined itself to peaceful measures, such as a petition for the repeal of the act. The other and later printed side of the sheet was headed, "Assert Your Rights." It stated reasons for alleging that anyone violated the Constitution when he refused to recognize "your right to assert your opposition to the draft," and went on: "If you do not assert and support your rights, you are helping to deny or disparage rights which it is the solemn duty of all citizens and residents of the United States to retain." It described the arguments on the other side as coming from cunning politicians and a mercenary capitalist press, and even silent consent to the Conscription Law as helping to support an infamous conspiracy. It denied the power to send our citizens away to foreign shores to shoot up the people of other lands, and added that words could not express the condemnation such cold-blooded ruthlessness deserves, etc., etc., winding up, "You must do your share to maintain, support, and uphold the rights of the people of this country." Of course the document would not have been sent unless it had been intended to have some effect, and we do not see what effect it could be expected to have upon persons subject to the draft except to influence them to obstruct the carrying of it out. . . .

But it is said, suppose that that was the tendency of this circular, it is protected by the 1st Amendment to the Constitution. Two of the strongest expressions are said to be quoted respectively from well-known men. It well may be that the prohibition of laws abridging the freedom of speech is not confined to previous restraints, although to prevent them may have been the main purpose. . . . We admit that in many places and in ordinary times the defendants, in saying all that was said in the circular, would have been within their constitutional rights. But the character of every act depends upon the circumstances in which it is done. The most stringent protection of free speech would not protect a man in falsely shouting fire in a theater, and causing a panic. It does not even protect a man from an injunction against uttering words that may have all the effect of force. The question in every case is whether the words used are used in such circumstances and are of such a nature as to create a clear and present danger that they will bring about substantive evils that Congress has a right to prevent. It is a question of proximity and degree. When a nation is at war many things that might be said in time of peace are such a hindrance to its effort that their utterance will not be endured so long as men fight, and that no court could regard them as protected by any constitutional right. It seems to be admitted that if an actual obstruction of the recruiting service were proved, liability for words that produced that effect might be enforced. The Statute of 1917 punishes conspiracies to obstruct as well as actual obstruction. If the act (speaking, or circulating a paper), its tendency and the intent with which it is done, are the same, we perceive no ground for saying that success alone warrants making the act a crime. . . .

Judgments affirmed.

168

A Soldier's View of the War (1918)

The First World War introduced new military technology, yet both sides employed age-old military tactics. The result was massive losses for all belligerents as the conflict stagnated in trench fighting (where battles were often fought to gain yards), and a war of attrition developed. The nature of the war changed in 1917, when Russia withdrew from the fighting (they signed a peace treaty with Germany) and the United States entered the war. The American Expeditionary Force (AEF) landed in France in June 1917, but the bulk of American troops did not arrive until early 1918. American participation was minimal until the Germans launched a massive offensive in March 1918, which the Americans helped repel. One of the nearly 2 million Americans who fought in the war was Captain Arthur P. Terry of Wytheville, Virginia. Terry entered the army shortly after graduation from Virginia Polytechnic Institute in 1916, and he arrived in France in May 1918. His diary accounts excerpted here present war from the soldier's perspective in the battles of Saint-Mihiel and Meuse-Argonne in 1918.

Questions to Consider

1. What are Captain Arthur Terry's views of the war?
2. What is the tone of his diary account?
3. What seems to be Terry's preoccupation in these excerpts?
4. What is his attitude about trench warfare?

AUGUST 6TH Yesterday Bob Patterson and I with thirty-five non-commissioned officers and a British Gas Officer were on our way to the front to witness a gas wave attack which was being launched last night by the British. The British Officer was for some reason very anxious to get to the lines before night fall. In going up we crossed over the heights to the right of Blairville and as we reached the top we were seen by a battery of German artillery, who opened fire on us. Two shots, three-inch shells, struck on each side of the path where we were walking but fortunately they were "duds." Lying on my stomach I could have touched where both shells struck. One of the men took oath to the fact that one of the shells passed between his legs. We ran to some trenches near by, where we had to remain from five o'clock until nine. We timed them and every seven minutes the enemy put over on the trenches a salvo of three inch shells. We escaped by simply outguessing the Germans by changing our positions, and too by "digging in." Several times officers were covered up by the earth thrown up by the bursting shells. Those were four long hours and in an exceedingly hot place. We expected every moment to be the last with some or all of us. . .

AUGUST 11TH We had quite a hot time last night. Colonel Parks and I were at the front and he had just sent out five patrols to try to get a German prisoner. They had not captured one in over three weeks. We wanted one so as to make him talk and get the dope on who was opposing us and what they were doing. Our patrols had just gone out when a message was received from the observation post reporting a great deal of activity in the German lines, and that he thought a relief was being made. We then ordered the artillery to open up, and in a minute—well it was wonderful but awful. With the opening of our guns "Jerry" sent up flares and rockets which lit up the entire country for miles. Then he retaliated [sic] with his guns. It was just one continuous roar with the screeching and whistling of the shells as they passed over. We were very anxious of our patrols but as the night passed on all of them checked in with no one hurt or missing. . . .

SEPTEMBER 25TH That night in Bois de Borrus—it can never be forgotten! It was ten forty-five; the regiment was forming in columns of squads when suddenly the silence of the night was broken by the now familiar hissing and whistling of an approaching shell; then the whole woods seemed to rock

Captain Arthur P. Terry, Diary, August–September 1918, Arthur P. Terry Collection, Box 1, Folder 1, George C. Marshall Research Foundation, Lexington, VA.

from a terrific explosion. Who will ever forget that moment? The crash of the shells; the cries of caution in the dark; the loud commands; for a time it seemed that we would die like rats in a trap. The first shell carried its death toll—it killed the first sergeant and the N. C. O's in a platoon of L Company. One of the men in Company F, in dodging a shell, fell by the side of me; just then the shell exploded, and he cried out "Mama." His cry was evidently a premonition of death, for we found him with a part of his head blown away. During the trying minutes which were ours here a very peculiar incident occurred. In jumping into a trench in dodging one of the shells a man of Company B landed on the legs of two other men, breaking one leg for each of them. In going to the head of the column with a message for Major Emory I had a very narrow escape. I had been jumping in and out of the trenches from the shells. At the end of the trench was a drain pool about fifteen feet deep, the bottom of which was filled with loose rock. It was dark and I could not see in it; over came a shell and I dived into it. The fall knocked me unconscious, but upon regaining same a few minutes later I fired my pistol and yelled for help. . . .

169

The Homefront War (1917–18)

When the United States declared war on Germany in April 1917, the nation was ill-prepared for such confrontation. Clearly, the military needed the necessary support in terms of manpower and supplies to fight a major war. The American economy needed to shift toward wartime production. And Woodrow Wilson's call for American involvement "to make the world safe for democracy" set idealistic goals for the conflict. Faced with fighting a war overseas and the need to generate wartime support on the homefront, the Wilson administration launched a publicity campaign. Part of this effort was the prominent display of posters that called for patriotic support and personal sacrifice to support the cause. Following are three posters that were part of this publicity campaign.

Questions to Consider

1. Based on a careful consideration of the second and third images, what conclusions can you draw about attitudes toward women at the time of the First World War?

2. What does the first image suggest about Germans? How accurate do you think this portrayal is?

3. What are the artists trying to accomplish in each of these posters?

4. Is it acceptable for the government to use propaganda to convince the public to support its policies? Are their limits to when it is acceptable?

394

Library of Congress, Prints and Photographs Division, LC-USZ62-19912

Frederick Strothmann,
artist (1918)

Library of Congress, Prints and Photographs Division, LC-USZ62-42150

Howard Chandler Christy,
artist (1917)

Edward Penfield, artist (1918)

Library of Congress, Prints and Photographs Division, LC-USZC4-3014

170

Opposition to the League of Nations (1919)

When the peace conference convened in France in 1919, President Woodrow Wilson attended and took an active role in negotiations in the hope of preserving his proposed idealistic blueprint for peacemaking, the Fourteen Points. The resulting Treaty of Versailles contained little of the original Fourteen Points except a League of Nations, which Wilson believed would correct the mistakes of the peace treaty. The heart of the new League of Nations was Article 10, which urged league members "to respect and preserve" the territory of members from external aggression. When Democrat Wilson submitted the treaty to the U.S. Senate for ratification, it came under the close scrutiny of Republican Henry Cabot Lodge, chair of the Foreign Relations Committee. Born in Massachusetts and Harvard educated (the first Ph.D. in political science), Lodge was known for his clear and forceful arguments in the 37 years he served in Congress. In a speech on the Senate floor, which is excerpted following, Lodge offered his reasons for opposing the Treaty of Versailles (and the League of Nations). The Senate would defeat the treaty ratification in two separate votes, mainly along partisan lines.

Questions to Consider

1. For what reasons does Henry Cabot Lodge oppose the treaty?
2. What changes would he make to the treaty?
3. How does he propose to maintain world peace? Is that possible?
4. Is Lodge an isolationist? What is the significance of his opposition to the ratification of the Treaty of Versailles?

I object in the strongest possible way to having the United States agree, directly or indirectly, to be controlled by a league which may at any time, and perfectly lawfully and in accordance with the terms of the covenant, be drawn in to deal with internal conflicts in other countries, no matter what those conflicts may be. We should never permit the United States to be involved in any internal conflict in another country, except by the will of her people expressed through the Congress which represents them.

With regard to wars of external aggression on a member of the league, the case is perfectly clear. There can be no genuine dispute whatever about the meaning of the first clause of article 10. In the first place, it differs from every other obligation in being individual and placed upon each nation without the intervention of the league. Each nation for itself promises to respect and preserve as against external aggression the boundaries and the political independence of every member of the league. . . .

Any analysis of the provisions of this league covenant, however, brings out in startling relief one great fact. Whatever may be said, it is not a league of peace; it is an alliance, dominated at the present moment by five great powers, really by three, and it has all the marks of an alliance. The development of international law is neglected. The court which is to decide disputes brought before it fills but a small place. The conditions for which this league really provides with the utmost care are political conditions, not judicial questions, to be reached by the executive council and the assembly, purely political bodies without any trace of a judicial character about them. Such being its machinery, the control being in the hands of political appointees whose votes will be controlled by interest and expedience it exhibits that most marked characteristic of an alliance—that its decisions are to be carried out by force. Those articles upon which the whole structure rests are articles which provide for the use of force; that is, for war. This league to enforce peace does a great deal for enforcement and very little for peace. It makes more essential provisions looking to war than to peace for the settlement of disputes. . . .

Taken altogether, these provisions for war present what to my mind is the gravest objection to this league in its present form. We are told that of course nothing will be done in the way of warlike acts without the assent of Congress. If that is true let us say so in the covenant. But as it stands there is no

---

"League of Nations," *Congressional Record*, 66th Congress, 1st session, part 4 (August 12, 1919), 3778–3784.

doubt whatever in my mind that American troops and American ships may be ordered to any part of the world by nations other than the United States, and that is a proposition to which I for one can never assent. . . .

Those of us, Mr. President, who are either wholly opposed to the league, or who are trying to preserve the independence and the safety of the United States by changing the terms of the league, and who are endeavoring to make the league, if we are to be a member of it, less certain to promote war instead of peace have been reproached with selfishness in our outlook and with a desire to keep our country in a state of isolation. So far as the question of isolation goes, it is impossible to isolate the United States. . . . But there is a wide difference between taking a suitable part and bearing a due responsibility in world affairs and plunging the United States into every controversy and conflict on the face of the globe. By meddling in all the differences which may arise among any portion or fragment of humankind we simply fritter away our influence and injure ourselves to no good purpose. . . .

. . . In the prosecution of the war we gave unstintedly American lives and American treasure. When the war closed we had 3,000,000 men under arms. We were turning the country into a vast workshop for war. We advanced ten billions to our allies. We refused no assistance that we could possibly render. All the great energy and power of the Republic were put at the service of the good cause. We have not been ungenerous. We have been devoted to the cause of freedom, humanity, and civilization everywhere. Now we are asked, in the making of peace, to sacrifice our sovereignty in important respects, to involve ourselves almost without limit in the affairs of other nations and to yield up policies and rights which we have maintained throughout our history. We are asked to incur liabilities to an unlimited extent and furnish assets at the same time which no man can measure. I think it is not only our right but our duty to determine how far we shall go. . . .

No doubt many excellent and patriotic people see a coming fulfillment of noble ideals in the words "league for peace." We all respect and share these aspirations and desires, but some of us see no hope, but rather defeat, for them in this murky covenant. For we, too have our ideals, even if we differ from those who have tried to establish a monopoly of idealism. Our first ideal is our country, and we see her in the future, as in the past, giving service to all her people and to the world. Our ideal of the future is that she should continue to render that service of her own free will. She has great problems of her own to solve, very grim and perilous problems, and a right solution, if we can attain to it, would largely benefit mankind. We would have our country strong to resist a peril from the West, as she has flung back the German menace from the East. We would not have our politics distracted and embittered by the dissensions of other lands. We would not have our country's vigor exhausted or her moral force abated, by everlasting meddling and muddling in every quarrel, great and small, which afflicts the world. Our ideal is to make her ever stronger and better and finer, because in that way alone, as we believe, can she be of the greatest service to the world's peace and to the welfare of mankind.

171

The New Negro (1925)

The First World War created both opportunity and despair for African Americans. In the years before the war; some blacks left the segregationist South and moved to the North for economic opportunity and the hope of a better life. When the war created labor shortages, however, this Great Migration swelled, as several thousand African Americans moved to the North to work in war industries. Blacks were drafted into the military, and segregated units fought in Europe. The migration continued after the war, as another 1 million African Americans migrated to the North, often crowding into urban ghettos such as New York's Harlem, Chicago's South Side, and Philadelphia's Seventh Ward. These ghettos became centers of African-American culture; storefront churches, newspapers, jazz and blues clubs, and literary salons helped form a black cultural identity. One of the observers of this movement was a Howard University philosophy professor and literary critic, Alain Locke. In 1925, Locke wrote The New Negro, *an essay that depicted the changes taking place.* The New Negro *is excerpted as follows.*

Questions to Consider

1. Who is the New Negro whom Locke depicts?
2. What resulted from the migration of African Americans to the cities of the North?
3. What is the significance of the "new spirit"?
4. How might W.E.B. DuBois ("On Race Relations," Document 147) have responded to Locke's views on the New Negro?

In the last decade something beyond the watch and guard of statistics has happened in the life of the American Negro and the three norns [one of the fates—past, present, future] who have traditionally presided over the Negro problem have a changeling in their laps. The Sociologist, the Philanthropist, the Race-leader are not unaware of the New Negro, but they are at a loss to account for him. He simply cannot be swathed in their formulae. For the younger generation is vibrant with a new psychology; the new spirit is awake in the masses, and under the very eyes of the professional observers is transforming what has been a perennial problem into the progressive phases of contemporary Negro life. . . .

Recall how suddenly the Negro spirituals revealed themselves; suppressed for generations under the stereotypes of Wesleyan hymn harmony, secretive,

Alain Locke, ed., *The New Negro: An Interpretation* (New York ,1925), 3–16.

half-ashamed, until the courage of being natural brought them out—and behold, there was folk-music. Similarly the mind of the Negro seems suddenly to have slipped from under the tyranny of social intimidation and to be shaking off the psychology of imitation and implied inferiority. By shedding the old chrysalis of the Negro problem we are achieving something like a spiritual emancipation. Until recently, lacking self-understanding, we have been almost as much of a problem to ourselves as we still are to others. But the decade that found us with a problem has left us with only a task. The multitude perhaps feels as yet only a strange relief and a new vague urge, but the thinking few know that in the reaction the vital inner grip of prejudice has been broken.

With this renewed self-respect and self-dependence, the life of the Negro community is bound to enter a new dynamic phase, the buoyancy from within compensating for whatever pressure there may be of conditions from without. The migrant masses, shifting from countryside to city, hurdle several generations of experience at a leap, but more important, the same thing happens spiritually in the life-attitudes and self-expression of the Young Negro, in his poetry, his art, his education and his new outlook, with the additional advantage, of course, of the poise and greater certainty of knowing what it is all about. From this comes the promise and warrant of new leadership. . . .

First we must observe some of the changes which since the traditional lines of opinion were drawn have rendered these quite obsolete. A main change has been, of course, that shifting of the Negro population which has made the Negro problem no longer exclusively or even predominantly Southern. Why should our minds remain sectionalized, when the problem itself no longer is? Then the trend of migration has not only been toward the North and the Central Midwest, but city-ward and to the great centers of industry—the problems of adjustment are new, practical, local and not peculiarly racial. Rather they are an integral part of the large industrial and social problems of our present-day democracy. And finally, with the Negro rapidly in process of class differentiation, if it ever was warrantable to regard and treat the Negro *en masse* it is becoming with every day less possible, more unjust and more ridiculous.

In the very process of being transplanted, the Negro is becoming transformed.

The tide of Negro migration, northward and city-ward, is not to be fully explained as a blind flood started by the demands of war industry coupled with the shutting off of foreign migration, or by the pressure of poor crops coupled with increased social terrorism in certain sections of the South and Southwest. Neither labor demand, the bollweevil nor the Ku Klux Klan is a basic factor, however contributory any or all of them may have been. The wash and rush of this human tide on the beach line of the northern city centers is to be explained primarily in terms of a new vision of opportunity, of social and economic freedom, of a spirit to seize, even in the face of an extortionate and heavy toll, a chance for the improvement of conditions.

With each successive wave of it, the movement of the Negro becomes more and more a mass movement toward the larger and the more democratic chance—in the Negro's case a deliberate flight not only from countryside to city, but from medieval America to modern.

Take Harlem as an instance of this. Here in Manhattan is not merely the largest Negro community in the world, but the first concentration in history of so many diverse elements of Negro life. It has attracted the African, the West Indian, the Negro American; has brought together the Negro of the North and the Negro of the South; the man from the city and the man from the town and village; the peasant, the student, the business man, the professional man, artist, poet, musician, adventurer and worker, preacher and criminal, exploiter and social outcast. Each group has come with its own separate motives and for its own special ends, but their greatest experience has been the finding of one another. Proscription and prejudice have thrown these dissimilar elements into a common area of contact and interaction. Within this area, race sympathy and unity have determined a further fusing of sentiment and experience. So what began in terms of segregation becomes more and more, as its elements mix and react, the laboratory of a great race-welding. Hitherto, it must be admitted that American Negroes have been a race more in name than in fact, or to be exact, more in sentiment than in experience. The chief bond between them has been that of a common condition rather than a common consciousness; a problem in common rather than a life in common. In Harlem, Negro life is seizing upon its first chances for group expression and self-determination. It is—or promises at least to be—a race capital. That is why our comparison is taken with those nascent centers of folk-expression and self-determination which are playing a creative part in the world to-day. Without pretense to their political significance, Harlem has the same role to play for the New Negro as Dublin has had for the new Ireland or Prague for the New Czechoslovakia. . . .

When the racial leaders of twenty years ago spoke of developing race-pride and stimulating race-consciousness, and of the desirability of race solidarity, they could not in any accurate degree have anticipated the abrupt feeling that has surged up and now pervades the awakened centers. Some of the recognized Negro leaders and a powerful section of white opinion identified with "race work" of the older order have indeed attempted to discount this feeling as a "passing phase," an attack of "race nerves" so to speak, an "aftermath of the war," and the like. It has not abated, however, if we are to gauge by the present tone and temper of the Negro press, or by the shift in popular support from the officially recognized and orthodox spokesmen to those of the independent, popular, and often radical type who are unmistakable symptoms of a new order. It is a social disservice to blunt the fact that the Negro of the Northern centers has reached a stage where tutelage, even of the most interested and well-intentioned sort, must give place to new relationships, where positive self-direction must be reckoned with in ever increasing measure. The American mind must reckon with a fundamentally changed Negro. . . .

172

The Red Scare (1920)

A series of labor strikes convulsed the country in 1919, and, influenced by the earlier Bolshevik Revolution in Russia, the American public came to believe that these strikes were the beginning of a communist revolution. When the U.S. Post Office discovered nearly 40 bombs addressed to various prominent officials (one was delivered and it exploded), many Americans were further convinced of a pending communist plot. These perceived communist tactics, the wartime hysteria against all things German (and foreign), the intolerance of dissenting opinions, and fervent nationalism all combined for an easy shift into the Red Scare. Recently appointed Attorney General A. Mitchell Palmer led a nationwide witch-hunt to find the "Reds" and prevent the perceived revolution. The main targets of this effort were radicals, recent immigrants, and some labor union leaders and members. Under Palmer's direction, the Justice Department launched several raids to round up and interrogate suspicious radicals and aliens. In the article excerpted following, journalist Frederick Barkley describes a Red Scare raid in Detroit for the news magazine, The Nation.

Questions to Consider

1. According to Barkley's account, how were the alleged radicals treated?
2. Does Barkley believe that a revolution was imminent?
3. What does he fear may result from the raids?
4. Why did the raids of the "Red Scare" cease?

On January 2 Arthur I. Barkey, chief agent of the Department of Justice in Detroit, received an order from Attorney General Palmer instructing Mr. Barkey, according to his own statement, to raid the headquarters of a group of interdicted organizations, principally the Communist party, "as long as they continue to meet," in a "supreme effort to break the back of radicalism" in Detroit. As a result, eight hundred men were imprisoned for from three to six days in a dark, windowless, narrow corridor running around the big central areaway of the city's antiquated Federal Building; they slept on the bare stone floor at night, in the heavy heat that welled sickeningly up to the low roof, just over their heads; they were shoved and jostled about by heavy-handed policemen; they were forbidden even the chance to perform a makeshift shave; they were compelled to stand in long lines for access to the solitary drinking fountain and the one toilet; they were denied all food for twenty hours, and after that were fed on what their families brought in; and they

Frederick R. Barkley, "Jailing Radicals in Detroit," *The Nation* 110 (January 31, 1920): 136–137. 22-30 were refused all communication with relatives or with attorneys. These eight hundred men, so closely packed that they had to step over one another's bodies to move about at all, included in their number citizens and aliens, college graduates and laborers, skilled mechanics making $15 a day and boys not yet out of short trousers. They were seized without warrant while attending dances and classes in physical geography and similar subjects; they were herded behind bars with no examination and no chance to inquire or explain; they were labeled in the newspapers as "Reds, Bolsheviks, Anarchists, Terrorists," and were left there for the jeering gaze of the credulous, befoozled public.

What was the crime of the eight hundred? The crime was that these men were attending a dance or studying physical geography and other sciences in a hall known as the House of the Masses, the headquarters of the Communist party—which has about one member for every thousand men in the country—in declaring, in stock phrases, for "proletarian revolution, the overthrow of capitalism, and the establishment of a dictatorship of the proletariat and destruction of the bourgeois state. . . ."

Among these families were the wives and children of American citizens, whom officials of the Department of Justice admitted they had no right to arrest. "Do you know how many citizens you've got up there?" Mr. Barkey was asked by a reporter on the third day after the first raid. "No, no," he replied nervously, "but don't say anything about citizens being held. We haven't any right to arrest citizens, you know, so don't say anything about that." When one newspaper reported Mr. Barkey to this effect, and told the conditions under which the men were being held, another journal reported his reply as follows: "The public should bear in mind that this is not a picnic, and the Department of Justice is not providing settees for criminals [350 of whom were later released for lack of evidence]. They have to sleep on the floor. That's right. But a stone bed in the post office probably isn't any harder than a board bed in the jail. The majority of them are getting better than their five-sleep-in-a-bed homes, and they have more food than they can eat. Relatives and friends have brought in whole boiled hams, boxes of oranges, and other delicacies." . . .

When the prisoners held in the "bull pen" were taken there from the Federal Building, camera men were on hand to film them. Six days' imprisonment without opportunity to shave, six nights of sleeping in their clothing on a stone floor, had prepared them well for the enforced role of "Bolshevik terrorists" with which the public is regaled. And these films, like the photographs taken at the House of the Masses, some Revolutionary War flintlocks, used in presenting costume plays, were found in a cupboard. Stacked before a great pile of books thrown from the institution's library and surmounted with framed pictures of Lenin, Trotsky, and Marx, they made a picture all too falsely convincing of the "menace of Bolshevism."

Today, January 19, the 300 men left of the 800 seized are housed in an old army fort here. In addition, about 140 are out on bond. Warrants for holding these 440 arrived from Washington on January 12, ten days after the raids. These warrants, the chief immigration inspector explained, "would block further efforts of attorneys to gain release for their clients through habeas corpus proceedings!" . . .

This is the situation in Detroit today. Nearly 400 men, citizens and aliens, are free again after being confined for one to two weeks under conditions of horror, confined because their peaceful assemblage, guaranteed by the Constitution, led the Department of Justice to suspect that their beliefs, also protected under the Constitution, were inimical to the peace and safety of 110,000,000 people. Nearly 400 men are free after a taste of "Americanization" that bodes ill for any future Americanizers who do not come backed by the clubs of the police and the constabulary.

Nearly 400 men, and hundreds more women and children, have had the seeds of hatred sown in their breasts. And probably 400 others, no more guilty of a crime than these, are waiting exile to Europe to spread those same seeds of hatred there. Thousands more of the city's great foreign-born population have had terror planted in their bosoms—terror like that which makes it impossible for the leaders of a sick benefit society to get its members together. And terror and hate are close akin. As for those Detroiters who may sometime have read the American Constitution and the Declaration of Independence, or remembered the proud boast that this was the land of freedom for exiles from autocratic Europe, a revulsion silent, but none the less deepseated and stern, has come. The Mayor, who speaks as strongly as he can, represents the indignation and resolution of others who speak not at all now, but who may speak at the ballot box at some not distant day. The people, sound at heart and steadfast for the right when they know the truth, will some day come to demand an accounting for this slaughter of Americanism to make a presidential candidate's holiday.

23

✳

The Return to "Normalcy"

During the 1920s, America withdrew from the world and attempted to return to a simpler, preprogressive time. The decade proved to be one of paradoxes. For many Americans, the time was one of abundance, where great fortunes were made, unprecedented mobility was enjoyed through the use of the automobile, and a new morality evolved. For other Americans, the decade had a far harsher reality. The reemergence of nativism led to the persecution of ethnic, religious, and racial minorities. In the countryside, farmers who had enjoyed boom years a decade earlier stood on the brink of financial ruin. The following documents bring the decade's many inconsistencies into sharp relief.

173

The Lure of Amusement Parks (1922)

In the early 20th century, a new urban mass culture emerged as more and more workers gained leisure time. Families and individuals found new ways to entertain themselves. The amusement park was one of the most popular forms of leisure. Often located near cities and connected to the downtown by the inexpensive subway or trolley system, amusement parks attracted millions of visitors from all walks of life during the summer. They offered thrilling rides such as the roller coaster, the Ferris Wheel (a popular carryover from the 1893 World's Columbian Exposition in Chicago), chutes, slides, and carrousels. They also featured exotic shows, dance halls, concerts, games of chance, food, unusual building architecture, and the extensive use of electricity. The most famous amusement park was Coney Island, built near New York City in the late 19th century. In the excerpted article, Edward F. Tilyou, the General Manager of Steeplechase Park, Coney Island and Steeplechase Pier, Atlantic City, New Jersey, offered his observations about the appeal of Coney Island and amusement parks for American Magazine. *His remarks came at the height of amusement park popularity; during the 1920s, attendance declined as the automobile and motion pictures provided competition.*

Questions to Consider

1. According to Tilyou, what made Coney Island and other amusement parks so attractive?
2. In what ways did amusement parks cater to the people?
3. What does the popularity of amusement parks suggest about urban life in the early 20th century?
4. What can you deduce about gender roles from this document?

. . . Those of us who run amusement parks see human nature with the brakes off, day after day, from May to September. People out for a good time forget all about the dress parade of business and social life. They cut loose from repressions and restrictions, and act pretty much as they feel like acting— since everyone else is doing the same thing.

There are five hundred amusement parks in the United States. At least two hundred and fifty of them are limited editions of Coney Island, with the same sort of fun-making devices, only fewer of them. I have visited many of these parks and have found people pretty much the same everywhere.

Our main advantage at Coney Island is in the size of the crowds. Often we have half a million people here on a Sunday or a holiday. In the course of the season the visitors are said to total between twenty-five and thirty million. In all the parks of the country, I suppose the seasonal attendance would exceed the total of our national population. These parks, therefore, furnish a gigantic laboratory of human nature—one which psychologists cannot afford to overlook. They would be especially interested in the way people cut loose from their usual repressions.

For instance, there was one amusement which took Surf Avenue, the main street of Coney, by storm several years ago. A number of "ballyhoo" men set up booths with shelves in the rear of them. These shelves were covered with imitation china dishes. In front of each booth was a liberal supply of missiles and a sign reading:

If you can't break up your own home, break up ours!

There wasn't a single prize offered. People paid their perfectly good money just for the savage joy of smashing dishes. They took an unholy glee in it—as if they were trying to make up for all the times they had felt like throwing things at home and decided that the gratification of their desire would be either ill bred or too expensive. . . .

I have heard people complain that amusement parks are speeding up more every year in glitter and racket. If that is true, it is because you people

Edward F. Tilyou, "Human Nature with the Brakes Off," *American Magazine* 94 (July 1922): 18–21, 86, 91–92, 94.

demand it. You respond instantly to incandescent cupolas, the blare of music, the slam of scenic railways, the beating of tom-toms; and we give you what you want. The most popular shows are those which give the keenest excitement. The tenseness of modern industry and business competition has keyed your nervous organism to such a pitch that you see a sharp stimulus. . . .

Those of us in the amusement business have studied your psychology, and tried to build our business on a few simple fundamentals. We know, for instance, that most people look back on childhood as the happiest period of their lives. They may be mistaken, but this is the mental attitude they like to adopt. So when they are out for a good time they get infinite joy out of acting like children again. That is why the slides, hobby horses, toy locomotives, and carrousels are always crowded at amusement parks.

Another thing we know is that the average person likes to have a share in making his own fun, instead of having attendants or mechanical contrivances do it all for him. People prefer to steer their own craft on the "Witching Waves," pilot their own airships, hold the reins of their own hobby horses, and find their own way out of the labyrinth.

Folks also take great glee in seeing other folks in embarrassing positions. Not only does it seem funny to them, but it stirs up a soothing complacency that *they* are not the victims. Spectators will stand for hours in front of the "Barrel of Fun," a revolving cylinder in which passers-through are likely to be rolled off their feet, or they will watch with equal intentness a narrow wooden lane which suddenly becomes movable, threatening to topple barrels from either side down onto the heads of luckless victims. . . .

Most amusement parks are built beside salt or fresh water beaches, and it is here that we have noticed a gradual but marked change in the habits of human beings. A few years ago the men at the beaches far outnumbered the women. Today there is about an equal division.

Most of us can remember the time when women were not expected to do any real swimming. They dressed for the *beach,* but not for the *water.* Satin beach slippers were quite the vogue. Such women as ventured into the waves were usually led by a protecting male hand. Today all this has changed. Most girls prefer the role of mermaid to that of beach flower. They dress suitably for real swimming, or they are not afraid of getting wet, or sunburned, or even dirty. . . .

Deliberate swindling at amusement places may be dead, but the harmless hoodwinking of the side shows will always live. People love to listen to the exaggerated promises of the "ballyhoo" man, and they enter his tent prepared to believe almost anything. There have been enough original "Wild Men of Borneo" to man a battleship.

"Only a dime, ladies and gentlemen, for the ravishing vision of Fatima, the beautiful Egyptian princess—direct descendent of Cleopatra!" shouts the "barker." You troop in, happy and unquestioning as children. Five minutes later you are rushing across the street to see the "Fire-Eating Fiji Islander."

"Show is about to begin! You'll have to hurry!" shouts another "barker." Experience may have taught you that shows begin only when tents are full—

but there is always the nervous rush to the door. You are children again, the same sort of children who used to pay "Five pins—no crooked ones taken!" for a peep through the hole in the mysterious chest carefully guarded by some youthful P. T. Barnum. As an amusement man, I thank heaven that we Americans never really grow up.

174

The Role of Advertising (1922)

One of the by-products of industrialization was the creation of the mass consumer culture. By the 1920s, increasing numbers of middle-class families had the income to purchase goods and services beyond basic necessities. Americans bought new appliances, such as the refrigerator and vacuum cleaner, and new products, such as cigarettes, toothpaste, and mouthwash. Such consumer spending helped fuel the changing American economy, but advertising was particularly influential in promoting the consumer economy and became a booming business in the 1920s. Advertisers found new and creative ways to market products, placing appealing ads in newspapers and magazines, erecting billboards along highways, and using air time on the recently developed radio broadcasts to acquaint the public with consumer items. Such efforts typically identified products with a certain lifestyle and persuaded potential customers that the purchase of the product would enrich their lives. In 1922, at the dawn of the advertising boom, journalist Roger Hoyt wrote about the importance of advertising in America. An excerpt of his article in The Outlook *is as follows.*

Questions to Consider

1. According to Roger C. Hoyt, what had advertising done for America?
2. Who would be reading this article? How would it shape their views?
3. Why are brand names and trademarks important to advertisers? Are they today?
4. Has advertising changed since this 1922 article was written? How?

Wherever one turns to–day, he is confronted by advertisements.

They fill up two-thirds of your favorite magazine or newspaper. They stare at you from enormous billboards and are painted on the sides of buildings. They glitter in huge electric signs which turn night into day. If you ride in a street car, your attention is caught by a many–colored card telling you to

---

Roger C. Hoyt, "A Plain Talk on Advertising," *The Outlook* 132 (September 20, 1922): 122–124.

"Chew Wrigley's Gum" or how to "Keep that Schoolgirl Complexion." Advertisements stare you out of countenance or sneak up on you surreptitiously. But you can't dodge them. You naturally ask, "What is this all about?" "Are such huge expenditures for advertising justified?" "Are these advertisements truthful or misleading?". . .

I think this whole subject can be greatly simplified if we consider legitimate advertising as just plain "news."

Let me carry this thought of "news" a little further. Consider life in a typical American home to-day as compared with that of a generation back. What has brought about the great change in the standard of living? I do not hesitate to attribute it largely to advertising, which is only another name for the dissemination of news regarding articles which make for a fuller and more enjoyable existence.

Very likely the maid is awakened in the morning by a Big Ben alarm clock. She hastens to prepare breakfast, consisting of Sunkist oranges, Yuban coffee, Quaker oats, toast made from Ward's bread, and some crisp strips of Beechnut bacon to serve on a Valsparred table. In the meantime the master of the house is bathing in a Standard sanitary tub with Ivory soap; shaving with Colgate's cream and a Gillette safety razor; donning his B.V.D.'s, Cluett shirt and collar, Holeproof hose, Hart, Schaffner, & Marx suit, and Regal shoes. After breakfast he grabs his Stetson hat, jumps into his Buick car, equipped with Goodyear tires, and rides over Barrett Tarviated roads. At the office he sits at a Globe Wernicke Desk and dictates letters through a Dictaphone, which are transcribed on an Underwood typewriter and filed away in a Library Bureau filing cabinet. On his way home he stops at the florist's to "Say It With Flowers," and in the evening enjoys his Robert Burns cigar while listening to the latest fox-trot on the Victrola. And advertising furnished the original impulse for this entire day's programme.

Advertising, because of its news value, has thus been a dominant factor in raising the standard of living and bringing greater comfort and a more healthful and happier life to millions of Americans.

But advertising must also justify itself from an economic standpoint. If it is a tax on the community in the form of higher prices for advertised products, as is frequently claimed, can it be justified? The old question arises, "Who pays for the advertising?" . . .

Suppose a manufacturer of a twenty-five-cent tooth-paste should decide that he could profitably spend $10,000 a month in advertising in periodicals. For this expenditure he could place his advertisement before approximately 20,000,000 readers. Now suppose only one out of every one hundred readers should buy a tube of the paste. He would then sell 200,000 tubes and his advertising would cost him five cents per tube. But many of these purchasers will be well satisfied if his tooth-paste is meritorious and will continue to use it. Thus the original cost of five cents a tube for advertising will be divided among subsequent sales and the cost per tube will steadily decrease. And so by advertising the manufacturer is steadily enlarging his market, making easier and larger sales, and decreasing the selling cost per unit. He can therefore do business at a lower total cost, and thus make a lower price to the consumer at the same time that he has created good will for his product and stabilized his business.

And this leads to a necessary corollary of advertising—maintenance of quality. One of the chief objects of the advertiser is to build up good will towards his product. His name and trade-mark become firmly established in the minds of the buying public and appear upon every package that he sells. He has thus put his name and reputation behind his goods and has in effect guaranteed a certain quality which the purchaser looks for and has a right to expect. No manufacturer can afford to place his trade-mark on an inferior article or allow the quality of an advertised brand to deteriorate. For the advertised article can be readily identified, and any falling off in quality would result in a quick decrease in sales. You can readily think of numerous advertised articles which you purchase because you recognize the reliability of the manufacturer, and which you would cease to purchase if the quality were not kept up to standard.

And so I think I may safely say that advertising renders a distinct and valuable service to the people of this country. Its news value has enabled progressive manufacturers to tell their story in the quickest and most economical manner. It has raised standards of living, developed a keener appreciation of the beautiful, promoted better health and sanitation, and greatly increased our National wealth.

Manufacturers of bath-tubs and soaps have advertised cleanliness into the consciousness of the American people. Tooth-paste manufacturers are preaching care of the teeth and proper dentistry; food manufacturers are teaching a more careful regulation of one's diet; the largest manufacturer of eye-glass lenses is now spending several hundred thousand dollars to educate people to take proper care of their eyes; a maker of beds talks about the hygienic value of restful sleep. . . .

Our wives are saved much drudgery by widely advertised appliances such as electric irons, stoves, washing-machines, vacuum cleaners, and kitchen cabinets. Electric fans keep us cool in the summer and heaters keep us warm in the winter. Our whole course of life from the hygienic nursing bottle to the copperlined casket is made smoother and richer by advertising news which tells us how to secure all those things which may make life really worth while.

And so when you pick up your favorite periodical to-night, don't tear out the advertising pages and cuss the publisher for wasting such a large amount of good white paper. But stop and consider these same advertisements as "news" announcements of the best things which human ingenuity has devised for your comfort, edification, and enrichment. If you will look at the advertisements from this point of view, you will be the gainer in wealth, and happiness.

175

The Impact of the Automobile (1922)

The most significant social and economic development of the 1920s was the automobile. It speeded transportation, created a movement for improved roads, helped accelerate suburban sprawl, and provided a sense of independence for American youth. The Ford Motor Company, founded by Henry Ford in 1903, revolutionized the auto industry with the assembly line and mass-production techniques used to make the Model T. Before stopping production of the "tin lizzie" after 20 years, Ford manufactured more than 15 million Model Ts, selling them for as little as $290 in 1927. Other automobile makers adopted the mass-production techniques, but fierce price competition and the large capital outlays required to maintain production reduced the number of companies from 253 in 1908 to 44 in 1929. The Big Three auto manufacturers—Ford, General Motors, and Chrysler—made 80 percent of the cars in the United States in the 1920s. In 1922, Allen D. Albert published the following article on the "social influence of the automobile" in Scribner's Magazine, *a popular news periodical. His article appeared as the popularity of the automobile became increasingly widespread.*

Questions to Consider

1. According to Allen D. Albert, what changes occurred as a result of the automobile?
2. What does Albert believe are the less desirable changes?
3. Why were Americans able to adjust so quickly to the automobile?
4. How might the automobile enhance democracy and individualism in American life? How might it undermine these traits?

We look along a perspective of lights dazzling in their intensity and realize wearily, any hot evening, that the procession along the boulevard will not cease till bedtime. Or we jerk ahead and wait, jerk ahead again and wait again, in a choke of purring cars after a football game. Or we look up from a hardware counter and see a farmer who has driven five miles from the harvest-field to get a ball of twine. Or we hunt for a parking space outside a Chautauqua tent. A dozen times a year, in as many situations, the newness and far reach of the motor-driven vehicle catch up our thought as does the airplane which lands in the field near our house.

"It is so wonderfully new," we say to ourselves time and again. Still we do not appreciate how new it really is! . . .

Are you still shocked by reading "Auto Bandits" in the head-lines? Have you passed at the side of a country road a car with no lights and two young figures shoulder against shoulder in a corner of the rear seat? Do you know that banks are still refusing to make loans for the buying of cars? Have you observed the bootlegger in the automobile, the doctor in his little coupé, the rural carrier in his Ford, the children in the school bus?

We have in 1921 about nine million motor-cars in the United States, hardly a third as many as our horses. Yet I think there can be no serious question that the motor-car has come to be more important to us socially than the horse.

The most comprehensive change it has wrought for us has been the general widening of the circle of our life. City folk feel this in the evening and at the week-end. Farmer folk feel it from early morning till bedtime every day.

Our mail comes to our R.F.D. box usually not later than eleven in the morning, and ours is the last delivery but one on our route. Some who work, in every town, now have year-round houses in the country. There is, in fact, a tangible and powerful movement directly opposite to that of the retired farmer. He came to town to rest; city folk are going to the country to rest, and in the era of the automobile they do not lose the diversions that appealed so strongly to the retired farmer. . . .

We have seen our architecture develop the garage in lieu of the old carriage-house and livery-barn. We have heard our speech enlivened with automobile terms, such as when our children describe a teacher of undistinguished personality as a "flat tire." We have noted the entire disappearance of the victoria before the "chummy car" or the "roadster," and some of us have sighed for an aristocracy that is never more to be.

Strange-looking driveways called "filling stations," with glowing lamps at night, long railroad-trains of tank-cars, streets painted with white lines to mark zones for safety for pedestrians and parking spaces for cars—how almost without a pause in our thinking have we adjusted our lives to these factors new since yesterday! . . .

We of the motor era do not bow to each other in passing on the highway as once we did. The car makes that impracticable. Sometimes we recognize the approaching machine and sometimes we make out the person who is driving. Before there can be any exchange of recognition, however, we have flown past each other. . . .

Automobile outlawry and lawlessness are now more serious, I believe, than they are to be hereafter. It is absurd to expect a great new social agency to come into use without abuse. Almost invariably abuse is the concomitant of use.

The same machine that hurries the surgeon to the bedside of the child with a broken foot will hurry the yeggman [slang for thief or burglar] in his getaway from a hold-up. The boy who acts the pig in his home will not suddenly become considerate of others when given absolute control of a vehicle swifter and heavier than the others on the street. Traffic squads are already making his control far from absolute in the more travelled thoroughfares. Within such limits it is to be expected that he and his highwayman associates will shortly be checked by some device that will stop all vehicular movement within a fixed limit on the sounding of an alarm. The car that persists in shooting ahead will thus be brought into clear view, while if the joy-rider or the thief stopped with the others ordinarily, he would only await capture. . . .

When the new defense is provided, as surely it will be, perhaps it may modify one of the new problems of education produced by the automobile. In an older day it was feasible for the college authorities to keep some sort of watch over their students. Now a boy at school in Connecticut can motor to New York City and back between his last lecture of one day and his first class of the next.

What are campus regulations to students who have the range of an extra-campus radius of one hundred miles? Assuredly the best answer will be the development of a motive in the life of the student that will keep him safe wherever he is. But while we wait for that approach to undergraduate perfection, there will be a value no male parent will question in the student's realization that the automobile thoroughfares around the campus are patrolled sensibly and sufficiently. Longer motor journeys will hasten the day of such control.

Bus lines are reporting to our village squares with little or no preliminary announcement. They make about the same time as accommodations trains, they travel more direct routes, they traverse a landscape unspoiled by cuts and fills and tracks, and they deliver us if not at our exact destinations into the very heart of town rather than at railway-stations away from the heart of town. . . .

Roads are improving farther from those busy streets. Touring-cars are improving likewise. One need not move around like a farm-hand on a load of hay, almost swamped by bulgy equipment. Compact outfits, touring vehicles as ingeniously designed as yachts, hotels cleanly kept and courteously managed, all promise a freer movement of the people to every interesting section of the country. In that freer movement the automobile will justify itself most of all, I believe, as an agent of the wholesome sociability in our modern life.

176

Religion and the Scopes Trial (1925)

The 1920s produced a cultural clash over the place of religion in America. Protestants were divided into two camps on the proper position of Christians toward modern science, evolution, and secular ideas. In one camp were the modernists, who were mostly middle-class people who had attempted to adapt their religion to the more scientific, modern world. In the other camp were the fundamentalists, who were mostly rural residents who sought to keep religion as the focal point in American life by reaffirming the literal interpretation of the Bible. Fundamentalists achieved a political victory when Tennessee outlawed the teaching of evolution in public schools. When biology teacher John T. Scopes was arrested for teaching evolution, it began the Scopes trial that had religion at its core. The trial attracted widespread media attention. Defending Scopes was the recently formed American Civil Liberties Union and prominent trial lawyer Clarence Darrow. Aiding the prosecution was William Jennings Bryan, a former presidential candidate and now an important fundamentalist spokesman. The trial's high point came when Darrow cross-examined Bryan, who defended the literal interpretation *of the Bible. Scopes was found guilty and fined $100. Bryan prepared a closing argument for the prosecution that he never delivered. Instead, the argument was printed in* The Memoirs of William Jennings Bryan *and is excerpted as follows.*

Questions to Consider

1. According to Bryan, what are the limits of science?
2. Why is evolution a danger to Christianity?
3. Why had the Scopes trial become so significant?
4. Does prosecuting Scopes constitute a threat to freedom of expression? Do Scopes's teachings pose a threat to freedom of religion?

Can any Christian remain indifferent? Science needs religion to direct its energies and to inspire with lofty purpose those who employ the forces that are unloosed by science. Evolution is at war with religion because religion is supernatural; it is, therefore, the relentless foe of Christianity, which is a revealed religion.

Let us, then, hear the conclusion of the whole matter. Science is a magnificent material force, but it is not a teacher of morals. It can perfect machinery, but it adds no moral restraints to protect society from the misuse of the machine. It can also build gigantic intellectual ships, but it constructs no moral rudders for the control of storm-tossed human vessels. It not only fails to supply the spiritual element needed but some of its unproven hypotheses rob the ship of its *compass* and thus endanger its cargo.

In war, science has proven itself an evil genius; it has made war more terrible than it ever was before. Man used to be content to slaughter his fellowmen on a single plain—the earth's surface. Science has taught him to go down into the water and shoot up from below, and to go up into the clouds and shoot down from above, thus making the battlefield three times as bloody as it was before; but science does not teach brotherly love. Science has made war so hellish that civilization was about to commit suicide; and now we are told that newly discovered instruments of destruction will make the cruelties of the late war seem trivial in comparison with the cruelties of wars that may come in the future. If civilization is to be saved from the wreckage threatened by intelligence not consecrated by love, it must be saved by the moral code of the meek and lowly Nazarene. His teachings, and His teachings alone, can solve the problems that vex the heart and perplex the world.

The world needs a Saviour more than it ever did before, and there is only one "Name under heaven given among men whereby we must be saved." It is this Name that evolution degrades, for, carried to its logical conclusion, it robs Christ of the glory of a virgin birth, of the majesty of His deity and mission, and of the triumph of His resurrection. It also disputes the doctrine of the atonement.

William Jennings Bryan and Mary Baird Bryan, *The Memoirs of Williams Jennings Bryan* (Chicago, 1925), 554–556.

It is for the jury to determine whether this attack upon the Christian religion shall be permitted in the public schools of Tennessee by teachers employed by the State and paid out of the public treasury. This case is no longer local; the defendant ceases to play an important part. The case has assumed the proportions of a battle-royal between unbelief that attempts to speak through so-called science and the defenders of the Christian faith, speaking through the Legislators of Tennessee. It is again a choice between God and Baal; it is also a renewal of the issue in Pilate's court. In that historic trial—the greatest in history—force, impersonated by Pilate, occupied the throne. Behind it was the Roman Government, mistress of the world, and behind the Roman Government were the legions of Rome. Before Pilate, stood Christ, the Apostle of Love. Force triumphed; they nailed Him to the tree and those who stood around mocked and jeered and said, "He is dead." But from that day the power of Caesar waned and the power of Christ increased. In a few centuries the Roman government was gone and its legions forgotten; while the crucified and risen Lord has become the greatest fact in history and the growing figure of all time.

Again force and love meet face to face, and the question, "What shall I do with Jesus?" must be answered. A bloody, brutal doctrine—Evolution—demands, as the rabble did nineteen hundred years ago, that He be crucified. That cannot be the answer of this jury representing a Christian State and sworn to uphold the laws of Tennessee. Your answer will be heard throughout the world; it is eagerly awaited by a praying multitude. If the law is nullified, there will be rejoicing wherever God is repudiated, the Saviour scoffed at and the Bible ridiculed. Every unbeliever of every kind and degree will be happy. If, on the other hand, the law is upheld and the religion of the school children protected, millions of Christians will call you blessed and, with hearts full of gratitude to God, will sing again that grand old song of triumph:

> Faith of our fathers, living still,
> In spite of dungeon, fire and sword;
> O how our hearts beat high with joy
> Whene'er we hear that glorious word—
> Faith of our fathers—holy faith;
> We will be true to thee til death!

177

The Ku Klux Klan's Perspective (1926)

In 1915, William J. Simmons revived the Ku Klux Klan. Patterned after the group formed during Reconstruction, the new Klan languished until a promotional campaign, several well-publicized investigations, and America's disillusionment following the First World War combined to boost membership into the millions (estimates range from 3 to 8 million). Appealing to America's nativistic tendencies and fears, the Klan spread beyond the South and became a powerful national organization that influenced state and local politics, conducted parades of members wearing white robes and hoods, and held rallies at which crosses were burned. In 1922, a revolt removed Simmons as Klan leader, and Hiram W. Evans, a dentist from Dallas, Texas, became the Klan's new Imperial Wizard. Evans oversaw much of the Klan's spectacular rise and its decline. In 1926, he published an article, excerpted following, in the respected North American Review, *which explained the Klan's purpose and moral agenda for America.*

Questions to Consider

1. What is the purpose of the Ku Klux Klan? How does it plan to carry out its goals?
2. What does the Klan oppose? Who would join the Klan? Why?
3. What does this document reveal about certain segments of American society in the 1920s?
4. How would Alain Locke, author of "The New Negro" (Document 171), respond to this document?

The Ku Klux Klan, in short, is an organization which gives expression, direction and purpose to the most vital instincts, hopes and resentments of the old stock Americans, provides them with leadership, and is enlisting and preparing them for militant, constructive action toward fulfilling their racial and national destiny. . . .

There are three of these great racial instincts, vital elements in both the historic and the present attempts to build an America which shall fulfill the aspirations and justify the heroism of the men who made the nation. These are the instincts of loyalty to the white race, to the traditions of America, and to the spirit of Protestantism, which has been an essential part of Americanism ever since the days of Roanoke and Plymouth Rock. They are condensed into the Klan slogan: "Native, white, Protestant supremacy."

First in the Klansman's mind is patriotism—America for Americans. He believes religiously that a betrayal of Americanism or the American race is treason to the most sacred of trusts, a trust from his fathers and a trust from God. He believes, too, that Americanism can only be achieved if the pioneer stock is kept pure. . . .

Americanism, to the Klansman, is a thing of the spirit, a purpose and a point of view, that can only come through instinctive racial understanding. It has, to be sure, certain defined principles, but he does not believe that many aliens understand those principles, even when they use our words in talking about them. Democracy is one, fairdealing, impartial justice, equal opportunity,

Hiram Wesley Evans, "The Klan's Fight for Americanism," *North American Review* 223 (March–April–May 1926): 33–61.

religious liberty, independence, self-reliance, courage, endurance, acceptance of individual responsibility as well as individual rewards for effort, willingness to sacrifice for the good of his family, his nation and his race before anything else but God, dependence on enlightened conscience for guidance, the right to unhampered development—these are fundamental. But within the bounds they fix there must be the utmost freedom, tolerance, liberalism. In short, the Klansman believes in the greatest possible diversity and individualism within the limits of the American spirit. But he believes also that few aliens can understand that spirit, that fewer try to, and that there must be resistance, intolerance even, toward anything that threatens it, or the fundamental national unity based upon it.

The second word in the Klansman's trilogy is "white." The white race must be supreme, not only in America but in the world. This is equally unde-batable, except on the ground that the races might live together, each with full regard for the rights and interests of others, and that those rights and interests would never conflict. Such an idea, of course, is absurd; the colored races today, such as Japan, are clamoring not for equality but for their supremacy. . . . The world has been so made that each race must fight for its life, must conquer, accept slavery or die. The Klansman believes that the whites will not become slaves, and he does not intend to die before his time.

Moreover, the future of progress and civilization depends on the contin-ued supremacy of the white race. . . . Until the whites falter, or some colored civilization has a miracle of awakening, there is not a single colored stock that can claim even equality with the white; much less supremacy.

The third of the Klan principles is that Protestantism must be supreme; that Rome shall not rule America. The Klansman believes this not merely because he is a Protestant, nor even because the Colonies that are now our nation were settled for the purpose of wresting America from the control of Rome and establishing a land of free conscience. He believes it also because Protestantism is an essential part of Americanism; without it America could never have been created and without it she cannot go forward. Roman rule would kill it.

Protestantism contains more than religion. It is the expression in religion of the same spirit of independence, self-reliance and freedom which are the highest achievements of the Nordic race. . . .

Let it be clear what is meant by "supremacy." It is nothing more than power of control, under just laws. It is not imperialism, far less is it autocracy or even aristocracy of a race or stock of men. What it does mean is that we insist on our inherited right to insure our own safety, individually and as a race, to secure the future of our children, to maintain and develop our racial heritage in our own, white, Protestant, American way, without interference. . . .

And we deny that either bigotry or prejudice enters into our intolerance or our narrowness. We are intolerant of everything that strikes at the founda-tions of our race, our country or our freedom of worship. We are narrowly opposed to the use of anything alien—race, loyalty to any foreign power or to any religion whatever—as a means to win political power. . . . This is our intolerance; based on the sound instincts which have saved us many times from the follies of the intellectuals. We admit it. More and worse, we are proud of it. . . .

The Negro, the Klan considers a special duty and problem of the white American. He is among us through no wish of his; we owe it him and to ourselves to give him full protection and opportunity. But his limitations are evident; we will not permit him to gain sufficient power to control our civilization. Neither will we delude him with promises of social equality which we know can never be realized. The Klan looks forward to the day when the Negro problem will have been saved on some much saner basis than miscegenation, and when every State will enforce laws making any sex relations between a white and a colored person a crime.

For the alien in general we have sympathy, opportunity, justice, but no permanent welcome unless he becomes truly American. It is our duty to see that he has every chance for this, and we shall be glad to accept him if he does. We hold no rancor against him; his race, instincts, training, mentality and whole outlook of life are usually widely different from ours. We cannot blame him if he adheres to them and attempts to convert us to them, even by force. But we must see that he can never succeed. . . .

178

The New Woman (1927)

The 1920s witnessed the emergence of the "new woman." Having achieved suffrage with the 19th Amendment, some women turned their attention to other feminine issues—such as political equality, economic independence, and improved relations between the sexes—to broaden their reform efforts, but this movement lacked cohesion. Some feminists advocated an equal rights amendment, individualism, female solidarity, and equality with men while retaining differences from men. Other women pursued reforms in the workplace and acceptance from men. Some young women—the "flappers"—received considerable press coverage for their revolution in morals: They wore lipstick, cut their hair short, smoked, drank alcohol, dressed in short skirts, attended wild parties, and were obsessed with sex. At the same time, other women, stagnating in male-dominated marriages that relegated them to care for the household and children, hoped to improve relations in the home. The new woman, then, worked for different agendas and with contrasting methods to challenge the prevailing convention. In an article published in Harper's Monthly Magazine, *Dorothy Dunbar Bromley promoted the "Feminist—New Style," a woman who understood the roots of feminism and was willing to make changes in her life.*

Questions to Consider

1. What is the purpose of Dorothy Dunbar Bromley's article?

2. What is the new style of feminist, and how does she differ from the old feminists and the new feminists?

3. How would men react to Bromley's article?

4. What can be deduced from this document about gender relations in the 1920s?

"Feminism" has become a term of opprobrium to the modern young woman. For the word suggests either the old school of fighting feminists who wore flat heels and had very little feminine charm, or the current species who antagonize men with their constant clamor about maiden names, equal rights, woman's place in the world, and many another cause . . . *ad infinitum*. . . .

But what of the constantly increasing group of young women in their twenties and thirties who are truly modern ones, those who admit that a full life calls for marriage and children as well as a career? These women if they launch upon marriage are keen to make a success of it and an art of child-rearing. But *at the same time* they are moved by an inescapable inner compulsion to be individuals in their own right. And in this era of simplified housekeeping they see their opportunity, for it is obvious that a woman who plans intelligently can salvage some time for her own pursuits. Furthermore, they are convinced that they will be better wives and mothers for the breadth they gain from functioning outside the home. In short, they are highly conscious creatures who feel obliged to plumb their own resources to the very depths, despite the fact that they are under no delusions as to the present inferior status of their sex in most fields of endeavor.

Numbers of these honest, spirited young women have made themselves heard in article and story. But since men must have things pointed out to them in black and white, we beg leave to enunciate the tenets of the modern woman's credo. Let us call her "Feminist—New Style."

First Tenet. Our modern young woman freely admits that American women have so far achieved but little in the arts, sciences, and professions as compared with men. . . .

But it remains true that a small percentage of women have proved the capacity, even the creative power of the feminine mind. Or have they not rather proved the fallacy of drawing a hard and fast distinction between the quality of men's minds and the quality of women's minds? . . .

Second Tenet. Why, then, does the modern woman care about a career or a job if she doubts the quality and scope of women's achievement to date? There are three good reasons why she cares immensely: first, she may be of that rare and fortunate breed of persons who find a certain art, science, or profession as inevitable a part of their lives as breathing; second, she may feel the need of a satisfying outlet for her energy whether or not she possesses creative ability; third, she may have no other means of securing her economic independence. And the latter she prizes above all else, for it spells her freedom as an individual, enabling her to marry or not marry, as she chooses, to terminate a marriage that has become unbearable, and to support and educate her children if necessary. . . .

Third Tenet. She will not, however, live for her job alone, for she considers that a woman who talks and thinks only shop has just as narrow a horizon as the housewife who talks and thinks only husband and children—perhaps more so, for the latter may have a deeper understanding of human nature. She will therefore refuse to give up all of her personal interests, year in and year out, for the sake of her work. . . .

Fourth Tenet. Nor has she become hostile to the other sex in the course of her struggle to orient herself. On the contrary, she frankly likes men and is grateful to more than a few for the encouragement and help they have given her.

In the business and professional world, for instance, Feminist—New Style has observed that more and more men are coming to accord women as much responsibility as they show themselves able to carry. She and her generation have never found it necessary to bludgeon their way, and she is inclined to think that certain of the pioneers would have got farther if they had relied on their ability rather than on their militant methods. . . .

Fifth Tenet. By the same corollary, Feminist—New Style professes no loyalty to women *en masse,* although she staunchly believes in individual women. Surveying her sex as a whole, she finds their actions petty, their range of interests narrow, their talk trivial and repetitious. As for those who set themselves up as leaders of the sex, they are either strident creatures of so little ability and balance that they have won no chance to "express themselves" (to use their own hackneyed phrase) in a man-made world; or they are brilliant, restless individuals who too often battle for women's rights for the sake of personal glory. . . .

Sixth Tenet. There is, however, one thing which Feminist—New Style envies Frenchwomen, and that is their sense of "chic." Indeed, she is so far removed from the early feminists that she is altogether baffled by the psychology which led some of then to abjure men in the same voice with which they aped them. Certainly their vanity must have been anaesthetized, she tells herself, as she pictures them with their short hair, so different from her own shingle, and dressed in their unflattering mannish clothes—quite the antithesis of her own boyish effects which are subtly designed to set off feminine charms. . . .

Seventh Tenet. Empty slogans seem to Feminist—New Style just as bad taste as masculine dress and manners. They serve only to prolong the war between the sexes and to prevent women from learning to think straight. Take these, for instance, "Keep your maiden name." "Come out of the kitchen." "Never darn a sock." . . .

Eighth Tenet. As for "free love," she thinks that it is impractical rather than immoral. With society organized as it is, the average man and woman cannot carry on a free union with any degree of tranquillity.

Incidentally, she is sick of hearing that modern young women are cheapening themselves by their laxity of morals. As a matter of fact, all those who have done any thinking, and who have any innate refinement, live by an aesthetic standard of morals which would make promiscuity inconceivable. . . .

Ninth Tenet. She readily concedes that a husband and children are necessary to the average woman's fullest development, although she knows well enough that women are endowed with varying degrees of passion and of maternal instinct. . . .

But no matter how much she may desire the sanction of marriage for the sake of having children, she will not take any man who offers. First of all a man must satisfy her as a lover and a companion. And second, he must have the mental and physical traits which she would like her children to inherit. . . .

This business of combining two careers presents its grave difficulties. In fact, it is a bigger job than any man has ever attempted. But because it *is* a big job, and because she has seen a few women succeed at it, Feminist—New Style will rise to the challenge. . . .

Tenth Tenet. But even while she admits that a home and children may be necessary to her complete happiness, she will insist upon *more freedom and honesty within the marriage relation*. . . .

Finally, Feminist—New Style proclaims that men and children shall no longer circumscribe her world, although they may constitute a large part of it. She is intensely self-conscious whereas the feminists were intensely sex-conscious. Aware of possessing a mind, she takes a keen pleasure in using that mind for some definite purpose; and also in learning to think clearly and cogently against a background of historical and scientific knowledge. . . . She knows that it is her American, her twentieth-century birth right to emerge from a creature of instinct into a full-fledged individual who is capable of molding her own life. And in this respect she holds that she is becoming man's equal.

If this be treason, gentlemen, make the most of it.

179

American Individualism (1928)

Herbert Hoover had a long and distinguished career as a government worker before seeking the presidency in 1928. Born in Iowa and raised as a Quaker, Hoover became a wealthy engineer-businessman before age 40. He headed the Food Administration during the First World War and used voluntary methods and a propaganda campaign to raise food production while reducing civilian consumption. Hoover served as secretary of commerce under Presidents Warren G. Harding and Calvin Coolidge, and he transformed

the insignificant department into one of the most dynamic agencies of the federal gov-
ernment: He helped promote new markets for business, developed industrial standardiza-
tion, and established regulations for the infant radio and aviation industries. Hoover
was well known to Americans, had established a reputation as a brilliant administrator,
and was a successful businessman when he ran for president against Democratic candi-
date Al Smith in 1928. Many argued that Hoover would "engineer" the country to
continued prosperity. Hoover concluded his presidential campaign in New York with
the following excerpted speech. It embodied Herbert Hoover's belief in American indi-
vidualism as well as the Republican party's philosophy in the 1920s.

Questions to Consider

1. According to Herbert Hoover, why did America have a strong economy in the 1920s?

2. What is Hoover's "American system"?

3. Why does Hoover fear government involvement in the economy? Is his argument valid?

4. How would the families discussed in the document "Urban Families in the Great Depression" (Document 180) have responded to Hoover's concept of "rugged individualism"?

When the war closed, the most vital of all issues both in our own country and throughout the world was whether governments should continue their war-time ownership and operation of many instrumentalities of production and distribution. We were challenged with a peace-time choice between the American system of rugged individualism and a European philosophy of diametri-cally opposed doctrines—doctrines of paternalism and state socialism. The acceptance of these ideas would have meant the destruction of self-government through centralization of government. It would have meant the undermining of the individual initiative and enterprise through which our people have grown to unparalleled greatness.

The Republican Party from the beginning resolutely turned its face away from these ideas and these war practices. . . . When the Republican Party came into full power it went at once back to our fundamental conception of the state and the rights and responsibilities of the individual. Thereby it restored confidence and hope in the American people, it freed and stimulated enter-prise, it restored the government to its position as an umpire instead of a player in the economic game. For these reasons the American people have gone forward in progress while the rest of the world has halted, and some of the countries have even gone backwards. . . .

There has been revived in this campaign, however, a series of proposals which, if adopted, would be a long step toward the abandonment of our

---

"Text of Hoover's Speech on Relation of Government to Industry," *New York Times,* October 23, 1928, p. 2. 23-32

American system and a surrender to the destructive operation of governmental conduct of commercial business. Because the country is faced with difficulty and doubt over certain national problems—that is prohibition, farm relief, and electrical power—our opponents propose that we must thrust government a long way into the businesses which give rise to these problems. In effect, they abandon the tenets of their own party and turn to state socialism as a solution for the difficulties presented by all three. It is proposed that we shall change from prohibition to the state purchase and sale of liquor. If their agricultural relief program means anything, it means that the Government shall directly or indirectly buy and sell and fix prices of agricultural products. And we are to go into the hydroelectric power business. In other words, we are confronted with a huge program of government in business.

There is, therefore, submitted to the American people a question of fundamental principle. That is: shall we depart from the principles of our American political and economic system, upon which we have advanced beyond all the rest of the world, in order to adopt methods based on principles destructive of its very foundations? And I wish to emphasize the seriousness of these proposals. I wish to make my position clear; for this goes to the very roots of American life and progress. . . .

Let us first see the effect upon self-government. When the Federal Government undertakes to go into commercial business it must at once set up the organization and administration of that business, and it immediately finds itself in a labyrinth, every alley of which leads to the destruction of self-government. . . .

Bureaucracy is ever desirous of spreading its influence and its power. You cannot extend the mastery of the Government over the daily working life of a people without at the same time making it the master of the people's souls and thoughts. Every expansion of Government in business means that Government in order to protect itself from the political consequences of its errors and wrongs is driven irresistibly without peace to greater and greater control of the nation's press and platform. Free speech does not live many hours after free industry and free commerce die.

It is a false liberalism that interprets itself into the government operation of commercial business. Every step of bureaucratizing the business of our country poisons the very roots of liberalism—that is, political equality, free speech, free assembly, free press, and equality of opportunity. It is the road not to more liberty, but to less liberty. Liberalism should be found not striving to spread bureaucracy but striving to set bounds to it. True liberalism seeks all legitimate freedom first in the confident belief that without such freedom the pursuit of all other blessings and benefits is vain. That belief is the foundation of all American progress, political as well as economic.

Liberalism is a force truly of the spirit, a force proceeding from the deep realization that economic freedom cannot be sacrificed if political freedom is to be preserved. Even if Governmental conduct of business could give us more efficiency instead of less efficiency, the fundamental objection to it would remain unaltered and unabated. It would destroy political equality. It would increase rather than decrease abuse and corruption. It would stifle initiative and invention. It would undermine the development of leadership. It would cramp and cripple the mental and spiritual energies of our people. It would extinguish equality and opportunity. It would dry up the spirit of liberty and progress. For these reasons primarily it must be resisted. For a hundred and fifty years liberalism has found its true spirit in the American system, not in the European systems. . . .

By adherence to the principles of decentralized self-government, ordered liberty, equal opportunity, and freedom to the individual, our American experiment in human welfare has yielded a degree of well-being unparalleled in all the world. It has come nearer to the abolition of poverty, to the abolition of fear of want, than humanity has ever reached before. Progress of the past seven years is the proof of it. This alone furnishes the answer to our opponents, who ask us to introduce destructive elements into the system by which this has been accomplished. . . .

I have endeavored to present to you that the greatness of America has grown out of a political and social system and a method of control of economic forces distinctly its own—our American system—which has carried this great experiment in human welfare farther than ever before in all history. We are nearer today to the ideal of the abolition of poverty and fear from the lives of men and women than ever before in any land. And I again repeat that the departure from our American system by injecting principles destructive to it which our opponents propose, will jeopardize the very liberty and freedom of our people, and will destroy equality of opportunity not alone to ourselves but to our children. . . .

24

✳

FDR and the New Deal

The uneven prosperity of the 1920s vanished with the onset of the Great Depression. As America's leaders searched for a solution to the crisis, large numbers of Americans sank into poverty. Thousands of Americans imbued with the values of rugged individualism begged for food, while many others wandered in search of opportunity. The Great Depression gave the Democrats political control of the country. Behind the leadership of President Franklin D. Roosevelt, the government energetically sought a variety of means to revive the economy and restore hope to the American people. Despite these efforts, political opposition and ecological difficulties hampered these attempts. The following documents depict the despair of many Americans and the varying efforts undertaken to alleviate these conditions.

180

Urban Families in the Great Depression (1931)

The economic boom of the 1920s vanished with the stock market crash in October 1929, and the country slid into the Great Depression. Although it was not the sole cause of the Great Depression, the crash revealed the unsound nature of business and helped trigger the economic collapse. Millions of workers lost their jobs as companies retrenched; prices dropped dramatically, but consumer spending virtually ceased. Thousands of businesses failed, and the banking system neared disintegration under the financial strain. At the nadir of the Great Depression, the standard of living had dropped by 50 percent and more than one-third of the workforce was fully unemployed (some received shorter work hours but were considered employed). Among the people hardest hit were the urban poor and those living on the margin of poverty. As the depression worsened, Congress heard testimony from numerous individuals operating private relief agencies about conditions for urban residents. Dorothy Kahn, executive director of the Jewish Welfare Society of Philadelphia, Pennsylvania, testified before the Senate Subcommittee on Unemployment Relief in December 1931. Her excerpted statement following reveals the plight of the urban family in the midst of the Great Depression.

Questions to Consider

1. What happened to urban families in Philadelphia in the Great Depression? How did they react to these circumstances?

2. According to Dorothy Kahn, what was the attitude of the unemployed?

3. Why does she explain this attitude to the congressional committee?

4. How would these families respond to Henry George's "*Progress and Poverty*" (Document 137)? How might they respond to the views contained in William Graham Sumner's "'The Forgotten Man'" (Document 138)?

THE CHAIRMAN: What happens to these families when they are evicted?

MISS KAHN: The families in Philadelphia are doing a number of things. The dependence of families upon the landlords, who seem to have a remarkable willingness to allow people to live in their quarters, rent free, is something that has not been measured. I think the only indication of it is the mounting list of sheriff's sales where property owners are simply unable to maintain their small pieces of property because rents are not being paid. Probably most of you saw in the newspapers the account of the "organized" representation of the taxpayers recently, where they vigorously and successfully opposed a rise in local taxes, largely because of the fact that they are under a tremendous burden through nonpayment of rents. That, of course, is the least of the difficulties, although I think this is the point at which we ought to stress one of the factors that Mr. West and other speakers have brought out in their testimony, that is the effect on families of the insecurity of living rent free, and in addition to that, the effect on their attitude toward meeting their obligations. Some of us would not be surprised if rent paying became an obsolete custom in our community. There are also, of course, evictions and the evictions in Philadelphia are frequently accompanied not only by the ghastly placing of a family's furniture on the street, but the actual sale of the family's household goods by the constable. These families are, in common Philadelphia parlance, "sold out."

One of the factors that is never counted in all of the estimates of relief in this country is the factor of neighborliness. That factor of neighborliness is a point that I would like to stress here, because it seems to us who are close to this problem that this factor has been stretched not only beyond its capacity but beyond the limits of human endurance. We have no measure in Philadelphia to-day of the overcrowding that is a direct or indirect result of our inability to pay rent for families. Only the other day a case came to my attention in which a family of 10 had just moved in with a family of 6 in a 3-room apartment. However shocking that may be to the members of this committee, it is almost an every-day occurrence in our midst. Neighbors do take people in. They

U.S. Congress, Senate, Subcommittee on Unemployment Relief, "Statement of Miss Dorothy Kahn," *Hearings before the Senate Subcommittee on Unemployment Relief, Senate Committee on Manufactures,* 72nd Congress, 1st session (28 December 1931), 73–77.

sleep on chairs, they sleep on the floor. There are conditions in Philadelphia that beggar description. There is scarcely a day that calls do not come to all of our offices to find somehow a bed or a chair. The demand for boxes on which people can sit or stretch themselves is hardly to be believed. . . .

Only the other day a man came to our office, as hundreds do day after day, applying for a job, in order not to have to apply for relief. I think we have already stressed the reluctance of individuals to accept relief, regardless of the source from which it comes. This man said to our worker: "I know you haven't any money to give us. I know there isn't enough money in the city to take care of the needs of everybody, but I want you to give me a job." Now, we have so many applications of that kind during the day that it has gotten to the point where we can scarcely take their names as they come in, because we have no facilities for giving jobs. In this particular case this individual interested me because when he heard that we had no jobs to give him, he said: "Have you anybody you can send around to my family to tell my wife you have no job to give me! Because she doesn't believe that a man who walks the street from morning till night, day after day, actually can't get a job in this town. She thinks I don't want to work." I think it is not necessary to dramatize the results of a situation like that. And there are thousands of them. It is only one illustration.

Another thing, it seems to me to be important to stress is the effect of this situation on the work habits of the next generation. I think it has not been brought out that in the early period of this so-called "depression" one of the most outstanding features of it was the fact that young people could get jobs even when old people of 40 years and over could not get jobs, and it has become quite customary for families to expect that their young members who are just coming of working age can replace the usual breadwinner, the father of the family. It is easy to forget about these young boys and girls reaching 14, 15, 16, 17, 18 years of age, who have had no work experience, and if we think of work not as merely a means of livelihood but as an aspect of our life and a part of our life, it has a good deal of significance that these young people are having their first work experience, and experience not with employment but with unemployment; that in addition to that they are looked to as potential breadwinners in the family; that they are under the same strain, the same onus that the father of the family is under, suspected of malingering, suspected of not wanting to work—all of these things which the average individual sees not as clearly as we see them in terms of millions of unemployed. . . .

181

Franklin D. Roosevelt's First Inaugural Address (1933)

The dominant issue in the presidential election in 1932 was the Great Depression. The Republicans renominated Herbert Hoover, who campaigned defensively on his record, while the Democrats selected New York Governor Franklin Delano Roosevelt, who offered few specific proposals to end the depression but radiated confidence as he pledged a New Deal for the American people. Roosevelt won the presidency in a landslide (472 electoral votes to 59), and the Democrats gained control of both houses of Congress. But in the four long months between the election and inauguration—soon remedied when the 20th Amendment moved the inauguration from March 4 to January 20—the Great Depression worsened: Unemployment increased, more businesses failed, and there were numerous "runs" on banks, as panicked depositors withdrew their life savings, which forced some banks to close their doors. On inauguration day, 80 percent of America's banks were closed (either by declared state holiday or by failure), and the country was near economic ruin. Roosevelt's inaugural address, excerpted as follows, exuded a sense of vigor and action at a time when Americans suffered a crisis of confidence.

Questions to Consider

1. In what ways does Franklin Roosevelt seek to build the American people's confidence?
2. What does Roosevelt believe are the significant problems facing the nation? How does he propose to solve them?
3. For what purposes does Roosevelt refer to the crisis as similar to war?
4. In what ways does Roosevelt differ from William Lloyd Garrison, Jr. ("A Businessman's View of the New Deal," Document 183) in his approach to America's economic problems?

I am certain that my fellow Americans expect that on my induction into the Presidency I will address them with a candor and a decision which the present situation of our Nation impels. This is preeminently the time to speak the truth, the whole truth, frankly and boldly. Nor need we shrink from honestly facing conditions in our country today. This great Nation will endure as it has endured, will revive and will prosper. So, first of all, let me assert my firm belief that the only thing we have to fear is fear itself—nameless, unreasoning, unjustified terror which paralyzes needed efforts to convert retreat into advance. In every dark hour of our national life a leadership of frankness and vigor has met with that understanding and support of the people themselves which is essential to victory. I am convinced that you will again give that support to leadership in these critical days.

In such a spirit on my part and on yours we face our common difficulties. They concern, thank God, only material things. Values have shrunken to fantastic levels; taxes have risen; our ability to pay has fallen; government of all kinds is faced by serious curtailment of income; the means of exchange are frozen in the currents of trade; the withered leaves of industrial enterprise

"Inaugural Address, March 4, 1933," *The Public Papers and Addresses of Franklin D. Roosevelt*, Vol. 2: *The Year of Crisis, 1933*, comp. Samuel I. Rosenman (New York, 1938), 11–16.

lie on every side; farmers find no markets for their produce; the savings of many years in thousands of families are gone.

More important, a host of unemployed citizens face the grim problem of existence, and an equally great number toil with little return. Only a foolish optimist can deny the dark realities of the moment.

Yet our distress comes from no failure of substance. We are stricken by no plague of locusts. Compared with the perils which our forefathers conquered because they believed and were not afraid, we have still much to be thankful for. Nature still offers her bounty and human efforts have multiplied it. Plenty is at our doorstep, but a generous use of it languishes in the very sight of the supply. . . .

Our greatest primary task is to put people to work. This is no unsolvable problem if we face it wisely and courageously. It can be accomplished in part by direct recruiting by the Government itself, treating the task as we would treat the emergency of a war, but at the same time, through this employment, accomplishing greatly needed projects to stimulate and reorganize the use of our natural resources.

Hand in hand with this we must frankly recognize the overbalance of population in our industrial centers and, by engaging on a national scale in a redistribution, endeavor to provide a better use of the land for those best fitted for the land. The task can be helped by definite efforts to raise the values of agricultural products and with this the power to purchase the output of our cities. It can be helped by preventing realistically the tragedy of the growing loss through foreclosure of our small homes and our farms. It can be helped by insistence that the Federal, State, and local governments act forthwith on the demand that their cost be drastically reduced. It can be helped by the unifying of relief activities which today are often scattered, uneconomical, and unequal. It can be helped by national planning for and supervision of all forms of transportation and of communications and other utilities which have a definitely public character. There are many ways in which it can be helped, but it can never be helped by merely talking about it. We must act and act quickly.

Finally, in our progress toward a resumption of work we require two safeguards against a return of the evils of the old order; there must be a strict supervision of all banking and credits and investments, so that there will be an end to speculation with other people's money; and there must be provision for an adequate but sound currency.

These are the lines of attack. I shall presently urge upon a new Congress, in special session, detailed measures for their fulfillment, and I shall seek the immediate assistance of the several States. . . .

I am prepared under my constitutional duty to recommend the measures that a stricken Nation in the midst of a stricken world may require. These measures, or such other measures as the Congress may build out of its experience and wisdom, I shall seek, within my constitutional authority, to bring to speedy adoption.

But in the event that the Congress shall fail to take one of these two courses, and in the event that the national emergency is still critical, I shall not evade the clear course of duty that will then confront me. I shall ask the Congress for the one remaining instrument to meet the crises—broad Executive power to wage a war against the emergency, as great as the power that would be given to me if we were in fact invaded by a foreign foe.

For the trust reposed in me I will return the courage and the devotion that befit the time. I can do no less.

We face the arduous days that lie before us in the warm courage of national unity; with the clear satisfaction that comes and precious moral values; with the clean satisfaction that comes from the stern performance of duty by old and young alike. We aim at the assurance of a rounded and permanent national life.

We do not distrust the future of essential democracy. The people of the United States have not failed. In their need they have registered a mandate that they want direct, vigorous action. They have asked for discipline and direction under leadership.

They have made me the present instrument of their wishes. In the spirit of the gift I take it.

In this dedication of a Nation we humbly ask the blessing of God. May He protect each and every one of us. May He guide me in the days to come.

182

The "Share Our Wealth" Plan (1933)

Franklin Delano Roosevelt's first New Deal attempted to restore economic confidence in the American people, provide relief to the unemployed, revive the sagging agricultural and business enterprises, and put people to work. Uneven in its impact and often contradictory and improvised, the New Deal "experiment" enjoyed massive public support during its inception. The New Deal, however, brought only limited recovery and, as the economic crisis waned, critics of the program emerged. Among the most prominent critics of Roosevelt and the New Deal was Louisiana Senator Huey P. Long. Nicknamed the "Kingfish," Long developed a fervent following from poor whites in Louisiana, was elected governor, and created a political machine that gave him almost dictatorial rule over the state. Elected senator in 1930, the demagogue used his popularity to spread his Share Our Wealth program, an implausibly simplistic plan that appealed to many Americans' resentment toward the wealthy. Long claimed that membership in the Share Our Wealth clubs exceeded 7 million. The 1933 Huey P. Long autobiography, Everyman a King, *excerpted as follows, promised economic security for all Americans with the proposed Share Our Wealth plan.*

Questions to Consider

1. Why would many Americans support this plan?
2. What would the people do to receive their share of the wealth? Could such a plan be successful?
3. How did Huey P. Long's plan challenge the New Deal? With what effect?
4. To what extent did Long's plan anticipate Lyndon Johnson's "Great Society"?

The increasing fury with which I have been, and am to be, assailed by reason of the fight and growth of support for limiting the size of fortunes can only be explained by the madness which human nature attaches to the holders of accumulated wealth.

What I have proposed is:—

THE LONG PLAN

1. A capital levy tax on the property owned by any one person of 1% of all over $1,000,000; 2% of all over $2,000,000 etc., until, when it reaches fortunes of over $100,000,000, the government takes all above that figure; which means a limit on the size of any one man's fortune to something like $50,000—the balance to go to the government to spread out in its work among the people.
2. An inheritance tax which does not allow any one person to receive more than $5,000,000 in a lifetime without working for it, all over that amount to go to the government to be spread among the people for its work.
3. An income tax which does not allow any one man to make more than $1,000,000 in one year, exclusive of taxes, the balance to go to the United States for general work among the people.

The foregoing program means all taxes paid by the fortune holders at the top and none at the bottom; the spreading of wealth among all the people and the breaking up of a system of Lords and Slaves in our economic life. It allows the millionaires to have, however, more than they can use for any luxury they can enjoy on earth. But, with such limits, all else can survive.

That the public press should regard my plan and effort as a calamity and me as a menace is no more than should be expected, gauged in the light of past events. According to Ridpath, the eminent historian:

Huey P. Long, *Everyman a King: The Autobiography of Huey P. Long* (New Orleans, 1933), 338–340. Copyright renewed 1961 by Russell B. Long. Reprinted by permission of Senator Russell B. Long.

The ruling classes always possess the means of information and the process by which it is distributed. The newspaper of modern times belongs to the upper man. The under man has no voice; or if, having a voice, he cries out, his cry is lost like a shout in the desert. Capital, in the places of power, seizes upon the organs of public utterance, and howls the humble down the wind. Lying and misrepresentation are the natural weapons of those who maintain an existing vice and gather the usufruct of crime.

—*Ridpath's History of the World,* page 410

In 1932, the vote for my resolution showed possibly a half dozen other Senators back of it. It grew in the last Congress to nearly twenty Senators. Such growth through one other year will mean the success of a venture, the completion of everything I have undertaken,—the time when I can and will retire from the stress and fury of my public life, maybe as my forties begin,— a contemplation so serene as to appear impossible.

That day will reflect credit on the States whose Senators took the early lead to spread the wealth of the land among all the people.

Then no tear dimmed eyes of a small child will be lifted into the saddened face of a father or mother unable to give it the necessities required by its soul and body for life; then the powerful will be rebuked in the sight of man for holding that which they cannot consume, but which is craved to sustain humanity; the food of the land will feed, the raiment clothe, and the houses shelter all the people; the powerful will be elated by the well being of all, rather than through their greed.

Then, those of us who have pursued that phantom of Jefferson, Jackson, Webster, Theodore Roosevelt and Bryan may hear wafted from their lips in Valhalla:

EVERY MAN A KING

183

A Businessman's View of the New Deal (1934)

The flood of legislation that produced the first New Deal sought to solve the economic problems created by the Great Depression. Although it enjoyed widespread public support, the program brought only modest economic recovery. The New Deal program, however, did change the role of government, especially the federal government. The National Recovery Administration, for example, had labor, business, and government officials draw up "codes of fair practices" to establish prices, wages, and hours in the workday. Participating businesses displayed the Blue Eagle crest to show "We Do Our Part." Congress also passed legislation and created bureaucracies to regulate the activities of banks and the stock exchange to prevent another economic collapse and to restore confidence in financial activities. In addition, Roosevelt dropped the gold standard and experimented with the value of the dollar to boost prices. Such activities enlarged the size of the federal government, broadened its scope, and greatly increased the debt. In

1934, The Nation *magazine published a series of articles by businessmen discussing various issues of the New Deal. Recently retired Boston investment banker, William Lloyd Garrison, Jr., grandson of the famed abolitionist, offered the following commentary on the New Deal.*

Questions to Consider

1. What are Garrison's views on the New Deal?
2. According to Garrison, what New Deal programs seem to be working?
3. What does he believe are the problems of the New Deal?
4. What does Garrison hope to accomplish with this article?

. . . What he [Roosevelt] chose to call the New Deal was, in part, his concept for coping with an acute and threatening emergency. Without delay he displayed his courage and vigor of action by his affirmative handling of the demoralized banking situation, then on the verge of collapse. His steady and confident temper generated a new hope which was immediately reflected in national sentiment and duly recorded in the quotations of the market-place. But that episode was merely a beginning. The New Deal, being both a philosophy and a mode of action, began to find expression in diverse forms which were often contradictory. Some assisted and some retarded the recovery of industrial activity. Bold and novel experiments on the part of the New Dealers soon began to startle the conservative element. An enormous outpouring of federal money for human relief and immense sums for public-works projects started to flow to all points of the compass. The nation began to think in terms of nine ciphers. Six billion dollars was added to the national debt, thereby offsetting in an incredibly short time the farsighted post-war reduction of that debt by the Coolidge Administration in the years of plenty. A bureaucracy in Washington grew by leaps and bounds, led and manned by the faithful, eager to make history. And finally, to lend the picture the heightened academic touch, John Maynard Keynes, of Cambridge, England, appeared in Washington and again commended the plan of buying Utopia for cash.

Meanwhile the old freedoms, or, if you prefer, the old anarchies, of the business world are in process of restraint. New statutes hedge about the activities of bankers, brokers, industrialists, and all those who direct the use of capital. Even the rights of sovereign States and their individual citizens seem to be somewhat dimmed. The lines of separation of governmental functions have become decidedly hazy. The President is almost a legislator. A bureau chief becomes the judicial interpreter of administrative law. A Supreme Court justice lends his wisdom to the administrative arm. Controls, restrictions, prohibitions, and warning become the order of the day. The American business man, once the symbol of free initiative, awakens to find himself "cribbed, cabined, and confined," shorn of much of his former prestige. If he possesses a sense of humor he must recognize, of course, that the old hand of the old dealers was obviously overplayed. The aberrations of the war markets, the dizzy height of commodity prices just prior to Armistice Day, the fantastic and frantic happenings from 1922 to 1929 explain for him the political earthquake of 1932. He is busy adjusting himself to the new circumstances as he gazed upon a situation where a huge unemployment dominates the necessities of political action, as poverty and distress on the grand scale have to be dealt with daily by the masters of the state.

Yet he finds the practical problem of producing profits at this juncture to be extremely difficult, save where government spending has happily flowed out in his direction. As matters stand today, an industrial or mercantile concern can only find its foreign markets sharply restricted but sees its home market adversely affected by serious drought and by widespread and militant strikes. It must reckon with higher taxes, higher material costs, and higher wages. It must carry on its business in terms of a dollar that is subject to further possible devaluation. It finds the government establishing or fostering competing agencies of business, and it fears further legislation hostile to its interests. On the other hand, the talons of the Blue Eagle look less terrifying since the bluff General Johnson relinquished his efforts to do the impossible. The voluntary cooperation of business developed under the NRA should stand as a permanent national benefit. The attempt at price-fixing will presumably go to the error side of the trial-and-error column. Likewise the attempt to advance wages ahead of the effective demand for goods has revealed its futility, to say nothing of its economic unorthodoxy.

The morale of the business man is, however, shaken as he observes increasingly in the government service, and in command of vastly powerful bureaus, men who are frankly Socialists in their economic faith. For the New Deal turned out to be a tripartite adventure which looked to results far beyond national recovery. It sought a recasting of our social scheme and embodied what is termed a "planned economy." . . .

What could be done to save us from such a calamity? The President alone has the power to give effective encouragement to business at this time. The business and banking community awaits some sincere assurance that there will be less interference by government agencies with the law of supply and demand. It wants to hear that an immediate effort will be made to check the flood of expenditures, thereby insuring an honest purpose to balance the budget.

A more hopeful and even more significant move would be the early inclusion among the President's advisers of more men of high reputation and long experience in the realm of practical affairs. The responsible man of affairs, with capital at risk in enterprise, who has known the alternations of hope and fear and has come to comprehend the significance of those consequences which tie together the periods of peak prosperity and panic decline, has procured an education through experience that has in it the beginnings of wisdom.

William Lloyd Garrison, Jr., "The Hand of Improvidence: What Businessmen Think,"
The Nation 139 (14 November 1934): 562–563. Reprinted with permission from the November 14, 1934 issue of *The Nation*.

To a man of such training, much of the hasty and emotional legislation of the New Deal is not only absurd but hopelessly obstructive to the government's own program of recovery. . . .

The democratic plan of government is not fool proof. It works very badly—panic succeeding prosperity. . . . But a mere transfer from individual monopoly to state monopoly, with its consequent regimentation and fettering of essential freedoms, can effect no cure of the malady. A democracy can be wrecked by bureaucrats, however high-sounding their ideals, who fail to conserve the nation's credit and thereby open wide the door, even if unintentionally, to the destructive forces of anarchy. When the history of our times is written, it is probable that the demoralization of the voters of the country by the distribution of floods of money from the public treasury, coupled with a false philosophy which declares that every man is entitled to be maintained out of the public funds, will be regarded as the most glaring of the political errors of our generation.

Even so, is there not some effective and hopeful means for dealing with our immediate national problems? As affairs now stand, specific recommendations seem well-nigh futile. So general has been the flouting of economic law that "confusion now hath made its masterpiece." The false price and wages levels decreed by the NRA; the disruptive and punitive character of the Securities Act and the Stock Exchange Act, with the consequent starving of the heavy industries; the prentice work of the New Deal surgeons upon the corpus of the public utilities—all suggest that time and reflection must first be permitted to color the thought and action of the Congress, the Cabinet and the Chief Executive.

We may be grateful, however, that some measure of recovery from the depths of depression is evident throughout the world. This tendency should help to carry us gradually, if haltingly, forward.

184

The "Dust Bowl" (1935)

The Great Plains region of Oklahoma, the Texas panhandle, Kansas, Colorado, and New Mexico is known for its sparse rainfall, thin soil, high winds, and expanse of natural prairie grasses. During the late 19th and early 20th centuries, the prairie grasses adequately supported the ranching industry, but during the First World War, farmers, who were enticed by high grain prices and using tractors, plowed up millions of acres of the grass cover to plant wheat. In doing so, they helped create an environmental tragedy. In the mid-1930s, a drought struck the region, and without the natural root system to keep the soil in place, high winds loosened the top soil and swirled it into great dust clouds called "black blizzards." As this article in Literary Digest *made clear to its readers, the continued winds wreaked havoc in what became known as the Dust Bowl. Nearly 60 percent of the area's population was driven out, and many, called Okies, moved to cities on the West Coast.*

Questions to Consider

1. What are the short-term effects of the Dust Bowl? The long-term effects?

2. What helped create this environmental tragedy? What would drought-relief programs do?

3. What does this document reveal about agriculture in the Great Plains in the 1930s?

4. Compare and contrast the description of the Great Plains found here and in "A Native American Remembers the Ghost Dance" (Document 132). Which approach to land use seems more ecologically sound?

Recurrent dry winds continued last week to spread a suffocating pall over more than a dozen States. AAA [Agricultural Adjustment Administration] officials said continuation of the great siege from the air would mean a new drought-relief grant. The Independent Kansas City *Star,* however, minimized the extent of the duststorms and their effect. Kansas City, it said, "sits in a vast empire of green, extending in every direction."

Others reported the sun hidden in several localities. Lands laid bare by the plow in the old cow-country to grow wheat during the War were surrendering top-soil to every breeze. People and animals were finding it difficult to breathe. Housewives were taping their windows to keep out the wind-blown soil, made so fine that it could sift in. Cow-country families were reported fighting their way eastward through the choking pall. Trains, struggling through, were several hours late.

"Noon was like night," said Walter Knudsen, Conductor of the Santa Fe Navajo, when the train reached Chicago six hours behind time. "There was no sun, and, at times, it was impossible to see a yard. The engineer could not see the signal-lights."

R. G. Goetze, Conductor of the Rock Island Colorado Express, which arrived in Chicago two and a half hours late, said, according to the Associated Press, which also had quoted Conductor Knudsen: "There was a heavy coating of dust on the streets when we left Denver. Then it snowed. The mixture put a plaster on the sides of the train."

In several places schools closed, and business was at a standstill. In Memphis, people covered their faces with handkerchiefs. Arkansas was covered by haze of dust. In Texas, birds feared to take wing. Texas State Senators put on surgical-masks. "Point of order," shouted Senator Ben G. Oneal of Wichita Falls, "the Governor is trying to gag the Senate."

The brunt of the storm, reports indicate, fell on Western Kansas, East Colorado and Wyoming, Western Oklahoma, virtually all of Texas, and parts of New Mexico. Dust swirled over Missouri, Iowa, and Arkansas, crossed the Mississippi, and sifted down on Illinois, Indiana, Kentucky, Tennessee, and Louisiana.

"Dust and the Nation's 'Bread-Basket,'" *Literary Digest* 119 (20 April 1935): 10.

Kenneth Welch, relief-administrator in Baca County, Colorado, reported that "dust-pneumonia is rapidly increasing among children." Scores of women and children had been sent out of the country.

Report had it, too, that some live stock had suffocated in Kansas. There was said to be a staggering crop-damage.

Walter Barlow of Amarillo, Texas, a grain-elevator operator, estimated that the wheat-crop damage in the Texas Panhandle was between $18,000,000 and $20,000,000. Harry B. Cordell, President of the Oklahoma State Board of Agriculture, said the last of that State's wheat-planting had virtually been destroyed by dust-storms of the last forty-eight hours. Government reports showed that much land in the nation's "bread-basket" was being abandoned.

Meanwhile, the Government was moving to expand its drought-relief program. Officials were planning to use $150,000,000 of work-relief money. Ten years, said Secretary of Agriculture Henry A. Wallace, would be required to make the program effective. Grass and other cover-crops, and tree-belts, will have to be planted; dams and terraces be constructed.

185

The Tennessee Valley Authority (1937)

Since the mid-1920s, regional planners had advocated a series of dams along the Tennessee River Valley to prevent flooding, enhance river navigation, and generate electrical power in the seven-state region. It was also hoped that the valley's economy, which was one of the poorest in the country, would improve. Progress on this regional plan was slow until Franklin Roosevelt took office. The Tennessee Valley Authority (TVA) was part of the first New Deal and was intended as a massive public works project and experiment in regional planning. Perhaps the TVA's most controversial aspect was this government agency's production and sale of electrical power to customers in the region. Dutch novelist and travel account author Odette Keun visited the Tennessee Valley in 1935 to observe the work of the TVA first hand. Excerpted as follows are comments from her book, A Foreigner Looks at the TVA.

Questions to Consider

1. According to Odette Keun, what did the TVA hope to accomplish?

2. Why did she support the generation and sale of electrical power?

3. Why was she so enthusiastic about the TVA? Was the TVA successful?

4. What do her observations reveal about tensions between government and private enterprise in the New Deal?

Since, according to its constitutional functions with respect to navigation and flood control, the TVA has constructed dams, it has almost limitless falling water at its disposal. Where there is falling water, there is power. Two things can be done with power: let it go to waste, or harness it and utilize it in the form of electricity by putting the water through turbines and generators. It is stupid to the point of being unthinkable that power should be allowed to go to waste when with an often relatively small additional equipment it can be harnessed and put into work in the form of electricity. Besides, it was imperative that the TVA should have some source of revenue. It has received, up to date, about 140 million dollars from the Federal government. But it must become more or less self-supporting, and to a large extent meet the expenses incurred by its activities. Neither its dams, nor its navigation scheme, nor its agricultural program, nor anything else, will bring in money. Quite the opposite: they all represent money that flows out. Only the sale of power is a financial asset. So, spurred on by common sense, economy and the spirit of the times, one of the aspects of which is electrification, Congress, by the Act of 1933 and successive amendments, gave the TVA the following powers:

Authority to dispose of all surplus electricity.

Authority directly to give preference to States, counties, municipalities, cooperative nonprofit organizations of citizens or farmers, and to domestic and rural customers rather than to commercial and industrial consumers.

Authority to construct transmission lines.

Authority to construct and operate rural distribution where farms and small villages are not already served at reasonable rates.

Authority to prescribe, in the power contracts, terms and conditions of resale including resale rates.

Authority to acquire existing electric facilities used in serving farms and small villages.

Authority to make loans to public agencies for the acquisition of existing distribution systems.

Authority to cancel the contracts made with public customers if these public customers practice discrimination against their own customers.

. . . The TVA stands upright for many noble and magnificent things, but for nothing more fervently than the abundant life and the happier social destiny which plentiful and cheap electricity can bring about. The fundamental mechanism for this electrical life is already here, in the dams, the turbines, the generators, the transmission lines, the motors. It is only partially utilized. The TVA holds that it must be fully utilized, and after it has been utilized to the full extent of its present capacity, it must be further developed. It must be

---

Odette Keun, *A Foreigner Looks at the TVA* (New York, 1937), 25–30, 44–45, 88–89. Reprinted by permission of Random House, Inc.

perpetually developed. And as it develops it has to be introduced, on a national scale, by appropriate social and political techniques, into the system of democracy which America represents. This system does not correspond today to the basic American faith in equality and liberty, nor to the natural and technical sciences and the social necessities of our times. To satisfy these imperatives, existing institutions must be adapted to a socialized organization of production and distribution, capable of maintaining secure abundance and of raising the material and cultural welfare of the people. It is important to make this transition as quickly as possible . . .

As I see it, the main points of the TVA's power policy are five. To make America electricity-conscious. To stimulate the electrification of industry. To put electricity and electricity-using appliances in every available home and farm. To reduce the costs of operation and the rates applied to the consumer. To create a market for as wide and cheap a consumption of electricity as possible. These points lend themselves to a lot of considerations . . .

. . . Enough has been said already . . . to prove that the TVA is a modern expression and practice of the *conservation movement.* The assumptions which form the basis of that movement are that the national resources of a country—minerals, soil, forests, waters—are not the possession of one generation alone but the inheritance of all the future generations of the people to whom that country belongs. Such a conception has just begun to dawn upon Americans, fascinated too long by the epic of the settler, the pioneer and the frontiersman who bequeathed to their descendants, together with heroic qualities of courage and self-reliance, a great deal of the philosophy of the brigand. The body of this land has been racked and torn and plundered, and in parts murdered by its children as mercilessly as by any foreign invader. It is a matter of vital national importance to preserve what is left, to heal it if possible, and to develop it wisely: quite as vital as to defend America against any enemy from overseas. The freedom of a nation is founded just as much upon its economy, which includes natural resources, as upon its armies. The TVA is doing invaluable work for the United States in checking floods and soil-erosion, promoting irrigation, planning the systematic use of rivers, husbanding the water-table. I hope I've shown that. But there is still another aspect of its water program which I want to mention. America has been pillaged by a lot of brutal and rapacious Americans, certainly, but she is also being depleted of the natural resources which are the origin of energy, by time itself. The whole world is being depleted in this manner, and a running-down process is perceptible everywhere. Everywhere, the products of the earth which are the origin of energy, coal, wood, oil, minerals, phosphates, are being exhausted. These materials are either non-replenishable or replenishable only over a period of so many centuries that it is essential to employ them with great foresight, prudence, and care. Only one source of energy is very easily replenishable, and that is falling water, for water is being ceaselessly restored to the world by the hydrologic cycle—the action of the sun which draws it up from the surface and lets it fall abundantly again. . . .

The Tennessee Valley Authority is laying it down. Handicapped and restricted though it is in all sorts of ways, it is the noblest, the most intelligent, and the best attempt made in this country or in any other democratic country, to economize, marshal and integrate the actual assets of a region, plan its development and future, ameliorate its standards of living, establish it in a more enduring security, and render available to the people the benefits of the wealth of their district, and the results of science, discovery, invention, and disinterested forethought. In its inspiration and its goal there is goodness, for goodness is that which makes for unity of purpose with love, compassion and respect for every life and every pattern of living. The economic machine, bad though it is, has not been smashed in the Tennessee Watershed; it is being very gradually, very carefully, very equitably reviewed and amended, and the citizens are being taught and directed, but not bullied, not coerced, not regimented, not frightened, within the constitutional frame the nation itself elected to build.

186

Frances Perkins Endorses
the Social Security Act (1935)

The Social Security Act (1935) was passed as part of the second New Deal, and it became the most significant social program in America. Franklin Roosevelt called it the "supreme achievement" of the New Deal, and it remains as an enduring legacy. The act represented a break with previous American practices of voluntarism and individualism and placed protection of all citizens—with old age insurance, unemployment compensation, disability pensions, and aid to dependents—under the government's auspices. Aware that Americans were traditionally suspicious of government social programs, an effort was made to inform the public about Social Security. In a national radio broadcast celebrating Labor Day 1935, Secretary of Labor Frances Perkins, the first woman to hold a cabinet position, took the opportunity to explain and to endorse the Social Security Act. Excerpted as follows is her address.

Questions to Consider

1. What is the purpose of Social Security? Who was to benefit?
2. What was the historical context for the Social Security Act?
3. In what ways does this act change the function of the federal government?
4. Was the passage of Social Security a positive development?

People who work for a living in the United States of America can join with all other good citizens on this forty-eighth anniversary of Labor Day in satisfaction that the Congress has passed the Social Security Act. This act establishes unemployment insurance as a substitute for haphazard methods of assistance in periods when men and women willing and able to work are without jobs. It provides for old aged pensions which mark great progress over the measures upon which we have hitherto depended in caring for those who have been unable to provide for the years when they no longer can work. It also provides security for dependent and crippled children, mothers, the indigent disabled and the blind.

Old people who are in need, unemployable, children, mothers and the sightless, will find systematic regular provisions for needs. The Act limits the Federal aid to not more that $15 per month in special cases and there is no requirement to allow as much as $15 from either State or Federal funds when a particular case has some personal provision and needs less than the total allowed.

Following essentially the same procedure, the Act as passed provides for Federal assistance to the States in caring for the blind, a contribution by the State of up to $15 a month to be matched in turn by a like contribution by the Federal Government. The Act also contains provision for assistance to the States in providing payments to dependent children under sixteen years of age. There also is provision in the Act for cooperation with medical and health organizations charged with rehabilitation of physically handicapped children. The necessity for adequate service in the fields of public and maternal health and child welfare calls for the extension of these services to meet individual community needs.

Consider for a moment those portions of the Act which, while they will not be effective this present year, yet will exert a profound and far-reaching effect upon millions of citizens. I refer to the provision for a system of old-age benefits supported by the contributions of employer and employees, and to the section which sets up the initial machinery for unemployment insurance.

Old-age benefits in the form of monthly payments are to be paid to individuals who have worked and contributed to the insurance fund in direct proportion to the total wages earned by such individuals in the course of their employment subsequent to 1936. The minimum monthly payment is to be $20, the maximum $85. These payments will begin in the year 1942 and will be to those who have worked and contributed. . . .

With the States rests now the responsibility of devising and enacting measures which will result in the maximum benefits to the American workman in the field of unemployment compensation. I am confident that impending State action will not fail to take cognizance of this responsibility. The people of the different States favor the program designed to bring them greater security in the future and their legislatures will speedily pass appropriate laws so that all may help to promote the general welfare.

Federal legislation was framed in the thought that the attack upon the problems of insecurity should be a cooperative venture participated in by both the Federal and State Governments, preserving the benefits of local

Frances Perkins, "The Social Security Act," *Vital Speeches of the Day* 1 (September 1935): 792–794.

administration and national leadership. It was thought unwise to have the Federal Government decide all questions of policy and dictate completely what the States should do. Only very necessary minimum standards are included in the Federal measure leaving wide latitude to the States. . . .

Our social security program will be a vital force working against the recurrence of severe depressions in the future. We can, as the principle of sustained purchasing power in hard times makes itself felt in every shop, store and mill, grow old without being haunted by the spectre of a poverty-ridden old age or of being a burden on our children.

The costs of unemployment compensation and old-age insurance are not actually additional costs. In some degree they have long been borne by the people, but irregularly, the burden falling much more heavily on some than on others, and none of such provisions offering an orderly or systematic assurance to those in need. The years of depression have brought home to all of us that unemployment entails huge costs to government, industry and the public alike.

Unemployment insurance will within a short time considerably lighten the public burden of caring for those unemployed. It will materially reduce relief costs in future years. In essence, it is a method by which reserves are built up during periods of employment from which compensation is paid to the unemployed in periods when work is lacking.

The passage of this act with so few dissenting votes and with so much intelligent public support is deeply significant of the progress which the American people have made in thought in the social field and awareness of methods of using cooperation through government to overcome social hazards against which the individual alone is adequate. . . .

187

Perspectives on the New Deal

Franklin D. Roosevelt's administration developed the New Deal to address the problems caused by the Great Depression. Some of the New Deal's innovative programs came from a group of college professor advisors known as the "brains trust," whereas other efforts revitalized Progressive-era proposals or expanded existing programs. Roosevelt experimented with a variety of New Deal programs, advancing some initiatives while abandoning those that did not stimulate the economy. The New Deal changed the role of the federal government, as new legislation and government agencies enlarged the size and regulatory scope of the government. Some Americans were alarmed at the growth of the government and its intrusion into everyday life, whereas others were troubled by the increasing debt and cost of government. In the first cartoon, Clifford Barryman of the Washington (DC) Evening Star *depicted Roosevelt's attitude toward the early New Deal programs. In the second cartoon, "Steve" Schilder used the 1937 dust storms to raise concerns about the New Deal.*

Questions to Consider

1. Compare and contrast these two images' view of the New Deal? Which do you think is more accurate?

2. What can you deduce from the first image about the growth of government bureaucracy resulting from the New Deal? Do conditions warrant such changes?

3. What can you deduce from the second image about the growth of taxes resulting from the New Deal? Do conditions warrant such changes?

4. Based on your consideration of these two images, to what extent would you regard the New Deal as an experiment?

Clifford Berryman for *The Evening Star* (Washington D.C.), April 26, 1934, p. 1. © 1934, *The Washington Post.* Reprinted with permission.

"It is Evolution, Not Revolution, Gentlemen"

Library of Congress, Prints and Photographs Division, LC-USZ62-95108 24-31

"Speaking of Dust Storms" by "Steve" Schilder (1937)

25

✳

Isolationism and World War II

By the late 1930s, the attention of the United States increasingly turned overseas. In both Europe and East Asia, states eager to seize territory and add to national glory had threatened the peace. America remained divided over whether it should become involved until being pulled into both European and Pacific theaters late in 1941 with the Japanese surprise attack at Pearl Harbor, Hawaii. The war forever changed American society. On the homefront, women replaced men in many occupations; on the battlefront, the skills of modern science were applied to create tools of massive destruction. The overwhelming majority of Americans heartily supported the war effort, even though thousands of their fellow citizens were deprived of their civil liberties. The following descriptions reveal some of the major issues and events of the war years.

188

The Four Freedoms (1941)

When the Second World War began in Europe, most Americans believed that a German victory would not threaten the United States, and so many supported the continued practice of diplomatic isolation. By mid-1940, German forces had swept across the continent, quickly conquering most of Europe and leaving Great Britain as the only country fighting the Nazis. It became evident that the United States was the only industrial power capable of producing enough war materiel to stop the Nazi war machine. When British officials requested ships, munitions, and other assistance to fight the Germans, the Roosevelt administration provided some war materiel under the strict cash-and-carry terms of the Neutrality Acts, but this response was not enough. Shortly after Franklin Roosevelt won an unprecedented third election in 1940, Great Britain informed the American president that they were nearly bankrupt and could not afford to purchase supplies to fight Germany. Although some Americans opposed providing any direct assistance to Great Britain, public opinion was shifting away from strict isolation. Roosevelt used his State of the Union address in early January 1941 to suggest a new American policy. His speech is excerpted as follows.

Questions to Consider

1. What does Roosevelt propose that America should do?

2. Why does he suggest this commitment?

3. What does Roosevelt hope to accomplish?

4. What is threatened by American inaction? Why?

. . . The need of the moment is that our actions and our policy should be devoted primarily—almost exclusively—to meeting this foreign peril. For all our domestic problems are now a part of the great emergency.

Just as our national policy in internal affairs has been based upon a decent respect for the rights and the dignity of all our fellow men within our gates, so our national policy in foreign affairs has been based on a decent respect for the rights and dignity of all nations, large and small. And the justice of morality must and will win in the end. . . .

I also ask this Congress for authority and for funds sufficient to manufacture additional munitions and war supplies of many kinds, to be turned over to those nations which are now in actual war with aggressor nations.

Our most useful and immediate role is to act as an arsenal for them as well as for ourselves. They do not need man power, but they do need billions of dollars worth of the weapons of defense. . . .

Let us say to the democracies: "We Americans are vitally concerned in your defense of freedom. We are putting forth our energies, our resources and our organizing powers to give you the strength to regain and maintain a free world. We shall send you, in ever-increasing numbers, ships, planes, tanks, guns. This is our purpose and our pledge." . . .

The happiness of future generations of Americans may well depend upon how effective and how immediate we can make our aid felt. No one can tell the exact character of the emergency situations that we may be called upon to meet. The Nation's hands must not be tied when the Nation's life is in danger.

We must all prepare to make the sacrifices that the emergency—almost as serious as war itself—demands. Whatever stands in the way of speed and efficiency in defense preparations must give way to the national need. . . .

For there is nothing mysterious about the foundations of a healthy and strong democracy. The basic things expected by our people of their political and economic systems are simple. They are:

Equality of opportunity for youth and for others.

Jobs for those who can work.

Security for those who need it.

The ending of special privilege for the few.

"State of the Union Address, January 1941," *Public Papers and Addresses of Franklin D. Roosevelt*, Vol. 9: *War – And Aid to Democracies*, comp. Samuel I. Rosenman (London, 1941), 663–672.

The preservation of civil liberties for all.

The enjoyment of the fruits of scientific progress in a wider and constantly rising standard of living.

These are the simple, basic things that must never be lost sight of in the turmoil and unbelievable complexity of our modern world. The inner and abiding strength of our economic and political systems is dependent upon the degree to which they fulfill these expectations.

Many subjects connected with our social economy call for immediate improvement.

As examples:

We should bring more citizens under the coverage of old-age pensions and unemployment insurance.

We should widen the opportunities for adequate medical care.

We should plan a better system by which persons deserving or needing gainful employment may obtain it.

I have called for personal sacrifice. I am assured of the willingness of almost all Americans to respond to that call. . . .

In the future days, which we seek to make secure, we look forward to a world founded upon four essential human freedoms.

The first is freedom of speech and expression—everywhere in the world.

The second is freedom of every person to worship God in his own way—everywhere in the world.

The third is freedom from want—which, translated into world terms, means economic understandings which will secure to every nation a healthy peacetime life for its inhabitants—everywhere in the world.

The fourth is freedom from fear—which, translated into world terms, means a world-wide reduction of armaments to such a point and in such a thorough fashion that no nation will be in a position to commit an act of physical aggression against any neighbor—anywhere in the world.

That is no vision of a distant millennium. It is a definite basis for a kind of world attainable in our own time and generation. That kind of world is the very antithesis of the so-called new order of tyranny which the dictators seek to create with the crash of a bomb.

To that new order we oppose the greater conception—the moral order. A good society is able to face schemes of world domination and foreign revolutions alike without fear.

Since the beginning of our American history, we have been engaged in change—in a perpetual peaceful revolution—a revolution which goes on steadily, quietly adjusting itself to changing conditions—without the concentration camp or the quick-lime in the ditch. The world order which we seek is the cooperation of free countries, working together in a friendly, civilized society.

This nation has placed its destiny in the hands and heads and hearts of its millions of free men and women; and its faith in freedom under the guidance of God. Freedom means the supremacy of human rights everywhere. Our support goes to those who struggle to gain those rights or keep them. Our strength is our unity of purpose.

To that high concept there can be no end save victory.

189

Isolation from the European War (1941)

When Europe erupted in war with Germany's invasion of Poland in September 1939, America, fearfully isolationist since the previous war, proclaimed neutrality. But when Germany swept over Europe, leaving Great Britain fighting alone, a growing number of Americans came to believe that the United States should support Britain's battle, provided America did not wage war. Capitalizing on this shifting mood, President Franklin Roosevelt described the country as "the great arsenal of democracy" and proposed that Great Britain have unlimited access to American supplies. Congress complied with the Lend-Lease Act (1941), providing aid to Great Britain and drawing America closer to war. Opposed to the possible American intervention into the war, the America First Committee, comprising some prominent midwestern businessmen and politicians, was organized in July 1940. Within one year, it claimed 450 chapters nationwide and a membership of several hundred thousand. National hero and aviator Charles A. Lindbergh was America First's most famous spokesman. One month after the passage of the Lend-Lease Act, Lindbergh addressed the New York chapter of the America First Committee. His speech, explaining the committee's position, was broadcast over the radio to a national audience.

Questions to Consider

1. What were Charles Lindbergh's reasons to oppose American intervention in this war?
2. What does Lindbergh hope to accomplish?
3. Did American citizens support the views of the America First Committee?
4. Is military preparedness a deterrent to war?

I know I will be severely criticized by the interventionists in America when I say we should not enter a war unless we have a reasonable chance of winning. That, they will claim, is far too materialistic a standpoint. . . . But I do

---

Charles Lindbergh, "We Cannot Win This War for England," *Vital Speeches of the Day* 7 (May 1941): 424–426.

not believe that our American ideals, and our way of life, will gain through an unsuccessful war. And I know that the United States is not prepared to wage war in Europe successfully at this time. . . .

I have said before, and I will say again, that I believe it will be a tragedy to the entire world if the British Empire collapses. That is one of the main reasons why I opposed this war before it was declared, and why I have constantly advocated a negotiated peace. I did not feel that England and France had a reasonable chance of winning. France has now been defeated; and . . . it is now obvious that England is losing a war. I believe this is realized even by the British Government. But they have one last desperate plan remaining. They hope that they may be able to persuade us to send another American Expeditionary Force to Europe and to share with England militarily, as well as financially, the fiasco of this war.

I do not blame England for this hope, or for asking for our assistance. . . .

. . . But we in this country have a right to think of the welfare of America first, just as the people in England thought first of their own country when they encouraged the smaller nations of Europe to fight against hopeless odds. When England asks us to enter this war, she is considering her own future, and that of her empire. In making our reply, I believe we should consider the future of the United States and that of the Western Hemisphere.

It is not only our right, but it is our obligation as American citizens to look at this war objectively and to weigh our chances for success if we should enter it. I have attempted to do this, especially from the standpoint of aviation; and I have been forced to the conclusion that we cannot win this war for England, regardless of how much assistance we send. . . .

. . . There is a policy open to this nation that will lead to success—a policy that leaves us free to allow our own way of life, and to develop our own civilization. It is not a new and untried idea. It was advocated by Washington. It was incorporated in the Monroe Doctrine. Under its guidance, the United States has become the greatest nation in the world.

It is based upon the belief that the security of a nation lies in the strength and character of its own people. It recommends the maintenance of armed forces sufficient to defend this hemisphere from attack by any combination of foreign powers. It demands faith in an independent American destiny. This is the policy of the America First Committee today. It is a policy not of isolation, but of independence; not of defeat, but of courage. It is policy that led this nation to success during the most trying years of our history, and it is a policy that will lead us to success again.

We have weakened ourselves for many months, and still worse, we have divided our own people by this dabbling in Europe's wars. While we should have been concentrating on American defense we have been forced to argue over foreign quarrels. We must turn our eyes and our faith back to our own country before it is too late. . . .

The United States is better situated from a military standpoint than any other nation in the world. Even in our present condition of unpreparedness no foreign power is in a position to invade us today. If we concentrate on our own defenses and build the strength that this nation should maintain, no foreign army will ever attempt to land on American shores.

War is not inevitable for this country. Such a claim is defeatism in the true sense. No one can make us fight abroad unless we ourselves are willing to do so. No one will attempt to fight us here if we arm ourselves as a great nation should be armed. Over a hundred million people in this nation are opposed to entering the war. If the principles of democracy mean anything at all, that is reason enough for us to stay out. If we are forced into a war against the wishes of an overwhelming majority of our people, we will have proved democracy such a failure at home that there will be little use fighting for it abroad.

The time has come when those of us who believe in an independent American destiny must band together and organize for strength. . . .

. . . These people—the majority of hardworking American citizens, are with us. They are the true strength of our country. And they are beginning to realize as you and I, that there are times when we must sacrifice our normal interests in life in order to insure the safety and the welfare of our nation. . . .

If you believe in an independent destiny for America, if you believe that this country should not enter the war in Europe, we ask you to join the America First Committee in its stand. We ask you to share our faith in the ability of this nation to defend itself, to develop its own civilization, and to contribute to the progress of mankind in a more constructive and intelligent way than has yet been found by the warring nations of Europe. We need your support, and we need it now. The time to act is here. I thank you.

190

Roosevelt's Declaration of War Message (1941)

For nearly a decade, the Japanese had been expanding into China while the United States worked to thwart the encroachment. Tensions between the two countries remained high, as negotiations either failed or were dismissed. When Japan imperialistically sought to consolidate all of East Asia under its domain in 1941, the United States responded with diplomatic pressure and economic embargoes on goods vital to the Japanese economy. Japanese leaders concluded that to preserve their empire they must fight the United States soon, so preparations were made to attack Pearl Harbor, Hawaii, and expand further in Asia. The United States had broken Japan's diplomatic secret code and knew that some attack was imminent, but the location was not known. American leaders guessed the attack would come in Southeast Asia (possibly Malaya), so only general warnings were sent to forces at Pearl Harbor. On Sunday morning, December 7, 1941, Japanese planes struck American forces at Pearl Harbor in two separate waves, crippling the Pacific fleet and killing more than 2,000 Americans. The next day, President Franklin Roosevelt gave the following speech to a joint session of Congress.

Questions to Consider

1. In what manner does Roosevelt characterize the actions of the Japanese?
2. Why does he offer a listing of locations where the Japanese have attacked?
3. How will the United States make "certain that this form of treachery shall never again endanger us"?
4. To what extent does Roosevelt's war message reflect the values expressed in "The Four Freedoms" (Document 188)?

Mr. Vice President, Mr. Speaker, members of the Senate and the House of Representatives:

Yesterday, Dec. 7, 1941—a date which will live in infamy—the United States of America was suddenly and deliberately attacked by naval and air forces of the empire of Japan.

The United States was at peace with that nation, and, at the solicitation of Japan, was still in conversation with its government and its Emperor looking toward the maintenance of peace in the Pacific.

Indeed, one hour after Japanese air squadrons had commenced bombing in the American island of Oahu the Japanese Ambassador to the United States and his colleague delivered to our Secretary of State a formal reply to a recent American message. And, while this reply stated that it seemed useless to continue the existing diplomatic negotiations, it contained no threat or hint of war or of armed attack.

It will be recorded that the distance of Hawaii from Japan makes it obvious that the attack was deliberately planned many days or even weeks ago. During the intervening time the Japanese Government has deliberately sought to deceive the United States by false statements and expressions of hope for continued peace.

The attack yesterday on the Hawaiian Islands has caused severe damage to American naval and military forces. I regret to tell you that very many American lives have been lost. In addition, American ships have been reported torpedoed on the high seas between San Francisco and Honolulu.

Yesterday the Japanese Government also launched an attack against Malaya.

Last night Japanese forces attacked Hong Kong.

Last night Japanese forces attacked Guam.

Last night Japanese forces attacked the Philippine Islands.

Last night Japanese attacked Wake Island.

And this morning the Japanese attacked Midway Island.

Japan has therefore undertaken a surprise offensive extending throughout the Pacific area. The facts of yesterday and today speak for themselves. The people of the United States have already formed their opinions and well understand the implications to the very life and safety of our nation.

"The President's Message," *New York Times*, December 9, 1941, pp. 1, 6.

As Commander in Chief of the Army and Navy, I have directed that all measures be taken for our defense, that always will our whole nation remember the character of the onslaught against us.

No matter how long it may take us to overcome this premeditated invasion, the American people, in their righteous might, will win through to absolute victory.

I believe that I interpret the will of the Congress and of the people when I assert that we will not only defend ourselves to the uttermost but will make it very certain that this form of treachery shall never again endanger us.

Hostilities exist. There is no blinking at the fact that our people, our territory and our interests are in grave danger.

With confidence in our armed forces, with the unbounding determination of our people, we will gain the inevitable triumph. So help us God.

I ask that the Congress declare that since the unprovoked and dastardly attack by Japan on Sunday, Dec. 7, 1941, a state of war has existed between the United States and the Japanese Empire.

191

Life in a Japanese Internment Camp (1942)

As World War II began, there were more than 100,000 people of Japanese descent living in the country, mainly along the West Coast. After the surprise attack on Pearl Harbor, rumors spread that Japanese in America would hinder the war effort through "fifth column" (espionage or sabotage) actions. Reacting to old suspicions, ignorant fears, and racial prejudice toward all Asians, the federal government ordered Japanese Americans—regardless of loyalty or American citizenship—to abandon their homes and businesses and be placed in "Relocation Centers." Nearly 110,000 people were incarcerated in centers that resembled concentration camps: They were located in remote areas and had armed guards, barbed-wire fencing, communal living arrangements in wooden barracks, and poor food. Among those relocated was Charles Kikuchi, an American-born child (Nisei) of Japanese immigrants (Issei), who kept a diary of his internment at Tanforan, a temporary assembly area in southern California. Kikuchi's diary, excerpted as follows, reveals the tensions of life in the camp as well as his own torn loyalties between his family and Japanese ancestry and his American citizenship.

Questions to Consider

1. Why does Charles Kikuchi believe the internment will be harmful to Japanese Americans? Where were Kikuchi's loyalties?

2. Why could Kikuchi see humor in some Americans' reaction to internment, yet be fearful of nativist groups like the Native Sons of the Golden West?

3. What does Kikuchi's diary reveal about the situation of Japanese Americans during World War II?

4. Were the relocation camps necessary?

S.F. Japanese Town certainly looks like a ghost town. All the stores are closed and the windows are bare except for a mass of "evacuation sale" signs. The junk dealers are having a roman holiday, since they can have their cake and eat it too. It works like this! They buy cheap from the Japanese leaving and sell dearly to the Okies coming in for defense work. Result, good profit. . . .

APRIL 30, 1942, BERKELEY   Today is the day that we are going to get kicked out of Berkeley. It certainly is degrading. I am down here in the control station, and I have nothing to do so I am jotting down these notes! The Army Lieutenant over there doesn't want any of the photographers to take pictures of these miserable people waiting for the Greyhound bus because he thinks that the American public might get a sympathetic attitude towards them.

I'm supposed to see my family at Tanforan as Jack told me to give the same family number. I wonder how it is going to be living with them as I haven't done this for years and years? I should have gone over to San Francisco and evacuated with them, but I had a last final to take. I understand that we are going to live in the horse stalls. I hope that the army has the courtesy to remove the manure first.

This morning I went over to the bank to close my account and the bank teller whom I have never seen before solemnly shook my hand and said, "Goodbye, have a nice time." I wonder if that isn't the attitude of the American people? They don't seem to be bitter against us, and I certainly don't think I am any different from them. . . .

MAY 3, 1942, SUNDAY   A lot of Nisei kids come in and mix their Japanese in with their English. Now that we are cut off from the Caucasian contacts, there will be a greater tendency to speak more and more Japanese unless we carefully guard against it. Someday these Nisei will once again go out into the greater American society and it is so important that they be able to speak English well—that's why education is so important. I still think it is a big mistake to evacuate *all* the Japanese. Segregation is the least desirable thing that could happen and it certainly is going to increase the problem of future social adjustments. How can we expect to develop Americanization when they are all put together with the stigma of disloyalty pointed at them? I am convinced that the Nisei could become good Americans, and will be, if they are not treated with much suspicion. The presence here of all those pro-Japan Issei certainly will not help things out any. . . .

There was a terrific rainstorm last night and we have had to wade through the "slush alleys" again. Everyone sinks up to the ankles in mud. Some trucks came in today with lumber to build new barracks, but the earth was so soft

Charles Kikuchi, *The Kikuchi Diary: Chronicle from an American Concentration Camp; The Tanforan Journals of Charles Kikuchi*, ed. John Modell (Urbana, IL, 1973), 51–52, 66, 73, 170, 229. Copyright © 1973 by the Board of Trustees of the University of Illinois. Used with permission of the University of Illinois Press.

that the truck sank over the hubs and they had a hell of a time pulling it out. The Army certainly is rushing things. About half of the Japanese have already been evacuated from the restricted areas in this state. Manzanar, Santa Anita, and Tanforan will be the three biggest centers. Now that S.F. has been almost cleared, the American Legion, the Native Sons of the Golden West, and the California Joint Immigration Committee are filing charges that the Nisei should be disfranchised because we have obtained citizenship under false pretenses and that "we are loyal subjects of Japan" and therefore should never have been allowed to obtain citizenship. This sort of thing will gain momentum and we are not in a very advantageous position to combat it. I get fearful sometimes because this sort of hysteria will gain momentum. . . . I think that they are stabbing us in the back and that there should be a separate concentration camp for these so-called Americans. They are a lot more dangerous than the Japanese in the U.S. ever will or have been. . . .

JULY 8, 1942 . . . I keep saying to myself that I must view everything intellectually and rationally, but sometimes I feel sentiments compounded of blind feelings and irrationality. Here all of my life I have identified my every act with America but when the war broke out I suddenly find that I won't be allowed to become an integral part of the whole in these times of national danger. I find I am put aside and viewed suspiciously. My set of values gets twisted; I don't know what to think. Yes, an American certainly is a queer thing. I know what I want, I think, yet it looks beyond my reach at times, but I won't accept defeat. Americanism is my only solution and I may even get frantic about it if thwarted. To retain my loyalty to my country, I must also retain my family loyalty or what else do I have to build upon? So I can't be selfish and individualistic to such a strong degree. I must view it from either angle and abide by the majority decision. If I am to be in a camp for the duration, I may as well have the stabilizing influence of the family. . . .

. . . There are so many interesting people in camp. They are Americans! Sometimes they may say things that arise out of their bewildered feelings, but they can't throw off the environmental effects of the American way of life which is ingrained in them. The injustices of evacuation will some day come to light. It is a blot upon our national life—like the Negro problem, the way labor gets kicked around, the unequal distribution of wealth, the sad plight of the farmers, the slums of our large cities, and a multitude of things. It would make me dizzy just to think about them now.

192

Women in the Homefront War Effort (1942)

World War II altered the economic status for many American women. As millions of men entered military service and the demand for labor increased dramatically, old stereotypes and barriers preventing women from entering the industrial workplace and the military were relaxed. Several hundred thousand women enlisted in the female ver-sions of the military (Army's WACS, Navy's WAVES, Women Marines, Coast Guard's SPARS), but the most significant change came when more than 6 million women joined the workforce. Most women found work in the defense industries, mainly building ships and airplanes, but some accepted employment in arduous occupa-tions—toolmaker, blacksmith, machinist, lumberjack—often reserved for men. A gov-ernment campaign to encourage hiring women made "Rosie the Riveter" a symbol for those in war work. By 1945, more than 50 percent of all employed workers in Amer-ica were women. Excerpted following is a 1942 Ladies' Home Journal *article des-cribing the new world of work for four women.*

Questions to Consider

1. According to the article, are the work opportunities for women limited because of gender?
2. What is the attitude of the women toward their work?
3. In what ways does the article suggest that the women retain their femi-ninity even though they work on the assembly line?
4. How do you think Betty Friedan, author of "The Problem that has No Name" (Document 205), would respond to this selection?

Marjory Kurtz, just 20, was a $15-a-week secretary in Absecon, N.J. Now she works in the Martin plant stock rooms.

Virginia Drummond, 30, ran a beauty shop in Punxsutawney, Pa. Today she wields an electric drill on the bomber assembly line.

Tommy Joseph, 24, of Clanton, Ala., wife of a young Army lieutenant in the Pacific, now drills bulkhead webs for Army planes.

Margaret Kennedy, 22, a Lancaster, Pa., schoolteacher till January, now works the midnight shift at the Glenn Martin plant.

When brisk Ginny Drummond and her covergirl roommate of the silky black hair and gentian-blue eyes, Tommy Joseph, sink dog-tired into bed these evenings, often as not a lively jive party is just starting in the adjoining room. Getting eight hours' sleep a night to bolster aching arms and feet for another eight hours' stand on the Glenn Martin aircraft-assembly line is practically impossible when four girls, sharing the same cramped one-bedroom apart-ment on Baltimore's sweltering Mt. Royal Avenue, keep working hours that stretch right around the clock.

Ginny and Tommy work six days in seven from 8:45 A.M. to 4:15 P.M. Their two other roommates, twenty-year-old Marge, daughter of a small-town mayor, and ex-schoolteacher Margaret Kennedy, are on the midnight shift, from 12:30 to 8:15 A.M. While waiting until it's time to leave for the

"This Changing World for Women," by Ruth Matthews and Betty Hannah, *Ladies' Home Journal* 59 (August 1942): 27–30. © Copyright 1942, Meredith Corporation. Used with the permission of *Ladies' Home Journal.*

plant, they try to subdue their chatter for the benefit of the two–day shift girls sharing the same lumpy bed in the next room. But long before the doorbell starts its nerve-shattering jangle over the bedroom door, and friends crash upstairs to drive Marge and Kennedy to work, the two sleepers are thoroughly awake.

"Daylight" nights pose even a greater problem for Marge and Kennedy. By the time these two are back, at 9:30 the following morning, the double bed is invitingly made up again, albeit with the same sheets. But by then the sun is warm and bright, and dawdling on the white front stoop is an irresistible temptation. All too often it's late afternoon before Marge and Kennedy drop into bed. By seven the apartment is filled with the rich odors of Ginny's cooking, and by the time everyone has eaten and the dishes are washed, a hoard of swains has arrived to keep them chattering and jiving way past the day shift's ten-o'clock bedtime. . . .

"You'll do a man's job and you'll get a man's paycheck," Glenn L. Martin tells his 4000 women employees, "but you'll be treated as the men are treated."

This means a full six-day week, taking the night shift when so assigned and, in the case of Tommy and Ginny, spending the forthcoming Thanksgiving, Christmas and New Year's holidays amid the terrific hubbub of hammers, cranes and electric drills.

Eighty per cent of the women at Martin are on the "small parts" assembly line, with a handful skilled enough to do the highly paid final installation jobs. From 3 to 5 per cent are engineers and inspectors. In aircraft manufacture for the United States as a whole, fewer than 2 per cent of the workers are women, compared with 40 to 80 per cent in some aircraft plants in Great Britain. But as more and more men are being taken into the armed forces, opportunities for women are booming. At least 2,000,000 women who have never drawn any kind of pay check in their lives—schoolgirls and housewives—will be in factories within the next year or two. They must be, if the war of production is to go forward.

Most Martin workers are between eighteen and twenty-four, although a few are over forty. Tommy, Ginny, Marge and Kennedy started off at the usual beginner's pay of 60 cents an hour with a guarantee of 75 cents an hour within three months. Already the older girls are doing skilled work such as drilling on bulkhead webs—part of the frame of a plane—and, with two raises, now net $32.67 a week. Marge and Kennedy are in the stock rooms. Although they both proudly wear bright nail polish, their hands are red and sore from handing out countless nuts, screws and bolts. (A Martin bomber has nearly 50,000 small parts, and each is nearly as important as a wing or propeller when a bomber goes into action.) They are now earning around $28 a week: "when we think what we used to make, that sure isn't hay."

An assembly-line worker has to buy her own tools, including electric hand drills, an investment that runs to about $30 cash if she's properly equipped. Tommy and Ginny say there are tools in their work kit they still don't know how to use—but they will before they're through at Martin: "There's no chance to get fed up with any particular job. The minute you've mastered one, they switch you to something harder."

Nobody at Martin has any doubt about the outcome of this war. When they watch those sleek-winged bombers line up, row on row, they feel they're helping to win it right now. . . .

And when the war is over? Some of the girls, and certainly the men they work beside, wonder just what all these women are going to do when the boys come home. Some, of course, will quit to get married. But not all of them will have husbands, because some of these boys aren't coming back. Tommy has faced that stark possibility with grim and self-searching courage. She, like many other of the women workers, may go on to a big supervisory job in aircraft production. As for the younger girls, "When the war's over we'll probably go home again and wash dishes."

"We'd better," Ginny advises with a wry smile. "It's the only way we'll ever get our hands clean again."

193

The Second World War Homefront (1941–45)

With America's entrance into World War II, there was a need to mobilize the economy for wartime production, to train men and women for military duty, and to maintain homefront support for the war effort. As in the First World War, the federal government began a media campaign to encourage women to take jobs in industry, to encourage a relaxation of racial tensions, and to call for patriotic support and personal sacrifice. Part of this publicity effort was the use of posters. Following are three posters that sought to muster public support for the war effort.

Questions to Consider

1. What can you deduce about gender roles during the 1940s from the first image?

2. What is the intent of the second image? How accurate is its portrayal of race relations?

3. Why is the third image comparing homefront sacrifice with that experienced by soldiers at the front?

4. What can you deduce about public support for the Second World War from these images?

Produced by Westinghouse for the War Production Co-Ordinating Committee. NARA Still Picture Branch, NWDNS-179-WP-1563

"We Can Do It!"
by J. Howard Miller.

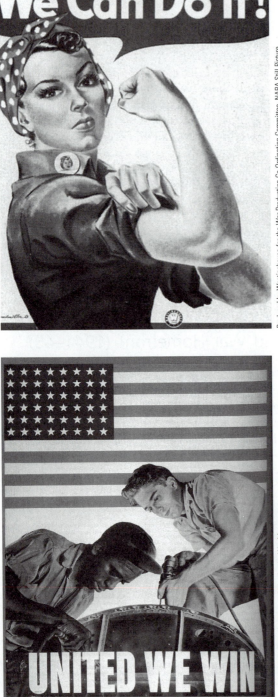

Printed by the Government Printing Office for the War Manpower Commission, NARA Still Picture Branch, NWDNS-44-PA-370

"United We Win"
Photograph by Alexander
Liberman (1943).

"You Talk of Sacrifice"

194

Truman's Decision to Drop the Bomb (1945)

At the behest of several refugee physicists from Europe who feared that Germany might develop an atomic bomb, President Franklin Roosevelt established the ultra-secret Manhattan Project to build a nuclear weapon for the United States. Racing against time, a team of physicists under the direction of J. Robert Oppenheimer produced a working bomb in the summer of 1945. But Germany had already surrendered, and Roosevelt had died three months earlier. The new inexperienced president,

Harry S Truman, who was completely uninformed about the bomb until he entered the White House, faced the decision of its use against Japan to both end the war and arrange the peace. Excerpted as follows is Truman's account of how he determined to use the atomic weapon.

Questions to Consider

1. According to Harry Truman, what did the advisory committee recommend?
2. What were Truman's alternatives to dropping the atomic bomb?
3. Was dropping the bomb needed to end the war? How did the bomb affect foreign relations after the war?
4. How do you think Charles Kikuchi, author of "Life in a Japanese Internment Camp" (Document 191), felt about President Truman's decision?

Stimson was one of the very few men responsible for the setting up of the atomic bomb project. He had taken a keen and active interest in every stage of its development. He said he wanted specifically to talk to me today about the effect the atomic bomb might likely have on our future foreign relations.

He explained that he thought it necessary for him to share his thoughts with me about the revolutionary changes in warfare that might result from the atomic bomb and the possible effects of such a weapon on our civilization.

I listened with absorbed interest, for Stimson was a man of great wisdom and foresight. He went into considerable detail in describing the nature and the power of the projected weapon. If expectations were to be realized, he told me, the atomic bomb would be certain to have a decisive influence on our relations with other countries. And if it worked, the bomb, in all probability, would shorten the war. . . .

My own knowledge of these developments had come about only after I became president, when Secretary Stimson had given me the full story. He had told me at that time that the project was nearing completion and that a bomb could be expected within another four months. It was at his suggestion, too, that I had then set up a committee of top men and had asked them to study with great care the implications the new weapon might have for us. . . .

It was their recommendation that the bomb be used against the enemy as soon as it could be done. They recommended further that it should be used without specific warning and against a target that would clearly show its devastating strength. I had realized, of course, that an atomic bomb explosion would inflict damage and casualties beyond imagination. On the other hand,

Harry S Truman, *Memoirs: Year of Decisions* (Garden City, NY, 1955), 10–11, 87, 418–421. Reprinted by permission of Margaret Truman Daniel.

the scientific advisers of the committee reported, "We can propose no technical demonstration likely to bring an end to the war; we see no acceptable alternative to direct military use." It was their conclusion that no technical demonstration they might propose, such as over a deserted island, would be likely to bring the war to an end. It had to be used against an enemy target.

The final decision of where and when to use the atomic bomb was up to me. Let there be no mistake about it. I regarded the bomb as a military weapon and never had any doubt that it should be used. The top military advisers to the President recommended its use, and when I talked to Churchill he unhesitatingly told me that he favored the use of the atomic bomb if it might aid to end the war. . . .

In deciding to use this bomb I wanted to make sure that it would be used as a weapon of war in the manner prescribed by the laws of war. That meant that I wanted it dropped on a military target. I had told Stimson that the bomb should be dropped as nearly as possibly upon a war production center of prime military importance. . . .

Four cities were finally recommended as targets; Hiroshima, Kokura, Nigata, and Nagasaki. They were listed in that order as targets for the importance of these cities, but allowance would be given for weather conditions at the time of the bombing. . . .

On August 6, the fourth day of the journey home from Potsdam, came the historic news that shook the world. I was eating lunch with members of the *Augusta's* crew when Captain Frank Graham, White House Map Room watch officer, handed me the following message:

TO THE PRESIDENT
FROM THE SECRETARY OF WAR
Big bomb dropped on Hiroshima August 5 at 7:15 P.M. Washington time. First reports indicate complete success which was even more conspicuous than earlier test.

I was greatly moved. I telephoned Byrnes aboard ship to give him the news and then said to the group of sailors around me, "This is the greatest thing in history. It's time for us to get home."

195

Remembering the Hiroshima Atomic Blast (1945)

On August 6, 1945, a B-29 Superfortress, the Enola Gay, *dropped a single atomic bomb on Hiroshima, Japan. The bomb emitted a sudden flash that demolished four square miles of the city, immediately killing nearly 80,000 people and setting fire to remaining structures. One of the survivors of this blast was Hiroko Nakamoto, a young, happy girl who came from a privileged family. Her powerful recollection of that day is excerpted as follows.*

Questions to Consider

1. What was most shocking to Hiroko Nakamoto about the atomic blast?

2. According to Nakamoto, was the bombing racially motivated?

3. Did American officials realize the destructiveness of the bomb? Was it necessary?

4. What can be deduced about Japanese views of the bombing of Hiroshima from Nakamoto's account?

Whenever I see strong sunshine, I remember the day very clearly, the day I will never forget as long as I live. That day, in one quick second, my world was destroyed. The day was August 6, 1945.

It was 8:15 in the morning, and I was on my way to work. I was walking. The night before, as usual, there had been alerts all night. I was groggy from lack of sleep. The all clear had sounded just as I left home. Now all seemed calm and quiet. I did not hear any sounds of airplanes overhead.

Suddenly, from nowhere, came a blinding flash. It was as if someone had taken a flashbulb picture a few inches from my eyes. There was no pain then.

Only a stinging sensation, as if I had been slapped hard in the face.

I tried to open my eyes. But I could not. Then I lost consciousness.

I do not know how I got there or how long it was before I awoke. But when I opened my eyes, I was lying inside a shattered house. I was dazed and in shock, and all I knew was that I wanted to go home. I pulled myself up and started stumbling down the street. The air was heavy with a sickening odor. It was a smell different from anything I had ever known before.

Now I saw dead bodies all about me. The buildings were in ruins, and from the ruins I could hear people crying for help. But I could not help them. Some people were trying, as I was, to walk, to get away, to find their homes. I passed a streetcar that was stalled. It was filled with dead people.

I stumbled on. But now a great fire came rolling toward us, and I knew it was impossible to get home.

I passed a woman on the street. She looked at me, then turned away with a gasp of horror. I wondered why. I felt as if one side of my face was detached, did not belong to me. I was afraid to touch it with my hand.

There was a river nearby, and the people who could walk began walking toward the river—burned people with clothes in shreds or no clothes at all, men and women covered with blood, crying children. I followed them. . . .

When I reached the river, I saw that the wooden bridge which I had crossed each day on my way to the factory was on fire. I stopped. And for the first time I looked at my body. My arms, legs and ankles were burned. And I realized that the left side of my face must be burned, too. There were strange burns. Not pink, but yellow. The flesh was hanging loose. I went down to the

Hiroko Nakamoto, as told to Mildred Mastin Pace, *My Japan, 1930–1951* (New York, 1970), 56–61, 64–66. Copyright held by the Estate of Mildred Mastin Pace. Reprinted by permission.

water's edge and tried to pat the skin back with salt water from the river, as I saw others doing.

But we could not stay by the river. The fire was coming closer, and the heat was more intense. Everyone started moving again, away from the fire, moving silently, painfully. . . .

I found myself on a wide street. I saw a number of burned people standing around a policeman. He had a small bottle of iodine, and some cotton he was dabbing it on the badly burned back of a man. I stared too dazed to realize how futile and pathetic it was. . . .

When I awoke again, I asked a man sitting next to me what had happened.

He said a bomb had destroyed almost the entire city. For the first time, my heart was filled with hate, bitter hate, for a people who could do this. I remembered a propaganda picture we had been shown of Americans laughing as they looked at corpses of Japanese soldiers. At the time I did not believe it. But I believed it now. . . .

By the time we reached the doctor's, his house, his office, even his yard were filled with people lying waiting for help. I lay in the yard and waited a long time. When at last he saw me, he did not even know what to do. These were burns such as no man had ever seen before. A nurse hastily put some oil on my burns, then hurried on to the next person. People were screaming; many were begging for water. And so few hands to help!

Some people were burned so black you could not tell whether they were lying face down or on their backs. It was hard to tell they were human beings.

But they were still alive.

More and more burned and injured kept arriving. . . .

Hiroshima was burning. The sky was red. Pine Street, its trees where I spent my childhood hours, the rice warehouse, the hotel, all were destroyed.

Friends and neighbors were dead. Everything we owned was gone. The rivers where we had enjoyed boating on summer evenings were filled with dead bodies floating in the water. People were screaming as they lay along the banks of the rivers. The dead and the half dead were lying among the wreckage in the streets.

The sky was red. Hiroshima was burning. My aunt, Teruko, and all the Kaitaichi relatives sat that night, in the darkened room, watching my face in silence.

26

✳

Postwar America

The Second World War transformed the United States as few events had in its history. The war years had boosted the economy, leaving the United States the world's most prosperous and powerful nation. Unlike in the 1920s, the nation did not withdraw from the world, but instead confronted its former wartime ally and new adversary, the Soviet Union, in the Cold War. Ideological differences (capitalism vs. communism), a tradition of suspicion and mistrust, and the perceived threat from this rival contributed to political maneuverings and initiated a massive arms and technology race. The Second World War also helped bring about important social changes, the most significant of which was the expansion of civil rights for African Americans. The following excerpts examine differing aspects of these major issues.

196

"Containment" (1946)

The conclusion of World War II left the United States and the Soviet Union as the two predominant world powers. But the former allies had ideological differences (capitalism and communism) and conflicting views of the postwar world, which made them adversaries in the Cold War, a conflict conducted on various levels although short of direct military clashes. Based in part on Soviet words and actions early in the Cold War, American leaders determined that the Soviet Union was bent on destroying capitalism and conquering the world. In 1946, George F. Kennan, a Soviet scholar and official in the American Embassy in Moscow, sent a "long telegram" to the State Department explaining the historic basis of Soviet foreign policy and warning of the Soviet threat to the United States. He also suggested how the United States could counter Soviet actions. Kennan's "long telegram"—and an article he published in Foreign Affairs in 1947 under the pseudonym "X"—became the foundation of America's new foreign policy of "containment," and Kennan, best known as "the father of containment," took a leading role in shaping many of the early Cold War policies. Excerpted as follows is his "long telegram" of February 1946.

Questions to Consider

1. According to George Kennan, what is the political ideology of the Soviet leaders, and how does this affect postwar relations with the United States?

2. What does Kennan believe are the purposes of Soviet foreign activities?

3. Why is "containment" significant to understanding Cold War activities?

4. To what extent does Kennan's policy reflect a desire to preserve Roosevelt's "Four Freedoms" (Document 188)?

At bottom of Kremlin's neurotic view of world affairs is traditional and instinctive Russian sense of insecurity. Originally, this was insecurity of a peaceful agricultural people trying to live on vast exposed plain in neighborhood of fierce nomadic peoples. To this was added, as Russia came into contact with economically advanced West, fear of more competent, more powerful, more highly organized societies in that area. But this latter type of insecurity was one which afflicted rather Russian rulers than Russian people; for Russian rulers have invariably sensed that their rule was relatively archaic in form, fragile and artificial in its psychological foundation, unable to stand comparison on contact with political system of Western countries. For this reason they have always feared foreign penetration, feared direct contact between Western world and their own, feared what would happen if Russians learned truth about world without or if foreigners learned truth about world within. And they have learned to seek security only in patient but deadly struggle for total destruction of rival power, never in compacts and compromises with it.

It was no coincidence that Marxism, which had smouldered ineffectively for half a century in Western Europe, caught hold and blazed for first time in Russia. Only in this land which had never known a friendly neighbor or indeed any tolerant equilibrium of separate powers, either internal or international, could a doctrine thrive which viewed economic conflicts of society as insoluble by peaceful means. After establishment of Bolshevist regime, Marxist dogma, rendered even more truculent and intolerant by Lenin's interpretation, became a perfect vehicle for sense of insecurity with which Bolsheviks, even more than previous Russian rulers, were afflicted. In this dogma, with its basic altruism of purpose, they found justification for their instinctive fear of outside world, for the dictatorship without which they did not know how to rule, for cruelties they did not dare not to inflict, for sacrifices they felt bound to demand. . . . This thesis provides justification for that increase of military and police power of Russian state, for that isolation of Russian population from outside world, and for that fluid and constant pressure to extend limits of Russian police power which are together the natural and instinctive urges of Russian rulers. Basically this is only the steady advance of uneasy Russian nationalism, a centuries old movement in which conceptions of offense and defense are inextricably confused. But in new guise of international Marxism, with its honeyed promises to a desperate and war torn outside world, it is more dangerous and insidious than ever before . . .

On official plane we must look for following:

(a) Internal policy devoted to increasing in every way strength and prestige of Soviet state: intensive military-industrialization; maximum development of armed forces; great displays to impress outsiders; continued secretiveness about internal matters, designed to conceal weaknesses and to keep opponents in dark.

(b) Wherever it is considered timely and promising efforts will be made to advance official limits of Soviet power. For the moment, these efforts are restricted to certain neighboring points conceived of here as being of immediate strategic necessity, such as Northern Iran, Turkey, possibly Bornholm. However, other points may at any time come into question, if and as concealed Soviet political power is extended to new areas. . . .

(c) Russians will participate officially in international organizations where they see opportunity of extending Soviet power or of inhibiting or diluting power of others. Moscow sees in UNO [United Nations Organization] not the mechanism for a permanent and stable world society founded on mutual interest and aims of all nations, but an arena in which aims just mentioned can be favorably pursued. . . .

(d) Toward colonial areas and backward or dependent peoples, Soviet policy, even on official plane, will be directed toward weakening of power and influence and contacts of advanced Western nations, on theory that in so far as this policy is successful, there will be created a vacuum which will favor Communist-Soviet penetration. Soviet pressure for participation in trusteeship arrangements thus represents, in my opinion, a desire to be in a position to complicate and inhibit exertion of Western influence at such points rather than to provide major channel for exerting of Soviet power. . . .

(e) Russians will strive energetically to develop Soviet representation in, and official ties with, countries in which they sense strong possibilities of opposition to Western centers of power. This applies to such widely separated points as Germany, Argentina, Middle Eastern countries, etc.

(f) In international economic matters, Soviet policy will really be dominated by pursuit of autarchy for Soviet Union and Soviet-dominated adjacent areas taken together. . . . Soviet foreign trade may be restricted largely to Soviet's own security sphere, including occupied areas in Germany, and that a cold official shoulder may be turned to principle of general economic collaboration among nations.

(g) With respect to cultural collaboration, lip service will likewise be rendered to desirability of deepening cultural contacts between peoples, but this will not in practice be interpreted in any way which could weaken security position of Soviet peoples. . . .

(h) Beyond this, Soviet official relations will take what might be called "correct" course with individual foreign governments, with great stress being laid on prestige of Soviet Union and its representatives and with punctilious attention to protocol, as distinct from good manners. . . .

PART 5:   [PRACTICAL DEDUCTIONS FROM STANDPOINT OF US POLICY]
In summary, we have here a political force committed fanatically to the belief that with US there can be no permanent modus vivendi, that it is desirable and necessary that the internal harmony of our society be disrupted, our traditional way of life be destroyed, the international authority of our state be broken, if Soviet power is to be secure. This political force has complete power of disposition over energies of one of world's greatest people and resources of world's richest national territory, and is borne along by deep and powerful currents of Russian nationalism. In addition, it has an elaborate and far flung apparatus for exertion of its influence in other countries, an apparatus of amazing flexibility and versatility, managed by people whose experience and skill in underground methods are presumably without parallel in history. Finally, it is seemingly inaccessible to considerations of reality in its basic reactions. For it, the vast fund of objective fact about human society is not, as with us, the measure against which outlook is constantly being tested and re-formed, but a grab bag from which individual items are selected arbitrarily and tendentiously to bolster an outlook already preconceived. This is admittedly not a pleasant picture. Problem of how to cope with this force [is] undoubtedly greatest task our diplomacy has ever faced and probably greatest it will ever have to face. It should be point of departure from which our political general staff work at present juncture should proceed. It should be approached with same thoroughness and care as solution of major strategic problem in war and if necessary, with no smaller outlay in planning effort. I cannot attempt to suggest all answers here. But I would like to record my conviction there are certain observations of a more encouraging nature I should like to make:

(1) Soviet power, unlike that of Hitlerite Germany, is neither schematic nor adventuristic. It does not work by fixed plans. It does not take unnecessary risks. Impervious to logic of reason, and it is highly sensitive to logic of force. For this reason it can easily withdraw—and usually does—when strong resistance is encountered at any point. Thus, if the adversary has sufficient force and makes clear his readiness to use it, he rarely has to do so. If situations are properly handled there need be no prestige-engaging showdowns.

(2) Gauged against Western World as a whole, Soviets are still by far the weaker force. Thus, their success will really depend on degree of cohesion, firmness and vigor which Western World can muster. And this is factor which it is within our power to influence.

(3) Success of Soviet system, as form of internal power, is not yet finally proven. It has yet to be demonstrated that it can survive supreme test of successive transfer of power from one individual or group to another. . . . In Russia, party has now become a great and—for the moment—highly successful apparatus of dictatorial administration, but it has ceased to be a source of emotional inspiration. Thus, internal soundness and permanence of movement need not yet be regarded as assured.

(4) All Soviet propaganda beyond Soviet security sphere is basically negative and destructive. It should therefore be relatively easy to combat it by any intelligent and really constructive program. For these reasons I think we may approach calmly and with good heart problem of how to deal with Russia. As to how this approach should be made, I only wish to advance, by way of conclusion, following comments:

(1) Our first step must be to apprehend, and recognize for what it is, the nature of the movement with which we are dealing. We must study it with same courage, detachment, objectivity, and same determination not to be emotionally provoked or unseated by it, with which doctor studies unruly and unreasonable individual.

(2) We must see that our public is educated to realities of Russian situation. I cannot over-emphasize importance of this. Press cannot do this alone. It must be done mainly by Government, which is necessarily more experienced and better informed on practical problems involved. . . .

(3) Much depends on health and vigor of our own society. World communism is like malignant parasite which feeds only on diseased tissue. This is point at which domestic and foreign policies meet. Every courageous and incisive measure to solve internal problems of our own society, to improve self-confidence, discipline, morale, and community spirit of our own people, is a diplomatic victory over Moscow worth a thousand diplomatic notes and joint communiques. . . .

(4) We must formulate and put forward for other nations a much more positive and constructive picture of sort of world we would like to see than we have put forward in past. It is not enough to urge people to develop political processes similar to our own. Many foreign peoples, in Europe at least, are tired and frightened by experiences of past, and are less interested in abstract freedom than in security. They are seeking guidance rather than responsibilities. We should be better able than Russians to give them this. And unless we do, Russians certainly will.

(5) Finally we must have courage and self-confidence to cling to our own methods and conceptions of human society. After all, the greatest danger that can befall us in coping with this problem of Soviet communism, is that we shall allow ourselves to become like those with whom we are coping.

197

Communists in the Government (1950)

The fight against communism in the Cold War abroad spread to domestic affairs in the second Red Scare. Losing Eastern Europe and China to communism and witnessing the Soviets develop an atomic bomb with alarming quickness convinced many Americans that secret information had been leaked. Adding to this situation were the relentless accusations from the House Committee on Un-American Activities that subversives were in the government, as well as several sensational "spy trials" involving secret documents allegedly sent to the Soviets. Early in 1950, an obscure Republican senator from Wisconsin, Joseph McCarthy, exploited this growing public fear. He launched an anticommunism campaign with a speech in Wheeling, West Virginia, excerpted following, which he later repeated in Congress because there was some discrepancy over the exact number of names of communists McCarthy possessed. The speech launched a four-year witch-hunt, during which outrageous accusations and fear of communist subversives in the government obscured evidence and substance.

Questions to Consider

1. To what does Joseph McCarthy attribute America's postwar problems?
2. Does McCarthy make a convincing argument that John S. Service should not work in the government?
3. What does this speech reveal about American fears in the early Cold War period?
4. Was Joseph McCarthy's influence on the United States positive or negative?

Five years after a world war has been won, men's hearts should anticipate a long peace and men's minds should be free from the heavy weight that comes with war. But this is not such a period—for this is not a period of peace. This is a time of the "cold war." This is a time when all the world is split into two vast, increasingly hostile armed camps—a time of great armaments race.

Today we can almost physically hear the mutterings and rumblings of an invigorated god of war. You can see it, feel it, and hear it all the way from the hills of Indochina, from the shores of Formosa, right over into the very heart of Europe itself.

The one encouraging thing is that the "mad moment" has not yet arrived for the firing of the gun or the exploding of the bomb which will set civilization about the final task of destroying itself. There is still a hope for peace

---

"Communists in Government Service," *Congressional Record*, 81st Congress, 2nd session, part 2 (February 20, 1950): 1952–1954.

if we finally decide that no longer can we safely blind our eyes and close our ears to those facts which are shaping up more and more clearly. And that is that we are now engaged in a show-down fight—not the usual war between nations for land areas or other material gains, but a war between two diametrically opposed ideologies. . . .

At war's end we were physically the strongest nation on earth and, at least potentially, the most powerfully intellectually and morally. Ours could have been the honor of being a beacon in the desert of destruction, a shining living proof that civilization was not yet ready to destroy itself. Unfortunately, we have failed miserably and tragically to arise to the opportunity.

The reason why we find ourselves in a position of impotency is not because our only powerful potential enemy has sent men to invade our shores, but rather because of the traitorous actions of those who have been treated so well by this Nation. It has not been the less fortunate or members of minority groups who have been selling this Nation out, but rather those who have had all the benefits that the wealthiest nation on earth has had to offer—the finest homes, the finest college education, and the finest jobs in Government we can give.

This is glaringly true in the State Department. There the bright young men who are born with silver spoons in their mouths are the ones who have been the worst.

Now I know it is very easy for anyone to condemn a particular bureau or department in general terms. Therefore, I would like to cite one rather unusual case—the case of a man who has done much to shape our foreign policy.

When Chiang Kai-shek was fighting our war, the State Department had in China a young man named John S. Service. His task, obviously, was not to work for the communization of China. Strangely, however, he sent official reports back to the State Department urging that we torpedo our ally Chiang Kai-shek and stating, in effect, that communism was the best hope of China.

Later, this man—John Service—was picked up by the Federal Bureau of Investigation for turning over to the Communists secret State Department information. Strangely, however, he was never prosecuted. However, Joseph Grew, the Under Secretary of State, who insisted on his prosecution, was forced to resign. Two days after Grew's successor, Dean Acheson, took over as Under Secretary of State, this man—John Service—who had been picked up by the FBI and who had previously urged that communism was the best hope of China, was not only reinstated in the State Department but promoted. And finally, under Acheson, placed in charge of all placements and promotions.

Today, ladies and gentlemen, this man Service is on his way to represent the State Department and Acheson in Calcutta—by far and away the most important listening post in the Far East.

Now, let's see what happens when individuals with Communist connections are forced out of the State Department. Gustave Duran, who was labeled as (I quote) "a notorious international Communist" was made assistant to the Assistant Secretary of State in charge of Latin American affairs. He was taken into the State Department from his job as lieutenant colonel in the Communist International Brigade. Finally, after intense congressional pressure and criticism, he resigned in 1946 from the State Department—and, ladies and gentlemen, where do you think he is now? He took over a high-salaried job as Chief of Cultural Activities Section in the office of the Assistant Secretary General of the United Nations. . . .

This, ladies and gentlemen, gives you somewhat of a picture of the type of individuals who have been helping to shape our foreign policy. In my opinion the State Department, which is one of the most important government departments, is thoroughly infested with Communists.

I have in my hand 57 cases of individuals who would appear to be either card carrying members or certainly loyal to the Communist Party, but who nevertheless are still helping to shape our foreign policy. . . .

As you hear this story of high treason, I know what you are saying to yourself, "Well, why doesn't the Congress do something about it?" Actually, ladies and gentlemen, one of the most important reasons for the graft, the corruption, the dishonesty, the disloyalty, the treason in high Government positions—one of the most important reasons why this continues—is a lack of moral uprising on the part of the 140,000,000 American people. In the light of history, however, this is not hard to explain.

It is the result of an emotional hang-over and a temporary moral lapse which follows every war. It is the apathy to evil which people who have been subjected to the tremendous evils of war feel. As the people of the world see mass murder, the destruction of defenseless and innocent people, and all of the crime and lack of morals which go with war, they become numb and apathetic. It has always been thus after war.

However, the morals of our people have not been destroyed. They still exist. This cloak of numbness and apathy has only needed a spark to rekindle them. Happily, this spark has finally been supplied. . . .

198

Governor Herman Talmadge's Statement on the *Brown* Decision (1954)

Beginning in the mid-1930s, the National Association for the Advancement of Colored People (NAACP) began to challenge school segregation in the hopes of ending the Jim Crow laws of the South. Their efforts culminated in the unanimous Supreme Court decision, Brown v. *Board of Education of Topeka, Kansas (1954), which ended the "separate but equal" doctrine of racial segregation in public schools. Positive and negative responses to this decision were immediate. Georgia Governor Herman E.*

Talmadge, Jr. was among the first southern politicians to issue a public statement, which came the day after the Brown *decision. Talmadge had deep political roots in Georgia: His father was elected governor three times, and the son filled the remainder of his father's last term, and then was elected governor. Talmadge was proud that he spent more on public education for blacks and whites in his six years as governor than all previous administrations combined. In 1956, he was elected to the Senate and became a prominent opponent of the Civil Rights Act of 1957. His* Brown *decision statement, offered following, reflected the sentiments of many whites in the lower South.*

Questions to Consider

1. On what basis did Herman Talmadge attack the Supreme Court's decision?
2. What is Georgia's "accepted pattern of life"?
3. Why did the NAACP choose public education to challenge existing segregation laws?
4. In what ways did the South resist the *Brown* decision?

The U.S. Supreme Court by its decision today has reduced our Constitution to a mere scrap of paper. It has blatantly ignored all law and precedent and usurped from the Congress and the people the power to amend the Constitution and from the Congress the authority to make the laws of the land. Its action confirms the worst fears of the motives of the men who sit on its bench and raises a grave question as to the future course of the nation.

There is no constitutional provision, statute or precedent to support the position the court has taken. It has swept aside 88 years of sound judicial precedent, repudiated the greatest legal minds of our age and lowered itself to the level of common politics.

It has attempted in one stroke to strike the 10th Amendment from the Constitution and to set the stage for the development of an all-powerful federal bureaucracy in Washington which can regulate the lives of all the citizens in the minutest detail.

The people of Georgia believe in, adhere to and will fight for their rights under the United States and Georgia constitutions to manage their own affairs. They cannot and they will not accept a bald political decree without basis in law or practicality which overturns their accepted pattern of life.

The court has thrown down the gauntlet before those who believe the Constitution means what it says when it reserves to the individual states the right to regulate their own internal affairs. Georgians accept the challenge and will not tolerate the mixing of the races in the public schools or any of its public tax–supported institutions. The fact that the high tribunal has seen fit to proclaim its views on sociology as law will not make any difference.

If adjustments in our laws and procedures are necessary, they will be made. In the meantime all Georgians will follow their pursuits by separate paths and in accepted fashion. The U.S. and Georgia Constitutions have not been changed. The Georgia Constitution provides for separation of the races. It will be upheld.

As governor and chairman of the State Commission on Education I am summoning that body into immediate session to map a program to insure continued and permanent segregation of the races. . . .

I urge all Georgians to remain calm and resist any attempt to arouse fear or hysteria. The full powers of my office are ready to see that the laws of our state are enforced impartially and without violence.

I was elected governor of Georgia on the solemn promise to maintain our accepted way of life. So long as I hold this office it shall be done.

199

An African-American Newspaper Editorial on the Little Rock Crisis (1957)

The Supreme Court's unanimous decision in the case of Brown v. *Board of Education of* Topeka, Kansas *(1954) generated cautious hope among African Americans that public facilities would be integrated. Although a few school districts in the South began integrating black and white students shortly after the decision, most remained segregated. State legislatures passed laws to circumvent the court's ruling, and white opposition groups formed to prevent integration. One of the first major tests of school integration came in Little Rock, Arkansas, in September 1957. When the school board moved to integrate nine black children into the all-white Central High School, Governor Orville Faubus called out the Arkansas National Guard to prevent the integration. When a mob of angry white protestors greeted the nine students, the event generated national attention and compelled President Dwight Eisenhower to act. The* Pittsburgh Courier *was one of the most widely respected and circulated African-American weekly newspapers. It had raised funds for the NAACP's legal battle to end segregation in public schools. The* Pittsburgh Courier *offered the following editorial on the Little Rock crisis.*

Questions to Consider

1. What were the critical issues in Little Rock, Arkansas, that prompted Eisenhower to act?
2. What actions did President Eisenhower take?

3. Why was Eisenhower's action so significant to the *Pittsburgh Courier*?

4. What were the impediments to integration in the South? How do you suppose Herman Talmadge ("Statement on the *Brown* Decision," Document 198) would have responded to President Eisenhower's actions?

Colored Americans everywhere join in saluting President Eisenhower for his forthright stand on the issue of public school integration despite caustic criticism from the hard core segregationist Southerners and their less vocal Northern sympathizers.

With the courage and determination of a great soldier and statesman, he has met the challenge to his authority without evasion or apologies.

Negroes understand full well his dilemma as Chief Executive of all the people, white and colored, dedicated to his duty to maintain internal peace and unity, and unwilling to make decisions that might well divide the nation; and therefore they are the more appreciative of his decisiveness.

It was said that he was temporizing and wishy-washy because he did not immediately take drastic action against those who challenged the Federal Courts and Administration authority and duty, and was considerate and patient beyond necessity.

He used the Federal power reluctantly and hesitantly because of his awful responsibility, but when this had no effect on the segregationists, their behind-the-scenes bosses, and their lower level stooges and goons, he acted with all the force and power at his disposal, which was plenty.

With the Little Rock mob flouting law and order, and about to institute a reign of terror, he flew the Army into the city, ringed Central High School with bayoneted paratroopers, and saw that the nine Negro children entered the school and attended their classes without opposition.

He Federalized the jim-crow Arkansas National Guard and saw that they performed their duty as Governor Faubus prevented them from doing; and when the Governor welshed on his pledged word to uphold the law if and when the Army was removed, he abruptly cancelled the removal indefinitely.

President Dwight D. Eisenhower, we salute you!

Since the Administration of President Grant, no other White House occupant has done as much to protect the rights of colored citizens to full citizenship in opposition to the unreconstructed Southern segregationists and their Northern supporters.

Here is a real man, not a time-serving trimmer, who dares to court unpopularity to perform his distasteful duty.

To quote Rabelais: "Happy is the country whose kings are philosophers, and whose philosophers are kings."

"Salute to the President," *Pittsburgh Courier,* October 12, 1957, p. 8. Copyright © 1957 by the *Pittsburgh Courier;* copyright renewed 1985 by *The New Pittsburgh Courier.* Reprinted by permission of GRM Associates, Inc., agents for the *Pittsburgh Courier.*

200

Suburbanization: Levittown, New York (1950)

Following World War II, many young couples, having saved a "nest egg" to buy a home, found few houses to purchase in the cities. Responding to this growing demand for new housing, William Levitt and his sons began construction of entirely new neighborhoods away from the cities. Levitt, a self-confident and wealthy New York developer who amassed a fortune building houses during the Great Depression and the war, introduced mass-production techniques to the housing industry, transforming what was once a cottage industry into a major manufacturing enterprise. In 1947, Levitt began work on his crowning achievement, Levittown, New York, whose construction and appearance are described in the 1950 Time *magazine article excerpted as follows. Home builders nationwide adopted Levitt's construction methods, producing numerous inexpensive houses and helping to promote a white, middle-class suburban revolution in the 1950s.*

Questions to Consider

1. Who was attracted to live in Levittown? Why?
2. How was a suburban mentality shaped in this community?
3. What enabled suburban communities like Levittown to develop?
4. According to the article, what were some of the criticisms of Levittown?
5. How might Odette Keun ("The Tennessee Valley Authority," Document 185) react to Levittown?

On 1,200 flat acres of potato farmland near Hicksville, Long Island, an army of trucks sped over new-laid roads. Every 100 feet, the trucks stopped and dumped identical bundles of lumber, pipes, bricks, shingles and copper tubing—all as neatly packaged as loaves from a bakery. Near the bundles, giant machines with an endless chain of buckets ate into the earth, taking just 13 minutes to dig a narrow, four-foot trench around a 25-by-32 ft. rectangle. Then came more trucks, loaded with cement, and laid a four-inch foundation for a house in the rectangle.

After the machines came the men. On nearby slabs already dry, they worked in crews of two and three, laying bricks, raising studs, nailing lath, painting, sheathing, shingling. Each crew did its special job, then hurried on to the next site. Under the skilled combination of men and machines, new houses rose faster than Jack ever built them; a new one was finished every 15 minutes. . . .

"Up From the Potato Fields," *Time* 56 (July 3, 1950): 67–72. © 1950 Time Inc. Reprinted by permission.

Levittown is known largely for one reason: it epitomizes the revolution which has brought mass production to the housing industry. Its creator, Long Island's Levitt & Sons, Inc., has become the biggest builder of houses in the U.S.

The houses in Levittown, which sell for a uniform price of $7,990, cannot be mistaken for castles. Each has a sharp-angled roof and a picture window, radiant heating in the floor, 12-by-16 ft. living room, bath, kitchen, two bedrooms on the first floor, and an "expansion attic" which can be converted into two more bedrooms and bath. The kitchen has a refrigerator, stove and Bendix washer; the living room a fireplace and a built-in Admiral television set. . . .

The influence of Levitt & Sons on housing goes much further than the thresholds of its own houses. Its methods of mass production are being copied by many of the merchant builders in the U.S., who are putting up four of every five houses built today. It is such mass production on one huge site which is enabling U.S. builders to meet the post-war demand and to create the biggest housing boom in U.S. history. . . .

At war's end, when the U.S. desperately needed 5,000,000 houses, the nation had two choices: the Federal Government could try to build the houses itself, or it could pave the way for private industry to do the job, by making available billions in credit. The U.S. wisely handed the job to private industry, got 4,000,000 new units built since the war, probably faster and cheaper than could have been done any other way.

The Government has actually spent little cash itself. By insuring loans up to 95% of the value of a house, the Federal Housing Administration made it easy for a builder to borrow the money with which to build low-cost houses. The Government made it just as easy for the buyer by liberally insuring his mortgage. Under a new housing act signed three months ago, the purchase terms on low-cost houses with Government-guaranteed mortgages were so liberalized that in many cases buying a house is now as easy as renting it. The new terms: 5% down (nothing down for veterans) and 30 years to pay. Thus an ex-G.I. could buy a Levitt house with no down payment and installments of only $56 a month.

The countless new housing projects made possible by this financial easy street are changing the way of life of millions of U.S. citizens, who are realizing for the first time the great American dream of owning their own home. No longer must young married couples plan to start living in an apartment, saving for the distant day when they can buy a house. Now they can do it more easily than they can buy a $2,000 car on the installment plan.

Like its counterparts across the land, Levittown is an entirely new kind of community. Despite its size, it is not incorporated, thus has no mayor, no police force, nor any of the other traditional city officers of its own. It has no movies, no nightclubs and only three bars (all in the community shopping centers).

And Levittown has very few old people. Few of its more than 40,000 residents are past 35; of some 8,000 children, scarcely 900 are more than seven years old. In front of almost every house along Levittown's 100 miles of winding streets sits a tricycle or a baby carriage. In Levittown, all activity stops from 12 to 2 in the afternoon; that is nap time. Said one Levittowner last week, "Everyone is so young that sometimes it's hard to remember how to get along with older people."

The community has an almost antiseptic air. Levittown streets, which have such fanciful names as Satellite, Horizon, Haymaker, are bare and flat as hospital corridors. Like a hospital, Levittown has rules all its own. Fences are not allowed (though here and there a home-owner has broken the rule). The plot of grass around each home must be cut at least once a week; if not, Bill Levitt's men mow the grass and send the bill. Wash cannot be hung out to dry on an ordinary clothesline; it must be arranged on rotary, removable drying racks and then not on weekends or holidays. . . .

Actually, Levittown's uniformity is more apparent than real. Though most of their incomes are about the same (average: about $3,800), Levittowners come from all classes, all walks of life. Eighty percent of the men commute to their jobs in Manhattan, many sharing their transportation costs through car pools. Their jobs, as in any other big community, range from baking to banking, from teaching to preaching. Levittown has also developed its own unique way of keeping up with the Joneses. Some Levittowners buy a new house every year, as soon as the new model is on the market. . . .

The most frequent criticism of Levittown and most other projects like it, is that it is the "slum of the future." Says Bill Levitt: "Nonsense." Many city planners agree with him, because they approve of Levittown's uncluttered plan and its plentiful recreational facilities. Nevertheless, in helping to solve the housing problem, Levittown has created other problems: new schools, hospitals, and sewage facilities will soon be needed; its transportation is woefully inadequate, even by Long Island standards. . . .

201

The Impact of Television (1955)

Experimentation with broadcast television began in the late 1920s, but a host of difficulties delayed its introduction to the public until after the Second World War. By the 1940s, the existing radio networks implemented their innovations in the fledgling broadcast television industry (e.g., programming, "prime time shows" commercials), while wartime electronics assembly lines shifted to begin mass production of television sets. After years of spending restraint in the Great Depression and Second World War, the postwar prosperity and the growing consumer culture helped fuel the dramatic growth of the television industry. Businesses found television to be a convenient vehicle on which to market their products, and millions of Americans discovered that it was an inexpensive form of entertainment. Shows appealing to women audiences, children's programs, and family shows were developed. In 1947, the opening of Congress was broadcast live on television, and some sporting events, such as baseball games, were televised. By 1949, about 1 million households owned a television, and ownership was growing dramatically. Intrigued by the growing popularity of television and its influence on American society, the popular news magazine U.S. News and World Report *produced a special report on the phenomenon. Excerpted following is the article that seeks to explain television's attraction and influence.*

Questions to Consider

1. According to the article, in what ways has television affected Americans?
2. How did Americans influence television?
3. Which of the three theories described in this selection seems most accurate?
4. To what extent is the commentary about television in this 1955 article relevant today?

The biggest of the new forces in American life today is television.

There has been nothing like it in the postwar decade, or in many decades before that—perhaps not since the invention of the printing press. Even radio, by contrast, was a placid experience.

The impact of TV on this country has been so massive that Americans are still wondering what hit them. . . .

Two out of three U.S. families now own their own sets, or are paying for them. In 32 million homes, TV dials are flicked on and off, from channel to channel, at least 100 million times between 8 a.m. and midnight.

Everywhere, children sit with eyes glued to screens—for three to four hours a day on average. Their parents use up even more time mesmerized by this new marvel—or monster. They have spent 15 billion dollars to look since 1946.

Now, after nearly 10 years of TV, people are asking: What hath TV wrought? What is this thing doing to us?" . . .

People have strong views. Here are some widely held convictions, both against and for television:

- That TV has kept people from going places and doing things, from reading, from thinking for themselves. Yet it is said also that TV has taken viewers vicariously into strange and fascinating spots and situations, brought distinguished and enchanting people into their living rooms, given them a new perspective.

- That TV has interfered with schooling, kept children from learning to read and write, weakened their eyesight and softened their muscles. But there are those who hold that TV has made America's youngsters more "knowing" about life, more curious, given them a bigger vocabulary. Teaching by TV, educators say, is going to be a big thing in the future.

"What TV is Doing to America," *U.S. News and World Report* 39 (September 2, 1955): 36–39. Copyright 1955 *U.S. News & World Report*, L.P. Reprinted by permission.

- That TV arouses morbid emotions in children, glorifies violence, causes juvenile crime—that it starts domestic quarrels, tend to loosen morals and make people lazy and sodden. However, it keeps families together at home, provides a realm of cheap entertainment never before available, stimulates new lines of conversation.

- That TV is giving the US an almost primitive language, made up of grunts, whistles, standardized wisecracks and clichés—that it is turning the average American into a stereotype. Yet it is breaking down regional barriers and prejudices, ironing out accents, giving people in one part of the country a better understanding of people in other parts.

- That TV is making politics "a rich man's game," turning statesmanship into a circus, handing demagogues a new weapon. But it is giving Americans their first good look at the inside of their Government, letting them judge the people they elect by sight as well as by sound and fury.

- That TV has distorted and debased salesmanship, haunting people with singing "commercials" and slogans. However, because or in spite of TV, people are buying more and more things they never before thought they needed or wanted. . . .

On an average evening, twice as many set owners will be watching TV as are engaged in any other form of entertainment or leisure activity, such as movie-going, card playing, or reading. Seven out of 10 American children watch TV between 6 and 8 o'clock most evenings.

Analysts are intrigued by the evidence that adults, not children, are the real television fans. The newest trend in viewing habits is a rise in the number of housewives who watch TV in the morning. One out of five with a set now watches a morning show with regularity. . . .

What does TV do to people? What do people do with TV? The researchers are digging into these questions all the time. In general, they come to theories, rather than conclusions. There are three main theories:

THEORY "A": This is widely held by people whose professions bring them into close contact with juveniles—judges, district attorneys, police officers, ministers. It assumes that TV is bound to be affecting the American mind and character because it soaks up one to five hours per day or more that used to be spent in outdoor play, in games requiring reasoning and imagination, or in reading, talking, radio listening, or movie-going.

Even the more passive of these pursuits, the theory runs, required more exercise of brain power than does TV watching. Then, too, many TV programs, the theorists say, are violent or in questionable taste.

Net effect, according to these people, is a wasting away or steady decline in certain basic skills among American youngsters. Children lose the ability to read, forfeit their physical dexterity, strength and initiative. . . .

THEORY "B": Mainly held by sociologists, communication economists, pollsters. This is that television is changing the American mind
and character, although nobody knows for sure just how. The evidence
is too fragmentary.

The analysts are disturbed by some aspects of TV's effect on viewers. Some think TV is conditioning Americans to be "other directed,"
that is, getting their ideas from someone else. . . .

A fancy name for this suspected effect of TV is "narcotic disfunc-
tion." This means that more and more men come home in the
evening, drop into a chair in front of the TV set after supper and slip
into a dream world of unreality. . . .

THEORY "C": This is what the TV people themselves like to think. It
is that television is rapidly becoming "one more service" to the US
public, another medium such as newspapers, magazines, radio. Some
people watch TV a lot, others very little. Most people want a set
around, but some don't lean on it. . . .

Three out of every four TV programs are entertainment shows. If
anything, the trend is toward a higher content of entertainment and a
lower slice of information.

In a typical week of the peak TV season, in January of last year,
crime, comedy, variety and Western shows accounted for 42.7 per cent
of all TV program time on New York City screens. News accounted
for 6.1 per cent of TV time—about the same share of time as was taken
by quiz, stunt and contest shows. Other informational types of TV
shows, such as interviews, weather reports, travelogues, children's instruc-
tional program and cooking classes, got 16.2 per cent of the time. . . .

. . . In a two-week period last June, when two comedy programs, the
"George Gobel Show" and "I Love Lucy," were at the top of the list, each
reaching more than 13 million homes, the top-ranking informational programs were way down the line. The "March of Medicine," for example, was
No. 62, "Meet the Press" was No. 150. . . .

The public is fickle. Top rating is hard to hold. The viewers tire rapidly of
a particular show unless the producers manage to come up with fresh material, new appeals.

202

Dwight D. Eisenhower's Farewell Address (1961)

*Dwight D. Eisenhower served two consecutive terms as president in the 1950s. He
brought to his job a wealth of military experience but virtually no political seasoning.
Born in Denison, Texas, but raised in Abilene, Kansas, Eisenhower finished West
Point in 1915 and remained a part of the military for most of his life, serving as*

supreme commander of Allied forces in Europe during World War II. Pressured to seek the presidency in 1952, the popular war hero won easily on the Republican ticket. Eisenhower's presidency was often nonpartisan and conservative, as he displayed the resourceful ability to stem domestic political and social forces, legitimatized many New Deal programs, and maintained many Cold War policies. Three days before he left office, Eisenhower gave his "farewell address," which was broadcast live over radio and television. Drawing on his knowledge of the military and changes that had taken place within the country, Eisenhower warned against dangers to American values and individual rights. His speech is excerpted as follows.

Questions to Consider

1. What changes have taken place regarding the military to prompt Eisenhower's warning?
2. What does he fear?
3. What does he ask Americans to do?
4. Do Eisenhower's concerns seem accurate today?

My fellow Americans:

Three days from now, after half a century in the service of our country, I shall lay down the responsibilities of office as, in traditional and solemn ceremony, the authority of the Presidency is vested in my successor. . . .

We now stand ten years past the midpoint of a century that has witnessed four major wars among great nations. Three of them involved our own country. Despite these holocausts America is today the strongest, the most influential and most productive nation in the world. Understandably proud of this pre-eminence, we yet realize that America's leadership and prestige depend, not merely upon our unmatched material progress, riches and military strength, but on how we use our power in the interests of world peace and human betterment.

Throughout America's adventure in free government, our basic purposes have been to keep the peace; to foster progress in human achievement, and to enhance liberty, dignity and integrity among people and among nations. To strive for less would be unworthy of a free and religious people. Any failure traceable to arrogance, or our lack of comprehension or readiness to sacrifice would inflict upon us grievous hurt both at home and abroad.

Progress toward these noble goals is persistently threatened by the conflict now engulfing the world. It commands our whole attention, absorbs our very beings. We face a hostile ideology—global in scope, atheistic in character, ruthless in purpose, and insidious in method. Unhappily the danger it poses promises to be of indefinite duration. To meet it successfully, there is

---

"Farewell Radio and Television Address to the American People," *Public Papers of the Presidents of the United States: Dwight D. Eisenhower, 1960–61* (Washington, DC, 1961), 1035–1040.

called for, not so much the emotional and transitory sacrifices of crisis, but rather those which enable us to carry forward steadily, surely, and without complaint the burdens of a prolonged and complex struggle—with liberty the stake. Only thus shall we remain, despite every provocation, on our charted course toward permanent peace and human betterment. . . .

A vital element in keeping the peace is our military establishment. Our arms must be mighty, ready for instant action, so that no potential aggressor may be tempted to risk his own destruction.

Our military organization today bears little relation to that known by any of my predecessors in peacetime, or indeed by the fighting men of World War II or Korea.

Until the latest of our world conflicts, the United States had no armaments industry. American makers of plowshares could, with time and as required, make swords as well. But now we can no longer risk emergency improvisation of national defense; we have been compelled to create a permanent armaments industry of vast proportions. Added to this, three and a half million men and women are directly engaged in the defense establishment. We annually spend on military security more than the net income of all United States corporations.

This conjunction of an immense military establishment and a large arms industry is new in the American experience. The total influence—economic, political, even spiritual—is felt in every city, every statehouse, every office of the federal government. We recognize the imperative need for this development. Yet we must not fail to comprehend its grave implications. Our toil, resources, and livelihood are all involved; so is the very structure of our society.

In the councils of government, we must guard against the acquisition of unwarranted influence, whether sought or unsought, by the military-industrial complex. The potential for the disastrous rise of misplaced power exists and will persist.

We must never let the weight of this combination endanger our liberties or democratic processes. We should take nothing for granted. Only an alert and knowledgeable citizenry can compel the proper meshing of the huge industrial and military machinery of defense with our peaceful methods and goals, so that security and liberty may prosper together.

Akin to, and largely responsible for the sweeping changes in our industrial-military posture, has been the technological revolution during recent decades.

In this revolution, research has become central; it also becomes more formalized, complex, and costly. A steadily increasing share is conducted for, by, or at the direction of, the federal government. . . .

It is the task of statesmanship to mold, to balance, and to integrate these and other forces, new and old, within the principles of our democratic system—ever aiming toward the supreme goals of our free society.

Another factor in maintaining balance involves the element of time. As we peer into society's future, we—you and I, and our government—must avoid the impulse to live only for today, plundering, for our own ease and convenience, the precious resources of tomorrow. We cannot mortgage the material assets of our grandchildren without risking the loss also of their political and spiritual heritage. We want democracy to survive for all generations to come, not to become the insolvent phantom of tomorrow.

Down the long lane of history yet to be written America knows that this world of ours, ever growing smaller, must avoid becoming a community of dreadful fear and hate, and be, instead, a proud confederation of mutual trust and respect.

Such a confederation must be one of equals. The weakest must come to the conference table with the same confidence as do we, protected as we are by our moral, economic, and military strength. That table, though scarred by many past frustrations, cannot be abandoned for the certain agony of the battlefield.

Disarmament, with mutual honor and confidence, is a continuing imperative. Together we must learn how to compose differences, not with arms, but with intellect and decent purpose. Because this need is so sharp and apparent I confess that I lay down my official responsibilities in this field with a definite sense of disappointment. As one who has witnessed the horror and the lingering sadness of war—as one who knows that another war could utterly destroy this civilization which has been so slowly and painfully built over thousands of years—I wish I could say tonight that a lasting peace is in sight.

Happily, I can say that war has been avoided. Steady progress toward our ultimate goal has been made. But, so much remains to be done. As a private citizen, I shall never cease to do what little I can to help the world advance along that road. . . .

27

✳

The Turbulent Sixties

Many Americans believed they stood at the beginning of a new era as the 1960s began. An exuberant belief that government could solve virtually any problem seemed to assure people that the nation would enjoy continued peace and prosperity, but the events of the decade quickly shattered these hopes. America's effort to check the spread of communism led it into Vietnam, an issue that ultimately divided the nation. On the domestic front, the fight for civil rights continued, despite an increase in violence. Many of the children who had grown up in prosperous surroundings of the 1950s entered colleges in record numbers and soon questioned many of the most cherished beliefs of their parents' generation. The following documents illustrate the idealism, disillusion, and turmoil that characterized the period.

203

Silent Spring (1962)

After the initial surge of public awareness about conservation in the early 20th century, the movement to conserve natural resources and preserve natural lands lost momentum. However, in the post–World War II period, the desire to improve the quality of life contributed to the emergence of a powerful environmental movement. The increased use of automobiles and emissions from some businesses polluted the air; many major cities, Los Angeles especially, experienced poor air quality. Certain industrial processes and the growing use of household washing machines dumped alarming amounts of chemicals into rivers and streams, contributing to water pollution. Nuclear weapons testing and the growth of atomic power plants generated alarms about radiation. And the use and disposal of some toxic chemicals was haphazard. In 1962, naturalist Rachel Carson sounded an alarm about the environment when she published Silent Spring, *one of the most influential books of the last half of the 20th century. Trained as a biologist and with gifted writing skills, Carson eloquently explained that the uncontrolled use of chemical pesticides, especially DDT, to improve crop yields or to eradicate harmful insects had disastrous environmental consequences. Her best-selling book helped spark the environmental movement in the 1960s. The following excerpt is from* Silent Spring.

Questions to Consider

1. According to Carson, in what ways was the pesticide aldrin most alarming?
2. Does Carson suggest alternatives to limiting harmful insects such as the Japanese beetle?
3. What does Carson hope to accomplish with her depiction?
4. How do think Carson might respond to the growth of suburbia? Why?
5. How might John Muir ("The American Forests," Document 161) react to Carson's depiction?

During the fall of 1959 some 27,000 acres in southeastern Michigan, including numerous suburbs of Detroit, were heavily dusted from the air with pellets of aldrin, one of the most dangerous of all the chlorinated hydrocarbons. The program was conducted by the Michigan Department of Agriculture with the cooperation of the United States Department of Agriculture; its announced purpose was control of the Japanese beetle. . . .

From its original point of entrance the Japanese beetle has spread rather widely throughout many of the states east of the Mississippi, where conditions of temperature and rainfall are suitable for it. Each year some outward movement beyond the existing boundaries of its distribution usually takes place. In the eastern areas where the beetles have been longest established, attempts have been made to set up natural controls. Where this has been done, the beetle populations have been kept at relatively low levels, as many records attest.

Despite the record of reasonable control in eastern areas, the midwestern states now on the fringe of the beetle's range have launched an attack worthy of the most deadly enemy instead of only a moderately destructive insect, employing the most dangerous chemicals distributed in a manner that exposes large numbers of people, their domestic animals, and all wildlife to the poison intended for the beetle. As a result these Japanese beetle programs have caused shocking destruction of animal life and have exposed human beings to undeniable hazard. Sections of Michigan, Kentucky, Iowa, Indiana, Illinois, and Missouri are all experiencing a rain of chemicals in the name of beetle control.

The Michigan spraying was one of the first large-scale attacks on the Japanese beetle from the air. The choice of aldrin, one of the deadliest of all chemicals, was not determined by any peculiar suitability for Japanese beetle control, but simply by the wish to save money—aldrin was the cheapest of the compounds available. While the state in its official release to the press acknowledged that aldrin is a "poison," it implied that no harm could come to human beings in the heavily populated areas to which the chemical was applied. (The official answer to the query "What precautions should I take?"

Excerpted from "Needless Havoc," from *Silent Spring* by Rachel Carson. Copyright © 1962 by Rachel L. Carson, renewed 1990 by Roger Christie. Reprinted by permission of Houghton Mifflin Company. All rights reserved.

was "For you, none.") An official of the Federal Aviation Agency was later quoted in the local press to the effect that "this is a safe operation" and a representative to the Detroit Department of Parks and Recreation added his assurance that "the dust is harmless to humans and will not hurt plants or pets." One must assume that none of these officials had consulted the published and readily available reports of the United States Public Health Service, the Fish and Wildlife Service, and other evidence of the extremely poisonous nature of aldrin.

Acting under the Michigan pest control law which allows the state to spray indiscriminately without notifying or gaining permission of individual landowners, the low-lying planes began to fly over the Detroit area. The city authorities and the Federal Aviation Agency were immediately besieged by calls from worried citizens. After receiving nearly 800 calls in a single hour, the police begged radio and television stations and newspapers to "tell the watchers what they were seeing and advise them it was safe," according to the Detroit *News*. . . as the planes went about their work the pellets of insecticide fell on beetles and humans alike, showers of "harmless" poison descending on people shopping or going to work and on children out from school for the lunch hour. Housewives swept the granules from porches and sidewalks, where they are said to have "looked like snow." As pointed out later by the Michigan Audubon Society, "In the spaces between shingles on roofs, in eaves-troughs, in the cracks in bark and twigs, the little white pellets of aldrin-and-clay, no bigger than a pin head, were lodged by the millions. . . . When the snow and rain came, every puddle became a possible death potion."

Within a few days after the dusting operation, the Detroit Audubon Society began receiving calls about the birds. According to the Society's secretary, Mrs. Ann Boyes, "The first indication that the people were concerned about the spray was a call I received on Sunday morning from a woman who reported that coming home from church she saw an alarming number of dead and dying birds. The spraying there had been done on Thursday. She said there were no birds at all flying in the area, that she had found at least a dozen [dead] in her backyard and that the neighbors had found dead squirrels." All other calls received by Mrs. Boyes that day reported "a great many dead birds and no live ones. . . . People who had maintained bird feeders said there were no birds at all at their feeders." Birds picked up in a dying condition showed the typical symptoms of insecticide poisoning—tremoring, loss of ability to fly, paralysis, convulsions.

Nor were birds the only forms of life immediately affected. A local veterinarian reported that his office was full of clients with dogs and cats that had suddenly sickened. Cats, who so meticulously groom their coats and lick their paws, seemed to be most affected. Their illness took the form of severe diarrhea, vomiting, and convulsions. The only advice the veterinarian could give his clients was not to let the animals out unnecessarily, or to wash the paws promptly if they did so. (But the chlorinated hydrocarbons cannot be washed even from fruits or vegetables, so little protection could be expected from this measure.)

Despite the insistence of the City-County Health Commissioner that the birds must have been killed by "some other kind of spraying" and that the outbreak of throat and chest irritations that followed the exposure to aldrin must have been due to "something else," the local Health Department received a constant stream of complaints. A prominent Detroit internist was called upon to treat four of his patients within an hour after they had been exposed while watching the planes at work. All had similar symptoms: nausea, vomiting, chills, fever, extreme fatigue, and coughing.

The Detroit experience has been repeated in many other communities as pressure has mounted to combat the Japanese beetle with chemicals. At Blue Island, Illinois, hundreds of dead and dying birds were picked up. Data collected by birdbanders here suggest that 80 per cent of the songbirds were sacrificed. In Joliet, Illinois, some 3000 acres were treated with heptachlor in 1959. According to reports from a local sportsmen's club, the bird population within the treated area was "virtually wiped out." Dead rabbits, muskrats, opossums, and fish were also found in numbers, and one of the local schools made the collection of insecticide-poisoned birds a science project. . . .

204

The Port Huron Statement (1962)

During the 1960s, record numbers of young Americans attended colleges and universities. Some found higher education to be insensitive, bureaucratic, and hierarchical, reflecting an American society they found dehumanizing and where the emerging "technocracy" subsumed the individual. For many of these students, the issues of the day—particularly the Civil Rights Movement and the Cold War, and later Vietnam—prompted a critical questioning of American values. One of the earliest statements on student disaffection came from the Students for a Democratic Society (SDS). In 1962, a group of students met at a United Auto Workers conference center in Port Huron, Michigan, to declare their disillusionment with society and prepare a political platform for the organization. Primarily written by Tom Hayden, the Port Huron Statement is a thoughtful critique of American life. The document helped influence many young activists, and the SDS became the principal organization of student radicalism. The Port Huron Statement is excerpted as follows.

Questions to Consider

1. According to the statement, what has created the discontent among SDS members?
2. Why are the paradoxes of the age so troubling?
3. What does the statement propose as the solution?

4. In what ways are the ideas expressed in the Port Huron Statement similar to those found in Roosevelt's "Four Freedoms" (Document 188)? How are they different?

We are people of this generation, bred in at least modest comfort, housed now in universities, looking uncomfortably to the world we inherit.

When we were kids the United States was the wealthiest and strongest country in the world; the only one with the atom bomb, the least scarred by modern war, an initiator of the United Nations that we thought would distribute Western influence throughout the world. Freedom and equality for each individual, government of, by, and for the people—these American values we found good, principles by which we could live as men. Many of us began maturing in complacency.

As we grew, however, our comfort was penetrated by events too troubling to dismiss. First, the permeating and victimizing fact of human degradation, symbolized by the Southern struggle against racial bigotry, compelled most of us from silence to activism. Second, the enclosing fact of the Cold War, symbolized by the presence of the Bomb, brought awareness that we ourselves, and our friends, and millions of abstract "others" we knew more directly because of our common peril might die at any time. We might deliberately ignore, or avoid, or fail to feel all other human problems, but not these two, for these were too immediate and crushing in their impact, too challenging in the demand that we as individuals take the responsibility for encounter and resolution.

While these and other problems either directly oppressed us or rankled our consciences and became our own subjective concerns, we began to see complicated and disturbing paradoxes in our surrounding America. The declaration "all men are created equal . . ." rang hollow before the facts of Negro life in the South and the big cities of the North. The proclaimed peaceful intentions of the United States contradicted its economic and military investments in the Cold War status quo.

We witnessed, and continue to witness, other paradoxes. With nuclear energy whole cities can easily be powered, yet the dominant nation-states seem more likely to unleash destruction greater than that incurred in all wars of human history. Although our own technology is destroying old and creating new forms of social organization, men still tolerate meaningless work and idleness. While two-thirds of mankind suffers undernourishment, our own upper classes revel amidst superfluous abundance. Although world population is expected to double in forty years, the nations still tolerate anarchy as a major principle of international conduct and uncontrolled exploitation governs the sapping of the earth's physical resources. Although mankind desperately needs revolutionary leadership, America rests in national stalemate, its goals ambiguous and tradition-bound instead of informed and clear, its democratic system apathetic and manipulated rather than "of, by, and for the people."

From Students for a Democratic Society (U.S.), *Port Huron Statement* (New York, 1962). Copyright © Tom Hayden. Reprinted by permission.

Not only did tarnish appear on our image of American virtue, not only did disillusion occur when the hypocrisy of American ideals was discovered, but we began to sense that what we had originally seen as the American Golden Age was actually the decline of an era. The worldwide outbreak of revolution against colonialism and imperialism, the entrenchment of totalitarian states, the menace of war, overpopulation, international disorder, supertechnology—these trends were testing the tenacity of our own commitment to democracy and freedom and our abilities to visualize their application to a world in upheaval.

Our work is guided by the sense that we may be the last generation in the experiment with living. But we are a minority—the vast majority of our people regard the temporary equilibriums of our society and world as eternally-functional parts. In this is perhaps the outstanding paradox: we ourselves are imbued with urgency, yet the message of our society is that there is no viable alternative to the present. Beneath the reassuring tones of the politicians, beneath the common opinion that America will "muddle through," beneath the stagnation of those who have closed their minds to the future, is the pervading feeling that there simply are no alternatives, that our times have witnessed the exhaustion not only of Utopias, but of any new departures as well. Feeling the press of complexity upon the emptiness of life, people are fearful of the thought that at any moment things might thrust out of control. They fear change itself, since change might smash whatever invisible framework seems to hold back chaos for them now. For most Americans, all crusades are suspect, threatening. The fact that each individual sees apathy in his fellows perpetuates the common reluctance to organize for change. The dominant institutions are complex enough to blunt the minds of their potential critics, and entrenched enough to swiftly dissipate or entirely repel the energies of protest and reform, thus limiting human expectancies. Then, too, we are a materially improved society, and by our own improvements we seem to have weakened the case for further change.

Some would have us believe that Americans feel contentment amidst prosperity—but might it not better be called a glaze above deeply felt anxieties about their role in the new world? And if these anxieties produce a developed indifference to human affairs, do they not as well produce a yearning to believe there *is* an alternative to the present, that something *can* be done to change circumstances in the school, the workplaces, the bureaucracies, the government? It is to this latter yearning, at once the spark and engine of change, that we direct our present appeal. The search for truly democratic alternatives to the present, and a commitment to social experimentation with them, is a worthy and fulfilling human enterprise, one which moves us and, we hope, others today. On such a basis do we offer this document of our convictions and analysis: as an effort in understanding and changing the conditions of humanity in the late twentieth century, an effort rooted in the ancient, still unfulfilled conception of man attaining determining influence over his circumstances of life. . . .

205

"The Problem That Has No Name" (1963)

The two decades following World War II marked the nadir of the feminist movement, as returning veterans and mass culture influenced women to assume domestic roles of mother and housewife and to forsake independent careers (even working mothers were criticized). Despite the prevailing attitude, significant changes were taking place: The number of women who received a college education increased rapidly, and more women, especially married women, joined the workforce. The feminist movement was revived in 1963 with Betty Friedan's best seller, The Feminine Mystique, *which is excerpted as follows. Friedan, a Smith College graduate, mother of three, and a freelance writer, based her book on a questionnaire she sent to former classmates asking about their lives after school and some further research. The book challenged the happy suburban housewife myth and found a receptive audience among many middle-class women who identified with its thesis. Friedan became an instant celebrity and spearheaded an active woman's rights campaign; in 1966, she helped found the National Organization for Women (NOW).*

Questions to Consider

1. According to Betty Friedan, how were women pressured into accepting the role of "housewife" in the post–World War II years?

2. What is the "problem that has no name"? What caused the problem? What solutions does Friedan suggest?

3. Who was the audience for Friedan's book?

4. In what ways are Friedan's ideas similar to those expressed by Jane Addams in "Why Women Should Vote" (Document 165)? How are they different? What conclusions might you draw about the changing status of women by comparing the two documents?

The problem lay buried, unspoken, for many years in the minds of American women. It was a strange stirring, a sense of dissatisfaction, a yearning that women suffered in the middle of the twentieth century in the United States. Each suburban wife struggled with it alone. As she made the beds, shopped for groceries, matched slipcover material, ate peanut butter sandwiches with her children, chauffeured Cub Scouts and Brownies, lay beside her husband at night—she was afraid to ask even of herself the silent question—"Is this all?"

For over fifteen years there was no word of this yearning in the millions of words written about women, for women, in all the columns, books and

From *The Feminine Mystique* by Betty Friedan. Copyright © 1983, 1974, 1973, 1963 by Betty Friedan. Used by permission of W. W. Norton & Company, Inc.

articles by experts telling women their role was to seek fulfillment as wives and mothers. Over and over women heard in voices of tradition and of Freudian sophistication that they could desire no greater destiny than to glory in their own femininity. Experts told them how to catch a man and keep him, how to breastfeed children and handle their toilet training, how to cope with sibling rivalry and adolescent rebellion; how to buy a dishwasher, bake bread, cook gourmet snails, and build a swimming pool with their own hands; how to dress, look, and act more feminine and make marriage more exciting; how to keep their husbands from dying young and their sons from growing into delinquents. They were taught to pity the neurotic, unfeminine, unhappy women who wanted to be poets or physicists or presidents. They learned that truly feminine women do not want careers, higher education, political rights—the independence and the opportunities that the old-fashioned feminists fought for. Some women, in their forties and fifties, still remembered painfully giving up those dreams, but most of the younger women no longer even thought about them. A thousand expert voices applauded their femininity, their adjustment, their new maturity. All they had to do was devote their lives from earliest girlhood to finding a husband and bearing children. . . .

In the fifteen years after World War II, this mystique of feminine fulfillment became the cherished and self-perpetuating core of contemporary American culture. Millions of women lived their lives in the image of those pretty pictures of the American suburban housewife, kissing their husbands goodbye in front of the picture window, depositing their stationwagonsful of children at school, and smiling as they ran the new electric waxer over the spotless kitchen floor. They baked their own bread, sewed their own and their children's clothes, kept their new washing machines and dryers running all day. They changed the sheets on the beds twice a week instead of once, took the rug-hooking class in adult education, and pitied their poor frustrated mothers, who had dreamed of having a career. Their only dream was to be perfect wives and mothers; their highest ambition to have five children and a beautiful house, their only fight to get and keep their husbands. They had no thought for the unfeminine problems of the world outside the home; they wanted the men to make the major decisions. They gloried in their role as women, and wrote proudly to make the major decisions. They gloried in their role as women, and wrote proudly on the census blank: "Occupation: housewife." . . .

If a woman had a problem in the 1950's and 1960's, she knew that something must be wrong with her marriage, or with herself. Other women were satisfied with their lives, she thought. What kind of a woman was she if she did not feel this mysterious fulfillment waxing the kitchen floor? She was so ashamed to admit her dissatisfaction that she never knew how many other women shared it. If she tried to tell her husband, he didn't understand what she was talking about. She did not really understand it herself. For over fifteen years women in America found it harder to talk about this problem than about sex. Even the psychoanalysts had no name for it. When a woman did, she would say, "I'm so ashamed," or "I must be hopelessly neurotic." . . .

Gradually I came to realize that the problem that has no name was shared by countless women in America. . . . The groping words I heard from other women, on quiet afternoons when children were at school or on quiet evenings when husbands worked late, I think I understood first as a woman long before I understood their larger social and psychological implications.

Just what was this problem that has no name? What were the words women used when they tried to express it? Sometimes a woman would say "I feel empty somehow . . . incomplete." Or she would say, "I feel as if I don't exist." Sometimes she blotted out the feeling with a tranquilizer. Sometimes she thought the problem was with her husband, or her children, or that what she really needed was to redecorate her house, or move to a better neighborhood, or have an affair, or another baby. Sometimes, she went to a doctor with symptoms she could hardly describe: "A tired feeling . . . I get so angry with the children it scares me . . . I feel like crying without any reason." (A Cleveland doctor called it "the housewife's syndrome.") . . .

It is no longer possible to ignore that voice, to dismiss the desperation of so many American women. This is not what being a woman means, no matter what the experts say. For human suffering there is a reason; perhaps the reason has not been found because the right questions have not been asked, or pressed far enough. I do not accept the answer that there is no problem because American women have luxuries that women in other times and lands never dreamed of; part of the strange newness of the problem is that it cannot be understood in terms of the age-old material problems of man: poverty, sickness, hunger, cold. . . .

It is no longer possible today to blame the problem on loss of femininity: to say that education and independence and equality with men have made American women unfeminine. I have heard so many women try to deny this dissatisfied voice within themselves because it does not fit the pretty-picture of femininity the experts have given them. I think, in fact, that this is the first clue to the mystery: the problem cannot be understood in the generally accepted terms by which scientists have studied women, doctors have treated them, counselors have advised them, and writers have written them. Women who suffer this problem in whom this voice is tiring, have lived their whole lives in the pursuit of feminine fulfillment. They are not career women (although career women may have other problems); they are women whose greatest ambition has been marriage and children. For the oldest of these women, these daughters of the American middle class, no other dream was possible. The ones in their forties and fifties who once had other dreams gave them up and threw themselves joyously into life as housewives. For the youngest, the new wives and mothers, this was the only dream. They are the ones who quit high school and college to marry, or marked time in some job in which they had no real interest until they married. These women are very "feminine" in the usual sense, and yet they still suffer the problem. . . .

If I am right, the problem that has no name stirring in the midst of so many American women today is not a matter of loss of femininity or too much education, or demands of domesticity. It is far more important than anyone recognizes. It is the key to women and their husbands and children, and puzzling their doctors and educators for years. It may well be the key to our future as a nation and a culture. We can no longer ignore that voice within women that says: "I want something more than my husband and my children and my home."

206

Letter from Birmingham Jail (1963)

The Civil Rights Movement made sporadic gains in the decade after the Brown decision, but not enough to satisfy many African Americans. Civil rights activism took the form of isolated local protests, which ultimately culminated in a massive social movement. The most famous incident was Rosa Parks' refusal to abandon her bus seat to a white rider (violating a city law) and the subsequent Montgomery bus boycott. One of the boycott's leaders was Martin Luther King, Jr. An eloquent Georgian who had recently received his Ph.D. in theology from Boston University, King served as a Baptist minister in Montgomery. King adopted the nonviolent resistance tactics of India's Mahatma Gandhi to the Civil Rights Movement with great success. He helped form and led the clergy-based Southern Christian Leadership Conference (SCLC), and he emerged as the most prominent spokesman for African Americans. The SCLC organized nonviolent direct action campaigns in cities throughout the South. When King was arrested for leading a Birmingham, Alabama, demonstration, several white clergymen wrote to King criticizing his tactics. King's response was his famous "Letter from Birmingham Jail," which is excerpted following.

Questions to Consider

1. What central issues does King address in his letter?
2. Why was King disappointed in moderate whites in the South?
3. What social changes does King hope to accomplish?
4. What does this document reveal about the King-led Civil Rights Movement?

You deplore the demonstrations taking place in Birmingham. But your statement, I am sorry to say, fails to express a similar concern for the conditions that brought about the demonstrations. I am sure that none of you would want to rest content with the superficial kind of social analysis that deals

Martin Luther King, Jr., *Why We Can't Wait* (New York, 1964), 77–100. Reprinted by arrangement with the Estate of Martin Luther King, Jr., c/o Writers House as agent for the proprietor. Copyright 1963 by Martin Luther King, Jr., copyright renewed 1991 by Coretta Scott King.

merely with effects and does not grapple with underlying causes. It is unfortunate that demonstrations are taking place in Birmingham, but it is even more unfortunate that the city's white power structure left the Negro community with no alternative.

In any nonviolent campaign there are four basic steps: collection of the facts to determine whether injustices exist; negotiation; self-purification; and direct action. We have gone through all these steps in Birmingham. There can be no gainsaying the fact that racial injustice engulfs this community. Birmingham is probably the most thoroughly segregated city in the United States. Its ugly record of brutality is widely known. Negroes have experienced grossly unjust treatment in the courts. There have been more unsolved bombings of Negro homes and churches in Birmingham than in any other city in the nation. These are the hard, brutal facts of the case. On the basis of these conditions, Negro leaders sought to negotiate with the city fathers. But the latter consistently refused to engage in good-faith negotiation. . . .

We have waited for more than 340 years for our constitutional and God-given rights. The nations of Asia and Africa are moving with jetlike speed toward gaining political independence, but we still creep at horse-and-buggy pace toward gaining a cup of coffee at a lunch counter. Perhaps it is easy for those who have never felt the stinging darts of segregation to say, "Wait." But when you have seen vicious mobs lynch your mothers and fathers at will and drown your sisters and brothers at whim; when you have seen hate-filled policemen curse, kick and even kill your black brothers and sisters; when you see the vast majority of your twenty million Negro brothers smothering in an airtight cage of poverty in the midst of an affluent society; when you suddenly find your tongue twisted and your speech stammering as you seek to explain to your six-year-old daughter why she can't go to the public amusement park that has just been advertised on television, and see tears welling up in her eyes when she is told that Funtown is closed to colored children, and see ominous clouds of inferiority beginning to form in her little mental sky, and see her beginning to distort her personality by developing an unconscious bitterness toward white people; when you have to concoct an answer for a five-year-old son who is asking: "Daddy, why do white people treat colored people so mean?"; when you take a cross-country drive and find it necessary to sleep night after night in the uncomfortable corners of your automobile because no motel will accept you; when you are humiliated day in and day out by nagging signs reading "white" and "colored"; when your first name becomes "nigger," your middle name becomes "boy" (however old you are) and your last name becomes "John," and your wife and mother are never given the respected title "Mrs."; when you are harried by day and haunted by night by the fact that you are a Negro, living constantly at tiptoe stance, never quite knowing what to expect next, and are plagued with inner fears and outer resentments; when you are forever fighting a degenerating sense of "nobodiness"—then you will understand why we find it difficult to wait. There comes a time when the cup of endurance runs over, and men are no longer willing to be plunged into the abyss of despair. I hope, sirs, you can understand our legitimate and unavoidable impatience.

You express a great deal of anxiety over our willingness to break laws. This is certainly a legitimate concern. Since we so diligently urge people to obey the Supreme Court's decision of 1954 outlawing segregation in the public schools, at first glance it may seem rather paradoxical for us consciously to break laws. One may well ask: "How can you advocate breaking some laws and obeying others?" The answer lies in the fact that there are two types of laws: just and unjust. I would be the first to advocate obeying just laws. One has not only a legal but a moral responsibility to obey just laws. Conversely, one has a moral responsibility to disobey unjust laws. I would agree with St. Augustine that "an unjust law is no law at all." . . .

I hope you are able to see the distinction I am trying to point out. In no sense do I advocate evading or defying the law, as would the rabid segregationist. That would lead to anarchy. One who breaks an unjust law must do so openly, lovingly, and with a willingness to accept the penalty. I submit that an individual who breaks a law that conscience tells him is unjust, and who willingly accepts the penalty of imprisonment in order to arouse the conscience of the community over its injustice, is in reality expressing the highest respect for law. . . .

I must make two honest confessions to you, my Christian and Jewish brothers. First, I must confess that over the past few years I have been gravely disappointed with the white moderate. I have almost reached the regrettable conclusion that the Negro's great stumbling block in his stride toward freedom is not the White Citizen's Counciler or the Ku Klux Klanner, but the white moderate, who is more devoted to "order" than to justice; who prefers a negative peace which is the absence of tension to a positive peace which is the presence of justice; who constantly says: "I agree with you in the goal you seek, but I cannot agree with your methods of direct action"; who paternalistically believes he can set the timetable for another man's freedom; who lives by a mythical concept of time and who constantly advises the Negro to wait for a "more convenient season."

Shallow understanding from people of good will is more frustrating than absolute misunderstanding from people of ill will. Lukewarm acceptance is much more bewildering than outright rejection. . . .

You speak of our activity in Birmingham as extreme. At first I was rather disappointed that fellow clergymen would see my nonviolent efforts as those of an extremist. I began thinking about the fact that I stand in the middle of two opposing forces in the Negro community. One is a force of complacency, made up in part of Negroes who, as a result of long years of oppression, are so drained of self-respect and a sense of "somebodiness" that they have adjusted to segregation; and in part of a few middle-class Negroes who, because of a degree of academic and economic security and because in some ways they profit by segregation, have become insensitive to the problems of the masses. The other force is one of bitterness and hatred, and it comes perilously close to advocating violence. It is expressed in the various black nationalist groups that are springing up across the nation, the largest and best-known being Elijah Muhammad's Muslim movement. Nourished by the Negro's frustration over the continued existence of racial discrimination, this movement is made up of people who have lost faith in America, who have absolutely repudiated Christianity, and who have concluded that the white man is an incorrigible "devil."

I have tried to stand between these two forces, saying that we need emulate neither the "do-nothingism" of the complacent nor the hatred and despair of the black nationalist. For there is the more excellent way of love and nonviolent protest. I am grateful to God that, through the influence of the Negro church, the way of nonviolence became an integral part of our struggle. . . .

I had hoped that the white moderate would see this need. Perhaps I was too optimistic; perhaps I expected too much. I suppose I should have realized that few members of the oppressor race can understand the deep groans and passionate yearnings of the oppressed race, and still fewer have the vision to see that injustice must be rooted out by strong, persistent and determined action. I am thankful, however, that some of our white brothers in the South have grasped the meaning of this social revolution and committed themselves to it. . . .

207

Malcolm X on Race Relations (1964)

Not all African Americans supported the nonviolent, direct-action campaigns of the mainstream Civil Rights Movement. Frustrated at the slow progress of change, some wanted a more demanding, more militant approach. Many of these advocates of black nationalism, or Black Power, as it came to be called, were inspired by Malcolm X. Born Malcolm Little, he was a high school dropout and was jailed for an attempted burglary. While serving a 10-year prison term, he was converted to the separatist doctrine of Elijah Muhammad and the Nation of Islam. He adopted "X" to replace "the white slave-master name which had been imposed upon my paternal forebears by some blue-eyed devil." Released from prison, Malcolm X became a popular and controversial Black Muslim spokesman, who attracted large audiences—both black and white—because of his fiery rhetoric, charisma, and militancy on such topics as black nationalism, self-help, and white racism. After a 1964 pilgrimage to Mecca, where he witnessed white Muslims who were free of prejudice, Malcolm X softened his attacks on whites, rejected black separatism, and considered political power as essential for black advances. He would eventually break from the Nation of Islam and form his own organization. In April 1964, just before leaving on his pilgrimage to Mecca, Malcolm X spoke to a New York audience, addressing issues of black nationalism and revolution. The speech is excerpted as follows.

Questions to Consider

1. What is the "black revolution" that Malcolm X discussed?
2. In what ways was he critical of the Civil Rights Movement?
3. How does Malcolm X believe the black revolution will come about?
4. How does this speech reveal both the militancy of Malcolm X as well as his moderating views toward whites?

1964 will be America's hottest year; her hottest year yet; a year of much racial violence and much racial bloodshed. But it won't be blood that's going to flow only on one side. The new generation of black people that have grown up in this country during recent years are already forming the opinion, and it's a just opinion, that if there is to be bleeding, it should be reciprocal—bleeding on both sides. . . .

So today, when the black man starts reaching out for what America says are his rights, the black man feels that he is within his rights—when he becomes the victim of brutality by those who are depriving him of his rights—to do whatever is necessary to protect himself. An example of this was taking place last night at this same time in Cleveland, where the police were putting water hoses on our people there and also throwing tear gas at them—and they met a hail of stones, a hail of rocks, a hail of bricks. A couple of weeks ago in Jacksonville, Florida, a young teen-age Negro was throwing Molotov cocktails.*

Well, Negroes didn't do this ten years ago. But what you should learn from this is that they are waking up. It was stones yesterday, Molotov cocktails today; it will be hand grenades tomorrow and whatever else is available the next day. The seriousness of this situation must be faced up to. You should not feel that I am inciting someone to violence. I'm only warning of a powder-keg situation. You can take it or leave it. If you take the warning, perhaps you can still save yourself. But if you ignore it or ridicule it, well, death is already at your doorstep. There are 22 million African-Americans who are ready to fight for independence right here. When I say fight for independence right here, I don't means any nonviolent fight, or turn-the-other-cheek fight. Those days are gone. Those days are over. . . .

This is a real revolution. Revolution is always based on land. Revolution is never based on begging somebody for an integrated cup of coffee. Revolutions are never fought by turning the other cheek. Revolutions are never based upon love-your-enemy and pray-for-those-who-spitefully-use-you. And revolutions are never waged singing "We Shall Overcome." Revolutions are based upon bloodshed. Revolutions are never compromising. Revolutions are never based upon negotiations. Revolutions are never based upon any kind of tokenism whatsoever. Revolutions are never even based upon that which is

---

*A crude hand grenade made with a bottle filled with a flammable liquid and a flaming rag inserted in the opening, that will ignite the liquid when the bottle is broken.

The Black Revolution," in *Malcolm X Speaks*, George Breitman and Betty Shabazz, eds., 45–59. Copyright 1965, 1989 by Betty Shabazz and Pathfinder Press. Reprinted by permission.

begging a corrupt society or a corrupt system to accept us into it. Revolutions overturn systems. And there is no system on this earth which has proven itself more corrupt, more criminal, than this system that in 1964 still colonizes 22 million African-Americans, still enslaves 22 million Afro-Americans.

There is no system more corrupt than a system that represents itself as the example of freedom, the example of democracy, and can go all over this earth telling other people how to straighten out their house, when you have citizens of this country who have to use bullets if they want to cast a ballot.

The greatest weapon the colonial powers have used in the past against our people has always been divide-and-conquer. America is a colonial power. She has colonized 22 million Afro-Americans by depriving us a first-class citizenship, by depriving us of civil rights, actually by depriving us of human rights. She has not only deprived us of the right to be a citizen, she has deprived us of the right to be human beings, the right to be recognized and respected as men and women. In this country the black can be fifty years old and he is still a "boy." . . .

All of our people have the same goals, the same objective. That objective is freedom, justice, equality. All of us want recognition and respect as human beings. We don't want to be integrationists. Nor do we want to be separationists. We want to be human beings. Integration is only a method that is used by some groups to obtain freedom, justice, equality and respect as human beings. Separation is only a method that is used by other groups to obtain freedom, justice, equality or human dignity. . . .

We have to keep in mind at all times that we are not fighting for integration, nor are we fighting for separation. We are fighting for recognition as human beings. We are fighting for the right to live as free humans in this society. In fact, we are actually fighting for rights that are even greater than civil rights and that is human rights. . . .

And today you have a new generation of black people who have come on the scene, who have become disenchanted with the entire system, who have become disillusioned over the system, and who are ready now and willing to do something about it.

So, in my conclusion, in speaking about the black revolution, America today is at a time or in a day or at an hour where she is the first country on this earth that can actually have a bloodless revolution. In the past, revolutions have been bloody. Historically you just don't have a peaceful revolution. Revolutions are bloody, revolutions are violent, revolutions cause bloodshed and death follows in their paths. America is the only country in history in a position to bring about a revolution without violence and bloodshed. But America is not morally equipped to do so. . . .

And the only way without bloodshed that this can be brought about is that the black man has to be given full use of the ballot in every one of the fifty states. But if the black man doesn't get the ballot, then you are going to be faced with another man who forgets the ballot and starts using the bullet. . . .

So you have a people today who not only know what they want, but also know what they are supposed to have. And they themselves are creating another generation that is coming up that not only will know what it wants and know what it should have, but also will be ready and willing to do whatever is necessary to see that what they should have materializes immediately. Thank you.

208

Lyndon Johnson on the Great Society (1964)

By the early 1960s, some paradoxes had developed in American society. Amid the prosperous times were growing numbers of people who lived in poverty; as the urban population increased, the infrastructure of roads and housing deteriorated; some public schools provided excellent educational opportunities, whereas others, often in poor areas, lagged behind. In race relations, the contrast between whites and blacks was increasingly apparent. The Kennedy administration believed that the federal government should become more active in resolving problems to create a better society and had conceived of some programs to effect change. When Lyndon B. Johnson became president after Kennedy's assassination, he was able to win support for many of Kennedy's proposals. He also began creating his own program, which he called the Great Society. In May 1964, Johnson spoke to students at the University of Michigan. The speech, excerpted following, provided a framework of the Great Society and its goals.

Questions to Consider

1. What is the Great Society that Johnson proposes?
2. Why does he target cities, rural areas, and education as the starting places for the Great Society?
3. How does he hope to accomplish the Great Society?
4. In what ways is the Great Society similar to the New Nationalism of Theodore Roosevelt (Document 163)? How is it different? In what ways is the Great Society similar to Franklin Roosevelt's New Deal ("Franklin D. Roosevelt's First Inaugural Address," Document 181)? How is it different?

The challenge of the next half century is whether we have the wisdom to use that wealth to enrich and elevate our national life, and to advance the quality of our American civilization.

Your imagination, your initiative, and your indignation will determine whether we build a society where progress is the servant of our needs, or a

---

"Remarks at the University of Michigan, May 22, 1964," *Public Papers of the Presidents of the United States, Lyndon B. Johnson, 1963–64* (Washington, 1965): 704–707.

society where old values and new visions are buried under unbridled growth. For in your time we have the opportunity to move not only toward the rich society and the powerful society, but upward to the Great Society.

The Great Society rests on abundance and liberty for all. It demands an end to poverty and racial injustice, to which we are totally committed in our time. But that is just the beginning.

The Great Society is a place where every child can find knowledge to enrich his mind and to enlarge his talents. It is a place where leisure is a welcome chance to build and reflect, not a feared cause of boredom and restlessness. It is a place where the city of man serves not only the needs of the body and the demands of commerce but the desire for beauty and the hunger for community.

It is a place where man can renew contact with nature. It is a place which honors creation for its own sake and for what it adds to the understanding of the race. It is a place where men are more concerned with the quality of their goals than the quantity of their goods.

But most of all, the Great Society is not a safe harbor, a resting place, a final objective, a finished work. It is a challenge constantly renewed, beckoning us toward a destiny where the meaning of our lives matches the marvelous products of our labor.

So I want to talk to you today about three places where we begin to build the Great Society—in our cities, in our countryside, and in our classrooms.

Many of you will live to see the day, perhaps 50 years from now, when there will be 400 million Americans—four-fifths of them in urban areas. In the remainder of this century urban population will double, city land will double, and we will have to build homes, highways, and facilities equal to all those built since this country was first settled. So in the next 40 years we must rebuild the entire urban United States. . . .

The catalog of ills is long: there is the decay of the centers and the despoiling of the suburbs. There is not enough housing for our people or transportation for our traffic. Open land is vanishing and old landmarks are violated.

Worst of all expansion is eroding the precious and time honored values of community with neighbors and communion with nature. The loss of these values breeds loneliness and boredom and indifference.

Our society will never be great until our cities are great. Today the frontier of imagination and innovation is inside those cities and not beyond their borders. . . .

A second place where we begin to build the Great Society is in our countryside. We have always prided ourselves on being not only America the strong and America the free, but America the beautiful. Today that beauty is in danger. The water we drink, the food we eat, the very air that we breathe, are threatened with pollution. Our parks are overcrowded, our seashores overburdened. Green fields and dense forests are disappearing.

A few years ago we were greatly concerned about the "Ugly American." Today we must act to prevent an ugly America.

For once the battle is lost, once our natural splendor is destroyed, it can never be recaptured. And once man can no longer walk with beauty or wonder at nature his spirit will wither and his sustenance be wasted.

A third place to build the Great Society is in the classroom of America. There your children's lives will be shaped. Our society will not be great until every young mind is set free to scan the farthest reaches of thought and imagination. We are still far from that goal.

Today, 8 million adult Americans, more than the entire population of Michigan, have not finished 5 years of school. Nearly 20 million have not finished 8 years of school. Nearly 54 million—more than one-quarter of all America—have not even finished high school. . . .

In many places, classrooms are overcrowded and curricula are outdated. Most of our qualified teachers are underpaid, and many of our paid teachers are unqualified. So we must give every child a place to sit and a teacher to learn from. Poverty must not be a bar to learning, and learning must offer an escape from poverty.

But more classrooms and more teachers are not enough. We must seek an educational system which grows in excellence as it grows in size. This means better training for our teachers. It means preparing youth to enjoy their hours of leisure as well as their hours of labor. It means exploring new techniques of teaching, to find new ways to stimulate the love of learning and the capacity for creation.

These are three of the central issues of the Great Society. While our Government has many programs directed at those issues, I do not pretend that we have the full answer to those problems. . . .

The solution to these problems does not rest on a massive program in Washington, nor can it rely solely on the strained resources of local authority. They require us to create new concepts of cooperation, a creative federalism, between the national Capital and the leaders of local communities. . . .

For better or for worse, your generation has been appointed by history to deal with those problems and to lead America toward a new age. You have the chance never before afforded to any people in any age. You can help build a society where the demands of morality, and the needs of the spirit, can be realized in the life of the Nation. . . .

209

"I Made Promises to Dead People" (1967–68)

The Domino Theory, which warned that communism must be halted before it spread, led U.S. policy makers to begin sending large numbers of U.S. troops to Vietnam in 1965. To many Americans, the Vietnam conflict seemed part of America's altruistic effort to make the world a better place, but increasingly, the war in Vietnam frustrated Americans. By 1968, more than 500,000 Americans were deployed in Southeast

Asia, and the United States' efforts to use its colossal military firepower and resources to defeat the communist Vietcong were ineffective. The war soon came to represent a hopeless cause that led to personal alienation and deep distrust of American institutions among many young Americans. The ensuing document records the insights of Jack McCloskey, an Army medic who served in Vietnam in 1967–68.

Questions to Consider

1. Why do you suppose that nonwhites and poor whites seem to account for most of the soldiers in Vietnam?

2. According to Jack McCloskey, why did Vietnam veterans become so alienated? How did returning veterans cope with this alienation?

3. What is the difference between McCloskey's war in Vietnam as perceived by his father and uncles?

4. After reading this document, how would you define *patriotism*?

What were your first impressions in Vietnam?

There was a lot of racial shit in Vietnam—in the rear especially. We'd go into Danang, and we'd see rebel flags and this bullshit. In the field, at least in my company, there was no racial tension whatsoever. I'd say 60 percent of my company was third world, Hispanic or black, and Native American. The rest were poor whites. . . .

What was that experience like? How did it affect you?

I remember the first guy I treated [voice cracks; tears in eyes]—a nineteen year-old Marine who stepped on a bouncing betty [a mine that explodes at groin level]. I remember running up and him saying, "Doc, doc, I'm going to live, ain't I?" I said, "Sure, babe," and he died. I remember crying, holding his hand, and crying. I cried at the next one, I cried at the next one, and I cried at the next one, until I got to a point where I wanted to either jump up and shoot myself or shut down.

Inevitably you get close to people in Vietnam. I got close to people, and they got killed. At that point, Vietnam had robbed me of one of the greatest human dignities a person can have—that's the ability to cry; that's the ability to feel. It got to a point where I didn't want to know where guys were from in the company. I didn't want to know their backgrounds. If they get hurt, I'll treat them; just don't talk to me.

There was also, though, in Vietnam. . . . [Breaks down.] I have never, ever, in my life, had a family like that, and that family was destroyed. When you're on the line like that, sharing like that, when your life depends on the other person and his life depends on you, you become so close. If I could gain that

From Jack McCloskey, "I Made Promises to Dead People," in *Winter Soldiers* by Richard Stacewicz, Twayne Publishers, © 1997, Twayne Publishers. Reprinted by permission of The Gale Group.

feeling now, that tightness that I had in Vietnam, I would do anything for that; but I can't get it anymore back here, and that's where the love-hate relationship comes in. . . .

Why?

This had become my family. By the time I returned to Vietnam, I was the senior medic in the company. There was a part of you that was God in Vietnam. You had to choose who would live and who would die. I went back because I thought I could make a better choice. I sometimes feel that was arrogance on my part. I felt that I was a very good medic. I did everything from tracheotomies to suturing people.

My last six months in Nam were with a helicopter assault battalion. We never had a base camp. We were aboard this ship called the *USS Tripoli,* and we would go all over, from Danang up to the DMZ [Demilitarized Zone], from three days to 30 days. We never knew where the fuck we were going. I remember being back on ship, never in the field that much. I'd start thinking of Casey and Allen [friends killed in action], remembering the good times, and I'd start shaking. I started using morphine. As a medic, I had an unlimited supply. I never mainlined; it was always in the asscheek or arm. Under that medication, I was able to remember the good times we had. I could get away from the horror. I could get away from their deaths. . . .

I'd say from July of 1969, when I got out of the service, to September 1969, I never talked to anybody. Nobody. I then went to school at City College here [New York City], getting my A.A. degree [an associate's degree]. I never mentioned to anybody in school that I was a Vietnam veteran. Until I got involved, all I would do was go to school and get drunk, go to school and get drunk. I was not involved in anything. It wasn't until Kent State and Cambodia that I started getting active again. When they turned the guns against their own people here at Kent State, when I saw American people believing the lies about Cambodia, that was it.

What compelled you to speak out? Why not just go on with your life?

When you're in Vietnam, you dream—dream about your girlfriend, dream about your wife—but you're dreaming of what it was before you left. When we came back to the world, it wasn't the world we left: your girlfriend's changed, you've changed—even though you don't think you've changed—so you go through this psychological "Hey, what the fuck is this back here in the world? This is the world I fought for?" I come back. I don't understand it; it doesn't understand me.

In Vietnam you came back as an individual. Seventy-two hours before, you're in combat. Seventy-two hours later, you're here in the world. What you learned for survival in Vietnam are not the norms for survival back here in the world. The Vietnam vet came back to a society, most especially to those among our own peer group, that in a lot of places in a lot of ways rejected them.

What do you do if you're eighteen or nineteen and you're from Harlem, you're a good machine gunner, you're a good medic, you're a good squad leader, you're a good mine-detector person, you're a good this, you're a good that? What do you do? For the first time in your life, you've been given responsibility, and you do a good job—and even if that good job means killing people, you've done a good job. [Then] you come back home, and you're just another nigger again?

You have to remember [that] the anger, the frustration, the alienation, that a lot of veterans came back with, to me are signs of sanity, not insanity. How else could you react to that situation?

This is why I'm very very proud that a lot of vets didn't fucking go off, didn't come back and start killing people, even as hurt and as painful as it was for them, they came back and didn't take their revenge out on the American public. In fact, they came back trying to change it.

You've got to remember that we were promised that if we go fight this war, we've got all this shit—we've got education, all these jobs waiting for us when we come home. What did it turn out to be? Bullshit. So I think it was a combination of seeing the war itself and understanding what that was about, and the other part of it, I think, for most white veterans that joined VVAW, was the shattering of the American dream. "I was given all these promises. I come home and they're not there."

I remember, when I first came back from Vietnam, trying to talk to my father, who had served in the Second World War; trying to talk to my uncles who had all served—but when I questioned my war, they thought I was questioning their war. They didn't want to hear it. I'm saying to them, "I'm not questioning your war. What you taught me, believing in America, believing in the Bill of Rights, I still believe in. The difference is [that] now I know my country can be wrong, and because I love my country, I want my country to start looking at that Bill of Rights." We did what we did because we loved our country and wanted our country to realize that it made mistakes. I am just as patriotic as my father or my uncle or anybody.

210

A Report on Racial Violence in the Cities (1968)

In the mid-1960s, a series of race riots convulsed America. Frustrated with the slow gains of the mainstream, nonviolent Civil Rights Movement and the raised hopes of President Lyndon Johnson's Great Society, urban African Americans took matters into their own hands. Beginning with the Watts riot in Los Angeles in August 1965, each of the next three summers witnessed the eruption of widespread violence, property destruction, and looting within the black neighborhoods of cities such as Detroit, Cleveland, Chicago, and Newark, New Jersey. Several hundred people died, thousands were injured, and millions of dollars worth of property was destroyed. President Johnson selected Otto Kerner, governor of Illinois and strong civil rights advocate, as chair of a federal commission to investigate the "civil disorders." The commission's published findings, often called the Kerner Report, offered the following explanation for the race riots of the 1960s.

Questions to Consider

1. According to the *Kerner Report,* what has helped shape white racial attitudes?
2. According to the report, who were the rioters and why did they riot?
3. What solutions does the report offer?
4. How might Herman Talmadge, author of "Statement on the *Brown Decision*" (Document 198), have responded to this report?

The record before this Commission reveals that the causes of recent racial disorders are imbedded in a massive tangle of issues and circumstances—social, economic, political, and psychological—which arise out of the historical pattern of Negro-white relations in America. . . .

Despite these complexities, certain fundamental matters are clear. Of these, the most fundamental is the racial attitude and behavior of white Americans toward black Americans. Race prejudice has shaped our history decisively in the past; it now threatens to do so again. White racism is essentially accumulating in our cities since the end of World War II. At the base of this mixture are three of the most bitter fruits of white racial attitudes:

PERVASIVE DISCRIMINATION AND SEGREGATION. The first is surely the continuing exclusion of great numbers of Negroes from the benefits of economic progress through discrimination in employment and education, and their enforced confinement in segregated housing and schools. The corrosive and degrading effects of this condition and the attitudes that underlie it are the source of the deepest bitterness and at the center of the problem of racial disorder.

BLACK MIGRATION AND WHITE EXODUS. The second is the massive and growing concentration of impoverished Negroes in our major cities resulting from Negro migration from the rural South, rapid population growth and the continuing movement of the white middle-class to the suburbs. The consequence is a greatly increased burden on the already depleted resources of cities, creating a growing crisis of deteriorating facilities and services and unmet human needs.

BLACK GHETTOS. Third, in the teeming racial ghettos, segregation and poverty have intersected to destroy opportunity and hope and to enforce failure. The ghettos too often mean men and women without jobs, families without men, and schools where children are processed instead of educated, until they return to the street—to crime, to narcotics, to dependency on welfare, and to bitterness and resentment against society in general and white society in particular.

These three forces have converged on the inner city in recent years and on the people who inhabit it. At the same time, most whites and many Negroes outside the ghetto have prospered to a degree unparalleled in the

National Advisory Commission on Civil Disorders, *Report of the National Advisory Commission on Civil Disorders* (Washington, DC, 1968), 203–206.

history of civilization. Through television—the universal appliance in the ghetto—and the other media of mass communications, this affluence has been endlessly flaunted before the eyes of the negro poor and the jobless ghetto youth.

As Americans, most Negro citizens carry within themselves two basic aspirations of our society. They seek to share in both the material resources of our system and its intangible benefits—dignity, respect and acceptance. . . .

Yet these facts alone—fundamental as they are—cannot be said to have caused the disorders. Other and more immediate factors help explain why these events happened now.

Recently, three powerful ingredients have begun to catalyze the mixture.

FRUSTRATED HOPES.   The expectations aroused by the great judicial and legislative victories of the civil rights movement have led to frustration, hostility and cynicism in the face of the persistent gap between promise and fulfillment. The dramatic struggle for equal rights in the South has sensitized Northern Negroes to the economic inequalities reflected in the deprivations of ghetto life.

LEGITIMATION OF VIOLENCE.   A climate that tends toward the approval and encouragement of violence as a form of protest has been created by white terrorism directed against nonviolent protest, including instances of abuse and even murder of some civil rights workers in the South; but the open defiance of law and federal authority by state and local officials resisting desegregation; and by some protest groups engaging in civil disobedience who turn their backs on nonviolence, go beyond the Constitutionally protected rights of petition and free assembly, and resort to violence to attempt to compel alteration of laws and policies with which they disagree. . . .

POWERLESSNESS.   Finally, many negroes have come to believe that they are being exploited politically and economically by the white "power structure." Negroes, like people in poverty everywhere, in fact lack the channels of communication, influence and appeal that traditionally have been available to ethnic minorities within the city and which enabled them—unburdened by color—to scale the walls of the white ghettos in an earlier era. The frustrations of powerlessness have led some to the conviction that there is no effective alternative to violence as a means of expression and redress, as a way of "moving the system." More generally, the result is alienation and the white society which controls them. This is reflected in the reach toward racial consciousness and solidarity reflected in the slogan "Black Power."

These facts have combined to inspire a new mood among Negroes, particularly among the young. Self-esteem and enhanced racial pride are replacing apathy and submission to "the system." Moreover, Negro youth, who make up over half of the ghetto population, share the growing sense of alienation felt by many white youth in our country. Thus, their role in recent civil disorders reflects not only a shared sense of deprivation and victimization by white society but also the rising youth throughout the society.

INCITEMENT AND ENCOURAGEMENT OF VIOLENCE. These conditions have created a volatile mixture of attitudes and beliefs which needs only a spark to ignite mass violence. Strident appeals to violence, first heard from white racists, were echoed and reinforced last summer in the inflammatory rhetoric of black racists and militants. Throughout the year, extremists crisscrossed the country preaching a doctrine of black power and violence. Their rhetoric was widely reported in the mass media; it was echoed by local "militants" and organizations; it became the ugly background noise of the violent summer. . . .

THE POLICE. It is the convergence of all these factors that makes the role of the police so difficult and so significant. Almost invariably the incident that ignites disorder arises from police action. Harlem, Watts, Newark and Detroit—all the major outbursts of recent years—were precipitated by routine arrests of Negroes for minor offenses by white police.

But the police are not merely the spark. In discharge of their obligation to maintain order and insure public safety in the disruptive conditions of ghetto life, they are inevitably involved in sharper and more frequent conflicts with ghetto residents than with the residents of other areas. Thus, to many Negroes police have come to symbolize white power, white racism and white repression. And the fact is that many police do reflect and express these white attitudes. The atmosphere of hostility and cynicism is reinforced by a widespread perception among Negroes of the existence of police brutality and corruption, and of a "double standard" of justice and protection—one for Negroes and one for whites.

211

Cesar Chavez and La Causa (1975)

For the thousands of migrant workers who toiled in the fields and orchards of California, life was difficult and demoralizing. Most of the migrants were Mexican Americans who received meager wages for backbreaking work, were forced to live in wretched migrant camps, and faced bitter racism that often excluded them from the democratic process or access to formal education. Cesar Chavez sought to correct this situation. Born in Arizona on his parents' farm that they lost during the Great Depression, the family became migrant workers in 1939, when Chavez was 12 years old. Chavez knew first-hand the hardships of Mexican-American workers. Leaving the fields, he worked as an organizer for the Community Service Organization, but he resigned his position as director in 1962 to create a union for migrant farm workers. He founded the Farm Workers Association (later called the United Farm Workers) that was known as La Causa. Chavez borrowed the tactics of nonviolent, direct-action campaigns from India's Mahatma Gandhi and merged them with traditional labor strategies of prolonged strikes to gain recognition of the union. He also relied on volunteers from universities and religious organizations to help organize national boycotts (against grapes

and then lettuce) to bring growers to the bargaining table. Chavez was able to negoti-
ate better wages and contracts for workers. In 1970, growers of California's table grapes
signed contracts with the United Farm Workers. In 1975, Chavez described his
accomplishments, as well as the future of the union, in his autobiography, which is
excerpted as follows.

Questions to Consider

1. What obstacles did Chavez overcome to build a farm workers' union?
2. Why does Chavez want the union to address the issues of political and economic power? How will this be done?
3. What does Chavez hope the union will accomplish?
4. In what ways is Chavez's description of the plight of immigrant labor similar to conditions described in "The Story of a Sweatshop Girl" (Document 150)? What conclusions can you draw from these similarities? What can you deduce about how American nationality is defined based on this document?

Once we have reached our goal and have farm workers protected by contracts, we must continue to keep our members involved. The only way is to continue struggling. It's just like plateaus. We get a Union, then we want to struggle for something else. The moment we sit down and rest on our laurels, we're in trouble.

Once we get contracts and good wages, we know the tendency will be for the majority to lose interest unless the Union is threatened or a contract is being renegotiated. The tendency will be for just a few to remain active and involved, while everybody else just holds out until something very big happens. That's true of other unions that we've seen; that's true of other institutions; that's true of our country.

To avoid that, to keep people's attention and continuing interest, we've got to expand and get them involved in other things. The Union must touch them daily.

Our best education, the most lasting, has been out on the picket line. But when the initial membership gets old and dies off, the new people coming in won't have had the same experience of building a Union. So we must get them involved in other necessary struggles.

Poor people are going to be poor for a long time to come, even though we have contracts, and economic action is an exciting thing for them. If they see an alternative, they will follow it. And we've probably got now the best organization of any poor people in all the country. That's why we can go any place in California where there are farm workers and get a whole group of people together and in action. We are hitting at the real core problems.

Cesar Chavez: Autobiography of La Causa, Jacques E. Levy, ed. (New York: W. W. Norton, 1975), 536–539. Reprinted by permission of Jacques E. Levy.

After we've got contracts, we have to build more clinics and co-ops, and we've got to resolve the whole question of mechanization. That can become a great issue, not fighting the machines, but working out a program ahead of time so the workers benefit.

Then there's the whole question of political action, so much political work to be done taking care of all the grievances that people have, such as the discrimination their kids face in school, and the whole problem of the police. I don't see why we can't exchange those cops who treat us the way they do for good, decent human beings like farm workers. Or why there couldn't be any farm worker judges.

We have to participate in the governing of towns and school boards. We have to make our influence felt everywhere and anywhere. It's a long struggle that we're just beginning, but it can be done because the people want it.

To get it done, there's a lot of construction work needed with our members. Many are not citizens, and others are not registered to vote. We must work toward the day when the majority of them are citizens with a vote.

But political power alone is not enough. Although I've been at it for some twenty years, all the time and the money and effort haven't brought about any significant change whatsoever. Effective political power is never going to come, particularly to minority groups, unless they have economic power. And however poor they are, even the poor people can organize economic power.

Political power by itself, as we've tried to fathom it and to fashion it, is like having a car that doesn't have any motor in it. It's like striking a match that goes out. Economic power is like having a generator to keep that bulb burning all the time. So we have to develop economic power to assure a continuation of political power.

I'm not advocating black capitalism or brown capitalism. At the worst it gets a black to exploit other blacks, or a brown to exploit others. At the best, it only helps the lives of a few. What I'm suggesting is a cooperative movement.

Power can come from credit in a capitalistic society, and credit in a society like ours means people. As soon as you're born, you're worth so much— not in money, but in the privilege to get in debt.

And I think that's a powerful weapon. If you have a lot of people, then you have a lot of credit. The idea is to organize that power and transfer it into something real. . . .

As a continuation of our struggle, I think that we can develop economic power and put it into the hands of the people so they can have more control of their own lives, and then begin to change the system. We want radical change. Nothing short of radical change is going to have any impact on our lives or our problems. We want sufficient power to control our own destinies. This is our struggle. It's a lifetime job. The work for social change and against social injustice is never ended.

I know we're not going to see the change, but if we can get an idea and put legs under it, that's all we want. Let it go. Let it start, like the Union. . . .

Actually, I can't see where the poor have fared that well under any political or economic system. But I think some power has to come to them so they can manage their lives. I don't care what system it is, it's not going to work if they don't have the power.

That's why if we make democracy work, I'm convinced that's by far the best system. And it will work if people want it to. But to make it work for the poor, we have to work at it full time. And we have to be willing to just give up everything and risk it all.

In the last twenty years, the farm workers' outlook has radically changed, just like day and night. Twenty years ago, to get one person to talk to me about the Union was an effort. They were afraid. Now, we've overcome that.

And the idea of serving without pay—they had never heard about that. Right now we need a good education program, a meaningful education, not just about the Union, but about the whole idea of the Cause, the whole idea of sacrificing for other people.

Fighting for social justice, it seems to me, is one of the profoundest ways in which man can say yes to man's dignity, and that really means sacrifice. There is no way on this earth in which you can say yes to man's dignity and know that you're going to be spared some sacrifice.

28

✳

The Rising Conservative Tide

Many of the leading issues from the 1960s continued to divide the United States during the 1970s and 1980s. In addition to the lingering turmoil from the 1960s, political corruption, a decline in the standard of living, and the failure of technology combined to erode the faith that many Americans had shared previously. Efforts to heal many of the divisions failed; new issues emerged that soon proved as divisive as the old. By the decade's end, many Americans had lowered their expectations for the future. Capitalizing on this malaise, the ascendance of conservatism in American life promoted a pro-business domestic stance, coupled with a strongly anticommunist foreign policy, in the hopes of reviving the nation's optimism. The ensuing selections reveal the issues that characterized this era.

212

Roe v. *Wade* (1973)

Perhaps the most controversial issue in modern America is abortion. The social role and legal status of abortion have varied throughout American history. In the first half of the 19th century, abortions were almost commonplace (abortionists advertised in newspapers), and there was frank discussion between women and their physicians about the procedure. In the late 19th century, state legislatures, pressured by the American Medical Association, which sought to upgrade and regulate medical practices, began to outlaw abortion unless a doctor deemed the procedure necessary. Despite the new laws, the practice of abortion continued "underground." As part of the women's movement of the 1960s and the medical community's change of opinion on abortion, some states relaxed or repealed their antiabortion laws. In 1973, the Supreme Court issued its decision in Roe v. Wade, *a case involving Norma McGorvey ("Roe"), who was denied an abortion under Texas law and sued the state. Justice Harry Blackmun wrote for the majority in the 7–2 opinion. Excerpted as follows is the majority opinion in* Roe v. Wade.

Questions to Consider

1. According to the Supreme Court's decision, why did states still retain laws prohibiting abortion?
2. Why did the court believe those reasons were no longer valid?
3. Upon what constitutional grounds does the court rest its decision? Why?
4. Why are supporters of *Roe* v. *Wade* so adamant that it remain in effect? Why are opponents of the decision so determined in condemning the decision?

We forthwith acknowledge our awareness of the sensitive and emotional nature of the abortion controversy, of the vigorous opposing views, even among physicians, and of the deep and seemingly absolute convictions that the subject inspires. One's philosophy, one's experiences, one's exposure to the raw edges of human existence, one's religious training, one's attitudes toward life and family and their values, and the moral standards one establishes and seeks to observe, are all likely to influence and to color one's thinking and conclusions about abortion.

In addition, population growth, pollution, poverty, and racial overtones tend to complicate and not to simplify the problem.

Our task, of course, is to resolve the issue by constitutional measurement, free of emotion and of predilection. We seek earnestly to do this, and, because we do, we have inquired into, and in this opinion place some emphasis upon, medical and medical-legal history and what that history reveals about man's attitudes toward the abortion procedure over the centuries. . . .

Three reasons have been advanced to explain historically the enactment of criminal abortion laws in the 19th century and to justify their continued existence.

It has been argued occasionally that these laws were the product of a Victorian social concern to discourage illicit sexual conduct. Texas, however, does not advance this justification in the present case, and it appears that no court or commentator has taken the argument seriously. . . .

A second reason is concerned with abortion as a medical procedure. When most criminal abortion laws were enacted, the procedure was a hazardous one for the woman. . . . Thus, it has been argued that a State's real concern in enacting a criminal abortion law was to protect the pregnant woman, that is, to restrain her from submitting to a procedure that placed her life in serious jeopardy.

Modern medical techniques have altered this situation. Appellants and various amici* refer to the medical data indicating that abortion in early preg-

---

*An uninvolved party that is allowed by the court to provide it with legal advice.
Roe v. *Wade*, 410 *U.S. Reports* 113 (1973).

nancy, this is, prior to the end of the first trimester, although not without its risk, is now relatively safe. Mortality rates for women undergoing early abortions, where the procedure is legal, appear to be as low as or lower than the rates for normal childbirth. Consequently, any interest of the State in protecting the woman from an inherently hazardous procedure, except when it would be equally dangerous for her to forgo it, has largely disappeared. Of course, important state interests in the area of health and medical standards do remain. . . .

The third reason is the State's interest—some phrase it in terms of duty—in protecting prenatal life. Some of the argument for this justification rests on the theory that a new human life is present from the moment of conception. The State's interest and general obligation to protect life then extends, it is argued, to prenatal life. Only when the life of the pregnant mother herself is at stake, balanced against the life she carries within her, should the interest in this area need not stand or fall on acceptance of the belief that life begins at conception or at some other point prior to live birth. . . .

The right of privacy, whether it be founded in the Fourteenth Amendment's concept of personal liberty and restrictions upon state action, as we feel it is, or, as the District Court determined, in the Ninth Amendment's reservation of rights of people, is broad enough to encompass a woman's decision whether or not to terminate her pregnancy. The detriment that the State would impose upon the pregnant woman by denying this choice altogether is apparent. Specific and direct harm medically diagnosable even in early pregnancy may be involved. Maternity, or additional offspring, may force upon a woman a distressful life and future. Psychological harm may be imminent. Mental and physical health may be taxed by child care. There is also the distress, for all concerned, associated with the unwanted child, and there is the problem of bringing a child into a family already unable, psychologically and otherwise, to care for it. In other cases, as in this one, the additional difficulties and continuing stigma of unwed motherhood may be involved. All these are factors the woman and her responsible physician necessarily will consider in consultation.

On the basis of elements such as these, appellant and some amici argue that the woman's right is absolute and that she is entitled to terminate her pregnancy at whatever time, in whatever way, and for whatever reason she alone chooses. With this we do not agree. . . .

We, therefore, conclude that the right of personal privacy includes the abortion decision, but that this right is not unqualified and must be considered against important state interests in regulation. . . .

Texas urges that, apart from the Fourteenth Amendment, life begins at conception and is present throughout pregnancy, and that, therefore, the State has a compelling interest in protecting that life from and after conception. We need not resolve the difficult question of when life begins. When those trained in the respective disciplines of medicine, philosophy, and theology are unable to arrive at any consensus, the judiciary, at this point in the development of man's knowledge, is not in a position to speculate as to the answer. . . .

With respect to the State's important and legitimate interest in the health of the mother, the "compelling" point, in the light of present medical knowledge, is at approximately the end of the first trimester. This is so because of the now-established medical fact that until the end of the first trimester mortality in abortion may be less than mortality in normal childbirth. It follows that, from and after this point, a State may regulate the abortion procedure to the extent that the regulation reasonably relates to the preservation and protection of maternal health. . . .

To summarize and to repeat:

1. A state criminal abortion statute of the current Texas type, that excepts from criminality only a *life-saving* procedure on behalf of the mother, without regard to pregnancy stage and without recognition of the other interests involved, is violative of the Due Process Clause of the Fourteenth Amendment.

    a. For the stage prior to approximately the end of the first trimester, the abortion decision and its effectuation must be left to the medical judgment of the pregnant woman's attending physician.

    b. For the stage subsequent to approximately the end of the first trimester, the State, in promoting its interest in the health of the mother, may, if it chooses, regulate the abortion procedure in ways that are reasonably related to maternal health.

    c. For the stage subsequent to viability, the State in promoting its interest in the potentiality of human life may, if it chooses, regulate, and even proscribe, abortion except where it is necessary, in appropriate medical judgment, for the preservation of the life or health of the mother. . . .

213

Richard Nixon and Watergate (1972–74)

In the presidential election of 1968, Republican Richard Nixon campaigned and won by advocating an end to the war in Vietnam and "law and order" in the United States. Four years later, in June 1972, several burglars were arrested after breaking into the Democratic National Headquarters in the Watergate apartment complex in Washington, DC. The burglars, it turned out, were employees of President Richard Nixon's reelection committee who planned to sabotage the Democratic party's campaign by "bugging" the office. There is no evidence to indicate that Nixon knew of the plans to break into the Watergate. However, Nixon had arranged to have all Oval Office conversations secretly tape recorded to use in writing the history of his presidency. When a White House aide told a congressional committee about these "White House tapes," they became the center of the investigation. Nixon refused to release the tapes, citing "executive privilege," but the Supreme Court ruled unanimously that he must turn over the tapes. The tapes revealed the inner workings of the Nixon White House and helped move Nixon to resign as president in 1974. The first cartoon, by Doug Marlette, addresses the central issues of the Nixon presidency and the Watergate affair. The second cartoon is by Herb Block of the Washington Post, *and it indicated the importance of the White House tapes.*

Questions to Consider

1. What do these two cartoons have to say about the ethical conduct of the Nixon administration?

2. Why does the first cartoon depict President Nixon as "Law-and-Order-Man"? What does this image suggest about his presidency?

3. What do these two cartoons suggest about Nixon's portrayal of his own ethical conduct?

4. What are the limits of presidential power and prerogative?

The Charlotte Observer, March 14, 1973. Reprinted by permission.

"Law and Order Man" by Douglas Marlette.

From *Herblock: A Cartoonist's Life* (New York, 1998). Reprinted by permission.

"Nixon hanging between the tapes" by Herb Block.

214

The Question of Reverse Discrimination (1978)

During the early 1970s, efforts were made to bring about a more integrated society. The Supreme Court ordered an end to segregation in public schools and required that students be bused out of their neighborhoods to achieve integration. Protests, especially from northern white families, led ultimately to a reversal on the "busing" issue. Also implemented in this period were affirmative action programs, which were designed to achieve racial equality in both the public and private sectors. Often, quotas—hiring a specific number of minorities—were adopted to fulfill the mandates. In 1973 and

1974, Allan Bakke, a white man in his late 20s, applied for admission to the Medical School of the University of California at Davis, but he was denied both times even though his admission rating was higher than minorities who were accepted. Bakke claimed the medical school's "special admissions program" for 16 minority students each year (out of an incoming class of 100) was illegal, and he sued for admission. The Supreme Court reached a decision in Regents of the University of California v. Bakke *in 1978. Excerpted as follows is the conservative* Chicago Tribune's *editorial on the verdict and its significance.*

Questions to Consider

1. Why was the Supreme Court so divided on this issue?
2. Did the decision affect affirmative action programs?
3. Is it ever legitimate to use affirmative action to redress racial inequality? Gender inequality? Income inequality?
4. Does this case represent a backlash against gains made from the Civil Rights Movement?

The Supreme Court's long awaited, delicately balanced ruling in the Bakke "reverse discrimination" case can be welcomed by the whole spectrum of public opinion except for the extremities. The ruling's impact on existing affirmative action programs is minimal. Though many university admissions offices show some discretionary favor to "disadvantaged" individuals, few use the explicit racial quotas that the medical school of the University of California at Davis has used. This Supreme Court decision, sharply focused on university admissions, means little for other "affirmative action" contexts.

Of course the ruling is disappointing both to those who hoped the court would legitimize racial quotas and to those who hoped the court would outlaw any consideration of race in allocation of scarce opportunities. But everyone else can welcome it.

The court was anything but united. The decision itself was 5 to 4, with six opinions written. In a sense, Justice Powell determined the court's position. He agreed with four colleagues that Mr. Bakke should be admitted and that explicit racial quotas are invalid, and with his other four colleagues that race may properly be a factor in university admissions. The first four held that the Civil Rights Act of 1964 precluded race as a legal factor in admissions. The other four found no constitutional or statutory obstacle to explicit racial quotas. Because of Justice Powell, neither bloc of four altogether prevailed or was altogether outvoted.

Justice Thurgood Marshall, the only black on the court, wrote a separate opinion eloquently reciting the history of blacks' victimization by invidious

---

"A well balanced Bakke decision," *Chicago Tribune,* June 30, 1978, section 5, 2. © Copyrighted 1978, Chicago Tribune Company, all rights reserved, used with permission.

racism. His reproaches of the Supreme Court's behavior in the decades following the Civil War are well justified. But his contention that court-countenanced discrimination then justifies court-countenanced reverse discrimination now is unconvincing. Two wrongs do not make a right. The objective of the courts and of society, when most faithful to our national aspirations, is justice. It is individuals who experience justice and injustice. Explicit racial quotas for admission to a medical school with no record of discriminating against a race are rightly held unfair to individual applicants [and all applicants are individuals] who had nothing to do with past discrimination against blacks.

But the bloc of four for which Justice Paul Stevens spoke is also unconvincing in its claim that Title VI of the Civil Rights Act of 1961 provides a sufficient basis for upholding Mr. Bakke and the California Supreme Court, and that no constitutional interpretation is necessary. The implication here is that, by definition, affirmative action is illegal. This would be intolerable. Congress has found no inconsistency in both enacting the Civil Rights Act and supporting affirmative action programs. For the court to have found some pervasive flaw in affirmative action programs, as many feared it might, would have a disastrous impact on current practice.

In a rather mysterious way, which resulted in the lonely position of a single justice becoming the decision of the court, the Supreme Court has rendered a balanced, judicious decision. As Atty. Gen. Griffin P. Bell, speaking for both himself and President Carter, said, the result is "a great gain for affirmative action"—as reasonably defined. It is a great gain, too, for academic freedom to exercise discretion. As Justice Powell affirmed, "The freedom of a university to make its own judgments as to education includes the selection of its student body"—as long as that selection is itself free from deliberate injustice and arbitrary quotas.

Because the Supreme Court's decision in the Bakke case was narrow rather than sweeping, it leaves numerous questions for later decision. It does not itself, one must hope, invite multiplied litigation. Academic admissions practices that comply with the Bakke decision can be so subjective, so plainly discretionary as to offer few handles for successful lawsuits. That may be frustrating to some of the losers, but any alternative would be damaging to many an individual and to both institutions and abstract justice.

215

Iranian Hostage Crisis (1979–81)

Since the early 1950s, the United States had supported the shah of Iran's government, mainly as a supplier of oil and as a check on the Soviet Union's influence in the Middle East. By the late 1970s, the shah had become increasingly unpopular in Iran because of his repressive control and his efforts to westernize the country. When public demonstrations broke out in early 1979, the shah fled Iran, and a powerful fundamentalist Islamic revolution, led by exiled religious leader, Ayatollah Khomeini, swept the country. Days after President Jimmy Carter permitted the shah to enter the United States for medical treatment, militant Iranian students stormed the U.S. Embassy and took Americans hostage. The students demanded the return of the shah to Iran in exchange for the hostages' freedom. To complicate matters, the Soviet Union invaded neighboring Afghanistan just a few weeks after the hostages were seized. President Carter tried unsuccessfully to negotiate the release of the hostages and even ordered a secret military rescue mission that failed. Finally, the hostages were released after 444 days in captivity. The following selection comes from a congressional hearing on the Iranian crisis, where former Secretary of State Edmund Muskie and deputy Secretary of State Warren Christopher testified on behalf of the Carter administration.

Questions to Consider

1. What are the central issues of this hearing?
2. What was the impact of the hostage crisis on the United States?
3. How does Secretary of State Muskie defend the American position?
4. Why was the hostage crisis significant?

MR. WINN. . . . What if President Carter had said that within 48 hours after the hostages were seized on November 4, 1979, that we would bomb Qum [a religious center] if they were not released? What if we had threatened the power that we have?

MR. MUSKIE. Well, then we would have been playing that old familiar game of chicken. If we made the threat and they did not respond to the threat we would have had to do it or we would not have had any credibility thereafter.

MR. WINN. Is it true the Russians told us within a week after that at the United Nations, "Do not have a military attack on Iran because of the hostages being seized, or we will have to retaliate."?

MR. MUSKIE. I am not aware of that, Congressman. I do not know about that. Chris?

MR. CHRISTOPHER. Nor am I.

MR. WINN. I was up there. The statement was not made but the rumors were pretty good. I do not know if they were throwing out smokescreens or not.

MR. MUSKIE. I may say this—and I am not sure I should say this much—but with respect to the situation in Iran following the invasion of Afghanistan, Iran became a very sensitive piece of real estate from our point of view in terms of Russian intentions, independent of the hostage situation—and I am sure it may have, from their point of view. The combination of the two has raised

---

"Iran's Seizure of the United States Embassy," *Hearings before the Committee on Foreign Affairs, February 17, 19, 25, and March 11, 1981* (Washington, DC, 1981): 171–177.

the visibility of Iran in terms of each country's perception of its security interests, I am sure. But I am not aware of any such exchange as you describe.

MR. CHRISTOPHER. Whether it was Monday morning or Tuesday morning or Wednesday morning or any day of the week I think it would have been a mistake to have given a 48-hour deadline with the consequences of our bombing Qum. My own judgment is Iran did not have the capacity at that time to bring itself to a decision to release the hostages and we would have been left in a situation where if we bombed the country, probably it would have cost the lives of all 53 hostages. I think it was a bad idea then and I think it is a bad idea now. . . .

MR. MICA. Thank you, Mr. Chairman. Up to this point we have focused mainly on the status quo financial situation with the United States, what the United States has gained or lost financially. The comment essentially, is "Iran has learned a lesson. We have not lost anything financially and we achieved our goal of getting the hostages released." The thought that has been going through my mind is what have we done to deter terrorism in the future and, in fact, could you make a list of what the terrorists, those students, have gained or what may have been gained through Iranian eyes, what may be perceived throughout the world, and maybe raise this question simply for the purpose of raising it. I say to you very respectfully, I have no answers to these but these are some of the thoughts that I just jotted down. The terrorists had an opportunity to air their grievances to the world. They paraded the so-called victims of the Shah and propagandized the Shah's regime very heavily for 444 days before the world. They forced nations around the world, like Mexico, to heed to their demand not to accept the Shah. They did indeed rally their countrymen for 444 days behind a very nebulous and questionable cause in leadership. And as you said, Mr. Secretary, they even put into place their political institutions. They—encouraged I think by the atmosphere—created assaults on at least two other embassies during the period the hostages were taken, and in one case a life was lost, a U.S. Marine. I think more importantly—and you alluded to this in your opening comments—they impacted the future of the United States. They altered the future of the United States by impacting a U.S. Presidential election, numerous House races and Senate races throughout this country. I think they probably created a better situation for the Russians to look at Afghanistan with their aggressive intentions and, not to mention the lives lost in the rescue attempt, created havoc and a very poor feeling about the United States throughout the world for a long time. Something that may take years to correct. So as Mr. Solarz indicated, when we talk about no negotiation versus extended or protracted negotiation, would these possible benefits to terrorists lead us to seek a new approach that may be somewhat other than bombing, but certainly not the type of public negotiation that would lead to the kind of situation we had?

MR. MUSKIE. You mentioned effects of the hostage crisis. Of course it had effects. It had effects on our political situation here in the United States. It resulted in a rescue attempt which cost some lives. It had effects. But none of those effects were included in the goals of those who seized the hostages. Their goals were to get the Shah back, to extract an apology from the United States, to achieve a condemnation of the United States worldwide on the basis of the years of the Shah's rule and our alleged involvement in his misrule. They did not achieve any of those goals that I can see. With respect to whether or not we have been diminished, that is a judgment call. I do not think we have. I think we might have been diminished if we had bombed Qum 48 hours later because they were in a position to respond to the threat. That might well have been perceived as misuse of power by one of the world's two superpowers. . . . So whatever means you use there are effects, but whether or not these militants achieved their goal is a different question. Of course they achieved some effect. They preoccupied our country for 14 months with an agonizing, frustrating situation that we would have preferred not to have lived through. But I do not see that as a benefit that offsets the costs which their country paid. Maybe they do. I would doubt it.

MR. MICA. The statement is that the terrorists have learned a lesson. Their goals, as you stated, were very finite; apology, return of some wealth, but instead they have achieved a stability that may not have ever been. It may fall tomorrow. Have they come out better, and have they really learned a lesson because we protracted these negotiations to the extent we did?

MR. MUSKIE. You speak of the incident and possible repetition of it as involving the same people. I do not know whether the same militants would try the same thing if we should reestablish diplomatic relations with Iran but with respect to acts of irrationality surely we live in a world in which we have seen it possible for people to create disruption, to threaten the peace, to disrupt communities. We have said it here in Washington. I saw nobody arguing we should not negotiate their release and the release was negotiated, as you can remember very well. . . . But the fact is Iran now is busy seeking to repair the rend in its relations, economic, diplomatic and otherwise with the rest of the world because it has come to learn it cannot live in a world alone. It lives in an interdependent world and if it fails to recognize that fact, Iran's real interests are seriously impacted. I think that is the lesson. Whether it would be a lesson terrorist minded people will absorb in the future I surely would not guarantee. . . .

216

The Reagan Revolution (1981)

As the 1980s began, a conservative mood pervaded the country, and Ronald Reagan both symbolized and galvanized this atmosphere. Reagan, born in Illinois and a devoted New Deal Democrat, began his career as a radio broadcaster, then became a Hollywood actor until he moved into television as an actor and program host. In the early 1960s, he switched to the Republican party and was elected to two terms as governor of California by appealing to middle-class resentments—taxes and big government. Using these issues again in 1980, Reagan won the Republican party nomination with the support of a powerful conservative coalition, and in the campaign against Democrat Jimmy Carter, he benefited from double-digit inflation and the Iranian hostage crisis associated with Carter. He won the election easily, beginning the "Reagan Revolution." Reagan's inaugural address, excerpted following, established the initial broad themes of his administration.

Questions to Consider

1. According to Reagan, what problems face the nation in 1981?

2. What does Reagan propose for the nation?

3. Who voted for Reagan in 1980? Why?

4. How might Lyndon Johnson, author of "The Great Society" (Document 208), have responded to this address?

To a few of us here today this is a solemn and most momentous occasion, and yet in the history of our nation it is a commonplace occurrence. The orderly transfer of authority as called for in the Constitution routinely takes place, as it has for almost two centuries, and few of us stop to think how unique we really are. In the eyes of many in the world, this every-4-year ceremony we accept as normal is nothing less than a miracle.

Mr. President, I want our fellow citizens to know how much you did to carry on this tradition. By your gracious cooperation in the transition process, you have shown a watching world that we are a united people pledged to maintaining a political system which guarantees individual liberty to a greater degree than any other, and I thank you and your people for all your help in maintaining the continuity which is the bulwark of our Republic.

The business of our nation goes forward. The United States are confronted with an economic affliction of great proportions. We suffer from the longest and one of the worst sustained inflations in our national history. It distorts our economic decisions, penalizes thrift, and crushes the struggling young and the fixed-income elderly alike. It threatens to shatter the lives of millions of our people.

Idle industries have cast workers into unemployment, human misery, and personal indignity. Those who do work are denied a fair return for their labor by a tax system which penalizes successful achievement and keeps us from maintaining full productivity.

But great as our tax burden is, it has not kept pace with public spending. For decades we have piled deficit upon deficit, mortgaging our future and

"Inaugural Address," *Public Papers of the Presidents of the United States: Ronald Reagan, 1981* (Washington, DC, 1982), 1–4.

our children's future for the temporary convenience of the present. To continue this long trend is to guarantee tremendous social, cultural, political, and economic upheavals.

In this present crisis, government is not the solution to our problem; government is the problem. From time to time we've been tempted to believe that society has become too complex to be managed by self-rule, that government by an elite group is superior to government for, by, and of the people. Well, if no one among us is capable of governing himself, then who among us has the capacity to govern someone else? All of us together, in and out of government, must bear the burden. The solutions we seek must be equitable, with no one group singled out to pay a higher price.

Well, this administration's objective will be a healthy, vigorous, growing economy that provides equal opportunity for all Americans, with no barriers born of bigotry or discrimination. Putting America back to work means putting all Americans back to work. Ending inflation means freeing all Americans from the terror of runaway living costs. All must share in the productive work of this "new beginning," and all must share in the bounty of a revived economy. With the idealism and fair play which are the core of our system and our strength, we can have a strong and prosperous America, at peace with itself and the world.

So, as we begin, let us take inventory. We are a nation that has a government—not the other way around. And this makes us special among the nations of the Earth. Our government has no power except that granted it by the people. It is time to check and reverse the growth of government, which shows signs of having grown beyond the consent of the governed.

It is my intention to curb the size and influence of the Federal establishment and to demand recognition of the distinction between the powers granted to the Federal Government and those reserved to the States or to the people. All of us need to be reminded that the Federal Government did not create the States; the States created the Federal Government.

Now, so there will be no misunderstanding, it's not my intention to do away with government. It is rather to make it work—work with us, not over us; to stand by our side, not ride on our back. Government can and must provide opportunity, not smother it; foster productivity, not stifle it.

It is no coincidence that our present troubles parallel and are proportionate to the intervention and intrusion in our lives that result from unnecessary and excessive growth of government. It is time for us to realize that we are too great a nation to limit ourselves to small dreams. We're not, as some would have us believe, doomed to an inevitable decline. I do not believe in a fate that will fall on us no matter what we do. I do believe in a fate that will fall on us if we do nothing. So, with all the creative energy at our command, let us begin an era of national renewal. Let us renew our determination, our courage, and our strength. And let us renew our faith and our hope.

We have every right to dream heroic dreams. Those who say that we're in a time when there are no heroes, they just don't know where to look. You can see heroes every day going in and out of factory gates. Others, a handful in number, produce enough food to feed all of us and then the world beyond. You meet heroes across a counter, and they're on both sides of that counter. There are entrepreneurs with faith in themselves and faith in an idea who create new jobs, new wealth and opportunity. They're individuals and families whose taxes support the government and whose voluntary gifts support church, charity, culture, art, and education. Their patriotism is quiet, but deep. Their values sustain our national life.

To those neighbors and allies who share our freedom, we will strengthen our historic ties and assure them of our support and firm commitment. We will match loyalty with loyalty. We will strive for mutually beneficial relations. We will not use our friendship to impose on their sovereignty, for our own sovereignty is not for sale.

As for the enemies of freedom, those who are potential adversaries, they will be reminded that peace is the highest aspiration of the American people. We will negotiate for it, sacrifice for it; we will not surrender for it, now or ever.

Our forbearance should never be misunderstood. Our reluctance for conflict should not be misjudged as a failure of will. When action is required to preserve our national security, we will act. We will maintain sufficient strength to prevail if need be, knowing that if we do so we have the best chance of never having to use that strength.

Above all, we must realize that no arsenal or no weapon in the arsenals of the world is so formidable as the will and moral courage of free men and women. It is a weapon our adversaries in today's world do not have. It is a weapon that we as Americans do have. Let that be understood by those who practice terrorism and prey upon other neighbors. . . .

217

Oliver North's Testimony at the Iran-Contra Hearings (1987)

The Reagan administration participated in several secret actions to support anticommunist movements in Central America. Of particular interest was Nicaragua, where the left-wing Sandinista government had established ties with communist nations. Using the Central Intelligence Agency (CIA) to conduct secret operations, the Reagan administration assisted the "contras" in their efforts to overthrow the Sandinista government. Alarmed at these covert operations, Congress passed the Boland Amendment, which explicitly prohibited the CIA or any other agency from spending money to support the contras. Meanwhile, the administration was frustrated in obtaining the release of American hostages held by Iranian-backed terrorists in Lebanon. Despite President Reagan's policy of refusing to negotiate with terrorists, some administration officials arranged an arms sale to Iran in exchange for the release of some hostages. These two issues converged when National Security Council (NSC) officials found a way to evade the

Boland Amendment by diverting profits from the arms sale to the contras. When these actions became known, Congress investigated. A central figure in the Iran-Contra hearings was Lieutenant Colonel Oliver North, an aggressive junior NSC officer, who helped engineer the deal. His testimony, excerpted as follows, describes some of his activities in the Iran-Contra affair.

Questions to Consider

1. What does North's testimony reveal about the conduct of the Reagan administration?
2. What is North's attitude during these hearings? Why did North shred documents?
3. Did Reagan approve the transfer of money to the contras?
4. What is the significance of the Iran-Contra affair?

MR. NIELDS: The American people were told by this government that our government had nothing to do with the Hasenfus airplane, and that was false. And it is a principal purpose of these hearings to replace secrecy and deception with disclosure and truth. And that's one of the reasons we have called you here, sir. And one question the American people would like to know the answer to is what did the President know about the diversion of the proceeds of Iranian arms sales to the contras. Can you tell us what you know about that, sir?

LT. COL. NORTH: You just took a long leap from Mr. Hasenfus' airplane. As I told this Committee several days ago, and if you'll indulge me, Counsel, in a brief summary of what I said, I never personally discussed the use of the residuals or profits from the sale of US weapons to Iran for the purpose of supporting the Nicaraguan resistance with the President. I never raised it with him and he never raised it with me during my entire tenure at the National Security Council; I assumed that the President was aware of what I was doing and had, through my superiors, approved it. . . .

MR. NIELDS: You testified that you assumed that the President had authorized the diversion. Lieutenant colonels in the Marine Corps do not divert millions of dollars from arm sales to Iran for the benefit of contras based on assumptions, do they? You had a basis for your assumption.

LT. COL. NORTH: I had the approval of my superiors. As I did for all the other things that I did, Mr. Nields.

MR. NIELDS: You had something else, didn't you, sir? You had a specific reason for believing that the President had approved. You wrote memoranda, did you not, seeking the President's approval for the diversion?

Joint Hearings before the Senate Select Committee on Secret Military Assistance to Iran and Nicaraguan Opposition and the House Select Committee to Investigate Covert Arms Transactions with Iran, 100th Congress, 1st session, part 1, 1987.

LT. COL. NORTH: I did.

MR. NIELDS: And indeed, you wrote more than one of them.

LT. COL. NORTH: I did.

MR. NIELDS: How many did you write?

LT. COL. NORTH: Again, I will estimate that there may have been as many as five . . .

MR. NIELDS: And these five were written, I take it, on each occasion where there was a proposed sale of arms to the Iranians that you felt had reached sufficiently final form to seek the President's approval?

LT. COL. NORTH: Yes . . .

MR. NIELDS: And you sent those memoranda up the line?

LT. COL. NORTH: It is my recollection that I sent each one of those up the line, and that on the three where I had approval to proceed, I thought that I had received authority from the President. I want to make it very clear that no memorandum ever came back to me with the President's initials on it, or the President's name on it, or a note from the President on it—none of these memoranda . . .

MR. NIELDS: . . . My question right now is, you sent these memoranda up to the National Security Adviser, is that correct?

LT. COL. NORTH: That is correct.

MR. NIELDS: For him to obtain the President's approval?

LT. COL. NORTH: Yes . . .

MR. NIELDS: Because you specifically wanted before proceeding on a matter of this degree of importance to have the President's approval?

LT. COL. NORTH: Yes . . .

MR. NIELDS: . . . [W]here are these memoranda?

LT. COL. NORTH: Which memoranda?

MR. NIELDS: The memoranda that you sent up to Admiral Poindexter seeking the President's approval.

LT. COL. NORTH: . . . I think I shredded most of that. Did I get 'em all? . . .

MR. NIELDS: Well, that was going to be my very next question, Colonel North, "Isn't it true that you shredded them?"

LT. COL. NORTH: I believe I did.

MR. NIELDS: And that would include the copies with the President—with a check mark where the lines say, "approved"?

LT. COL. NORTH: That would have included all copies of—I tried, as I was departing the NSC, a process which began as early as October, to destroy all references to these covert operations. I willingly admit that. . . .

MR. NIELDS: . . . Are you here telling the Committee that you don't remember whether on November 21st there was a document in your files reflecting Presidential approval of the diversion?

Lt. Col. North: As a matter of fact, I'll tell you specifically that I thought they were all gone, because by the time I was told that some point early on November 21st that there would an inquiry conducted by Mr. Meese, I assured Admiral Poindexter—incorrectly it seems—that all of those documents no longer existed. And so that is early on November 21st because I believe the decision to make an inquiry, to have the Attorney General or Mr. Meese in his role as friend to the President conduct a fact-finding excursion on what happened in September and November in 1985. I assured the Admiral, "Don't worry, it's all taken care of."

Mr. Nields: You had already shredded them?

Lt. Col. North: I thought. That's right . . .

Mr. Nields: And, you were aware, were you not, sometime during the day on Friday, November 21st, that the Attorney General's people were going to come in and look at documents over the weekend?

Lt. Col. North: That is correct.

Mr. Nields: And, you shredded documents before they got there?

Lt. Col. North: I would prefer to say that I shredded documents that day like I did on all other days, but perhaps with increased intensity, that is correct.

Mr. Nields: So that the people you were keeping these documents from, the ones that you shredded, were representatives of the Attorney General of the United States?

Lt. Col. North: They worked for him. . . .

Mr. Nields: . . . My question to you is this: Isn't it true—and I'll put it that others above you, by putting out this version of the facts, were committing the President of the United States to a false story.

Lt. Col. North: Yes, that's true.

Mr. Nields: Did you ever say to any of those people, "you can't do that without asking the President"?

Lt. Col. North: No, I did not.

Mr. Nields: Did you ever say, "you can't do that, it's not true and you cannot commit the President of the United States to a lie"?

Lt. Col. North: I don't believe that I ever said that to anyone, no.

Mr. Nields: Did anybody else in your presence say that?

Lt. Col. North: No.

Mr. Nields: So none of these people—Director of Central Intelligence, two National Security Advisors, Attorney General—none of them ever made the argument, "it's not true, you can't say it"?

Lt. Col. North: No, and in fairness to them, I think that they had a darn good reason for not putting the straight story out, and their reasons might have been the same as mine, they may have been different. And you'd have to ask them. The fact is, I think there were good and sufficient reasons at that time.

Mr. Nields: Did anybody ask the President?

Lt. Col. North: I did not.

Mr. Nields: Do you know if anyone else did?

Lt. Col. North: I do not.

218

An Editorial on the Removal of the Berlin Wall (1989)

For more than 40 years, the Cold War had divided much of the world into two oppos-ing camps. In Europe, the division was along the "iron curtain" boundary separating the communist East, under Soviet influence, from the capitalistic West, under American influence. Even Germany and its old capital of Berlin were divided along these lines. In 1985, Soviet leader Mikhail Gorbachev began policies called perestroika *(eco-nomic restructuring) and* glasnost *(openness) to revitalize the Soviet Union's sagging economy and to achieve better relations—especially trade—with the West. These poli-cies triggered dissent, then growing demands for more rapid reforms both within the Soviet Union and in Eastern Europe. When Gorbachev agreed not to intervene in the affairs of East-bloc countries in 1989, popular uprisings ended Communist party rule and new governments were formed. Perhaps the most sensational incident of this col-lapse came in November 1989, when the Berlin Wall—the symbol of the Cold War since its erection in 1961—was removed and the borders between the two Germanies opened. Excerpted as follows is a* New York Times *editorial, which places the removal of the Berlin Wall in an historical perspective.*

Questions to Consider

1. The *New York Times* editorial argues that the destruction of the Berlin Wall ended 75 years of European catastrophes. Is this true?

2. What else did destruction of the Berlin Wall signify?

3. How did the United States react to creation of "a European house"?

4. What is the significance of this event?

Crowds of young Germans danced on top of the hated Berlin wall Thursday night. They danced for joy, they danced for history. They danced because the tragic cycle of catastrophes that first convulsed Europe 75 years ago, embrac-ing two world wars, a Holocaust and a cold war, seems at long last to be nearing an end.

"The End of the War to End Wars," *New York Times,* November 11, 1989, p. 26. Copyright © 1989 by The New York Times Company. Reprinted by permission.

November 11, now named Veterans Day, is the day of the armistice that ended World War I. But that war to end wars was lost when the victors bungled the peace. They exacted heavy reparations from Germany, paving the way to chaos and the rise of National Socialism. The years between the two wars turned out to be merely a truce. Hitler in 1940 received the surrender of the French forces in the same railroad car in which Germany's delegates surrendered in 1918, and Europe was again plunged into strife.

Some 20 million people died in World War I, perhaps 50 million in World War II, but even these two appalling acts of miscalculation and bloodletting did not bring Europe's torments to an end. The tragedy had a third act: the cold war divided a Europe freed from Hitler's tyranny from a Europe bowed under Stalin's. The Berlin wall, erected by Erich Honecker in 1961, stood as the foremost symbol of that division and the Continent's continuing stasis.

The reveling crowds of Berliners mingling from East and West could scarcely believe that the hated wall had at last been breached. Those watching them around the world could only share their delight—and their wonder at the meaning of it all.

If the horrifying cycle that began in 1914 is at last completed, what new wheels have begun to turn? Instability in Eastern Europe has seldom brought good news. But this dissolution may lead to settlement, even if the settlement's shape remains unclear.

Armistice is only the laying down of arms, not peace. And for as long as it has stood, the Berlin wall has symbolized a Europe not at peace, and a world polarized by Soviet-American rivalry.

Mikhail Gorbachev has spoken of a European house. No one, not even he, can yet be sure how the rooms might fit together. Still, no house has a wall through its middle, and for the first time in a generation, neither does Europe.

29

✳

Society and Culture at Century's End

In the last 30 years, American society and culture has changed dramatically. The 1970s witnessed an economic malaise caused, in part, by the rising price of petroleum; the 1990s experienced an economic boom that prompted some consumer excesses. Many of the "baby boomers" were central in bringing about the economic and social changes. The country also experienced the impact of growing numbers of immigrants as well as an adjustment to the internal migration of people to the "Sunbelt." In many areas, new arrangements involving immigration, class structure, gender roles, homosexuality, race relations, and health care were formed. The documents that follow reveal some aspects of American culture and society at century's end.

219

Soaring Energy Costs (1974)

Since World War II, the American standard of living rose continuously, in part because of inexpensive oil. The United States had become increasingly dependent on petroleum to fuel the economy. Americans, long accustomed to plentiful abundance in most material goods, naively believed that natural resources, especially petroleum, were boundless. As domestic oil production declined in the 1960s, demand skyrocketed. The United States began importing increasingly larger amounts of foreign oil, especially from the Middle East. In October 1973, this dependency was made shockingly apparent to the American public when several Arab nations imposed an oil embargo on countries that supported Israel in the Yom Kippur War. After several months, the embargo was lifted, but the Organization of Petroleum Exporting Countries (OPEC) increased the price of crude oil. Excerpted as follows is an article from Newsweek, *a popular news magazine, which examined the oil price increase and its impact on America.*

Questions to Consider

1. How much were oil prices affected initially?
2. What was America's response to rising oil prices?

3. What were the long-term implications of OPEC's action?

4. How has America altered its "energy-hoggish ways"? With what success?

In two stunning strokes last week, the Mideast masters of the world's most productive oil fields dramatically altered the international energy equation for years to come—and in so doing, forced Americans one step closer to a profound change in the way they live. In the short run, the Arab coup will mean higher prices for gasoline, fuel oil and petroleum-based products ranging from plastic toys to polyester-fiber suits. But in the long term, it presages an end to what economist Walter Heller characterizes as America's "energy-hoggish ways"—a life-style exemplified by thriving gasoline stations on nearly every corner and noxious expressways crammed curb to curb with overpowered but underpopulated automobiles.

In the first of their moves, the Muslim rulers of Iran, Iraq, Kuwait, Saudi Arabia, Qatar and Abu Dhabi quite simply ended the long era of cheap energy. They raised the posted price of Persian Gulf crude oil to $11.65 a barrel—a whopping 131 per cent increase. . . .

. . . Gasoline at the pump could jump as much as 9 cents a gallon in some areas of the country, pushing prices well above 50 cents a gallon. And should the Administration's newly announced contingency plan for gas rationing actually go into effect, the price of some gas could go up another 25 cents to 75 cents per gallon. The price of heating oil could well climb by 7 cents above the average of 30 cents per gallon. Just what effect the oil-price increase will have on the price of the thousands of other consumer goods that use oil as either a raw material or as an energy source in their manufacture is difficult to measure. But there is no doubt that nearly everything will be much more expensive. . . .

In Washington, energy czar William E. Simon underscored the potential seriousness of the petroleum situation by unveiling the Administration's stand-by rationing scheme. If and when it goes into effect, the program might limit licensed drivers over 18 to between 32 and 35 gallons of gasoline per month, require a bureaucracy of 17,000 to administer and enforce, and cost at least $1.5 billion. . . .

But Simon also cautioned that the nation was "far from being out of the woods"—and he stressed the need for consumers to continue curbing their appetites for energy to trim the gap between supply and demand. . . . Beyond gestures, Simon declared that he may later recommend such fuel-saving measures as closing gas stations another day in addition to Sunday or perhaps even proposing a partial ban on driving one day a week. "If the American public continues to cooperate," Simon emphasized, "we can avoid more stringent measures."

"Energy: How High Is Up," *Newsweek* 83 (January 7, 1974): 18–22. © 1974, Newsweek, Inc. All rights reserved. Reprinted by permission.

The Administration is depending on more than mere public cooperation with voluntary conservation measures. This weekend, for instance, year-round daylight-saving time takes effect, an action energy experts estimate could conserve the equivalent of 95,000 barrels of oil daily. And for all its apparent inequities and loopholes, the government's allocation program—now scheduled to be operative on Jan. 15—appears tough in many ways. Not only will it cut airline fuel supplies, but fuel-oil dealers will be allocated oil only on the basis of reduced indoor temperatures in homes and business establishments. Crude-oil allocations for refineries will be strictly controlled. As far as gasoline is concerned, 5 per cent of 1972 production will be diverted to the production of home-heating oil—in effect, Simon says, "a moderate form of [gas] rationing." . . .

But the most devastating problem facing American consumers, at least during the first half of the year, is inflation. Invariably, the higher cost of imported oil will ripple through the entire U.S. economy, sending prices soaring. While Administration economists are understandably reluctant to predict how much, the rate seems likely to top the pace for the last six months of 9.7 per cent. . . .

. . . The higher prices they now charge for their oil will unquestionably speed the development of economically viable substitute fuels, probably somewhat sooner than would otherwise have been possible. Perhaps most important of all, the decibel level seems finally to have lowered when the Arab oil question is discussed and debated, suggesting that the Arab leaders have come to recognize their own enormous stake in fostering stable relations with the industrialized West.

"We don't want to hurt the industrialized world," the Shah of Iran promised last week, following his announcement of the higher oil prices. "We will be one of them soon. What good will it do if the present industrialized world is crushed and terminated? What will replace it?"

220

A Migration to the "Sunbelt" (1976)

Americans have always been a people on the move, seeking a better life elsewhere in the country. The steady westward migration, the gold and silver rushes of the 19th century, and the Great Migration of African Americans to northern industrial cities during and after the First World War are but a few examples of this mobile society. Starting in the early 1970s, another significant demographic shift took place. Large numbers of people abandoned the industrial cities of the North and East and moved to the South and the Southwest, the so-called Sunbelt. Their migration, like the earlier movements, brought notable changes to those areas they left and to those areas they inhabited. The following article excerpted from Time, *a popular news magazine, sought to explain this migration and its impact. The country is still adjusting to this demographic shift.*

Questions to Consider

1. According to this article, why were people migrating to the Sunbelt?
2. How has this migration changed the region?
3. How has it changed the North and East?
4. What is the significance of this migration?

All of these people are examples of a special breed that is rapidly increasing across the U.S.: the new American migrants. They are pulling themselves up by their roots in order to pursue the good life in places that are smaller, sunnier, safer, and perhaps saner than those they left. Their desire to move onward has spawned an exodus that is causing major changes in American society. Because of the migration, many once great cities are falling into ever more serious decline; scores of little-known communities are either booming or feeling the pains of all-too-sudden growth (or both); and millions of Americans have profoundly altered their way of life.

Americans have always been a restlessly mobile people, but their new migratory habits are quite different from those of the past. There are three interrelated patterns of movement:

OUT OF THE BIG CITIES. Where once Americans thronged to the big cities and their immediate suburbs in search of jobs, education and excitement, they are now moving to smaller cities and towns. Between 1970 and 1974, over 1.7 million more Americans left the big metropolitan areas than moved to them. Through migration, the New York Area alone lost half a million people more than it gained; similarly, Chicago lost a quarter of a million. Of the 16 metropolitan areas that have more than 2 million people each, eight have lost population since 1970. . . .

TO THE COUNTRYSIDE. After declining for most of this century, the nation's rural areas since 1970 have been growing faster than its urban areas. The Census Bureau defines metropolitan areas as those counties that have cities of 50,000 people or more; counties with no communities of that size are predominantly rural. . . .

TO THE SOUTH AND SOUTHWEST. Americans are rapidly leaving the Northern and Eastern regions, the old industrial quadrant from St. Louis and Chicago to Philadelphia and Boston, and increasingly heading toward the South and West. Between 1970 and last year, 2,537,000 people migrated from the Northeastern and North Central states to the Southern and Western states. . . . By far the nation's fastest-developing new boom region is the Sunbelt—the lower arc of warmlands stretching from Southern California to the Carolinas.

These new migrations suggest a major change in Americans' expectations— what they want from their careers and communities and what they are willing

"Americans on the Move," *Time* 107 (March 15, 1976): 55–64. Copyright ©1976 Time, Inc. Reprinted by permission.

to give up to get it. Says Pollster Louis Harris: "Most Americans don't want more quantity of anything, but more quality in what they've got."

In such impulses is a certain chastened spirit, a feeling—no doubt a residue of the manic '60s—that smaller and quieter home pleasures are more important than acquisitiveness and ambition. This is not necessarily an edifying spiritual development in America so much as a self-interested calculation that a 90-minute commute or a triple-bolted apartment door is not worth the trouble if one can escape. The ethic suggests that bigness is no longer better, that mere dollars do not mean a more satisfying life, that success is more a matter of enjoying where one is than moving ahead. Those sentiments, of course, can carry a troubling complacency. The frankly escapist note is one theme of some of the new migrations—a kind of premature retirement, a dropping-out. That is a sweet and organically grown estimate of life, but in some cases it smacks of elitism gone to the country of the cure. Many are migrating, however, for somewhat opposite reasons. They find that in the smaller cities and towns there is more scope for their ambition, more room for competition and expansion.

"In a way it is certainly a middle-class migration," says Queens College Political Scientist Andrew Hacker. "Those who are moving out are looking for a kind of middle-class subcountry, a place where it is safer, and where there is more predictable service, and where the school system is less problematic." . . .

Employees who made the move are usually happy with their new lives. Others who relocate on their own often have to take pay cuts, but in most cases they find that the dollar goes further. People in the South and West spend comparatively less for taxes, housing, fuel, clothing and most services. The Bureau of Labor Statistics estimates that the cost of maintaining a high standard of living for a family of four in New York City is 33% higher than in Houston or Nashville. Air conditioning has made the long, hot summers bearable. And for some people the way of life—a moderate climate, plenty of outdoor activity, the residual Southern graces—is an attractive alternative to the iron chill of the North. . . .

In many ways, the migrants from the North and the East are helping to alter the character of the South, which is becoming more sophisticated and more homogenized. On the whole, Yankees who move there find themselves welcomed, mostly because they bring new money, skills and opportunity with them. At the same time, the South is changing the carpetbaggers in a number of respects. Sometimes there is no Southerner more given to Southern style and sense of place than the Confederate from, say, Chicago—the Yankee Good Ole Boy.

Whatever economic advantages they bring, however, the newcomers sometimes threaten to perpetuate in new territory many of the offenses of urban sprawl around the big cities. Especially in many communities of the Sunbelt, oldtimers have grown bitterly aware that the massive invasions have overloaded public services, overwhelmed police and fire departments, water supplies and sewage systems. . . .

Another and in some ways more urgent problem is what the new migrations are doing to the big industrial cities, especially those of the Northeast quadrant. They are hemorrhaging. Economist Thomas Muller of the Urban Institute in Washington lists nine "municipal danger signals." Among them: substantial long-term outmigration, loss of private employment, high debt service, high unemployment, high tax burden, increasing proportion of low-income population. . . .

It is possible to be too apocalyptic about the big cities' prospects. They still have tremendous force, and the bulk of the nation's industry and financial power. But the migratory trend is disturbing to people who have a stake in the big old cities. The automobile has in many ways rendered them obsolete. Along the highways circling them have arisen "ring cities," shopping centers, medical complexes and the rest, which provides the services that long gave the central city its *raison d'etre*. . . .

The U.S. is more than ever a nation of immigrants, and the new internal migration is a pursuit, as much psychological as geographical, of the remaining pockets of Frederick Jackson Turner's frontier. The migration is also the last march of a kind of expansionist privilege: the old American idea that all mistakes are canceled by the horizon, by more room, by moving out. Great population movements are hardly unique in a nation that was built by its restless energy. Never before, however, have so many Americans been able to change their lives quite so quickly, and to base their decisions about where to live on the amenities they desire.

221

Discos (1977)

Music that was popular among the youth in the late 1960s underwent a transformation. Whereas rock music of the 1960s tended to follow traditional folk ballads or talking blues and came to be identified with protest messages of the counterculture, the disco movement of the 1970s combined music and dance that shifted from the old music forms. Although some critics condemned disco music as ordinary, they were also quick to note its popularity as dance music. Millions flocked to discos or clubs, as the music's popularity grew dramatically in a short period. Attending a disco became a unique form of expression. The 1977 movie hit, Saturday Night Fever, *starring John Travolta and Karen Gorney, captured the popularity of disco music. Also in 1977, Sally Helgesen reported on the disco culture for* Harper's Magazine. *An excerpt of her article is as follows.*

Questions to Consider

1. According to Helgesen, for what reasons do people go to discos?

2. In what ways does Helgesen describe gays who frequent discos? Straights?

3. What does the popularity of discos reveal about America in the 1970s?

4. Compare the attitudes about gays found in this document to those found in "The Issue of Gay Marriage" (Document 227).

. . . I had only recently become aware myself that men and women who did not consider themselves homosexuals were routinely spending time at discos where most of the clientele were gay; that their persistence in doing this was becoming a problem for the owners and patrons of these clubs; that their presence had about it an ambiguity of purpose, for while they might say they were there only as watchers, only as voyeurs, they were also becoming partic- ipants, regulars in a scene which could never be theirs, outlaws in what has always been an outlaw world.

Infinity is a disco in Lower Manhattan. It is 3:00 a.m. Friday, the dead of night, but the evening is not yet half over and there are still 2,000 people here. Perhaps a third of them are crowded against the shoulders-high ban- quette that rims the floor, from which they can watch those parading before them or simply stare at themselves in the wall-to-wall mirrors which reflect unending images across the huge loft spaces. The mirrors are part of the show at Infinity, for not only can you watch your own image change beneath the flashing strobes, you can also dance with yourself, especially if you have brought a fan, or a tambourine, or a pole, or a great big hat. Such props give you something with which to balance your act, provide an acceptable foil. With the mirrors all around, you really don't need a partner. . . .

To walk through the crowd at Infinity tonight is to walk through an exotic aviary where every variety of species is on display, usually single exam- ples of each, but occasionally exhibited with an identical mate for the admi- ration of the passing public. A large German male dressed as a cowgirl watches a Spanish couple fox-trotting in black cutaways and patent pumps. A woman wearing a transparent plastic rain cape with only a garter belt and black stockings underneath wanders about alone. A young man in saddle shoes has strapped a life-size female doll to his ankles and wrists, and he moves lightly across the floor with her, unencumbered by the weight of any human shape. There is here a standard of conformity to the outrageous; one must put on a passing pleasing show. . . .

Infinity is not a gay disco, although it may appear that way at first because the gays display the most exotic plumage, and put on the best show. Then too, each of the two bars at Infinity is bracketed by a huge pair of pink neon phalluses which a glow in the night like homosexual icons. Infinity drew a gay crowd when it opened, but as so often happens at discos in New York, the party crowd followed them there, straight society people. After the place had been written up, and everybody knew it was chic, what is known on the scene as "the scurve" arrived, singles who live with roommates on the Upper East Side or in the middle-class neighborhoods of New Jersey and Long

Sally Helgesen, "Disco," *Harper's Magazine* 255 (October 1977): 20–24. Copyright © 1977 by *Harper's Magazine*. All rights reserved. Reproduced from the October issue by special permission.

Island, people drifting around and trying to get picked up. Now middle-class young men cruise the banquettes each weekend, but the tone of the place is sufficiently gay that a woman can protect herself by adopting a fierce glare to indicate dykishness, or by staring fixedly at herself in the mirror, for self-absorption is respected here.

The music never stops at a disco, not for a single minute. Each song segues right into the next, the monotony of the bass pedal smoothing the transition. The lights are synchronized with the sound, and they never stop flashing except during the percussive interludes, when everything falls dark; then the whistles blow and the crowd yelps and hoots and barks as if hinting that a bacchanal is about to begin, but it never, never does begin, although everyone seems to be waiting for something to happen. After you've been in a disco for a while, after your senses have been operated upon by those *bodies*, . . . you may begin to feel a disorientation of fancy within yourself, and you may attune yourself to the repetitive shifts of this electronic music of the spheres and fall into a kind of disco trance in which your brain turns off and you give yourself up to the sensations which envelop you. And suddenly whoever you thought you were when you walked in the door may no longer seem very important. . . .

On the afternoon before the opening of a new disco, Rene, the makeup man at Fiorucci, is very busy. Fiorucci is a clothing store, all mirrors and steel and hard, mean edges, where the disco heavies hang out during the day, and many of the regulars have Rene do their makeup for them in the afternoons. Rene is only twenty-one, but he says he's been going to discos four nights a week for eight years, before the straight crowd picked up on the scene. He likes only the fanciest places, where he can wear the most outrageous costumes and live out whatever fantasy might strike him on a particular evening. . . .

That cabdriver who had driven me to the disco late one Wednesday night had said of the women who went there, "What I want to ask them is, Why do they go?"

Hollywood says she goes because gay men are better at creating fantasies, and she needs fantasy in her life. Discos are nothing if not a fantasy world, where you can change your identity by changing your costume. Fantasy travels light.

If you want to travel light, you must not carry a sense of yourself too heavily. Mike O'Harro, the "Disco King" of Washington D. C., tells me that, as discos spread to every city in America, "you'll be able to know that you can get a good time anywhere by just walking into a disco, because it will be just like every other disco," and O'Harro is right; but to "get a good time" anywhere, any time, you must not consider too closely where you came from or where you are going, or why you are making this particular stop along the way. You must let the music take your mind, so that those "bodies without, which are commonly called Objects," may work on your senses so you can forget that deepest part that once felt most like yourself. That part is heavy baggage, and you don't want it when you are traveling light.

222

A Perspective on AIDS (1987)

The Acquired Immune Deficiency Syndrome (AIDS) epidemic brought significant change to accepted social and medical norms. First detected in 1981, the human immunodeficiency virus (HIV) that leads to AIDS breaks down the body's immune system with fatal results. Initially, the disease was associated with male homosexuals and drug addicts who used "dirty" needles. It intensified animosity toward the homosexual community (Patrick Buchanan, White House director of communications, said homosexuals had "declared war on nature, and now nature is extracting an awful retribution"), but as the HIV virus spread through blood or sexual contact to infect alarming numbers of heterosexual individuals, this attitude softened. To help limit the spread of the virus and calm popular fear of AIDS, the federal government launched an education campaign about the disease and encouraged "safe sex" through the use of condoms. Sexual experimentation and promiscuity declined. With escalating medical costs to treat the disease and few advances toward a cure, AIDS remains a frightening problem. Excerpted as follows is David C. Jones's 1987 speech to medical students at Duke University about AIDS. Jones is from the North Carolina AIDS Service Coalition.

Questions to Consider

1. Why does Jones argue that AIDS will alter existing health insurance and health care?

2. Why does he believe that HIV antibody testing could lead to blatant discrimination?

3. What six-point proposal does Jones make to change attitudes about AIDS?

4. Have attitudes about AIDS changed? Why?

Too many of my friends have died and far too many more are ill or living in fear. You are being pulled into a maelstrom of controversy about the disease that is killing them. In fact, I believe that Society is setting you up to have to deal with its own doubt, fear and anger. I believe that you are going to have to be the arbiters of some very profound and even radical questions that will shake the very foundations of the delivery of health care as we know it. . . .

First, who will get what care? Some of the ethical dilemmas you will face will be generated by the creeping obsolescence of insurance as we know it. Health insurance as we know it today will not exist twenty years from now. AIDS is not the first but it is the most startling example of a confluence of

---

David C. Jones, "Perspective on AIDS: Ethical, Socioeconomic and Political Aspects," *Vital Speeches of the Day* 54 (1987): 176–179. Reprinted by permission.

forces that will change dramatically how we will decide who is going to get what medical care. Let me explain.

We believe that society should share the burden of injury or loss. So we have insurance. . . .

Now comes AIDS. It seems universally fatal, there is not much we can do and care costs a great deal. The financial impact on an insurance company can be great.

The first response of some companies fell somewhere between silly and sinister. My favorite is the letter that one company sent to agents telling them to be suspicious of single men ". . . in such occupations that do not require physical exertion . . . such as antique dealers, interior decorators or florists."

Then there came a blood test to detect antibodies to the virus that causes AIDS also with epidemiological data indicating that large numbers of people with antibodies are infected, and that a growing portion of them are going to die very expensive deaths.

Insurance companies fought for the right to use the antibody test to deny new coverage. Their position is simple and traditional: it identifies a new potential risk. . . .

We are standing on the brink of an explosion of diagnostic capability. This will be possible as a result of breakthroughs in our ability to read and understand our genetic program, and the technological elegance of rapidly evolving new generations of precise, affordable diagnostic systems. . . .

We will be able to run a series of tests and print out the probable health events of an individual. We will have a good picture of what diseases this person is likely to experience naturally, and others that will probably be experienced should certain environmental conditions be encountered.

What this means, based on the structure and management of private insurance today, is that a staggering number of people will be uninsurable and many will be unemployable. We face the very real possibility of creating an entire caste of non-persons, people for whom there is no work, no promise, no place. . . .

I will go so far as to say that society will not tolerate it. The only question in my mind is how soon people will react. It may be soon as thoughtful people begin to recognize the implications of financing care the way we have always done it when this information is available. Or it may be after millions of people are forced into poverty and we face a cataclysmic reaction from society. How we respond to AIDS now and the problem of a growing number of terminally ill Americans without insurance will tell us a lot about what our future holds.

We will finally be forced to resolve a debate that has been simmering in this country for years. Is good health care a right or a privilege? We were going to have to face up to this sooner or later. AIDS has just made it sooner. . . .

The HIV antibody test represents the first time that medical information has been used widely as the basis for social and political discrimination of an unpopular minority. Society's reaction to homosexuality as a lifestyle ranges from acceptance to scorn. AIDS has even brought forth again the condemnation of those with the astonishing arrogance to claim God's proxy to judge. . . .

But we have to look at the real world in which this disease is spreading. AIDS is not like any other disease. Punitive discrimination does occur, regularly. And now we hear threats of prison. Now we have added fear upon fear. And it is fear that will assure that this system, in this environment, in this state, simply will not work. Fewer people will seek testing, fewer people will know that they are infected, and more people will die from the complications of an acquired immune deficiency.

The members of the AIDS Service Coalition have been dealing with AIDS for a long time. We know how terrible it is and we want to do everything we can to see that no one is ever consumed by it again. We would like to make a specific six-point proposal that should be part of public health policy. We believe it will cause the largest number of people to change the behavior that places them at risk and to seek information, counseling and medical care.

First, a statewide AIDS education program should be the state's first priority. Education is the only hope we have of preventing people from being infected in the first place. Further, people are more likely to seek counseling or testing when they are told that they may have been exposed if they have already received some education about AIDS.

Second, adequate counseling must be available, both before and after testing. . . .

Third, anonymous testing for HIV should continue to be available to all who seek it. It should be the policy of the state to require informed consent before any person is tested, and that every person tested in any setting should be notified of the result.

Fourth, a system of contact notification should be developed that emphasizes voluntary self-referral, with the option of notification by trained AIDS counseling specialists at the state level. Counseling should include both the necessity of informing sexual and needle contacts, and effective and sensitive techniques for notifying others. . . .

Fifth, we must dispel the fear of losing one's apartment or job by making it clear that North Carolina prohibits discrimination based on a positive HIV test or a diagnosis of AIDS.

Sixth, we should reduce the financial burden of AIDS by making alternatives to extended hospitalization available, and thereby make more resources available for controlling AIDS. . . .

. . . The forces that have been unleashed by AIDS are so powerful that if we do not find a way to harness them productively, and with dignity, we shall all be consumed by them.

All I can really ask you to do is to ask the questions now, over and over, in good faith, within a framework that recognized a respect for people and a commitment to do no harm, a framework that causes us to act in the interests of others and share the benefits and the burdens of what we do. Please deal with them now, while you may still have time.

223

A View on Hispanic Assimilation (1991)

Since the early 1980s, immigration into the United States had increased dramatically. Most of the legal immigrants were Hispanic (from Spanish-speaking countries of Latin America, mainly Mexico) and Asian. Their numbers had swollen to nearly 600,000 per year. In addition, there were illegal immigrants, mostly Mexicans, moving across the border. Many native-born Americans ("Anglos") were alarmed as increasing numbers of immigrants moved into the areas where they lived. The Anglos believed they would become a minority in their own cities and that American values would be threatened. Such fears prompted efforts to assimilate the newcomers faster, bar Spanish in public schools, and restrict or prohibit government services provided to the immigrants. Clearly, cultural differences were divisive. In 1991, Linda Chavez published Out of the Barrio, *a study of Hispanics in American society. Chavez served in several federal government posts in the Reagan administration and was the first woman appointed to the Civil Rights Commission. In the following selection, Chavez offers a conservative commentary on the role of Hispanics and of government.*

Questions to Consider

1. According to Chavez, why should Hispanics assimilate?
2. What is the role of government, according to Chavez? Why does she oppose affirmative action programs?
3. Should Hispanics follow the example of previous immigrants to America?
4. In what ways would Cesar Chavez ("Cesar Chavez and La Causa," Document 211) disagree with Linda Chavez? How do you account for these differences?

Assimilation has become a dirty word in American politics. It invokes images of people, cultures, and traditions forged into a colorless alloy in an indifferent melting pot. But, in fact, assimilation, as it has taken place in the United States, is a far more gentle process, by which people from outside the community gradually became part of the community itself. Descendants of the German, Irish, Italian, Polish, Greek and other immigrants who came to the United States bear little resemblance to the descendants of the countrymen their forebears left behind. America changed its immigrant groups—and was changed by them. Some groups were accepted more reluctantly than others—the Chinese, for example—and some with great struggle. Blacks, whose

---

Linda Chavez, *Out of the Barrio: Toward a New Politics of Hispanic Assimilation* (New York, 1991), 161–171. Copyright © 1991 by Basic Books, a division of HarperCollins Publishers, Inc. Reprinted by permission of Basic Books, a member of Perseus Books, L.L.C.

ancestors were forced to come here, have only lately won their legal right to full participation in this society; and even then civil rights gains have not been sufficiently translated into economic gains. Until quite recently, however, there was no question but that each group desired admittance to the mainstream. No more. Now ethnic leaders demand that their groups remain separate, that their native culture and language be preserved intact, and that whatever accommodation takes place be on the part of the receiving society. . . .

The government should not be obliged to preserve any group's distinctive language or culture. Public schools should make sure that all children can speak, read, and write English well. When teaching children from non-English-speaking backgrounds, they should use methods that will achieve English proficiency quickly and should not allow political pressure to interfere with meeting the academic needs of students. No children in an American school are helped by being held back in their native language when they could be learning the language that will enable them to get a decent job or pursue higher education. More than twenty years of experience with native-language instruction fails to show that children in these programs learn English more quickly or perform better academically than children in programs that emphasize English acquisition.

If Hispanic parents want their children to be able to speak Spanish and know about their distinctive culture, they must take the responsibility to teach their children these things. Government simply cannot—and should not—be charged with this responsibility. Government bureaucracies given the authority to create bicultural teaching materials homogenize the myths, customs, and history of the Hispanic peoples of this hemisphere, who, after all, are not a single group but groups. It is only in the United States that "Hispanics" exist; a Cakchiquel Indian in Guatemala would find it remarkable that anyone could consider his culture to be the same as a Spanish Argentinean's. The best way for Hispanics to learn about their native culture is in their own communities. Chinese, Jewish, Greek, and other ethnic communities have long established after-school and weekend programs to teach language and culture to children from these groups. Nothing stops Hispanic organizations from doing the same things. . . .

Politics has traditionally been a great equalizer. One person's vote was as good as another's regardless of whether the one was rich and the other poor. But politics requires that people participate. The great civil rights struggles of the 1960s were fought in large part to guarantee the right to vote. Hispanic leaders demand representation but do not insist that individual Hispanics participate in the process. The emphasis is always on rights, never on obligations. Hispanic voter organizations devote most of their efforts toward making the process easier—election law reform, postcard registration, election materials in Spanish—to little avail; voter turnout is still lower among Hispanics than among blacks or whites. Spanish posters urge Hispanics to vote because it will mean more and better jobs and social programs, but I've never seen one that mentions good citizenship. Hispanics (and others) need to be reminded that if they want the freedom and opportunity democracy offers, the least they can do is take the time to register and vote. These are the lessons with which earlier immigrants were imbued, and they bear reviving. . . .

The government can do only so much in promoting higher education for Hispanics or any group. It is substantially easier today for a Hispanic student to go to college than it was even twenty or thirty years ago, yet the proportion of Mexican Americans who are graduating from college today is unchanged from what it was forty years ago. When the former secretary of education Lauro Cavazos, the first Hispanic ever to serve in the Cabinet, criticized Hispanic parents for the low educational attainment of their children, he was roundly attacked for blaming the victim. But Cavazos's point was that Hispanic parents must encourage their children's educational aspirations and that, too often, they don't. Those groups that have made the most spectacular socioeconomic gains—Jews and Chinese, for example—have done so because their families placed great emphasis on education.

Hispanics cannot have it both ways. If they want to earn as much as non-Hispanic whites, they have to invest the same number of years in schooling as these do. The earnings gap will not close until the education gap does. Native-born Hispanics are already enjoying earnings comparable to those of non-Hispanic whites, once educational differences are factored in. If they want to earn more, they must become better educated. But education requires sacrifices, especially for persons from lower-income families. Only a substantial commitment to the education of their children on the part of this generation of Hispanic parents will increase the speed with which Hispanics improve their social and economic status.

Affirmative action politics treats race and ethnicity as if they were synonymous with disadvantage. The son of a Mexican American doctor or lawyer is treated as if he suffered the same disadvantage as the child of a Mexican farm worker; and both are given preference over poor, non-Hispanic whites in admission to most colleges or affirmative action employment programs. Most people think this is unfair, especially white ethnics whose own parents and grandparents also faced discrimination in this society but never became eligible for the entitlements of the civil rights era. It is inherently patronizing to assume that all Hispanics are deprived and grossly unjust to give those who aren't preference on the basis of disadvantages they don't experience. Whether stated or not, the essence of affirmative action is the belief that Hispanics—or any of the other eligible groups—are not capable of measuring up to the standards applied to whites. This is a pernicious idea.

Ultimately, entitlements based on their status as "victims" rob Hispanics of real power. The history of American ethnic groups is one of overcoming disadvantage, of competing with those who were already here and proving themselves as competent as any who came before. Their fight was always to be treated the same as other Americans, never to be treated as special, certainly not to turn the temporary disadvantages they suffered into the basis for permanent entitlement. Anyone who thinks this fight was easier in the early part of this century when it was waged by other ethnic groups does not know history. Hispanics have not always had an easy time of it in the United States. Even through discrimination against Mexican Americans and Puerto Ricans was not as severe as it was against blacks, acceptance has come only with struggle, and some prejudices still exist. Discrimination against Hispanics, or any other group, should be fought, and there are laws and a massive administrative apparatus to do so. But the way to eliminate such discrimination is not to classify all Hispanics as victims and treat them as if they could not succeed by their own efforts. Hispanics can and will prosper in the United States by following the example of the millions before them.

223

"Dr. Wen Ho Lee as the Model Minority for the 21st Century" (2002)

Increasing ethnic identity in the United States led many members of minority groups to question the idea of an American "melting pot" that was inclusive of all. But the experience of Asian Americans has led them to be labeled a "model minority" whose success proved that American society could successfully accommodate Americans who were not of European descent. Despite the sense that East Asians had arrived, the emergence of China as an important force in global affairs cast suspicions on some Chinese Americans as to their true loyalties. The case of Wen Ho Lee in 1999 brought this issue to a head. Dr. Lee, a nuclear physicist employed by the Los Alamos National Laboratory, was indicted on 59 counts of violating the Federal Atomic Energy Act and the Federal Espionage Act. The FBI would eventually drop the charges, acknowledging their mishandling of the case. The ensuing essay recounts the history of white racism toward Chinese Americans and criticizes the Chinese-American community's response to the arrest as an example of the "model minority" acquiescing to a stereotype. Author Ling-Chi Wang is a professor and former chair of the Department of Ethnic Studies at the University of California at Berkeley and a leading spokesperson on Chinese American and East Asian issues.

Questions to Consider

1. How does the treatment of Chinese Americans depicted in this document compare with the descriptions found in "W.E.B. DuBois on Race Relations" (Document 147) or "A View of Hispanic Assimilation" (Document 223)?

2. Why is Dr. Wang so critical of the concept of the "model minority"?

3. What does the author recommend as the best course of action for Chinese Americans?

4. Based on your reading of this document, how widespread is the acceptance of East Asians as "real Americans"?

The sad truth about Chinese Americans is our inability and unwillingness to assert our rights and to scream and protest when our constitutional rights as American citizens are trampled upon and taken away. We can't even express our anger openly when an injustice is inflicted us. Let me venture into an explanation from a historical perspective.

Since the California gold rush in mid-19th century, Chinese in the U.S. have been brow-beaten by the media, white working class, opportunistic politicians, and all three branches of the U.S. government. Chinese labor was decisively indispensable for the economic development of the American West, especially in California. They were recruited to mine mines, build railroads, reclaim and work on the rich delta land, and man the sweatshop manufacturing industries, like garment, shoes, boots, wool, and cigar. Yet, when their labor was deemed no longer necessary or worse, a threat, especially in times of economic slow-downs, they were told to pack up and go back to where they came from. Cries of "Yellow Peril" and Chinese heathenism and non-assimilability inspired exclusionary and punitive laws designed to stop further Chinese immigration, to deny them the fundamental rights guaranteed by the U.S. constitution, and indeed, to purge them from the U.S. population. Observing the rapid decline of Chinese population by 1904, Chan Kiu Sing declared, "They call it exclusion; but it is not exclusion, it is extermination."

The denial of our constitutional and political rights was so pervasive that by 1860s, the colloquial expression, "Not a Chinaman's Chance," became an integral part of American language. That's right: to be a Chinese in the U.S. was to have no chance at all. Being Chinese, therefore, is to know your subservient place and alien status in the society, to stay out of the way, to remain invisible and unobtrusive, to be only useful, but never competitive.

That, in essence, is the place and plight of Chinese in the U.S. in the 19th and first half of the 20th centuries. Even though African American struggles for civil and political rights after World War II have significantly benefited Chinese American advancement in the U.S., the old attitudes and racist stereotypes of Chinese remain alive and well in the white society and in American national consciousness.

What is most alarming is how the stereotypes, like Chinaman, non-assimilability, and Yellow Peril, persist to this date. For example, the post–World War era brought new types of Chinese immigrants to the U.S., many of whom were the cream of China (including the best and the brightest from Taiwan, Hong Kong, and Chinese throughout Southeast Asia). Chinese

Ling-Chi Wang, "Dr. Wen Ho Lee as the Model Minority of the 21st Century," adapted from a posting to Huaren.org c. September 2002. Used by permission of Ling-Chi Wang.

Americans were celebrated because they were quiet and docile, they studied and worked hard, they never complained and talked back to their colleagues and supervisors, they respected authorities, they rarely expressed their feelings and thoughts, and they raised solid families with well-behaved, hard-working, and high-achieving children. Best of all, as reliable and productive employees, they were more than willing to work overtime when asked to do so, they never asked for raises, and they never complained even if they were bypassed for promotions.

The best recent examples of Chinese American plight are Vincent Chin and Wen Ho Lee. Vincent Chin was a Chinese American engineer working in early 1980s in Detroit, Michigan, the automobile manufacturing center of the U.S. He was brutally killed by two unemployed white auto workers because he was presumed to be not just "a foreigner" but worse, a highly competitive "Japanese" responsible for their job loss. The two first-degree murderers, through plea-bargaining, were eventually allowed to plead guilty to "involuntary manslaughter," fined about $3000 each, placed on a three-year probation, and then freed without serving one day in jail. This is exactly what "Not a Chinaman's Chance" is all about! Disgusted, Chin's mother returned to China at a time when many Chinese were frantically trying to find ways to go to the Gold Mountain. When asked at the airport why she was returning to China, she tersely stated, "There is no justice for Chinese in the U.S."

As for Wen Ho Lee, he is the personification of the "model minority" stereotype. For 20 years, he worked diligently in the most secretive nuclear weapon lab, the Los Alamos National Laboratory, where he received the highest level of security clearance. Amidst national hysteria over an alleged theft of W-88 miniature multi-warhead design by China, Wen Ho Lee was fingered by the *New York Times* on March 6, 1999 as the prime suspect responsible for the loss of America's most advanced nuclear secret, characterized by his prosecutors and lab bosses as "the crown jewel" of America's nuclear arsenal. He was instantly treated as a foreigner and pronounced guilty in the court of public opinion. He was placed in solitary confinement for nine months while he waited for the trial to begin. No wonder federal Judge James Parker, in freeing him in September 2000, apologized to Wen Ho Lee and launched an unprecedented attack on the federal prosecutors for misleading him and the top leaders in Washington, DC. for acting shamefully and irresponsibly!

Did Wen Ho Lee come out of the jail attacking the U.S. government for unjustly prosecuting and persecuting him? Not at all! He smiled and thanked the people who defending him. He did not criticize or sue the government for wrongful prosecution and false imprisonment. He just smiled in front of national TV coverage. What a model minority!

What was the response from Chinese America? When I proposed a national mobilization to defend Wen Ho Lee in April 1999, I was greeted with strong opposition or stone silence from all the Asian American civil rights organizations. When I launched a movement to obtain both freedom and justice for Wen Ho Lee and I urged all Asian American scientists and engineers to boycott the national labs as a protest for the mistreatment of Wen Ho Lee and all Chinese American scientists in March 2000, I was soundly criticized by many a Chinese American civil rights leader because the boycott was considered offensive and ineffective. In effect, when the Wen Ho Lee case surfaced, most Asian American leaders ran for cover and effectively either remained silent or distanced themselves from the case. Some even advised me to stay out of the case for fear my reputation would be tainted or worse, ruined. They bought the government propaganda about Wen Ho Lee's guilt. They further suggested that the boycott movement would bring about a backlash against Chinese Americans. They obviously did not even understand what had already happened to Wen Ho Lee: convicted without a trial and subjected to cruel and unusual punishment without a conviction. In fact, through racial profiling, all the Chinese American scientists and engineers became thieves and spies in the eyes of their colleagues in the labs and in the public at large.

It seems like the only remedy suggested by some of our national leaders is to hoist and wave the American flag on July 4, 2000 as if that act alone will deliver us from racism, racial profiling, selective prosecution, and unjust treatment and punishment. I don't think our leaders understand what it means to be an American and what it means to assert our constitutional rights, including the right of dissent on behalf of truth, equality, and justice, even it means to be a pain in the ass, to stick out like a sore thumb, or to be thorn in the flesh.

When we look at the elected Chinese American politicians across the U.S., most of them depend heavily on Chinese American political contributions to get elected, sometimes as much as 90% of their total in-takes. Yet, these same Chinese American politicians are expected to go out of their way not to represent and articulate Chinese or Asian American concerns for fear of antagonizing the white voters among their constituencies. In other words, they want Chinese Americans to contribute money to their campaigns in order for them to be celebrities! Have we no shame? Have we no self-respect?

Is there hope for Chinese Americans? Or, are we relegated forever to live by the model minority status, personified by the new icon of the 21st century, Wen Ho Lee? It is a strange, if not abnormal un-American thing!

225

The Changing Demographics of America (1999)

In the period following the Second World War, the United States experienced the beginnings of a demographic shift that had implications for future generations of Americans. The promise of rising incomes fueled suburbanization, which combined with the desire for early marriage and starting a family to produce the "Baby Boom." The Baby

Boomers, as this large group is often identified, have wielded significant influence, in part, because of their numbers relative to the rest of American society. As they have grown older, the Baby Boomers have helped shape the political, social, and economic landscape of America in the second half of the 20th century and, by and large, enjoyed the fruits of this considerable influence. By the late 20th century, as the Baby Boomers neared retirement, some predicted the demise of Social Security and a possible generational conflict between the Baby Boomers and the subsequent generations over taxes, jobs, and resources. In the following excerpt, Thomas G. Donlan, an editor at Barron's, a business and financial weekly newspaper, offered some commentary on the demographic changes taking place at the end of the 20th century.

Questions to Consider

1. Do Baby Boomers seem selfish?
2. To what extent can one stereotype according to age?
3. What does the author see as having more impact than the Baby Boomer generation?
4. Why do you think the author is so critical of the Baby Boomer generation? To what extent is this criticism warranted?

For their whole lives, Baby Boomers have been the 400-pound canaries of American society. The generations of children born between 1946 and 1964 have been the birds who sit anywhere they want, whose whims rule the nation. When they were children, the country moved to the suburbs and forced municipalities to build thousands of new schools. The government built the Interstate Highway system, which let Mom and Dad take them on a new kind of vacation. When they were teenagers, the country went youth-crazy and idolized idealistic college students. The government provided a new system of college loans and subsidized the construction of college facilities. When they were young adults, the country changed its banking system to provide credit cards and mortgages so they could go deeply into debt to have it all right then and there. The government changed the bankruptcy laws and eventually taxed everybody to bail out the thousands of lenders who accommodated profligate Boomers. When they reached middle age, Wall Street rebuilt itself to provide mutual finds and brokerage accounts to help them pay off debts and build some wealth. The government created new tax-advantaged retirement accounts and enhanced the attractiveness of the old ones.

What other generation has had its music playing on the radio for their whole lives? There were no big band oldies stations when the Boomers were kids, but every city now has two or three oldies stations playing the Boomers' favorites.

Thomas G. Dolan, "Demographics and Destiny: A New Chapter in the Story of the Generations," *Barron's,* October 25, 1999, p. 25. Reprinted by permission.

What other generation enjoyed a (so far) 17-year bull market, marred only by one big recession and one little one? Their parents weathered three recessions during the Eisenhower Administration alone. Sure, it's coincidence that microchip technology got started when the Boomers were teens, and just good luck for everybody that shrinking transistors made computing and communications ever more powerful, as if on a schedule. But it's not coincidence that the national economy struggled when the Boomers were young and inexperienced, and took off as the Boomers hit their productive stride.

Boomers are frequently condemned, even by their own pundits, as spoiled, self-absorbed and greedy. Some say they were nursed on demand feeding according to the theories of Dr. Spock and they never got over it. But with all their annoying flaws, Boomers in their vast numbers are the best thing that ever happened to the American economy. The demand of 77 million credit-card-wielding consumers, many of them well-educated to demand the best, has driven producers all over the world to do their best on price and performance. And the engineers, scientists, doctors and managers turned out by those expanded schools and colleges have provided the means to design and supply better products and services valued around the world.

That's a trend that ought to continue for as much as two more decades. But it's equally true that Boomers will impose at least one more major shift on the American economy, and this one not for the better. As they retire, the Boomers will convert themselves from producers to pure consumers. Some huge percentage of U.S. cash flow will be devoted to paying their Social Security and their Medicare.

It has never been clear how this will be done. Without changes in the programs, Social Security and Medicare will shoulder aside most other non-defense government spending by the 2030s, or impose huge tax increase on younger generations of working people.

But it has always seemed clear that this would be done, somehow. The Boomers are too many to mess with, and they have always gotten their way.

More recently, we have also heard that the Boomers pose another financial threat, to themselves and other investors. Private retirement savings, though for the most part fully funded, are funded in securities markets, and some analysts have warned that as Boomers tap pensions, they will drain capital from the markets and cause a Wall Street Crash of 2020, or thereabouts.

In a variation on the old Wall Street joke, they ask: Since the generation following the Boomers is so much smaller, who will buy all the securities the Boomers want to sell?

It seems logical, even just, and certainly a bit ironic. If Boomers' saving and investing have driven the market up tenfold from the base of 1982, and even if that goes smoothly for many more years, won't Boomers' dis-saving and disinvesting ultimately tank the market? . . .

Even if demography is destiny, and even if Boomers want to sell in a mad rush, there will be buyers. Foreign buyers, putting newly earned wealth to work in the safest markets in the world. As long as the U.S. government does not do anything to spoil the national economic reputation, Boomers in their millions will be able to sell to foreign investors in even greater millions.

Perhaps more interesting to American trend-spotters, there will be lots of American investors too. The overlooked demographic feature of 21st America is this: The Baby Boom recently ceased to be the most numerous generation in U.S history.

The aging of America has been a widely expected trend, but the 21st century will not be ruled by graying Boomers after all. The Boomers must make way for Generations X and Y, otherwise known as the Birth Dearth and the Baby Rebound.

Generation X followed the Baby Boom and its spokesmen were feeling lost and unloved in the early Nineties when they named it. We don't know what Y stands for—neither do they as yet—we just know it follows X.

En masse, Boomers had fewer children, but they also delayed having families, so lots of their kids missed Generation X and are concentrated in the cohorts born after 1980. Joining them in Generation Y are the children of immigrants who came in the large waves of migrants, legal and illegal, arriving here since 1975.

The result is that there are roughly 77 million Boomers, born between 1947 and 1964, 60 million Gen X-ers, born between 1965–1980, and 80 million members of Generation Y, born between 1980–1999. Immigration will continue to swell the ranks of Generation Y for years to come.

If demographics is destiny, then the United States could have a very different destiny than the one we have expected. Perhaps the Baby Boomers will not be permitted to tax Generations X and Y into poverty, or to bind the government to the bidding of the American Association of Retired Persons and its allied groups of lobbyists for greedy geezers.

The first members of Generation Y, including a young man who lived in our house for 18 years, have just arrived at college. Their wings are still wet. They are all promise, all potential. It will take 20 more years for the last members of Generation Y to come of age.

It's their job to find their own definitional cliché, but we note with interest that they are a generation brought up with no illusions of Social Security. As matters stand, they can expect to be taxed heavily to support it, and receive little if any benefit from it. What they do about that will mark them forever.

226

Consumer Choice in Automobiles and Its Impact (2000)

Americans have been infatuated with the automobile for nearly a century. For millions of Americans, their vehicle is a transportation necessity; they need it to travel to work, to shop, to go on vacation, to simply move from one location to another. But the automobile is often much more than a mode of convenient transportation. Since the early 20th century, automobile manufacturers have appealed to shifting consumer tastes by producing a rainbow of color options, changing body styles, offering a variety of engine sizes, and providing conveniences such as automatic transmissions, radios, and more glamorous and comfortable interiors. Manufacturers also produced a variety of price ranges for different models, hoping to appeal to consumer's pocketbooks. For many Americans, the automobile became a fashion statement: the type of car you drove reflected who you were or how you wanted to be perceived. In the late 1980s, a new type of vehicle appeared—the sports utility vehicle, or SUV—which catered to the tastes of affluent middle-class Americans. In the following excerpt, Keith Bradsher, the Detroit, Michigan bureau chief for the New York Times *and author of numerous newspaper articles on the automobile industry, comments on the impact of the SUV in his book* High and Mighty.

Questions to Consider

1. Who does the author blame for some of the excesses in SUV design?
2. Do consumers have a responsibility to fellow citizens to drive safe, non-polluting, fuel-efficient automobiles?
3. How might Thomas Donlan, author of "The Changing Demographics of America" (Document 225), respond to this essay?
4. What counterarguments might be made in favor of driving SUVs?

Sport utility vehicles have taken over America's roads during the last decade, and are on their way to taking over the world's roads. The four-wheel-drive vehicles offer a romantic vision of outdoor adventure to deskbound baby boomers. The larger models provide lots of room for families and their gear. Their size gives them an image of safety. The popularity of SUVs has revived the economy of the upper Midwest and has helped power the American economy since the early 1990s.

Yet the proliferation of SUVs has created huge problems. Their safe image is an illusion. They roll over too easily, killing and injuring occupants at an alarming rate, and they are dangerous to other road users, inflicting catastrophic damage to cars that they hit and posing a lethal threat to pedestrians. Their "green" image is also a mirage, because they contribute far more than cars to smog and global warming. Their gas-guzzling designs increase American dependence on imported oil at a time when anti-American sentiment is prevalent in the Middle East.

The success of SUVs comes partly from extremely cynical design and marketing decisions by automakers and partly from poorly drafted government regulations. The manufacturers' market researchers have decided that millions of baby boomers want an adventurous image and care almost nothing about putting others at risk to achieve it, so they have told auto engineers to design

High and Mighty: SUVs—The World's Most Dangerous Vehicles by Keith Bradsher (New York, 2000), xiii–xvii. Copyright © by Keith Bradsher. Reprinted by permission of Public Affairs, a member of Perseus Books, L.L.C.

vehicles like the Dodge Durango, with its grille resembling a jungle cat's teeth and its flared fenders that look like bulging muscles in a savage jaw.

Automakers are able to produce behemoths that guzzle gas, spew pollution and endanger their occupants and other motorists because of loopholes in government regulations. When the United States imposed safety, environmental and tax rules on automobiles in the 1970s, much tougher standards were set for cars than for pickup trucks, vans and the off-road vehicles that have since evolved into sport utility vehicles. Many of these loopholes still exist, and have spread to other countries that have copied American regulations. The result has been a public policy disaster, with automakers given an enormous and unintended incentive to shift production away from cars and toward inefficient, unsafe, heavily polluting SUVs. . . .

The height and width of the typical SUV make it hard for car drivers behind it to see the road ahead, increasing the chance that they will be unable to avoid a crash, especially a multi-vehicle pileup. The stiff, truck-like underbody of an SUV does little to absorb that force of collision with trees and other roadside objects. Its size increases traffic congestion, because car drivers tend to give sport utility vehicles a lot of room, so fewer vehicles can get through each green light at an intersection. Most of the nation's roadside guardrails were built for low-riding cars, and may flip an SUV on impact instead of deflection it safely back into its lane of traffic. The trucklike brakes and suspensions of SUVs mean that their stopping distances are longer than for a family car, making it less likely that an SUV driver will be able to stop before hitting a car. And when SUVs do hit pedestrians, they strike them high on the body, inflicting worse injuries than cars, which have low bumpers that flip pedestrians onto the relatively soft hood.

For all their deadliness to other motorists, SUVs are no safer than cars for their own occupants. Indeed, they are less safe. The occupant death rate per million SUVs is actually 6 percent higher than the occupant death rate per million cars. The biggest SUVs, which pose the greatest hazards to other motorists, have an 8 percent higher death rate for their occupants than minivans and the larger midsize cars like the Ford Taurus and Pontiac Grand Prix. How is this possible? SUV occupants simply die differently, being much more likely than car occupants to die in rollovers, as well as being much more likely to send other drivers to the grave. . . .

There are 20 million SUVs on the nation's roads and more than half of them are less than five years old. Three-quarters of the full-size SUVs, the largest models, are also under five years old. As affluent, cautious-driving baby boomers begin to sell their SUVs or turn them in at the end of leases, the used-vehicle market will be flooded with these vehicles. Falling prices will make them more attractive to younger drivers and drivers with poor safely records—including drunk drivers. The only thing more frightening for traffic safely experts than a drunk driver or young person behind the wheel of a new SUV is a drunk or young person behind the wheel of an old SUV with failing brakes and other maintenance problems. . . .

SUVs are terrible not just for traffic safely but for the environment. Because of their poor gas mileage, they emit a lot of carbon dioxide, a gas linked to global warming. A midsize SUV puts out roughly 50 percent more carbon dioxide per mile than the typical car, while a full-size SUV may emit twice as much. The Sierra Club likes to point out that driving a full-size SUV for a year instead of a midsize car burns as much extra energy as leaving a refrigerator door open for six years. SUVs also spew up to 5.5 times as much smog-causing gases per mile as cars. . . .

227

The Issue of Gay Marriage (2003)

Throughout the 20th century, most gays and lesbians remained silent about their sexual orientation for fear of persecution and violent backlash, although homosexual communities existed in most major cities. Inspired by the Civil Rights Movement, some gays and lesbians began to publicly demand tolerance and hopefully reshape homophobic views. This movement made news when gays at the Stonewall Bar in New York City fought back against a particularly violent police raid in June 1969. In the aftermath of this incident, the Gay Liberation Front made gains by advocating "gay rights," while more and more homosexuals "came out of the closet" and argued that their sexual orientation was legitimate. In the 1990s, gay men and lesbians became more prominent in public venues such as movies, television shows, and politics, which helped dispel some homophobic stereotypes. Despite instances of violence toward homosexuals and less subtle forms of discrimination, increasing numbers of Americans supported gay rights. In 2000, Vermont became the first state to grant legal status to same-sex marriages. As other states considered extending rights to gays and lesbians, Ramesh Ponnuru, writing for the conservative magazine, The National Review, *offered the following editorial on gay marriage.*

Questions to Consider

1. Why does the author believe that "Gay Marriage is on the Way"?
2. In what ways is the Gay Rights Movement similar to other similar civil rights movements? How is it different?
3. In what ways do you think the AIDS crisis affected the issue of gay marriage?

For social conservatives, it seems that the battle over gay rights is nearing an end before it has even fairly begun. It is true that a small majority of the American public continues to believe, as the poll question puts it, that "sexual relations between two adults of the same sex" are "always wrong." It is true,

Ramesh Ponnuru, "Coming Out Ahead: Why Gay Marriage is on the Way," *National Review* 55 (July 28, 2003): 24–26. © 2003 by National Review Inc., 215 Lexington Avenue, New York, NY 10016. Reprinted by permission.

as well, that a slightly larger majority believes that persons of the same sex should not be allowed to marry.

But public opinion has been moving with stunning rapidity. In the 1970s and '80s, the percentage of Americans who believed gay sex was "always wrong" barely budged. The National Opinion Research Center found that 73 percent held that belief in 1973, and 76 percent did in 1990. By 2000, that number had fallen by 16 points. It fell another 6 in the next two years. In 1996, Gallup found that 26 percent of the public supported same-sex marriage. In late June of this year, 39 percent did. Young people support it more than their elders. The trend lines favor gay marriage.

So do legal developments, . . . Elite, including legal-elite, opinion favors gay rights more than public opinion does. Still, public opinion influences the courts. If courts had imposed gay marriage in 1990, there would have been a substantial public backlash. Now the idea looks less radical. If the courts move this year, or two years from now, there may yet be a backlash—but perhaps not one large enough to be effective. Three decades after Roe, almost three years after *Bush v. Gore,* no one is shocked when the courts make the weightiest political decisions.

Another shift in public sentiment is less easily captured in poll numbers: the rise of what one might call an "anti-anti-gay" bloc. People in this group may have qualms about homosexuality and may not support gay marriage. But they are at least as uncomfortable with anything that strikes them as hostile to gay people, with rhetoric that singles them out for criticism, with political figures who seem to spend too much time worrying about them. It is this group—more than gays themselves or even unequivocal supporters of gay rights—that has caused the Bush White House to take a moderate line on gay issues.

President Bush opposes gay marriage, "hate crimes" legislation, and even the Employment Non-Discrimination Act. But he has also appointed openly gay officials, refrained from picking fights with the gay lobby, and generally frustrated social-conservative groups. . . .

Again, most people continue to agree with social conservatives that marriage should be reserved for heterosexual couples. But they do not agree with the premises that underlie that conclusion. The traditional moral argument against homosexual sex has been part of a larger critique of non-marital sex—and, classically, of sex that is not oriented toward procreation within marriage. Social conservatives need no instruction on how the links among sex, procreation, and marriage have been weakened among heterosexuals. They know that many people have adopted what might be called a privatized view of marriage, as an institution whose contours are plastic, whose purpose is to provide emotional satisfaction to the persons concerned, and whose terms are negotiable (and revocable). But they have been slow to see some of the political effects of these social changes.

The logic of the argument against homosexuality now implicates the behavior of a lot of heterosexuals. If the argument is made openly, and cast as a case for traditional sexual morals in general, a large part of the public will flinch. If the argument is made so as to single out gays, the logic vanishes.

Social conservatives begin to look as though they are motivated not by principle but by the desire to persecute a minority. If no effective public argument can be made, the prohibition on gay marriage must survive based on tradition and unarticulated reasons. These are weak defenses in a rationalistic and sexually liberated era. . . .

At the same time that social conservatives were reaching this dead end, the agenda of gay-rights organizations was changing, too. What, after all, have been gays' great demands in recent years? They have asked for the opportunity to serve in the armed forces, to lead Boy Scout troops, to marry and adopt. Social-conservative rhetoric on homosexuality remained stuck in the 1970s, presenting gays as sexual radicals. Social conservatives were really the last squares. . . .

The most effective gay strategy was not a political strategy at all. It was the choice of individuals to identify themselves openly as homosexuals. Scores of millions of Americans now have friends and relatives whom they know are gay. Perhaps as a strict matter of logic, that should not have affected their views on sexual morality. But logic and eros have never been easy bedfellows, have they?

It was perhaps impossible for social conservatives to resist a tide so strong. But their failure was partly of their own making. They were simultaneously too loving and too hateful. The second point is familiar enough to everyone. For the reasons outlined above, persuasive social-conservative rhetoric on gay rights is difficult to devise. But the rhetoric the social Right actually adopted had the additional burden of lending itself to easy caricature as spiteful, harsh, and obsessive—in part because it was not infrequently all of those things. The Religious Right's love for gays, meanwhile, was not the sort that homosexuals could recognize. It took the form of wanting to save their souls. What religious conservatives wanted was for gays to become ex-gays. The unspoken wish of many other conservatives was for gays to re-closet themselves. Neither had any chance of happening in large numbers. . . .

When the Massachusetts supreme court brings full-fledged gay marriage to an American state for the first time, the issue will heat up. Anyone who expects President Bush's storied quest for the Catholic vote to strengthen the hand of social conservatives has not been looking at the survey data. *Catholic World Report* recently commissioned a survey that suggested that students at Catholic colleges became more liberal during their time on campus. The freshmen were pro-life, and the seniors pro-choice. What was even more interesting was that a majority of Catholic-college freshmen already favored gay marriage when they got to campus. I suspect that even conservative Catholics who oppose gay marriage are especially sensitive to rhetoric that seems intolerant toward gays as persons.

After Massachusetts, will Republicans find a way to object forcefully to gay marriage and to push for the marriage amendment, without looking intolerant? That would be a tall order even for people who thought deeply about these matters. Social conservatives have not yet lost this battle, and their defeat is not quite inevitable. But that is the way to bet.

30

✳

Our Times

A merica's role as the world's lone superpower was accompanied by
domestic concerns at the turn of the 21st century. The American
economy boomed, in part because the increasing globalization of
trade and the computer revolution created new business and jobs, but the
president was embroiled in a scandal that led to his impeachment. The collapse
of the Soviet Union produced new relationships in the post–Cold War era,
but the terrorists' attacks on September 11, 2001, caused many Americans to
reconsider America's place in the world. Within a 12-year period, the United
States fought three wars (1991 Gulf War, Afghanistan, and the 2003 Iraq War)
in the Middle East in efforts to curb the power of an expansion-minded dictator or to remove terrorist threats. At home, Congress passed legislation that
broadened investigative powers to thwart potential terrorist threats. The following selections reveal some of the themes that defined the times.

228

"A New World Order" (1991)

*The dramatic and rapid breakdown of communist rule in Europe in 1989–90 indi-
cated that the Cold War was concluding and that neither the Soviet Union nor the
United States could control world events. The new Eastern European governments, the
remarkable reunification of Germany, and the disintegration of the Soviet Union into
15 republics revealed an increasingly fractured and unpredictable Europe that asserted
newfound autonomy. An abortive democratic reform movement in China, however, and
communist control of Cuba, Angola, and North Korea demonstrated that communism
still persisted. Meanwhile, African, Middle Eastern, and Latin American countries,
freed from the Cold War tensions, became more self-reliant. Clearly, a new era of international relations had begun, and world inclination viewed the United States as the
model for modern society. In the context of these turbulent times, President George
Bush addressed the United Nations General Assembly on his vision of "a new world
order," as what he called the "renewal of history" changed global relationships.
Excerpted as follows is his speech.*

Questions to Consider

1. Why does George Bush believe history has resumed?
2. According to Bush, what opportunities and perils exist in the post–Cold War era?
3. What role should the United Nations play in the "new world order"? In what instances should the United States become involved in maintaining the new order?
4. What is the significance of Bush's proclamation of a new world order?

My speech today will not sound like any you've heard from a President of the United States. I'm not going to dwell on the superpower competition that defined international politics for half a century. Instead, I will discuss the challenges of building peace and prosperity in a world leavened by the Cold War's end and the resumption of history.

Communism held history captive for years. It suspended ancient disputes; and it suppressed ethnic rivalries, nationalistic aspirations, and old prejudices. As it has dissolved, suspended hatreds have sprung to life. People who for years have been denied their pasts have begun searching for their own identities—often through peaceful and constructive means, occasionally through factionalism and bloodshed.

This revival of history ushers in a new era, teeming with opportunities and perils. And let's begin by discussing the opportunities.

First, history's renewal enables people to pursue their natural instincts for enterprise. Communism froze that progress until its failures became too much for even its defenders to bear.

And now citizens throughout the world have chosen enterprise over envy; personal responsibility over the enticements of the state; prosperity over the poverty of central planning. . . .

Frankly, ideas and goods will travel around the globe with or without our help. The information revolution has destroyed the weapons of enforced isolation and ignorance. In many parts of the world technology has overwhelmed tyranny, proving that the age of information can become the age of liberation if we limit state power wisely and free our people to make the best use of new ideas, inventions and insights.

By the same token, the world has learned that free markets provided levels of prosperity, growth and happiness that centrally planned economies can never offer. Even the most charitable estimates indicate that in recent years the free world's economies have grown at twice the rate of the former communist world. . . .

I cannot stress this enough: Economic progress will play a vital role in the new world. It supplies the soil in which democracy grows best.

George Bush, "The Challenge of Building Peace: A Renewal of History," *Vital Speeches of the Day* 58 (1991): 2–4.

People everywhere seek government of and by the people. And they want to enjoy their inalienable rights to freedom and property and person. . . .

The challenge facing the Soviet peoples now—that of building political systems based upon individual liberty, minority rights, democracy and free markets—mirrors every nation's responsibility for encouraging peaceful, democratic reform. But it also testifies to the extraordinary power of the democratic ideal.

As democracy flourishes, so does the opportunity for a third historical breakthrough: international cooperation. A year ago, the Soviet Union joined the United States and a host of other nations in defending a tiny country against aggression—and opposing Saddam Hussein. For the very first time on the matter of major importance, superpower competition was replaced with international cooperation.

The United Nations, in one of its finest moments, constructed a measured, principled, deliberate and courageous response to Saddam Hussein. It stood up to an outlaw who invaded Kuwait, who threatened many states within the region, who sought to set a menacing precedent for the post–Cold War World. . . .

We will not revive these ideals if we fail to acknowledge the challenge that the renewal of history presents.

In Europe and Asia, nationalist passions have flared anew, challenging borders, straining the fabric of international society. At the same time, around the world, many age-old conflicts still fester. You see signs of this tumult right here. The United Nations has mounted more peacekeeping missions in the last 36 months than during its first 43 years. And although we now seem mercifully liberated from the fear of nuclear holocaust, these smaller, virulent conflicts should trouble us all.

We must face this challenge squarely: first, by pursuing the peaceful resolution of disputes now in progress; second, and more importantly, by trying to prevent others from erupting.

No one here can promise that today's borders will remain fixed for all time. But we must strive to ensure the peaceful, negotiated settlement of border disputes.

We also must promote the cause of international harmony by addressing old feuds. . . .

Government has failed if citizens cannot speak their minds; if they can't form political parties freely and elect governments without coercion; if they can't practice their religion freely; if they can't raise their families in peace; if they can't enjoy a just return from their labor; if they can't live fruitful lives and, at the end of their days, look upon their achievements and their society's progress with pride.

The renewal of history also imposes an obligation to remain vigilant about new threats and old. We must expand our efforts to control nuclear proliferation. We must work to prevent the spread of chemical and biological weapons and the missiles to deliver them.

We can never say with confidence where the next conflict may arise. And we cannot promise eternal peace—not while demagogues peddle false promises to people hungry with hope; not while terrorists use our citizens as pawns, and drug dealers destroy our peoples. We, as a result—we must band together to overwhelm affronts to basic human dignity.

It is no longer acceptable to shrug and say that one man's terrorist is another man's freedom fighter. Let's put the law above the crude and cowardly practice of hostage-holding.

The United Nations can encourage free-market development through its international lending and aid institutions. However, the United Nations should not dictate the particular forms of government that nations should adopt. But it can and should encourage the values upon which this organization was founded. Together, we should insist that nations seeking our acceptance meet standards of human decency.

Where institutions of freedom have lain dormant, the United Nations can offer them new life. These institutions play a crucial role in our quest for a new world order, an order in which no nation must surrender one iota of its own sovereignty; an order characterized by the rule of law rather than the resort to force; the cooperative settlement of disputes, rather than anarchy and bloodshed; and an unstinting belief in human rights.

Finally, you may wonder about America's role in the new world that I have described. Let me assure you, the United States has no intention of striving for a Pax Americana. However, we will remain engaged. We will not retreat and pull back into isolationism. We will offer friendship and leadership. And in short, we seek a Pax Universalis built upon shared responsibilities and aspirations.

To all assembled, we have an opportunity to spare our sons and daughters the sins and errors of the past. We can build a future more satisfying than any our world has ever known. The future lies undefined before us, full of promise; littered with peril. We can choose the kind of world we want; one blistered by the fires of war and subjected to the whims of coercion and chance, or one made more peaceful by reflection and choice. Take this challenge seriously. Inspire future generations to praise and venerate you, to say: On the ruins of conflict, these brave men and women built an era of peace and understanding. They inaugurated a new world order, an order worth preserving for the ages.

216

Clinton White House Response
to *The Starr Report* (1998)

Shortly after Bill Clinton took office, the Clintons became embroiled in a series of scandals. First was the Clintons' involvement in "Whitewater," a label for a fraudulent real estate investment along the Whitewater River in Arkansas that became intertwined with a failed savings and loan business that misused funds. An independent counsel, headed by Kenneth Starr, was formed to investigate. In 1994, former state employee, Paula Jones, filed a civil suit for sexual harassment against Bill Clinton, claiming he made unwanted sexual advances to her while he was governor of Arkansas. In January 1998, it was learned that Monica Lewinsky had had a sexual relationship with Bill Clinton while she was a White House intern. Clinton denied having sex, but later described his relations with Lewinsky as "inappropriate" and said that his behavior was motivated by a desire to protect his family and "myself from the embarrassment of my own conduct." Meanwhile, Whitewater independent counsel Kenneth Starr continued his methodical investigation, now broadened to include the Jones and Lewinsky scandals. In September 1998, Starr submitted his report to Congress. Throughout his presidency, Bill Clinton personally employed a team of lawyers to assist in defending himself. The day after Starr submitted his report to Congress, the Clinton legal team issued a public response. The following selection is from their response.

Questions to Consider

1. What *Starr Report* charges does this response address?

2. What does this document suggest about the Starr investigation?

3. On what basis does this response argue that Clinton should not be impeached?

4. What are the limits of the public's right to know about elected officials?

. . . It has come down to this.

After four years, scores of FBI agents, hundreds of subpoenas, thousands of documents, and tens of millions of dollars. After hiring lawyers, accountants, IRS agents, outside consultants, law professors, personal counsel, ethics advisers, and a professional public relations expert. After impaneling grand juries and leasing office space in three jurisdictions, and investigating virtually every aspect of the President's business, financial, political, official and, ultimately, personal life, the Office of Independent Counsel [OIC] has presented to the House a Referral that no prosecutor would present to any jury.

The President has admitted he had an improper relationship with Ms. Lewinsky. He has apologized. The wrongfulness of that relationship is not in dispute. And yet that relationship is the relentless focus of virtually every page of the OIC's Referral.

In 445 pages, the referral mentions Whitewater, the failed land deal which originated its investigation, twice. It never once mentions other issues it has been investigating for years—matters concerning the firing of employees of the White House travel office and the controversy surrounding the FBI files.

"Response of President's Lawyers to Independent Counsel's Report," *New York Times*, September 13, 1998, pp. 37–39.

By contrast, the issue of sex is mentioned more than 500 times, in the most graphic, salacious and gratuitous manner.

The Office of Independent Counsel is asking the House of Representatives to undertake its most solemn and consequential process short of declaring war: to remove a duly, freely and fairly elected President of the United States because he had—as he has admitted—an improper, illicit relationship outside of his marriage. Having such a relationship is wrong. Trying to keep such a relationship private, while understandable, is wrong. But such acts do not even approach the Constitutional test of impeachment—"treason, bribery, or other high crimes and misdemeanors."

The founders were wise to set such a high standard, and were wise to vest this awesome authority in the hands of the most democratic and accountable branch of our Government, and not in the hands of unaccountable prosecutors.

We have sought in this Initial Response to begin the process of rebutting the OIC's charges against the President—charges legal experts have said would not even be brought against a private citizen. The President did not commit perjury. He did not obstruct justice. He did not tamper with witnesses. And he did not abuse the power of the office of the Presidency.

230

Bill Gates and Microsoft (1998)

The most visible and dramatic aspect of the technological revolution in the late 20th century was the personal computer. The development of the microprocessor—a tiny computer on a silicon chip—paved the way for the personal computer, and, as microprocessors became faster and contained more memory, the functions and uses of the personal computer expanded. Gathering momentum in the 1980s, the computer revolutionized almost every facet of life. In the early 1990s, increasing numbers of personal computers were connecting to the Internet, a worldwide network of computers and databases. Soon e-mail was replacing the telephone and traditional mail (which some now called "snail mail") services, and Web pages became commonplace. Some individuals called the Internet the "information superhighway." One of the key individuals in the development of the personal computer was Bill Gates. He dropped out of Harvard University and, with Paul Allen, formed Microsoft to develop the software to run the hardware of the early personal computers. Microsoft developed many new software programs, often with business applications, and came to dominate the software industry for the personal computer. In March 1998, Bill Gates testified before a Senate committee on Microsoft, its place in the computer industry, and a Department of Justice antitrust suit against his company. His prepared statement is excerpted as follows.

Questions to Consider

1. How does Gates describe the computer and software industries? What are his examples?
2. On what basis does Gates argue that Microsoft is not a monopoly?
3. What does Gates envision as the future of computers?
4. Should Microsoft face an antitrust suit?
5. How does Gates' testimony compare to that given by John D. Rockefeller nearly 100 years earlier ("The Success of Standard Oil," Document 133)?

. . . Mr. Chairman, in the computer software industry, rapid and unpredictable changes constantly create new market opportunities and threaten the position of existing competitors. The position of a product—no matter how popular—is never secure because it is impossible to know when the next new idea will come along that could render that entire product category less important or even obsolete. Few industries face this kind of intense competitive pressure, even those in other parts of the high technology sector. The computer industry is littered with examples of companies that enjoyed great success for a short time, only to be overtaken by new technologies that better served consumers' needs.

For instance, as inexpensive microprocessors became available in the 1970s, Wang, IBM and others developed computers dedicated to a single task: word processing. Demand for electronic typewriters soon declined sharply, and sales of dedicated devices from Wang and IBM rose sharply. (At one time Wang was nearly synonymous with word processing.) In the 1980s, however, demand for these single-task devices declined dramatically as personal computers became available that could perform a wide range of functions in addition to word processing. In the space of just a few years, Wang went from market leader to bankruptcy. . . .

The advent of the PC industry itself is perhaps the best example of rapid and unpredictable technological change taking established market leaders by surprise. In the 1960s and 1970s, IBM and a few other large vendors such as Sperry Rand, Honeywell, Burroughs, Control Data and NCR were the titans of the computer industry. . . . The PC was derided by many manufacturers of "big iron" mainframe computers as a "toy" (which it was, at first). IBM and others were slow to appreciate the potential of distributing computing power to individuals. IBM is still a very powerful force in the computer industry. But none of the traditional mainframe or minicomputer manufacturers fully embraced personal computers in a timely way, and many faltered as a result. Today, the computer industry is populated by many high volume manufacturers that did not even exist twenty-five years ago, such as Compaq, Dell, Gateway 2000, and Micron Technologies.

U.S. Congress, Senate, *Competition, Innovation, and Public Policy in the Digital Age: Hearings Before the Committee on the Judiciary,* "Prepared Statement of Bill Gates," March 3, 1998 (Washington, DC, 1998), 89–96.

The era of hobbyists working in garage operations that nobody ever heard of and developing the next new product to take the industry by storm is not simply a legend from days gone by, it's a story we hear all the time in this industry. Take Scott Cook of Intuit, for example. Scott developed the enormously popular Quicken personal finance software sitting at his kitchen table. And the precursor of Netscape Navigator was designed by undergraduate students at the University of Illinois in Champaign-Urbana who worked for the National Center for Supercomputing Applications. . . .

Microsoft's acute awareness that today's success story could easily become tomorrow's has-been is reflected in the company's stark rallying cry: "Innovate or Die!" Nowhere is that attitude more evident than in Microsoft's response to the emergence of the Internet as a powerful new force in computing. Microsoft has always recognized that there would be a very large network developed to interconnect computers around the world, i.e., the network commonly referred to as the Information Superhighway, but it is no secret that we did not immediately recognize that the Internet would become that network. . . .

The swiftness with which people around the world have taken to the Internet is simply amazing and is powerful evidence that no company in the computer software industry can afford complacency. Microsoft is working hard to identify and pursue the many long-term opportunities that the Internet affords. Virtually everything we do these days at Microsoft reflects our conviction that the Internet is going to continue to grow. I believe that almost everyone in the developed world and huge numbers of people in the developing world will be using the Internet within the foreseeable future. Access to these technologies and the benefits they offer promises to have far-reaching effects on the way we live and work and learn, many of which we cannot even imagine today. . . .

To remain competitive and to continue to provide consumers with high quality, low cost, innovative products, Microsoft and other U.S. software companies must retain the ability to design their products free from government interference. The current case is a good example: the DOJ [Department of Justice] is attempting to require Microsoft to offer Windows without important Internet-related aspects of the operating system, depriving consumers and software developers of the benefits of compatibility provided by a common platform like Windows. If the DOJ succeeds with its efforts to limit Microsoft's ability to improve Windows, software developers will be less likely to create innovative new products that take full advantage of Windows and consumers will be unsure whether applications will work properly with the version of Windows installed on their PC. . . .

In short, while I certainly agree that the government should work to ensure that competition is not stifled by collusion or other plainly illegal activities, I think that the government should be extremely wary of interceding in an industry like computer software that is working so well on its own. As I hope my testimony today has made clear, the computer software industry is not broken, and there is no need to fix it. It is a thriving and vibrant sector of the U.S. economy and the envy of the rest of the world. . . .

Mr. Chairman, let me be very clear on this point—Microsoft does not have monopoly power in the business of developing and licensing computer operating systems. As you know, a monopolist, by definition, is a company that has the ability to restrict entry by new firms and unilaterally control prices. Microsoft can do neither. Software exhibits none of the barriers to entry that characterize traditional industries like mining or manufacturing. A new competitor needs little in the way of physical infrastructure. Distribution costs are low (software can be transmitted around the world nearly instantaneously). The principal assets required to create excellent software are human intelligence, creativity, and a willingness to assume entrepreneurial risk, all of which are in abundant supply in this country. A software product is the copyrighted expression in lines of code of ideas. No one can monopolize new ideas that can be implemented in software.

With regard to pricing, the market pressures we face compel Microsoft to price Windows competitively. In fact, the price of Windows has remained virtually unchanged over the years, while its performance and features have increased dramatically. Today Microsoft Windows is one of the central technologies contained in most new PCs, yet it accounts for less than 3 percent of the cost of a typical PC.

If Microsoft truly had monopoly power, it would be free to increase the prices for its operating systems with no need to innovate. A monopolist is lazy, charging prices above competitive levels for products that are rarely improved because no one else can offer alternative products to consumers. In contrast, Microsoft spends ever larger sums each year on research and development to deliver better operating system technology at affordable prices.

Mr. Chairman, I have been tremendously fortunate to be a part of an incredible industry like computer software during such an exciting period, but I firmly believe that we have only just scratched the surface; the greatest advances in the computer industry are yet to come. And Microsoft is working hard to unleash the power of personal computing to the benefit of everyone. Already we are working on operating systems that will enable personal computers to recognize users when they enter a room, respond accurately to voice and handwritten commands, and serve as highly efficient communication, productivity and entertainment devices. And, of course, we are devoting significant resources to developing the technology that will enable users of the Internet to realize its full potential. There is much more we can and will do to make the Internet more accessible and to give consumers good reasons to want to use it more. . . .

Mr. Chairman, Microsoft will continue to compete vigorously in the computer software industry, listen to our customers, and work hard to create new and innovative products at low prices. If Microsoft fails to keep pace with technological change and is outstripped by its competitors, let it be because we failed to innovate fast enough, not because we were hobbled by government intervention in our efforts to develop new products that meet the needs of consumers. . . .

231

George W. Bush Responds to the Terrorist Attacks (2001)

Throughout most of American history, the United States has been relatively free of direct military attack or acts of terrorism. The country benefited from this isolation. At the end of the 20th century, the United States was the wealthiest, strongest, and most powerful nation on earth. But some had come to loath the United States and its global influence. One such individual was Osama bin Laden, a wealthy Saudi Arabian who had embraced a fundamentalist, antimodern view of Islam. Enraged at the presence of American troops in Saudi Arabia after the Gulf War (1991), America's support of Israel, and the spread of American popular culture throughout the world, bin Laden found refuge in Taliban-dominated Afghanistan, from which he masterminded several terrorist attacks against American interests in the 1990s. By 1998, bin Laden formed an extremist Islamic organization called al-Qaeda (Arabic for "The Base") to recruit, train, and finance fighters who wanted to strike at the United States. On September 11, 2001, nineteen al-Qaeda members hijacked four passenger jets and used them as suicide missiles in a coordinated attack on the United States. Two planes were flown into the twin towers of the World Trade Center in New York City; within two hours, both 110-story buildings collapsed. The third plane smashed into the Pentagon. A fourth plane, headed for Washington, DC, crashed in a Pennsylvania field after passengers rushed the cockpit. Speaking to the nation a short time after the terrorist attacks, President George W. Bush offered the following response.

Questions to Consider

1. Why does Bush give the Taliban an ultimatum?

2. In what ways does Bush commit the United States to a war on terrorism? To what effect?

3. In what ways does America change after these attacks?

4. Compare and contrast President Bush's remarks with "Woodrow Wilson's Declaration of War Message" (Document 166) and with "Roosevelt's Declaration of War Message" (Document 190). How are they similar? Different?

On September the eleventh, enemies of freedom committed an act of war against our country. Americans have known wars—but for the past 136 years,

"Address of George W. Bush, President of the United States, Delivered to a Joint Session of Congress and the American People, Washington, D.C., September, 20, 2001," *Vital Speeches of the Day* 67 (October 2001): 760–763.

they have been wars on foreign soil, except for one Sunday in 1941. Americans have known the casualties of war—but not at the center of a great city on a peaceful morning. Americans have known surprise attacks—but never before on thousands of civilians. All of this was brought upon us in a single day—and night fell on a different world, a world where freedom itself is under attack.

Americans have many questions tonight. Americans are asking:

Who attacked our country?

The evidence we have gathered all points to a collection of loosely affiliated terrorist organization known as al-Qaida. They are the same murderers indicted for bombing American embassies in Tanzania and Kenya, and responsible for the bombing of the U.S.S. Cole.

Al-Qaida is to terror what the mafia is to crime. But its goals is not making money; its goal is remaking the world—and imposing its radical beliefs on people everywhere.

The terrorists practice a fringe form of Islamic extremism that has been rejected by Muslim scholars and the vast majority of Muslim clerics—a fringe movement that perverts the peaceful teachings of Islam. The terrorists' directive commands them to kill Christians and Jews, to kill all Americans and make no distinctions among military and civilians, including women and children.

This group and its leader—a person named Usama bin Ladin—are linked to many other organizations in different countries, including the Egyptian Islamic Jihad and the Islamic Movement of Uzbekistan. . . .

The leadership of al-Qaida has great influence in Afghanistan, and supports the Taliban regime in controlling most of that country. . . .

The United States respects the people of Afghanistan—after all, we are currently its largest source of humanitarian aid—but we condemn the Taliban regime. It is not only repressing its own people, it is threatening people everywhere by sponsoring and sheltering and supplying terrorists. By aiding and abetting murder, the Taliban regime is committing murder. And tonight, the United States of America makes the following demands on the Taliban:

Deliver to United States authorities all the leaders of al-Qaida who hide in your land.

Release all foreign nationals—including American citizens—you have unjustly imprisoned, and protect foreign journalists, diplomats, and aid workers in your country.

Close immediately and permanently every terrorist training camp in Afghanistan and hand over every terrorist, and every person in their support structure, to appropriate authorities.

Give the United States full access to terrorist training camps, so we can make sure they are no longer operating.

These demands are not open to negotiation or discussion. The Taliban must act and act immediately. They will hand over the terrorists, or they will share in their fate.

I also want to speak tonight directly to Muslims throughout the world: We respect your faith. It is practiced freely by many millions of Americans, and by millions more in countries that America counts as friends. Its teachings are good and peaceful, and those who commit evil in the name of Allah blaspheme the name of Allah. The terrorists are traitors to their own faith, trying, in effect, to hijack Islam itself. The enemy of America is not our many Muslim friends; it is not our many Arab friends. Our enemy is a radical network of terrorists, and every government that supports them.

Our war on terror begins with al-Qaida, but it does not end there. It will not end until every terrorist group of global reach has been found, stopped, and defeated. . . .

Our response involves far more than instant retaliation and isolated strikes. Americans should not expect one battle, but a lengthy campaign, unlike any other we have seen. It may include dramatic strikes, visible on television, and covert operations, secret even in success. We will starve terrorists of funding, turn them one against another, drive them from place to place, until there is no refuge or rest. And we will pursue nations that provide aid or safe haven to terrorism. Every nation, in every region, now has a decision to make. Either you are with us, or you are with the terrorists. From this day forward, any nation that continues to harbor or support terrorism will be regarded by the United States as a hostile regime.

Our nation has been put on notice: We are not immune from attack. We will take defensive measures against terrorism to protect Americans.

Today, dozens of federal departments and agencies, as well as state and local governments, have responsibilities affecting homeland security. These efforts must be coordinated at the highest level. So tonight I announce the creation of a Cabinet-level position reporting directly to me—the Office of Homeland Security. . . .

This is not, however, just America's fight. And what is at stake is not just America's freedom. This is the world's fight. This is civilization's fight. This is the fight of all who believe in progress and pluralism, tolerance and freedom.

We ask every nation to join us. We will ask, and we will need, the help of police forces, intelligence services, and banking systems around the world. . . .

The civilized world is rallying to America's side. They understand that if this terror goes unpunished, their own cities, their own citizens may be next. Terror, unanswered, can not only bring down buildings, it can threaten the stability of legitimate governments. And we will not allow it. . . .

Great harm has been done to us. We have suffered great loss. And in our grief and anger we have found our mission and our moment. Freedom and fear are at war. The advance of human freedom—the great achievement of our time, and the great hope of every time—now depends on us. Our nation—this generation—will lift a dark threat of violence from our people and our future. We will rally the world to this cause, by our efforts and by our courage. We will not tire, we will not falter, and we will not fail. . . .

232

A Response to the USA-Patriot Act (2001)

In the wake of the September 11, 2001 attacks, the federal government moved quickly to toughen national security. More than 1,000 individuals, mostly Arab and Muslim men who were suspected of having some connection to terrorist organizations, were detained and interrogated. Airport security became more rigorous (and soon fell under the jurisdiction of the new federal agency, the Transportation Safety Administration), and a more careful screening of applications by foreigners to travel or study in the United States began. Congress passed the USA-Patriot Act, which authorized law enforcement officials to use broader investigative powers to thwart potential terrorist threats. Such expansion of powers exposes the delicate balance between the need for national security in crisis times and the protection of individual rights under the Constitution and the Bill of Rights. Since its creation in response to the Red Scare of 1919–20, the American Civil Liberties Union (ACLU) has been a staunch advocate of protecting individuals' rights. In the excerpted speech, Anthony D. Romero, Executive Director of the ACLU, offered the following comments about the USA-Patriot Act in a speech to The City Club of Cleveland, Ohio.

Questions to Consider

1. For what reasons does Romero believe the climate of opinion and tolerance is different from earlier times in American history?

2. In what ways does Romero believe the USA–Patriot Act is a threat to liberties?

3. What is the proper balance between national security and protecting individual rights?

4. Is Romero's "proactive agenda" an appropriate course of action in a time of crisis? Why or why not?

If one can talk of good news amidst such tragedy, these actions would be the topic. And there is more good news in the form of statements by President Bush and many public officials, who urge Americans to respect the rights of others and warn that attacks on Arabs and Muslims "will not stand." Although that is exactly what a US President should be saying, the fact is that it has not always been the case. We know from our history that in times of national emergencies government officials have targeted particular groups for harassment or outright discrimination. . . .

Anthony D. Romero, "In Defense of Liberty," *Vital Speeches of the Day* 68 (January 2002): 169–172. Reprinted by permission.

The terrorists apparently took insidious advantage of this tolerance, living in our communities and enjoying our freedoms. Does that mean that those freedoms are somehow at fault? Or that respecting the rights of others is wrong? The answer is an emphatic "No." These fundamental values, established in our Constitution, are the bedrock of our country. They are what truly distinguish us; they are the source of our unique strength; they are our legacy to the world.

I also think there is another reason for the greater measure of tolerance and respect we have witnessed so far. That is, that our message—and by "our," I refer to the ACLU and other civil liberties groups—has actually gotten through. We may be the favorite whipping post of conservative editors and the best laugh-line for late-night talk show hosts, but our efforts have not been in vain. Our defense of liberty for over 80 years has succeeded in raising people's consciousness of the Bill of Rights as something more than an appendage to the Constitution. Our efforts have kept the spotlight on these guarantees, reminding people that constitutional principles exist to be exercised, and that they are not subject to the whims of government.

Which brings me to the current debate over the appropriate balance between liberty and security in a time of national crisis. After weeks of negotiation, the USA-Patriot Act was signed into law last Friday. Notwithstanding the rhetoric and lip service paid to civil liberties by our nation's leaders, the new law gives government expanded power to invade our privacy, imprison people without meaningful due process, and punish dissent.

The ACLU has been in the forefront of those arguing that this is no time for Congress to be pushing through new laws that would seriously diminish our civil liberties. This is a time for reason, not hysteria. The US is facing a serious threat to its security. However, that threat is directed as well to our democratic values, our freedoms, our diversity, our equality.

There are many provisions that simply do not meet the basic test of maximizing our security and preserving our civil liberties.
I would list the following five proposals as among the most offensive:

1. The overly broad definition of "terrorism"—A definition that could easily be used against many forms of civil disobedience, including legitimate and peaceful protest. The language is so ambiguous that it is possible that if an organized group of peace demonstrators spray painted a peace sign outside of the State Department, they could be charged as terrorists for their actions.

2. Indefinite detention of immigrants based on the Attorney General's certification of a danger to national security—A harmful provision with language so vague that even the existence of judicial review would provide no meaningful safeguard against abuse.

3. Expanded wiretap authority—The new legislation minimized judicial supervision of law enforcement wiretap authority by permitting law enforcement to obtain the equivalent of blank warrants in the physical world; authorizing intelligence wiretaps that need not specify the phone

to be tapped or require that only the target's conversations be eaves-dropped on. And the new law extends lower surveillance standards to the Internet.

Let me explain with regard to the Internet, since it can be rather complicated. Under current law, authorities can require a telephone company to reveal numbers dialed to and from a particular phone by simply certifying that this information is "relevant to an ongoing crimi-nal investigation." This is far less than the probable cause standard that governs most searches and seizures. The new law extends this low level of proof to Internet communications, which unlike a telephone num-ber—reveal personal and private information, such as which Internet sites an individual has visited. Once that lower standard is applied to the Internet, law enforcement officers would have unprecedented power to monitor what citizens do on the Net, thereby opening a "back door" on the content of personal communications.

4. The use of "sneak and peek" searches to circumvent the Fourth Amend-ment—Under this segment of the legislation, law enforcement officials could enter your home, office or other private place and conduct a search, take photographs and download your computer files without notifying you until after the fact. This delayed notice provision undercuts the spirit of the Fourth Amendment and the need to provide information to citizens when their privacy is invaded by law enforcement authorities.

5. Eviscerating the wall between foreign surveillance and domestic crimi-nal investigation—The new legislation gives the Director of the Central Intelligence the power to manage the gathering of intelligence in America and mandate the disclosure of information obtained by the FBI about terrorism in general—even if it is about law abiding Ameri-can citizens—to the CIA. . . .

Terror, by its very nature, is intended not only to destroy, but also to intim-idate a people; forcing them to take actions that are not in their best interest.

That's why defending liberty during a time of national crisis is the ulti-mate act of defiance. It is the ultimate act of patriotism. For, if we are intim-idated to the point of restricting our freedoms, the terrorists have won.

Security and liberty do not have to be at odds, nor put on a collision course. We must act to defend against any assault on civil liberties. However, we should be prepared not only to react, but also to be proactive, offering alternative solutions where feasible.

So what do we do? A proactive agenda has several parts:

First, we need to urge our fellow Americans to think carefully and clearly about the tradeoffs between national security and individual freedom, and to understand that some will seek to restrict freedom for ideological and other reasons that have little to do with security.

Second, we need to stay informed and involved in the current congres-sional deliberations over anti-terror legislation. We have to let our elected officials know that our eyes are on them. . . .

Third, we must demand that government take the necessary efforts to prevent and punish unwarranted, bigoted attacks on fellow citizens of Arab descent and members of religious minorities, including Muslims and Sikhs. . . . They are our neighbors, friends, co-workers, not the enemy. . . .

Fourth, we must keep the pressure on other issues. We do not have the luxury of putting other civil liberties on the backburner. We must not lose the momentum on important struggles like the death penalty or electoral reform. . . .

Fifth, we must demand government accountability and responsiveness to civil liberties. The American people have a right to know that our basic protections are in place. . . .

Finally, we should establish guidelines for evaluating new proposals that would affect our basic civil liberties. At the very least, proposed changes to restrict liberty should be examined and debated in public . . . .

The American people must be reassured that constitutional guarantees will apply in times of crisis and tranquility alike. . . .

233

The United States and the World (2003)

Since World War II, the United States experienced economic expansion that provided job opportunities for its growing population. This economic growth helped shape a society that became increasingly consumer oriented and remarkably affluent. At the same time, American products, technology, and culture were spread throughout the world. Many American citizens enjoyed the fruits of this prosperity and global trade, and they came to believe that the American way of life, its core values and beliefs, and its culture were good for the world. What Americans saw as sharing the benefits of the good life was, however, often viewed as a new form of imperialism. But rather than taking or occupying foreign lands, as happened in an earlier imperialistic impulse, American culture, technology, economic presence, and its military permeated nearly every corner of the globe and seemingly dominated world affairs. In the wake of the September 11, 2001 terrorist attacks, Americans began to question why the country was attacked and why many in the world held the United States in contempt. In the excerpted article, Fareed Zakaria, the international editor for the news magazine, Newsweek, *offered an explanation of America's place in the world.*

Questions to Consider

1. How do you think the average SUV owner as described in "Consumer Choice in Automobiles and its Impact" (Document 226) would respond to this essay?

2. Compare and contrast the ideas expressed here with those found in George Hoar's "An Anti-Imperialist Perspective"(Document 154). How are they similar? Different?

3. What does the author have to say that is positive about the United States? In what ways is he critical?

Most Americans have never felt more vulnerable. September 11 was not only the first attack on the American mainland in 150 years, but it was also sudden and unexpected. Three thousand civilians were brutally killed without any warning. In the months that followed, Americans worried about anthrax attacks, biological terror, dirty bombs and new suicide squads. Even now, the day-to-day rhythms of American life are frequently interrupted by terror alerts and warnings. The average American feels a threat to his physical security unknown since the early years of the republic.

Yet after 9-11, the rest of the world saw something quite different. They saw a country that was hit by terrorism, as some of them had been, but that was able to respond on a scale that was almost unimaginable. Suddenly terrorism was the world's chief priority, and every country had to reorient its foreign policy accordingly. Pakistan had actively supported the Taliban for years; within months it became that regime's sworn enemy. Washington announced that it would increase its defense budget by almost $50 billion, a sum greater than the total defense budget of Britain or Germany. A few months later it toppled a regime 6,000 miles away—almost entirely from the air—in Afghanistan, a country where the British and Soviet empires were bogged down at the peak of their power. It is now clear that the current era can really only have one name, the unipolar world—an age with only one global power. America's position today is unprecedented. A hundred years ago, Britain was a superpower, ruling a quarter of the globe's population. But it was still only the second or third richest country in the world and one among many strong military powers. The crucial measure of military might in the early 20th century was naval power, and Britain ruled the waves with a fleet as large as the next two navies put together. By contrast, the United States will spend as much next year on defense as the rest of the world put together (yes, all 191 countries). And it will do so devoting 4 percent of its GDP, a low level by postwar standards.

American dominance is not simply military. The U.S. economy is as large as the next three—Japan, Germany and Britain—put together. With 5 percent of the world's population, this one country accounts for 43 percent of the world's economic production, 40 percent of its high-technology production and 50 percent of its research and development. If you look at the indicators of future growth, all are favorable for America. It is more dynamic economically, more youthful demographically and more flexible culturally than any other part of the world. It is conceivable that America's

Fareed Zakaria, "The Arrogant Empire," *Newsweek*, March 24, 2003, 18–33. © 2003 Newsweek, Inc. All rights reserved. Reprinted by permission.

lead, especially over an aging and sclerotic Europe, will actually increase over the next two decades.

Given this situation, perhaps what is most surprising is that the world has not ganged up on America already. Since the beginnings of the state system in the 16th century, international politics has seen one clear pattern—the formation of balances of power against the strong. Countries with immense military and economic might arouse fear and suspicion, and soon other coalesce against them. . . . At this point, most Americans will surely protest: "But we're different!" Americans—this writer included—think of themselves as a nation that has never sought to occupy others, and that through the years has been a progressive and liberating force. But historians tell us that all dominant powers thought they were special. Their very success confirmed for them that they were blessed. But as they became ever more powerful, the world saw them differently. . . .

. . . When America had the world as its feet, Franklin Delano Roosevelt and Harry Truman chose not to create an American imperium, but to build a world of alliances and multilateral institutions. They formed the United Nations, the Bretton Woods system of economic cooperation and dozens of other international organizations. America helped get the rest of the world back on its feet by pumping out vast amounts of aid and private investment. The centerpiece of this effort, the Marshall Plan, amounted to $120 billion in today's dollars. . . .

Of course, all these exertions served our interests, too. They produced a pro-American world that was rich and secure. They laid the foundations for a booming global economy in which America thrives. But it was an enlightened self-interest that took into account the interests of others. Above all, it reassured countries—through word and deed, style and substance—that America's mammoth power need not be feared. . . .

In its first year the [George W. Bush] administration withdrew from five international treaties—and did so as brusquely as it could. It reneged on virtually every diplomatic effort that the Clinton administration has engaged in, from North Korea to the Middle East, often overturning public statements from Colin Powell supporting these efforts. It developed a language and diplomatic style that seemed calculated to offend the world. . . .

September 11 only added a new layer of assertiveness to Bush's foreign policy. Understandably shocked and searching for responses, the administration decided that it needed total freedom of action. . . .

. . . Because of 9-11, it has had to act forcefully on the world stage and assert American power. But that should have been all the more reason to adopt a posture of consultation and cooperation while doing what needed to be done. The point is to scare our enemies, not terrify the rest of the world. . . .

The real question is how America should wield its power. For the past half century it has done so through alliances and global institutions and in a consensual manner. Now it faces new challenges—and not simply because of what the Bush administration has done. The old order is changing. The alliances forged during the cold war are weakening. Institutions built to reflect the realities of 1945—such as the U.N. Security Council—risk becoming anachronistic. But if the administration wishes to further weaken and indeed destroy these institutions and traditions—by dismissing or neglecting them—it must ask itself: What will take their place? By what means will America maintain its hegemony?

For some in the administration, the answer is obvious: America will act as it chooses, using what allies it can find in any given situation. As a statement of fact this is sometimes the only approach Washington will be able to employ. But it is not a durable long-term strategy. It would require America to build new alliances and arrangements every time it faced a crisis. More important, operating in a conspicuously unconstrained way, in service of a strategy to maintain primacy, will paradoxically produce the very competition it hopes to avoid. . . .

There are many specific ways for the United States to rebuild its relations with the world. It can match its military buildup with diplomatic efforts that demonstrate its interest and engagement in the world's problems. It can stop over-subsidizing American steelworkers, farmers and textile-mill owners, and open its borders to goods from poorer countries. But above all, it must make the world comfortable with its power by leading through consensus. America's special role in the world—its ability to buck history—is based not simply on its great strength, but on a global faith that this power is legitimate. If America squanders that, the loss will outweigh any gains in domestic security. And this next American century could prove to be lonely, brutish, and short.

THOMSON
WADSWORTH

AMERICAN JOURNEY ONLINE

H I S T O R Y   I N   Y O U R   H A N D S

VISIT: http://ajaccess.wadsworth.com

The landmark events of American history recorded by eye-witnesses . . . the great themes of the American experience according to those who lived it . . . these are captured in the 16 primary source collections that make up American Journey Online. Each key topic in American history and culture addressed by the series encompasses hundreds of carefully selected, rare documents, pictures, and archival audio and video. Essays, headnotes, and captions by scholars set the sources in context. Full text searchability and extensive hyperlinking provide fast and easy access and cross-referencing. The scope of the collections and the power of online delivery make American Journey Online a unique and unprecedented tool for historical inquiry for today's researchers.

New World War II Module

INTRODUCTION   CONTENTS   SEARCH   INDEX

World War II
Michelle Fleischer & Barbara Rader, General Editors

AMERICAN JOURNEY ONLINE

World War II
General Editor: Michelle Fleischer and Barbara Rader

This collection of primary source materials covers every major aspect of America's involvement in World War II. Beginning with an examination of America's isolationist policies, this title brings the user through the bombing of Pearl Harbor, the fighting in Europe and Asia, the conferences of "The Big Three", the effect of the war on the home front and the use of the atomic bomb.

Introduction | Contents | Search | Index

© Copyright 1999 Primary Source Media All rights reserved.

The 16 Modules and Contributors

African American Experience: General Editor: Michele Stepto, Yale University

American Revolution: General Editor: Norman Desmarais, Brown University

Asian-American Experience: Produced in association with the Asian American Studies Center, UCLA

Civil Rights in the United States: General Editor: Jay Sigler, emeritus, Rutgers University

Civil War: General Editor: Rachel Filene Seidman, Carleton College

Cold War: General Editor: Walter Hixson, University of Akron

Constitution and Supreme Court: General Editors: Lance Banning, University of Kentucky; Kermit L. Hall, Ohio State University; and Jack N. Rakove, Stanford University

Great Depression and New Deal: General Editor: Otis L. Graham, University of North Carolina, Wilmington

Hispanic-American Experience: De Varona, Professor of Education, Florida International University; Frank Menchaca, Vice President of Publishing, Scribners and Macmillan Library Reference; Bryce Milligan, Editor/Publisher of Wings Press; Victor Montejo, University of California, Davis; and Alan West

Immigrant Experience: General Editor Thomas Archdeacon, University of Wisconsin, Madison

Native American Experience: General Editor: Jace Weaver, Yale University

Westward Expansion: General Editor: John Bowman

Women in America: General Editor: Elizabeth Frost-Knappman, New England Press Association

World War I and the Progressive Era: General Editor: Patrick Reagan, Tennessee Technological University

World War II: Michelle Fleischer and Barbara Rader   NEW!

Vietnam Era: General Editors: George Herring, University of Kentucky and Clarence Wyatt, Centre College Robert K. Brigham, Vassar College

HISTORY ■ http://history.wadsworth.com

THOMSON
✦
WADSWORTH

New Online Interactive Video Exercises:

- Alger Hiss Accused of Espionage
- Alger Hiss and Whittaker Chambers Testify
- Army of the Republic of Vietnam (ARVN), 1957 (Images only, no audio)
- Atomic Bomb Drill Conducted in New York City
- Berlin Airlift
- Blacks in Postwar America
- Blaming Reds for 1919 Strikes
- Book Burning in the 1930s
- Eisenhower Publicly Responds to Sputnik Launch
- French-Indochina War Begins
- Germany Admitted to NATO
- Grand Coulee Dam (Images only, no audio)
- Guardian at the Gate (Video in 4 seperate segments)
- Guardian at the Gate: Lyndon B. Johnson's Closing Remarks
- Hydrogen Bomb Is Tested
- Inaugurating the National American Indian Memoria (Images only, no audio)
- Integration of Central High School, Little Rock (Images only, no audio)
- Internment of Japanese Americans
- James Meredith Enters the University of Mississippi
- Jazz--Music of the People
- Korean War Begins
- Ku Klux Klan in the 1920s
- Lindbergh's Welcome Home in New York City
- Lyndon B. Johnson Speaks to American Students
- Lyndon Johnson Signs Civil Rights Act, 1964

- Mesa Verde: 1 and Mesa verde: 2, Di Peso, Charles C (Images only, no audio)
- Prohibition
- Protest in Washington, DC, 1930
- Protests of Sentencing of Sacco and Vanzetti
- Rebuilding Indian Country: 1
- Rebuilding Indian Country: 2
- Revolt in Hungary, 1956
- Roosevelt Dedicating the Mark Twain Memorial Bridge (Images only, no audio)
- Roosevelt Reviewing the Pacific Fleet (Images only, no audio)
- Roosevelt's Tour of Bonneville Dam (Images only, no audio)
- Rosenbergs Convicted and Executed
- Saigon during the Tet Offensive, 1968 (Images only, no audio)
- Satellite Tracking Becomes Part of the Cold War
- Scopes (Monkey) Trial
- Senator Joseph R. McCarthy Is Condemned
- South Vietnam's Independence Day Celebrations, 1962 (Images only, no audio)
- Strikes in the South
- Suffragettes Marching, 1920
- Tempera Painting by Quincy Tahoma, a Navajo Indian: 1
- Tempera Painting by Quincy Tahoma, a Navajo Indian: 2
- The Charleston
- The Stock Market Crash of 1929
- The United Nations Is Formed
- Yosemite National Park

American Journey User's Guide:

American Journey Online User's Guide with Activities
Instructor ISBN: 0-534-18759-5   **Student ISBN:** 0-534-17433-7
The User's Guide consists of 17 chronological chapters covering major eras in U.S. history, each of which contains 10 guided activities using American Journey Online. In the front matter are an introduction to American Journey Online and a guide to navigating within its databases.

Available With The Following Text:

Liberty, Equality, Power: A History of the American People, 4e ©2005
urrin, Paul Johnson, James McPherson, Gary Gerstle, Emily S. Rosenberg, and Norman Rosenberg
Complete: 0-534-62730-7; Vol. I: 0-534-64182-2; Vol. II: 0-534-64218-7
Bundled with User Guide Complete: 0-534-64173-3, Vol.I: 0-534-04571-5, Vol.II: 0-534-04589-8

American Passages: A History of the American People, 2e ©2004
Edward L. Ayers, Lewis L.Gould, David H.Oshinsky, and Jean R. Soderlund
Complete: 0-534-16949-X, Vol. I: 0-534-16953-8, Vol. II: 0-534-60743-8
Compact Edition Complete:0-534-64791-X, Vol. I: 0-534-64792-8, Vol. II: 0-534-64793-6
Bundled with User Guide Complete: 0-534-07922-9, Vol. I: 0-534-07931-8, Vol. II: 0-534-07949-0
Compact Edition Complete: 0-534-64784-7, Vol. I: 0-534-64137-7, Vol. II: 0-534-64146-6

The American Past: A Survey of American History, 7e ©2004
Joseph Conlin
Complete: 0-534-62136-8, Vol. I: 0-534-62137-6, Vol. II: 0-534-62138-4
Bundled with User Guide Complete: 0-534-07985-7, Vol.I: 0-534-08003-0, Vol.II: 0-534-08021-9

Liberty, Equality, Power: A History of the American People, 3e Concise Editon
John Murrin, Paul Johnson, James McPherson, Gary Gerstle, Emily S. Rosenberg, and Norman Rosenberg
Complete: 0-534-26462-X, Vol. I: 0-534-26463-8, Vol. II: 0-534-26464-6, ©2001
Bundled with User Guide Complete: 0-534-08030-8, Vol.I 0-534-08039-1, Vol.II: 0-534-0-534-08048-0

American Passages, Brief ©2003
Edward L. Ayers, Lewis L.Gould, David H.Oshinsky, and Jean R. Soderlund
Complete: 0-15-504951-8, Vol. I: 0-15-505117-2, Vol. II: 0-15-505123-7
Bundled with User Guide Complete: 0-534-04966-4, Vol.I 0-534-04975-3, Vol.II: 0-534-04984-2

We the People: A Brief American History ©2003
Peter N. Carroll
Complete: 0-534-59355-0, Vol. I: 0-534-59356-9, Vol. II: 0-534-59357-7
Bundled with User Guide Complete: 0-534-04993-1, Vol.I 0-534-05002-6, Vol.II: 0-534-05011-5